Discover Your
Inner
Hermit Crab

Other Books by Jim Toomey

Sherman's Lagoon: Ate That, What's Next?
Poodle: The Other White Meat
An Illustrated Guide to Shark Etiquette
Another Day in Paradise
Greetings from Sherman's Lagoon
Surf's Up!
The Shark Diaries
Catch of the Day
A Day at the Beach
Surfer Safari
Planet of the Hairless Beach Apes
Yarns & Shanties (and Other Nautical Baloney)
Sharks Just Wanna Have Fun
Confessions of a Swinging Single Sea Turtle

Treasuries

Sherman's Lagoon 1991 to 2001:
Greatest Hits and Near Misses
In Shark Years I'm Dead: Sherman's Lagoon Turns Fifteen

Discover Your
Inner
Hermit Crab

**The Fifteenth Sherman's Lagoon Collection
by Jim Toomey**

**Andrews McMeel
Publishing, LLC**
Kansas City • Sydney • London

Sherman's Lagoon is syndicated internationally by King Features Syndicate, Inc. For information, write King Features Syndicate, Inc., 300 West Fifty-Seventh Street, New York, New York 10019.

Andrews McMeel Publishing, LLC
an Andrews McMeel Universal company
1130 Walnut Street, Kansas City, Missouri 64106

www.andrewsmcmeel.com

11 12 13 14 WKT 10 9 8 7 6 5 4 3 2

ISBN: 978-0-7407-9110-9

Library of Congress Control Number: 2010921935

Sherman's Lagoon may be viewed on the Internet at
www.shermanslagoon.com.

———— **ATTENTION: SCHOOLS AND BUSINESSES** ————

Andrews McMeel books are available at quantity discounts with bulk purchase for educational, business, or sales promotional use. For information, please e-mail the Andrews McMeel Publishing Special Sales Department:
specialsales@amuniversal.com

Foreword

In William Shakespeare's *King Lear*, the Fool with his witty foolery shows the audience the wisdom that can be found in comic relief. The Fool, companion and advisor to Lear, counsels and plays with the king and exposes the king's foolishness with the wit of a great satirist. Not that this is news or anything, but the fact that the Bard in the greatest of his works, his tragedies, uses fools as Renaissance gurus or various purveyors of truth, speaks to the importance of these courtly funnymen. Humor, their tool of trade, slices through the dense overgrowth of ambiguity and falseness like a scythe exposing the fertile ground of a universally understood morality, which all too often has been trod upon and muddied repeatedly by most of the other characters. (I know: It's a heck of a tool, that one.) Of course, ol' Shakespeare did not invent the tool but followed in the footsteps of great writers from even as early as the Greek and Roman periods. However, he wonderfully tweaked the art of using humor to reveal the realities of the human condition and, of course, has been followed himself; consider Joseph Heller's Yossarian or Ken Kesey's McMurphy, just to name a few of the more memorable, later jokesters.

So, OK, what does all of this have to do with Jim Toomey's latest collection, *Discover Your Inner Hermit Crab*, or for that matter, *Sherman's Lagoon*? It's a good and fair question—and with it, you may be ahead of me here—but in answering it and before we get too far, I must assure you that my Shakespeare allusion has nothing to do with Toomey being a fool; quite the contrary. As a fan of Jim's work, you have probably already subscribed to his silliness. (A shark as conduit, as bearer of insights, to *humans*? How silly is that? Hasn't Toomey seen *Jaws*, for Pete's sake?) Plus, you have probably grasped the wit contained within the wonderfully drawn frames of sea life, or one might say, windows into Jim's bizarre maritime imagination. But, you may not have seen a method behind Jim's madness, if you will. In addition to a goal confessed by him in an earlier collection to present a story of uncuddly beasts in order to make them more cuddly, Jim hopes to, well, make them more cuddly! Think about it: He gives us, to ponder and laugh with, quirky yet sincere fish and other inner space dwellers, those creatures we land-borne hairless apes, as Toomey likes to call us, don't see very often. Why? Because those critters need to be seen more often, and when I write *seen*, I mean *felt*. Jim Toomey truly cares about Sherman's, Megan's, Hawthorne's, and the rest of the crew's animate doppelgängers out there in the real oceans and seas. And, he doesn't just sympathize, he acts. That story of Jim's action will have to wait for another day, but let it be known that as Jim Toomey gives us the gift—the necessity, rather—of laughter with *Sherman's Lagoon*, he provides for us a porthole to see and understand and feel the truth of our fellow animals; comic relief for the soul on one hand, and hopeful visions of happy, cuddly (yes, *cuddly*) critters on the other. Jim, as artfully as the Bard before him, uses humor to reveal wisdom and demonstrate with certainty (finally!) that he's no fool.

Andrew M. Sidle
Alexandria, Virginia

January 31, 2010

P.S. Fillmore, that erudite sea turtle, begged me to open with Shakespeare, and I caved.

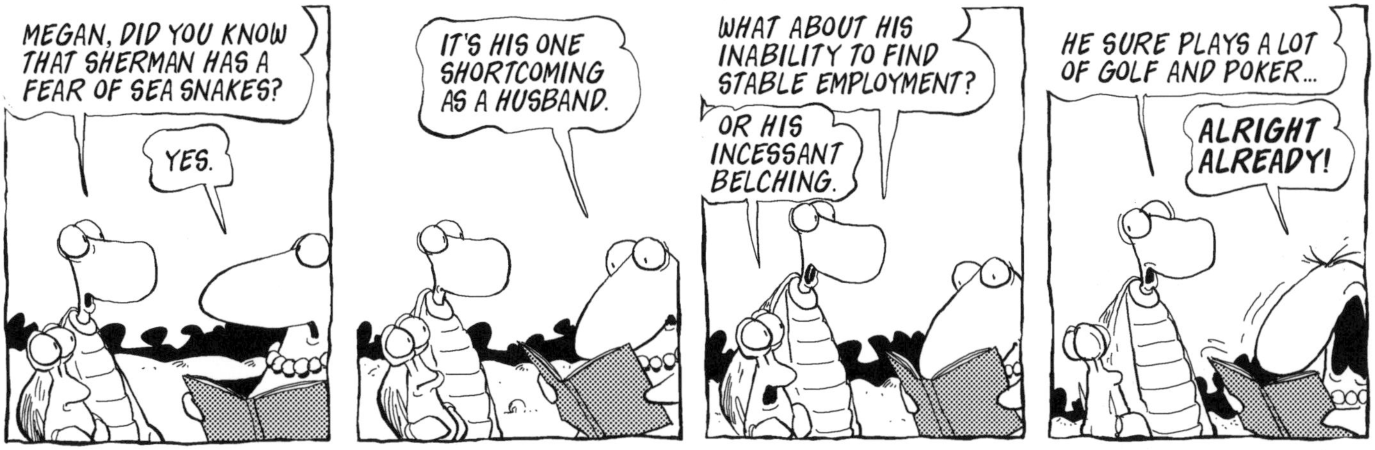
MEGAN, DID YOU KNOW THAT SHERMAN HAS A FEAR OF SEA SNAKES?
YES.
IT'S HIS ONE SHORTCOMING AS A HUSBAND.
WHAT ABOUT HIS INABILITY TO FIND STABLE EMPLOYMENT?
OR HIS INCESSANT BELCHING.
HE SURE PLAYS A LOT OF GOLF AND POKER...
ALRIGHT ALREADY!

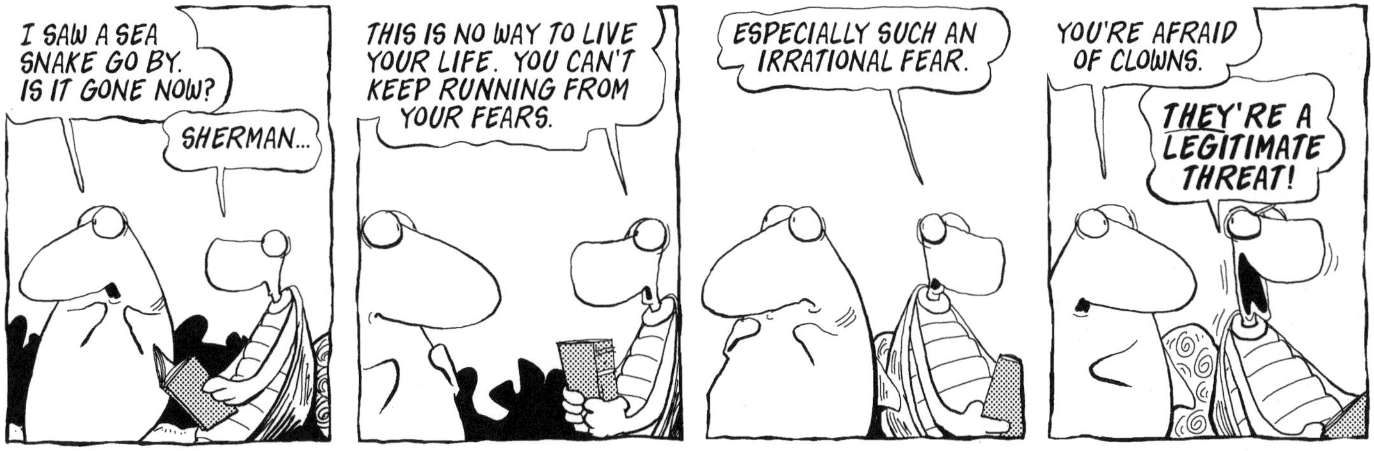
I SAW A SEA SNAKE GO BY. IS IT GONE NOW?
SHERMAN...
THIS IS NO WAY TO LIVE YOUR LIFE. YOU CAN'T KEEP RUNNING FROM YOUR FEARS.
ESPECIALLY SUCH AN IRRATIONAL FEAR.
YOU'RE AFRAID OF CLOWNS.
THEY'RE A LEGITIMATE THREAT!

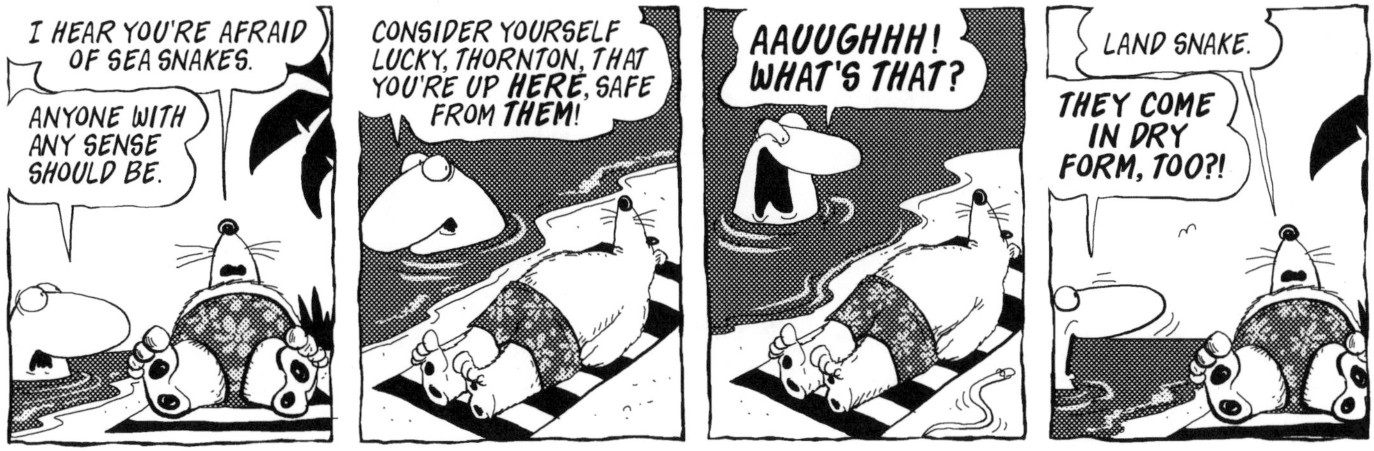
I HEAR YOU'RE AFRAID OF SEA SNAKES.
ANYONE WITH ANY SENSE SHOULD BE.
CONSIDER YOURSELF LUCKY, THORNTON, THAT YOU'RE UP HERE, SAFE FROM THEM!
AAUUGHHH! WHAT'S THAT?
LAND SNAKE.
THEY COME IN DRY FORM, TOO?!

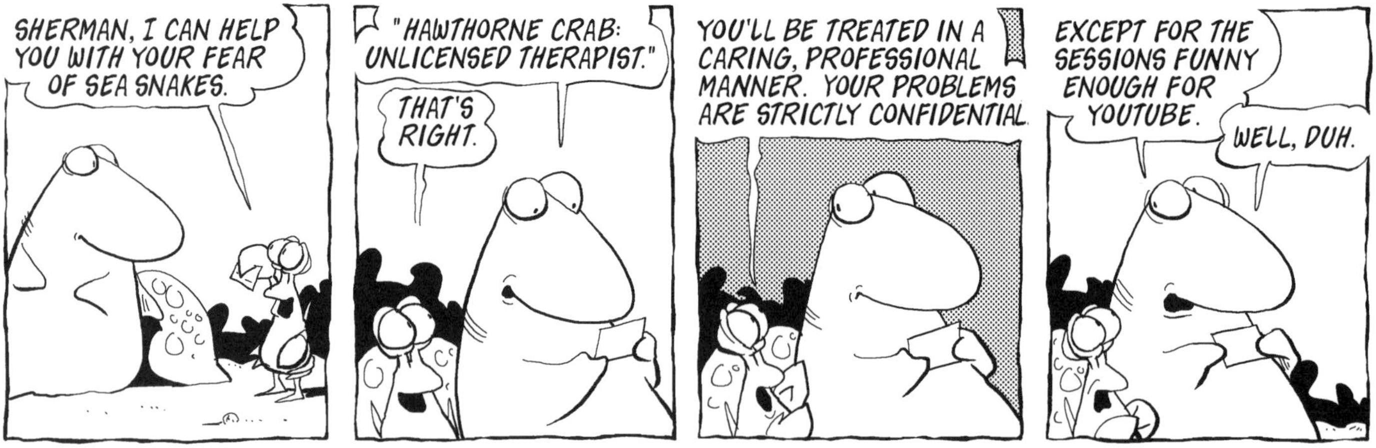
SHERMAN, I CAN HELP YOU WITH YOUR FEAR OF SEA SNAKES.
"HAWTHORNE CRAB: UNLICENSED THERAPIST."
THAT'S RIGHT.
YOU'LL BE TREATED IN A CARING, PROFESSIONAL MANNER. YOUR PROBLEMS ARE STRICTLY CONFIDENTIAL.
EXCEPT FOR THE SESSIONS FUNNY ENOUGH FOR YOUTUBE.
WELL, DUH.

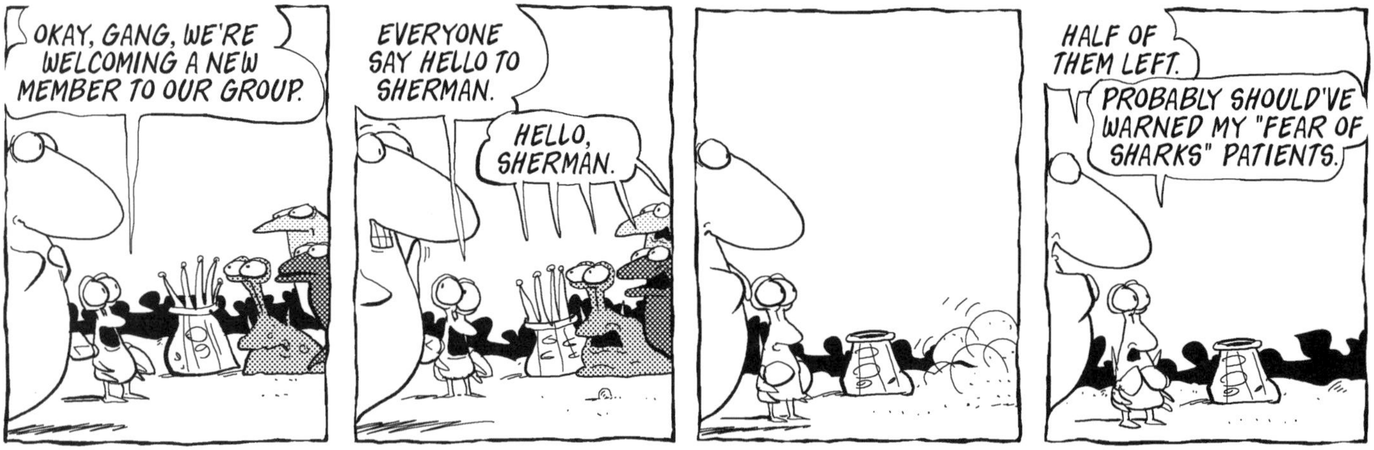
OKAY, GANG, WE'RE WELCOMING A NEW MEMBER TO OUR GROUP.
EVERYONE SAY HELLO TO SHERMAN.
HELLO, SHERMAN.
HALF OF THEM LEFT.
PROBABLY SHOULD'VE WARNED MY "FEAR OF SHARKS" PATIENTS.

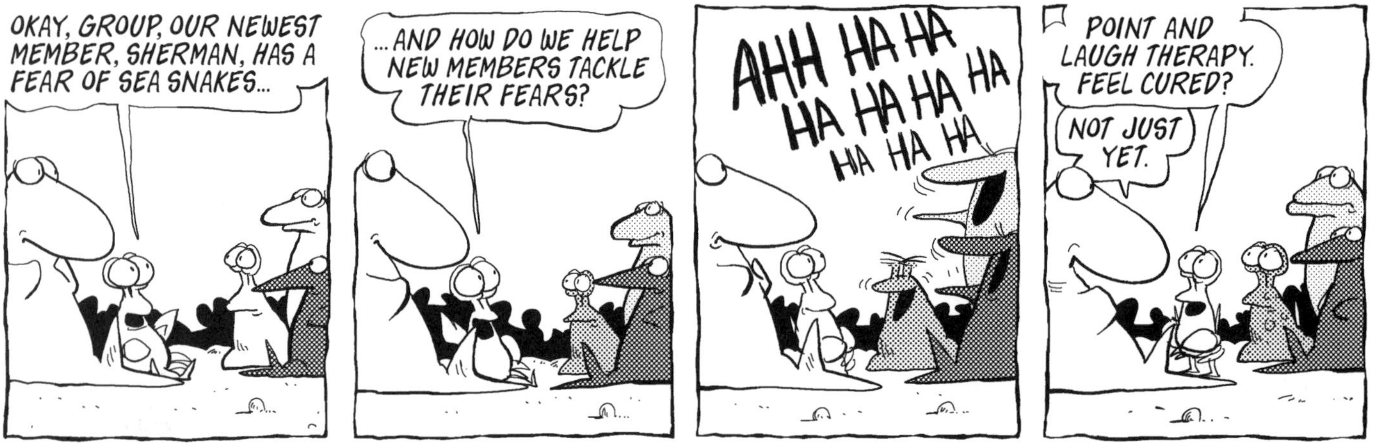
OKAY, GROUP, OUR NEWEST MEMBER, SHERMAN, HAS A FEAR OF SEA SNAKES...
...AND HOW DO WE HELP NEW MEMBERS TACKLE THEIR FEARS?
AHH HA HA HA HA HA HA HA HA HA
POINT AND LAUGH THERAPY. FEEL CURED?
NOT JUST YET.

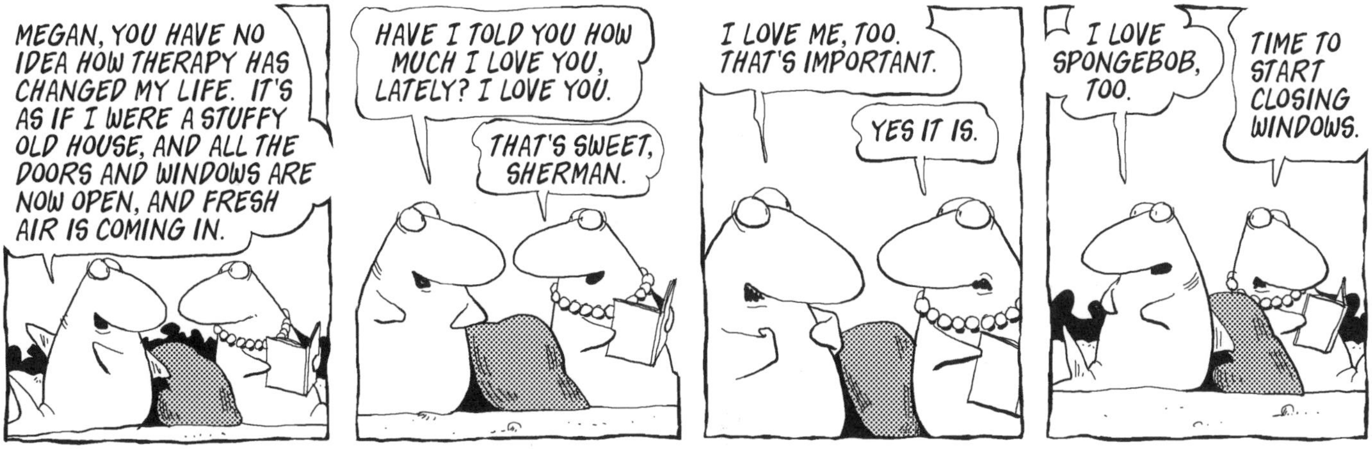
MEGAN, YOU HAVE NO IDEA HOW THERAPY HAS CHANGED MY LIFE. IT'S AS IF I WERE A STUFFY OLD HOUSE, AND ALL THE DOORS AND WINDOWS ARE NOW OPEN, AND FRESH AIR IS COMING IN.
HAVE I TOLD YOU HOW MUCH I LOVE YOU, LATELY? I LOVE YOU.
THAT'S SWEET, SHERMAN.
I LOVE ME, TOO. THAT'S IMPORTANT.
YES IT IS.
I LOVE SPONGEBOB, TOO.
TIME TO START CLOSING WINDOWS.

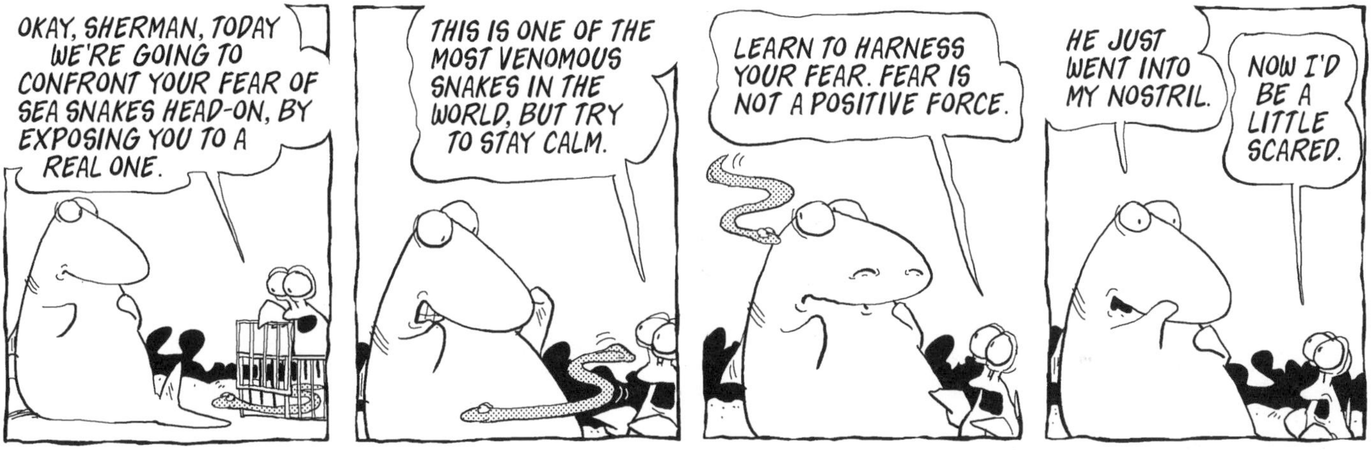
OKAY, SHERMAN, TODAY WE'RE GOING TO CONFRONT YOUR FEAR OF SEA SNAKES HEAD-ON, BY EXPOSING YOU TO A REAL ONE.
THIS IS ONE OF THE MOST VENOMOUS SNAKES IN THE WORLD, BUT TRY TO STAY CALM.
LEARN TO HARNESS YOUR FEAR. FEAR IS NOT A POSITIVE FORCE.
HE JUST WENT INTO MY NOSTRIL.
NOW I'D BE A LITTLE SCARED.

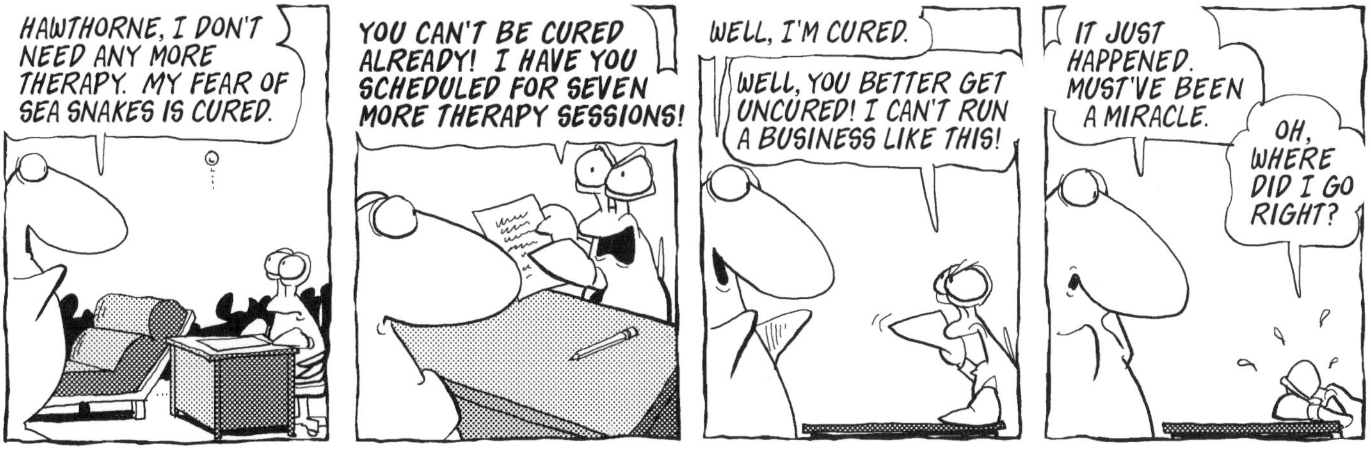
HAWTHORNE, I DON'T NEED ANY MORE THERAPY. MY FEAR OF SEA SNAKES IS CURED.
YOU CAN'T BE CURED ALREADY! I HAVE YOU SCHEDULED FOR SEVEN MORE THERAPY SESSIONS!
WELL, I'M CURED.
WELL, YOU BETTER GET UNCURED! I CAN'T RUN A BUSINESS LIKE THIS!
IT JUST HAPPENED. MUST'VE BEEN A MIRACLE.
OH, WHERE DID I GO RIGHT?

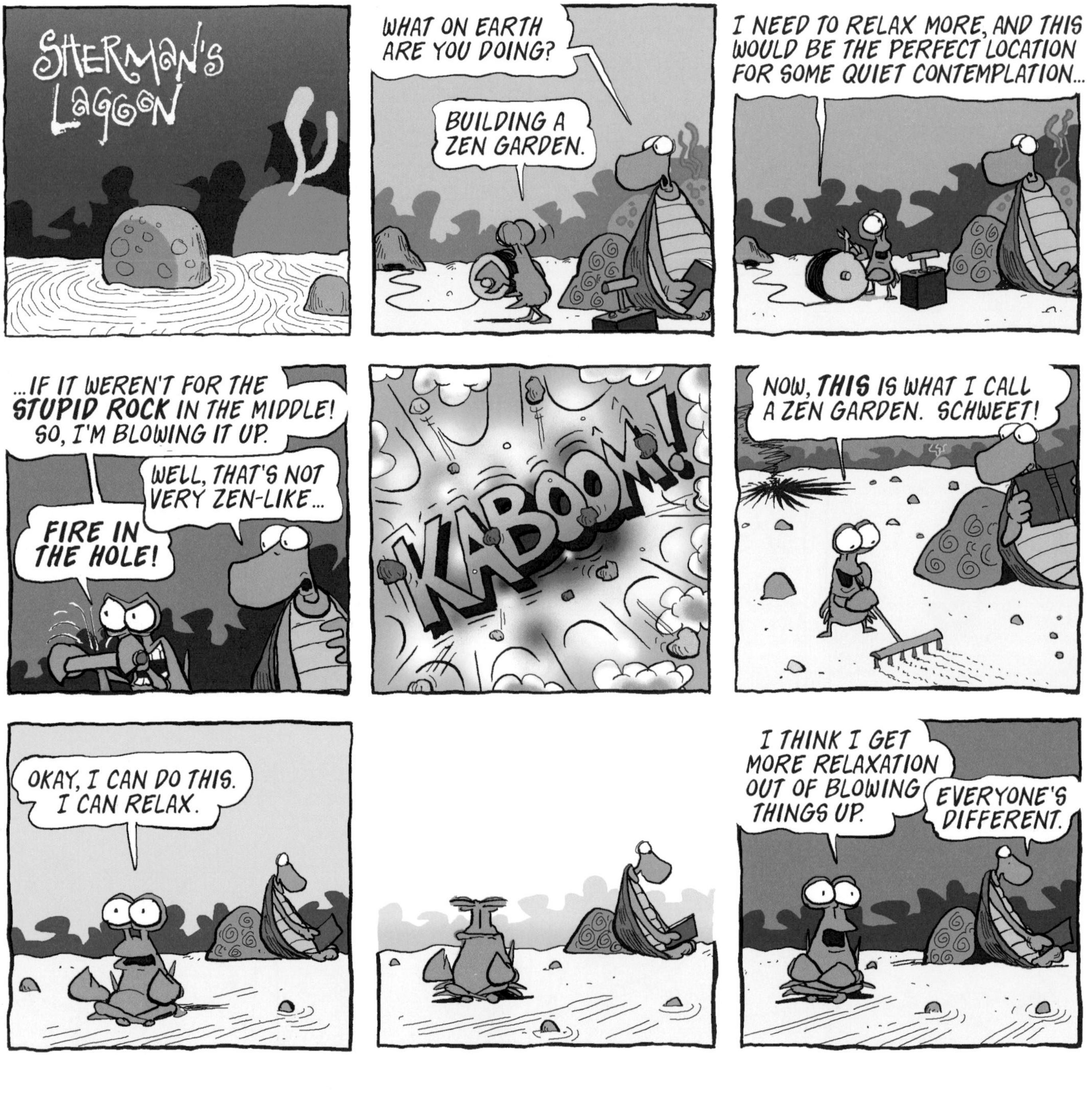
SHERMAN'S LAGOON
WHAT ON EARTH ARE YOU DOING?
BUILDING A ZEN GARDEN.
I NEED TO RELAX MORE, AND THIS WOULD BE THE PERFECT LOCATION FOR SOME QUIET CONTEMPLATION...
...IF IT WEREN'T FOR THE **STUPID ROCK** IN THE MIDDLE! SO, I'M BLOWING IT UP.
WELL, THAT'S NOT VERY ZEN-LIKE...
FIRE IN THE HOLE!
KABOOM!
NOW, **THIS** IS WHAT I CALL A ZEN GARDEN. SCHWEET!
OKAY, I CAN DO THIS. I CAN RELAX.
I THINK I GET MORE RELAXATION OUT OF BLOWING THINGS UP.
EVERYONE'S DIFFERENT.

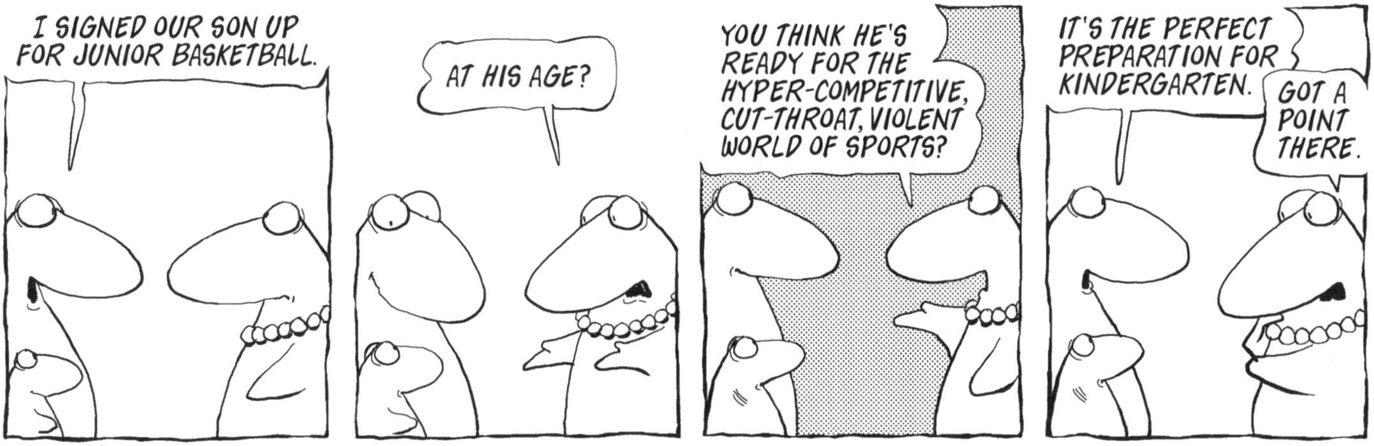
I SIGNED OUR SON UP FOR JUNIOR BASKETBALL.
AT HIS AGE?
YOU THINK HE'S READY FOR THE HYPER-COMPETITIVE, CUT-THROAT, VIOLENT WORLD OF SPORTS?
IT'S THE PERFECT PREPARATION FOR KINDERGARTEN.
GOT A POINT THERE.

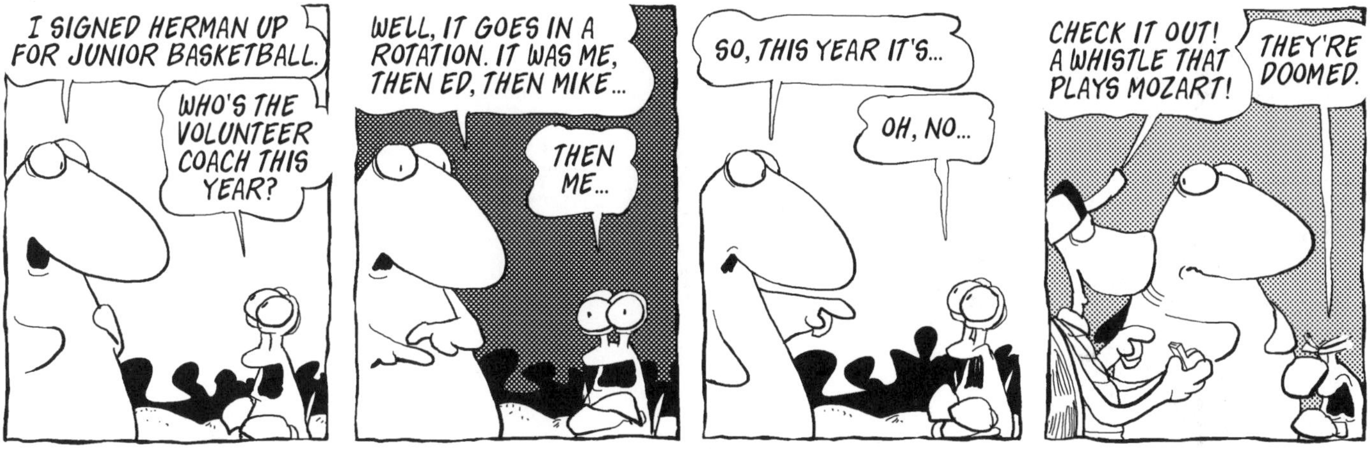
I SIGNED HERMAN UP FOR JUNIOR BASKETBALL.
WHO'S THE VOLUNTEER COACH THIS YEAR?
WELL, IT GOES IN A ROTATION. IT WAS ME, THEN ED, THEN MIKE...
THEN ME...
SO, THIS YEAR IT'S...
OH, NO...
CHECK IT OUT! A WHISTLE THAT PLAYS MOZART!
THEY'RE DOOMED.

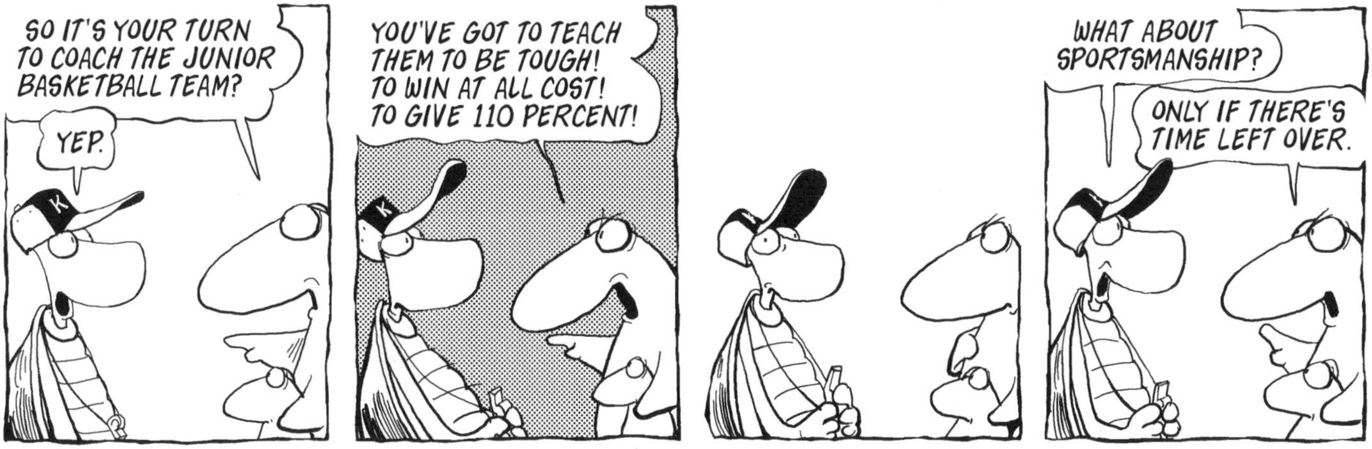
SO IT'S YOUR TURN TO COACH THE JUNIOR BASKETBALL TEAM?
YEP.
YOU'VE GOT TO TEACH THEM TO BE TOUGH! TO WIN AT ALL COST! TO GIVE 110 PERCENT!
WHAT ABOUT SPORTSMANSHIP?
ONLY IF THERE'S TIME LEFT OVER.

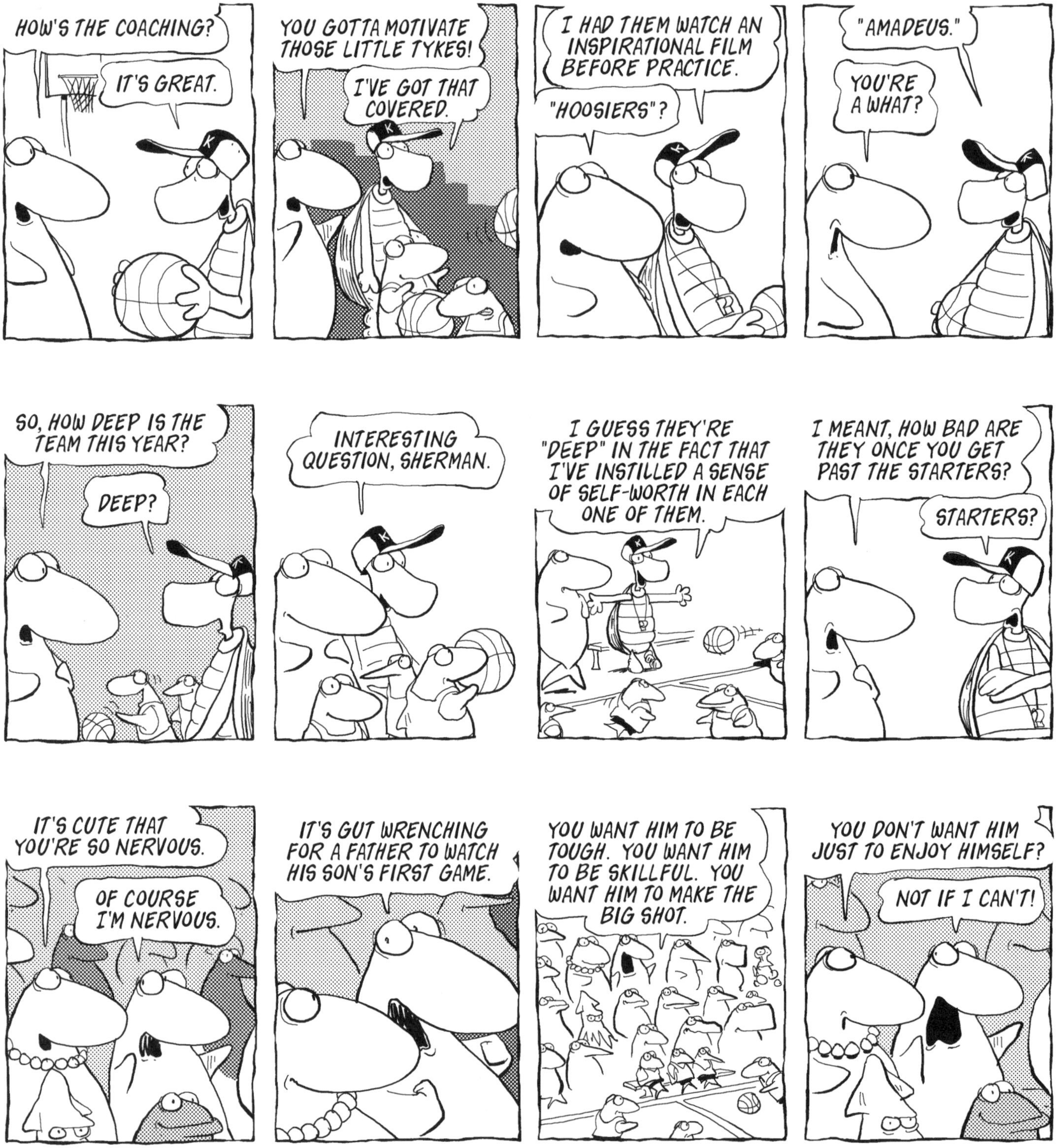
HOW'S THE COACHING?
IT'S GREAT.
YOU GOTTA MOTIVATE THOSE LITTLE TYKES!
I'VE GOT THAT COVERED.
I HAD THEM WATCH AN INSPIRATIONAL FILM BEFORE PRACTICE.
"HOOSIERS"?
"AMADEUS."
YOU'RE A WHAT?
SO, HOW DEEP IS THE TEAM THIS YEAR?
DEEP?
INTERESTING QUESTION, SHERMAN.
I GUESS THEY'RE "DEEP" IN THE FACT THAT I'VE INSTILLED A SENSE OF SELF-WORTH IN EACH ONE OF THEM.
I MEANT, HOW BAD ARE THEY ONCE YOU GET PAST THE STARTERS?
STARTERS?
IT'S CUTE THAT YOU'RE SO NERVOUS.
OF COURSE I'M NERVOUS.
IT'S GUT WRENCHING FOR A FATHER TO WATCH HIS SON'S FIRST GAME.
YOU WANT HIM TO BE TOUGH. YOU WANT HIM TO BE SKILLFUL. YOU WANT HIM TO MAKE THE BIG SHOT.
YOU DON'T WANT HIM JUST TO ENJOY HIMSELF?
NOT IF I CAN'T!

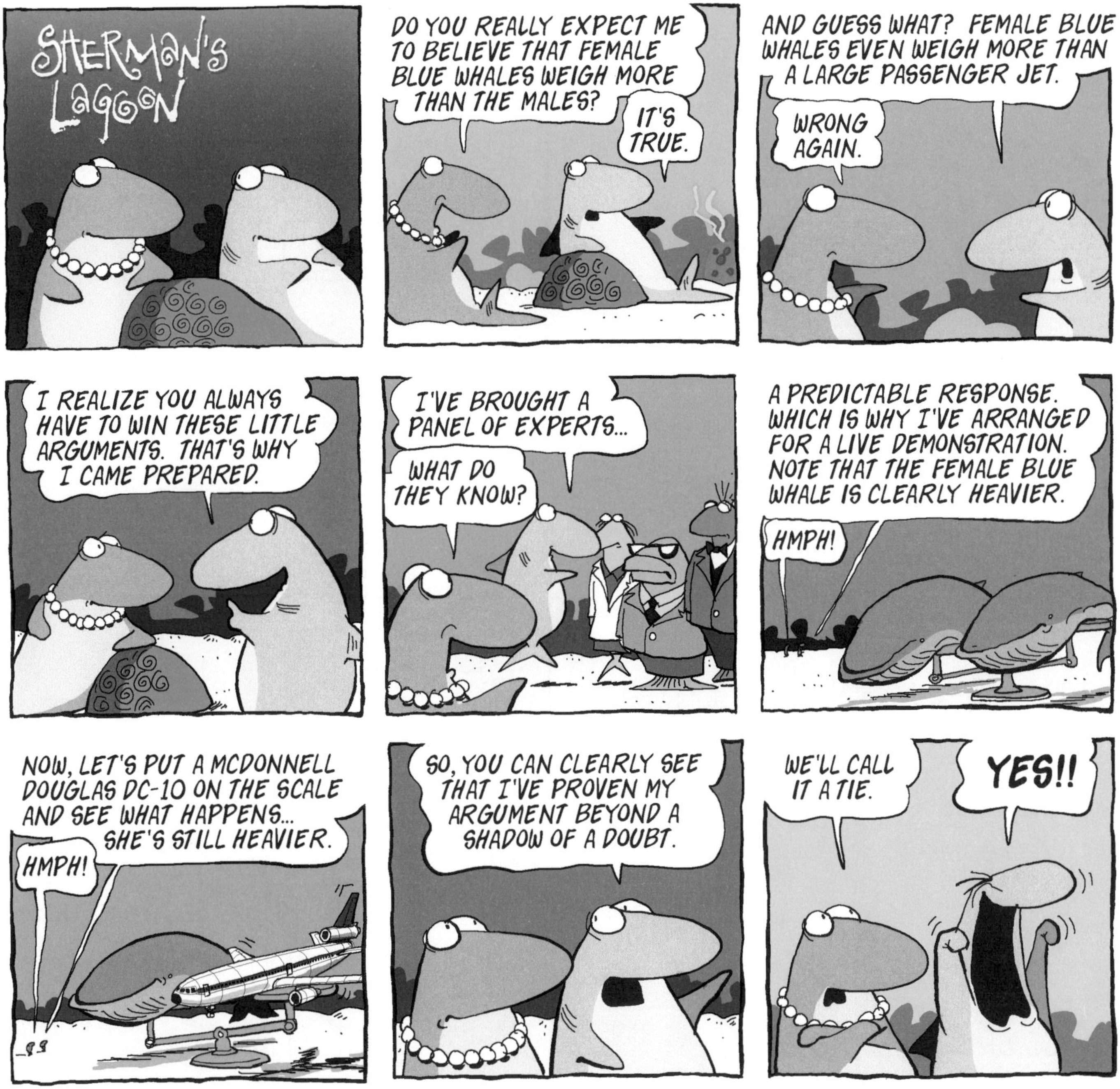
SHERMAN'S LAGOON
DO YOU REALLY EXPECT ME TO BELIEVE THAT FEMALE BLUE WHALES WEIGH MORE THAN THE MALES?
IT'S TRUE.
AND GUESS WHAT? FEMALE BLUE WHALES EVEN WEIGH MORE THAN A LARGE PASSENGER JET.
WRONG AGAIN.
I REALIZE YOU ALWAYS HAVE TO WIN THESE LITTLE ARGUMENTS. THAT'S WHY I CAME PREPARED.
I'VE BROUGHT A PANEL OF EXPERTS...
WHAT DO THEY KNOW?
A PREDICTABLE RESPONSE. WHICH IS WHY I'VE ARRANGED FOR A LIVE DEMONSTRATION. NOTE THAT THE FEMALE BLUE WHALE IS CLEARLY HEAVIER.
HMPH!
NOW, LET'S PUT A MCDONNELL DOUGLAS DC-10 ON THE SCALE AND SEE WHAT HAPPENS... SHE'S STILL HEAVIER.
HMPH!
SO, YOU CAN CLEARLY SEE THAT I'VE PROVEN MY ARGUMENT BEYOND A SHADOW OF A DOUBT.
WE'LL CALL IT A TIE.
YES!!

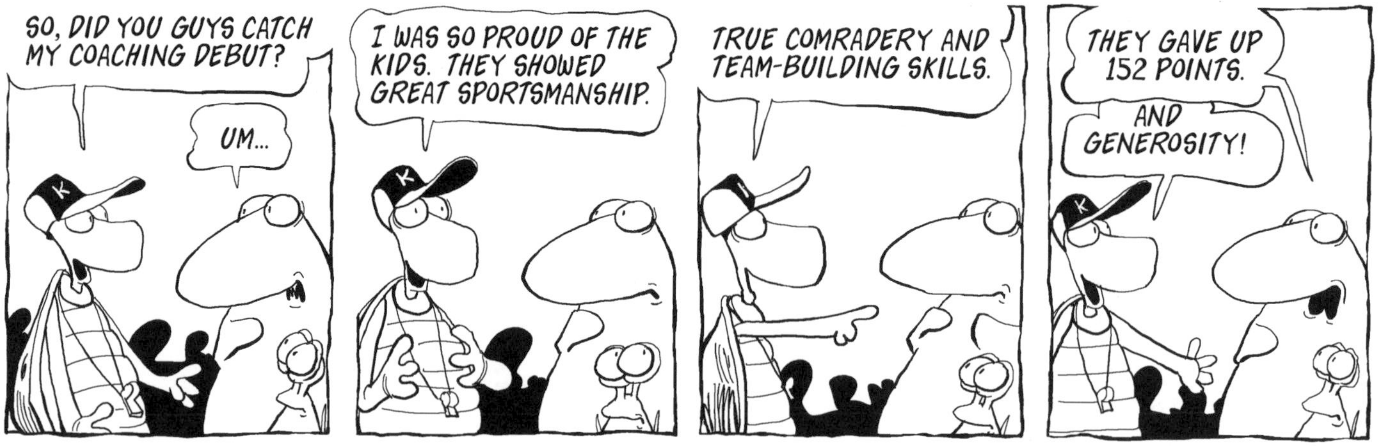
SO, DID YOU GUYS CATCH MY COACHING DEBUT?
UM...
I WAS SO PROUD OF THE KIDS. THEY SHOWED GREAT SPORTSMANSHIP.
TRUE COMRADERY AND TEAM-BUILDING SKILLS.
THEY GAVE UP 152 POINTS.
AND GENEROSITY!

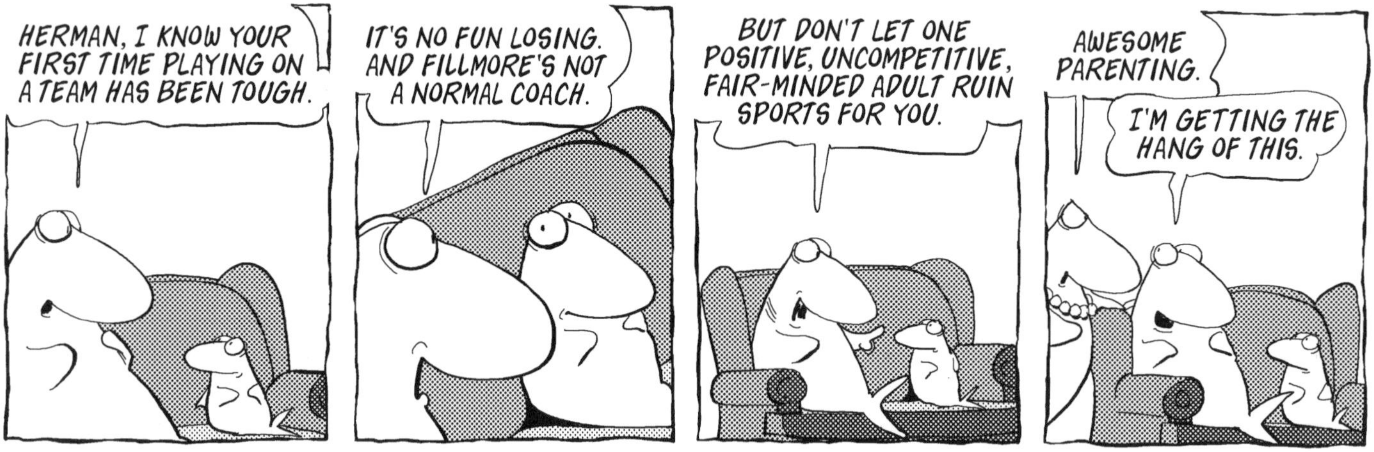
HERMAN, I KNOW YOUR FIRST TIME PLAYING ON A TEAM HAS BEEN TOUGH.
IT'S NO FUN LOSING. AND FILLMORE'S NOT A NORMAL COACH.
BUT DON'T LET ONE POSITIVE, UNCOMPETITIVE, FAIR-MINDED ADULT RUIN SPORTS FOR YOU.
AWESOME PARENTING.
I'M GETTING THE HANG OF THIS.

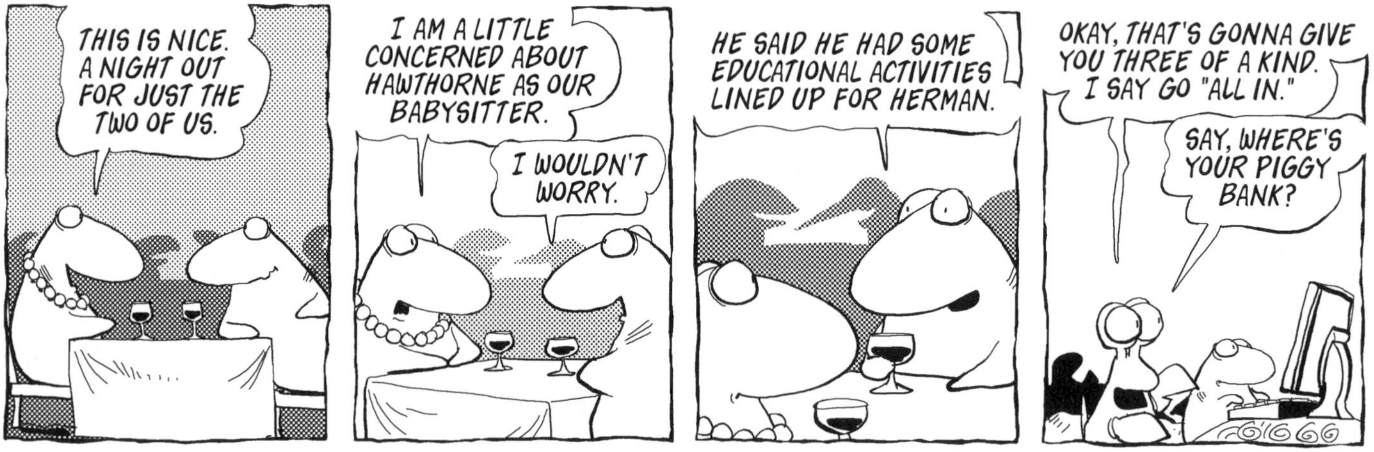
THIS IS NICE. A NIGHT OUT FOR JUST THE TWO OF US.
I AM A LITTLE CONCERNED ABOUT HAWTHORNE AS OUR BABYSITTER.
I WOULDN'T WORRY.
HE SAID HE HAD SOME EDUCATIONAL ACTIVITIES LINED UP FOR HERMAN.
OKAY, THAT'S GONNA GIVE YOU THREE OF A KIND. I SAY GO "ALL IN."
SAY, WHERE'S YOUR PIGGY BANK?

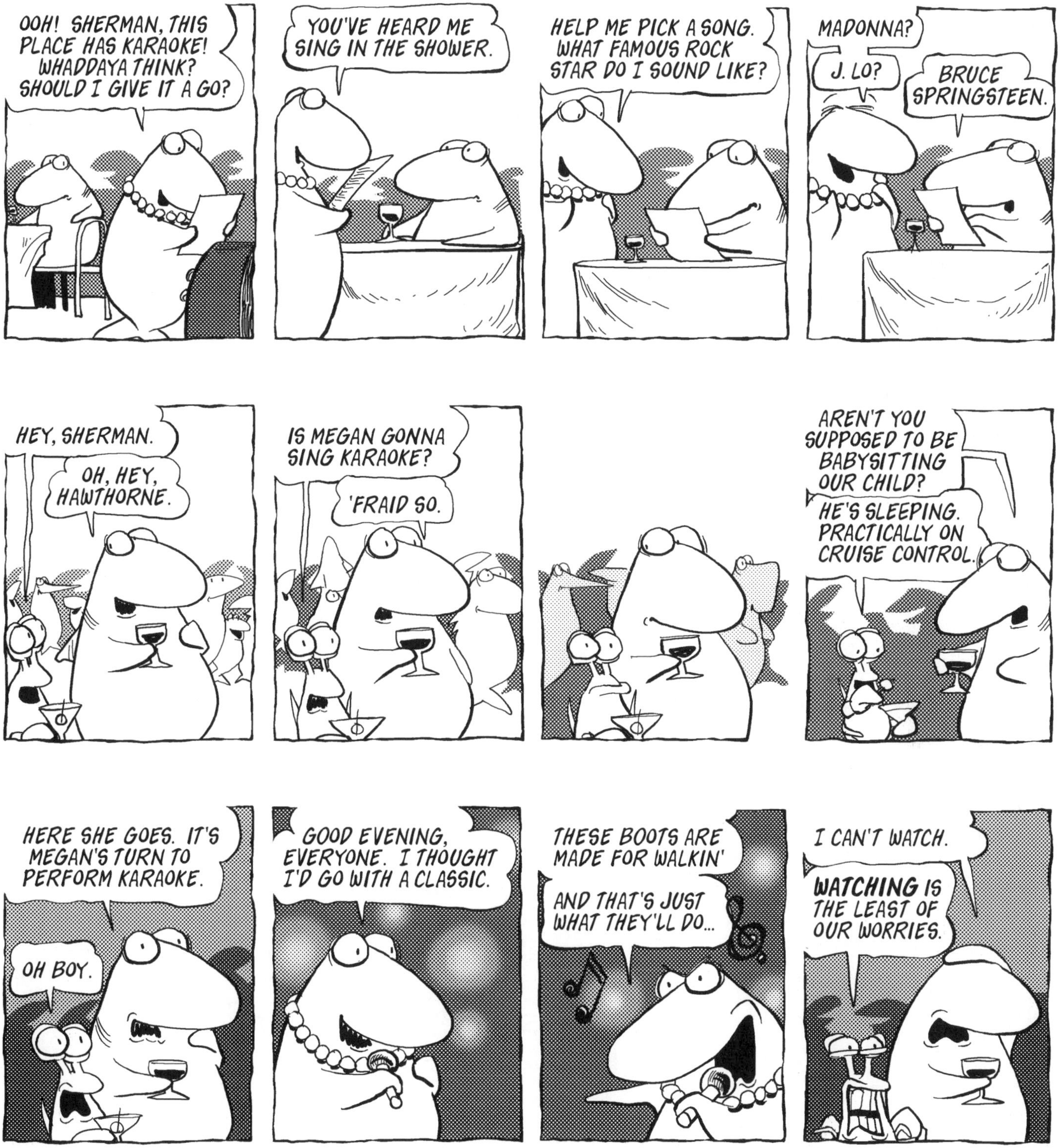
OOH! SHERMAN, THIS PLACE HAS KARAOKE! WHADDAYA THINK? SHOULD I GIVE IT A GO?
YOU'VE HEARD ME SING IN THE SHOWER.
HELP ME PICK A SONG. WHAT FAMOUS ROCK STAR DO I SOUND LIKE?
MADONNA?
J. LO?
BRUCE SPRINGSTEEN.
HEY, SHERMAN.
OH, HEY, HAWTHORNE.
IS MEGAN GONNA SING KARAOKE?
'FRAID SO.
AREN'T YOU SUPPOSED TO BE BABYSITTING OUR CHILD?
HE'S SLEEPING. PRACTICALLY ON CRUISE CONTROL.
HERE SHE GOES. IT'S MEGAN'S TURN TO PERFORM KARAOKE.
OH BOY.
GOOD EVENING, EVERYONE. I THOUGHT I'D GO WITH A CLASSIC.
THESE BOOTS ARE MADE FOR WALKIN'
AND THAT'S JUST WHAT THEY'LL DO...
I CAN'T WATCH.
WATCHING IS THE LEAST OF OUR WORRIES.

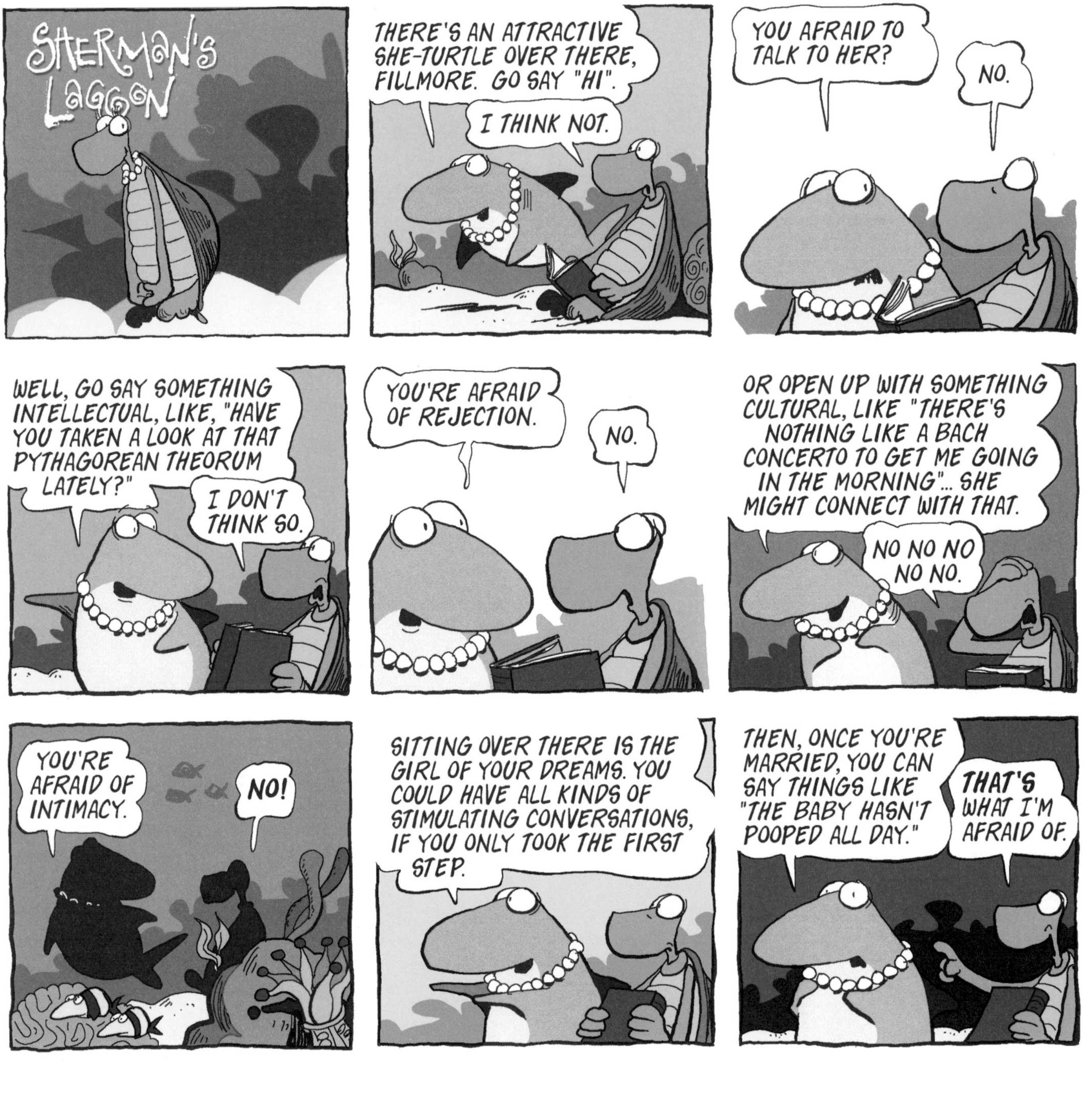
SHERMAN'S LAGOON
THERE'S AN ATTRACTIVE SHE-TURTLE OVER THERE, FILLMORE. GO SAY "HI".
I THINK NOT.
YOU AFRAID TO TALK TO HER?
NO.
WELL, GO SAY SOMETHING INTELLECTUAL, LIKE, "HAVE YOU TAKEN A LOOK AT THAT PYTHAGOREAN THEORUM LATELY?"
I DON'T THINK SO.
YOU'RE AFRAID OF REJECTION.
NO.
OR OPEN UP WITH SOMETHING CULTURAL, LIKE "THERE'S NOTHING LIKE A BACH CONCERTO TO GET ME GOING IN THE MORNING"... SHE MIGHT CONNECT WITH THAT.
NO NO NO NO NO.
YOU'RE AFRAID OF INTIMACY.
NO!
SITTING OVER THERE IS THE GIRL OF YOUR DREAMS. YOU COULD HAVE ALL KINDS OF STIMULATING CONVERSATIONS, IF YOU ONLY TOOK THE FIRST STEP.
THEN, ONCE YOU'RE MARRIED, YOU CAN SAY THINGS LIKE "THE BABY HASN'T POOPED ALL DAY."
THAT'S WHAT I'M AFRAID OF.

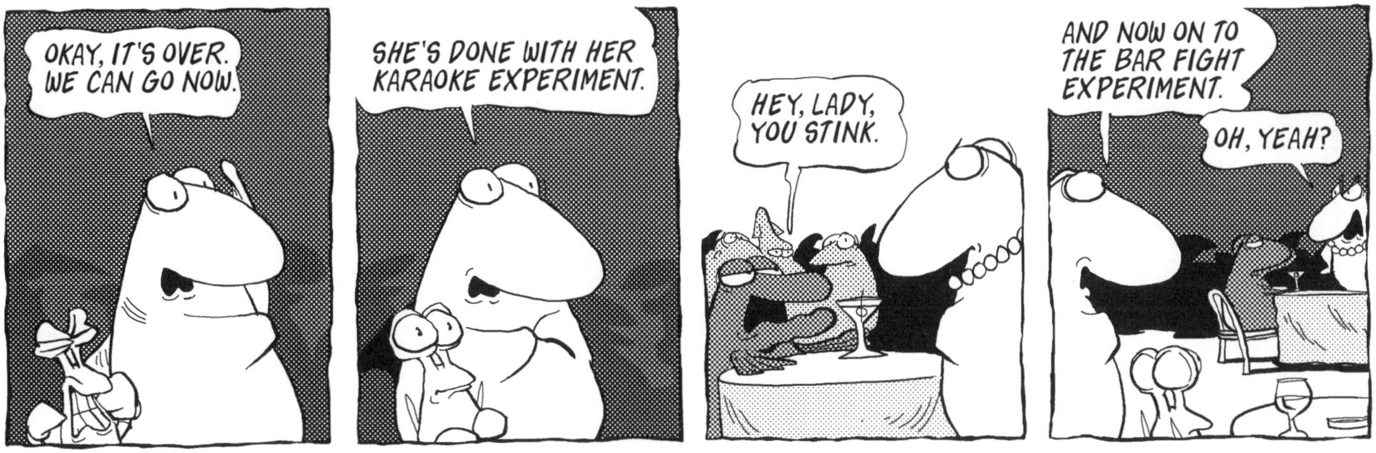
OKAY, IT'S OVER. WE CAN GO NOW.
SHE'S DONE WITH HER KARAOKE EXPERIMENT.
HEY, LADY, YOU STINK.
AND NOW ON TO THE BAR FIGHT EXPERIMENT.
OH, YEAH?

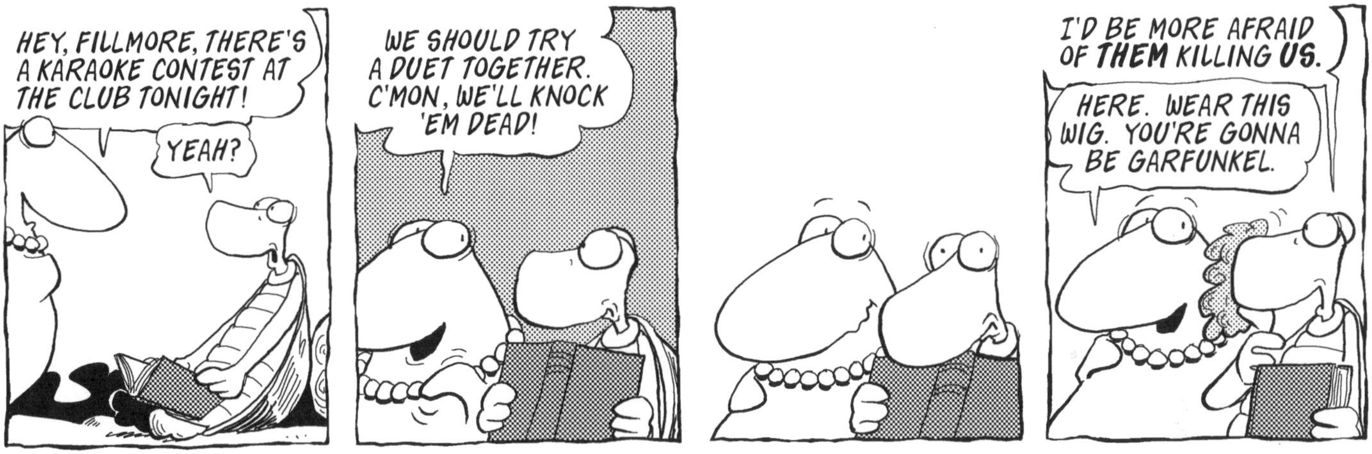
HEY, FILLMORE, THERE'S A KARAOKE CONTEST AT THE CLUB TONIGHT!
YEAH?
WE SHOULD TRY A DUET TOGETHER. C'MON, WE'LL KNOCK 'EM DEAD!
I'D BE MORE AFRAID OF **THEM** KILLING **US**.
HERE. WEAR THIS WIG. YOU'RE GONNA BE GARFUNKEL.

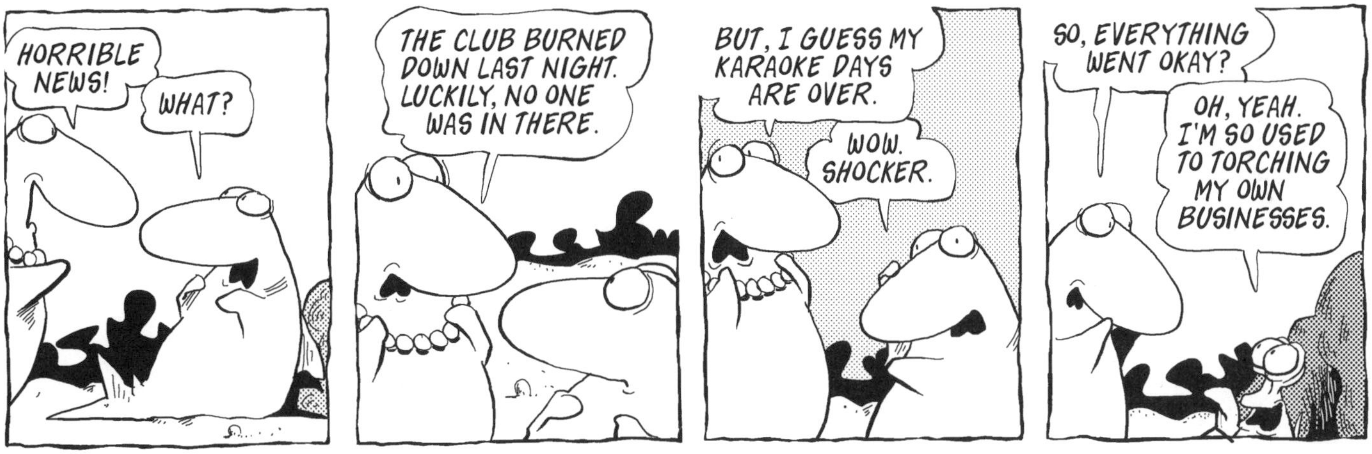
HORRIBLE NEWS!
WHAT?
THE CLUB BURNED DOWN LAST NIGHT. LUCKILY, NO ONE WAS IN THERE.
BUT, I GUESS MY KARAOKE DAYS ARE OVER.
WOW. SHOCKER.
SO, EVERYTHING WENT OKAY?
OH, YEAH. I'M SO USED TO TORCHING MY OWN BUSINESSES.

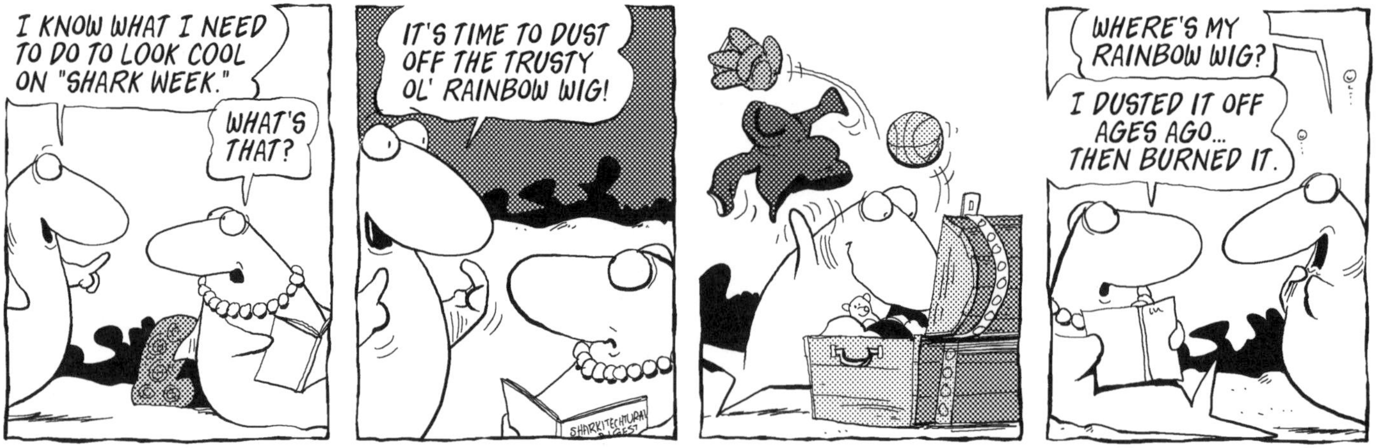
I KNOW WHAT I NEED TO DO TO LOOK COOL ON "SHARK WEEK."
WHAT'S THAT?
IT'S TIME TO DUST OFF THE TRUSTY OL' RAINBOW WIG!
WHERE'S MY RAINBOW WIG?
I DUSTED IT OFF AGES AGO... THEN BURNED IT.

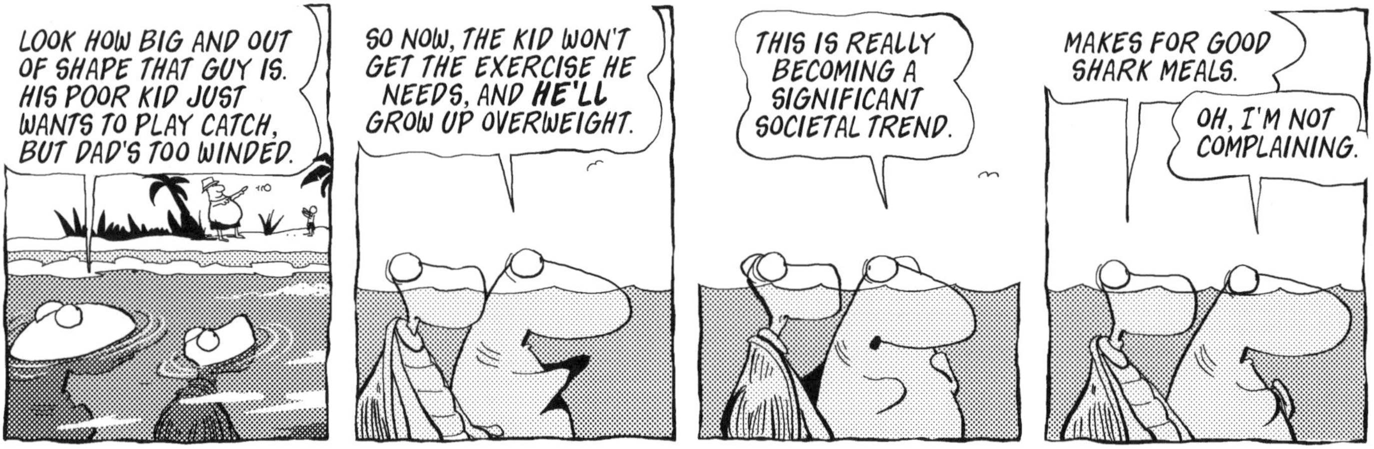
LOOK HOW BIG AND OUT OF SHAPE THAT GUY IS. HIS POOR KID JUST WANTS TO PLAY CATCH, BUT DAD'S TOO WINDED.
SO NOW, THE KID WON'T GET THE EXERCISE HE NEEDS, AND HE'LL GROW UP OVERWEIGHT.
THIS IS REALLY BECOMING A SIGNIFICANT SOCIETAL TREND.
MAKES FOR GOOD SHARK MEALS.
OH, I'M NOT COMPLAINING.

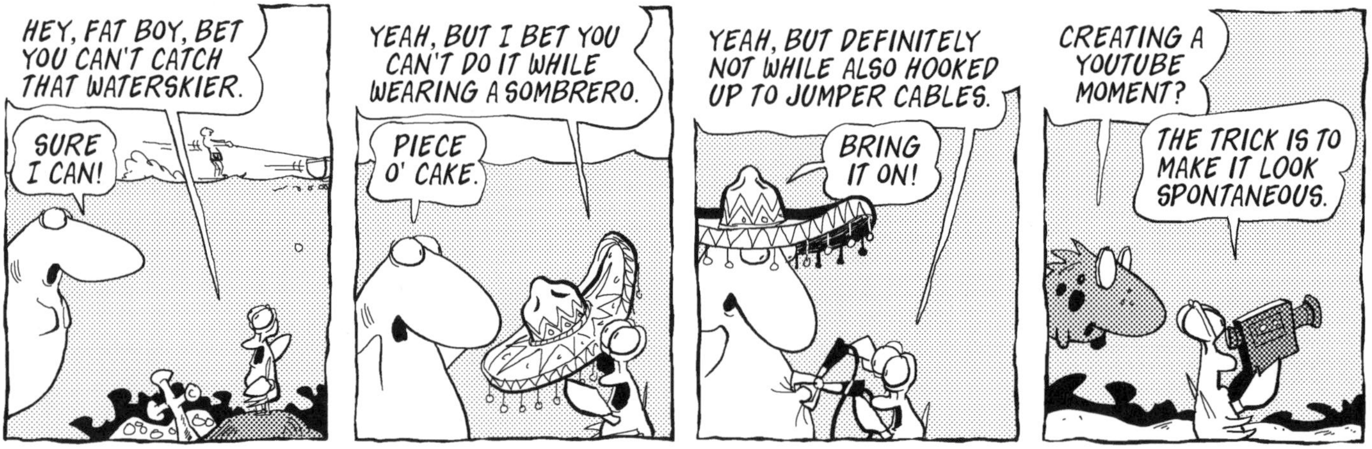
HEY, FAT BOY, BET YOU CAN'T CATCH THAT WATERSKIER.
SURE I CAN!
YEAH, BUT I BET YOU CAN'T DO IT WHILE WEARING A SOMBRERO.
PIECE O' CAKE.
YEAH, BUT DEFINITELY NOT WHILE ALSO HOOKED UP TO JUMPER CABLES.
BRING IT ON!
CREATING A YOUTUBE MOMENT?
THE TRICK IS TO MAKE IT LOOK SPONTANEOUS.

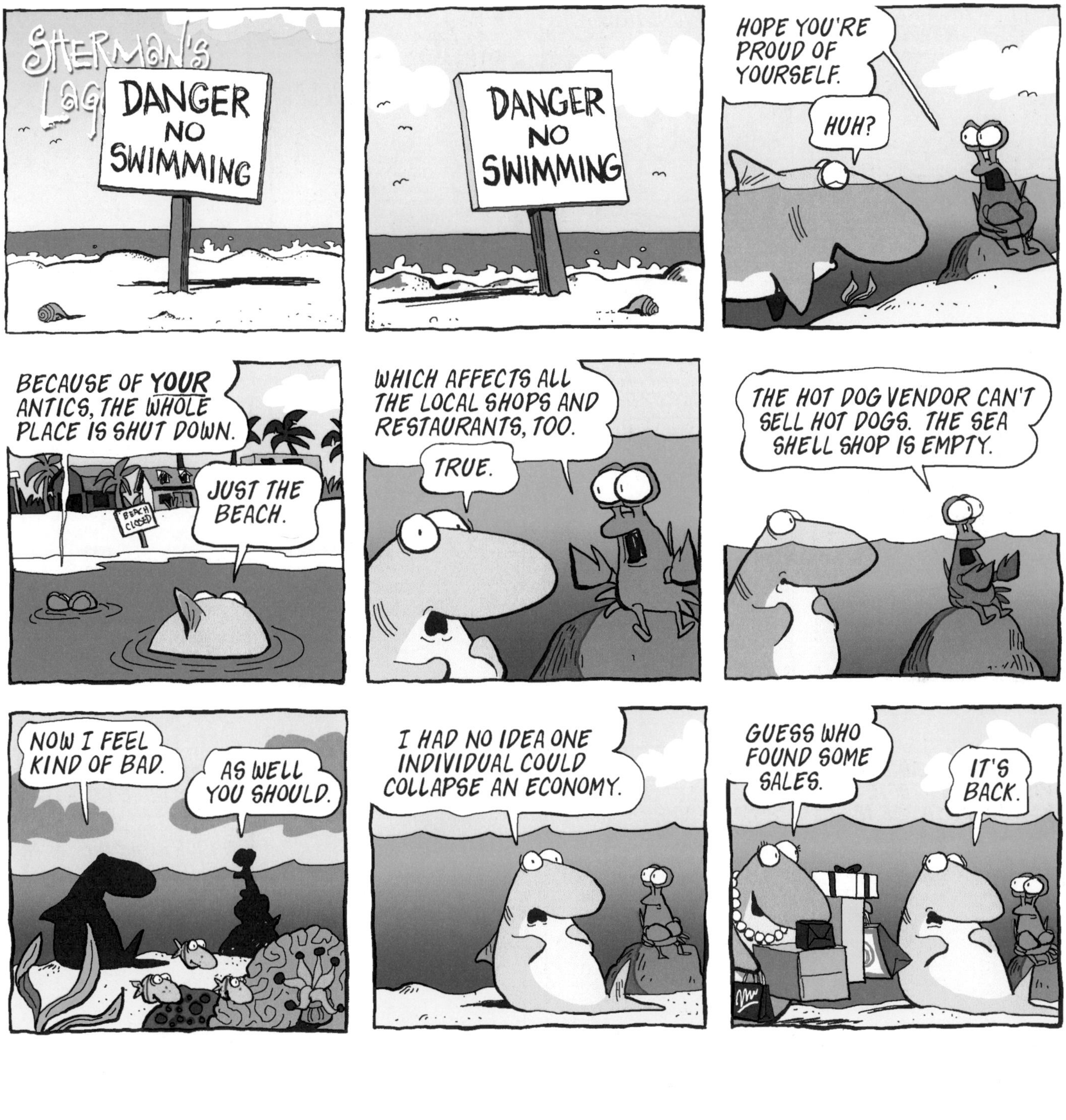
SHERMAN'S LAGOON
DANGER NO SWIMMING
DANGER NO SWIMMING
HOPE YOU'RE PROUD OF YOURSELF.
HUH?
BECAUSE OF YOUR ANTICS, THE WHOLE PLACE IS SHUT DOWN.
BEACH CLOSED
JUST THE BEACH.
WHICH AFFECTS ALL THE LOCAL SHOPS AND RESTAURANTS, TOO.
TRUE.
THE HOT DOG VENDOR CAN'T SELL HOT DOGS. THE SEA SHELL SHOP IS EMPTY.
NOW I FEEL KIND OF BAD.
AS WELL YOU SHOULD.
I HAD NO IDEA ONE INDIVIDUAL COULD COLLAPSE AN ECONOMY.
GUESS WHO FOUND SOME SALES.
IT'S BACK.

NICE GLASSES, DOOFUS.
THEY'RE FOR READING.
AND I HAD TO BUY OVER THE COUNTER SINCE THE LAGOON HAS NO OPTOMETRIST.
DING
WAS THAT AN EVIL "DING"?
IS THERE ANOTHER KIND?
I NEED TO HAVE MY EYES CHECKED.
DO YOU HAVE INSURANCE?
Hawthorne Optometry
WELL, I DID. BUT THEN THE COMPANY WENT BANKRUPT.
OH, WELL, THEN I CAN'T...
BUT THEN THEY GOT A HUGE BAILOUT CHECK!
OH, WELL, GREAT! WE CAN...
Hawthorne Optometry
BUT THEN THEY BLEW IT ALL AT THE HORSE TRACK.
OH, WELL, THEN I CAN'T...
Hawthorne Optometry
LET'S RUN SOME PRELIMINARY TESTS ON YOUR EYES TO SEE IF YOU NEED GLASSES.
OKAY.
Hawthorne Optometry
LOOK THROUGH THE LENS, AND TELL ME WHAT YOU SEE...
JESSICA SIMPSON IN DAISY DUKE SHORTS.
WHOOPS. WRONG SLIDE SHOW.

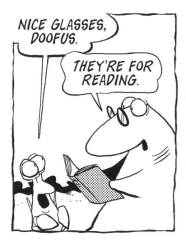

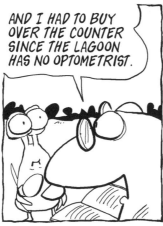

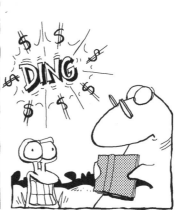

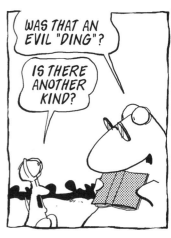

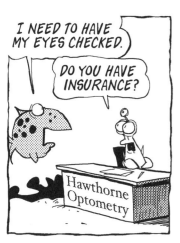

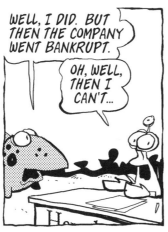

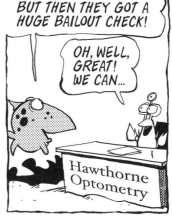

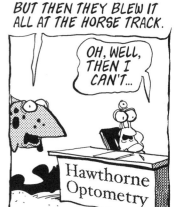

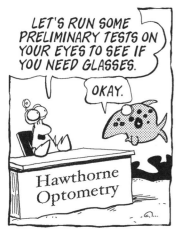

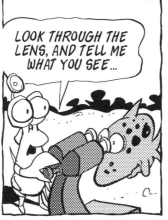

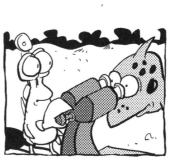

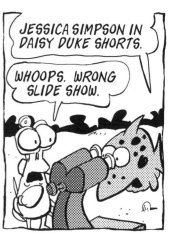

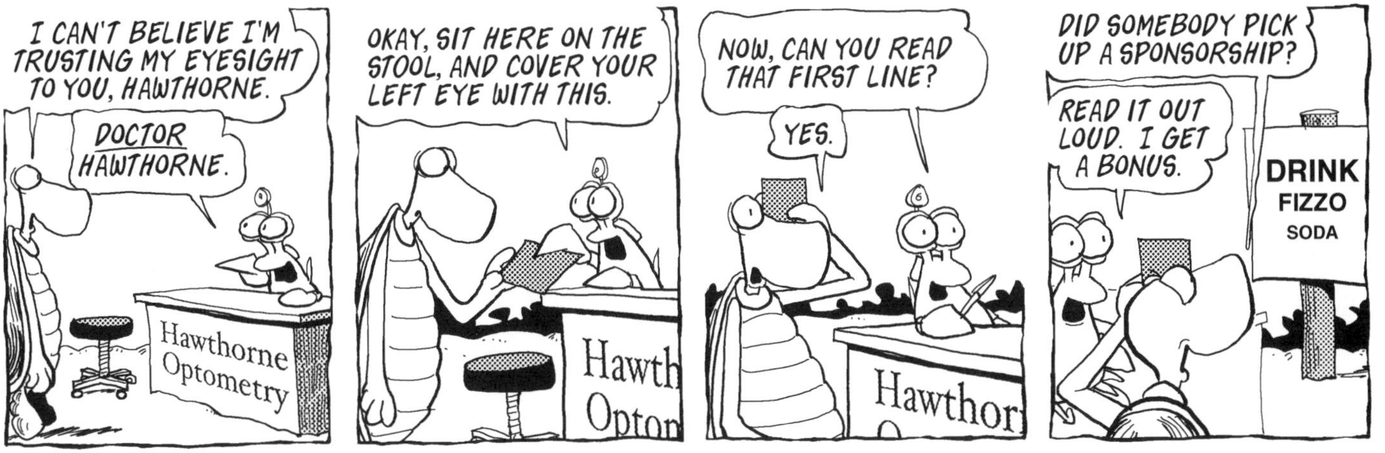
I CAN'T BELIEVE I'M TRUSTING MY EYESIGHT TO YOU, HAWTHORNE.
DOCTOR HAWTHORNE.
Hawthorne Optometry
OKAY, SIT HERE ON THE STOOL, AND COVER YOUR LEFT EYE WITH THIS.
NOW, CAN YOU READ THAT FIRST LINE?
YES.
DID SOMEBODY PICK UP A SPONSORSHIP?
READ IT OUT LOUD. I GET A BONUS.
DRINK
FIZZO
SODA

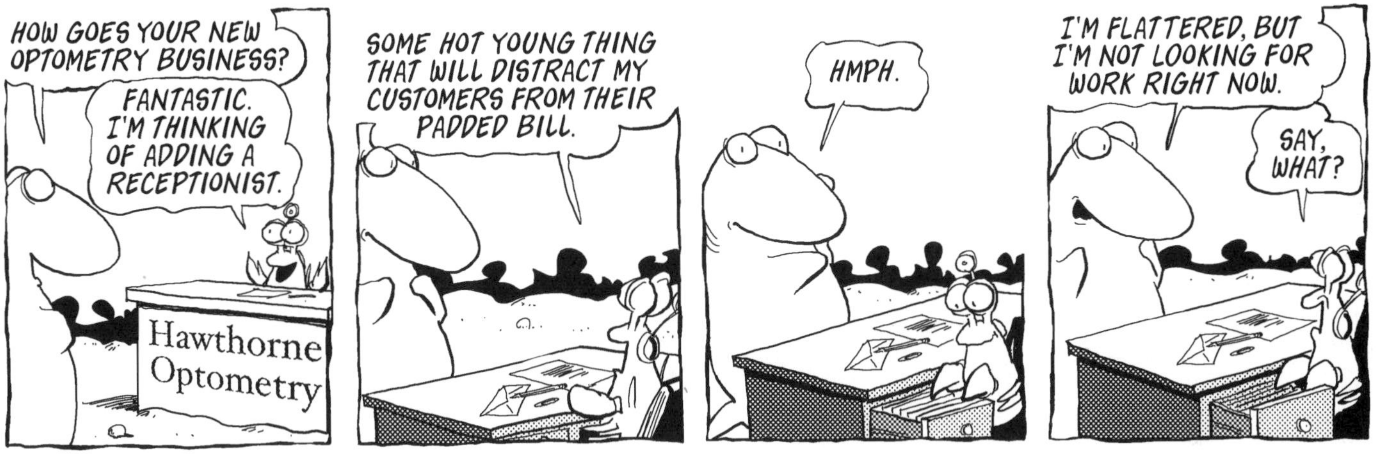
HOW GOES YOUR NEW OPTOMETRY BUSINESS?
FANTASTIC. I'M THINKING OF ADDING A RECEPTIONIST.
Hawthorne Optometry
SOME HOT YOUNG THING THAT WILL DISTRACT MY CUSTOMERS FROM THEIR PADDED BILL.
HMPH.
I'M FLATTERED, BUT I'M NOT LOOKING FOR WORK RIGHT NOW.
SAY, WHAT?

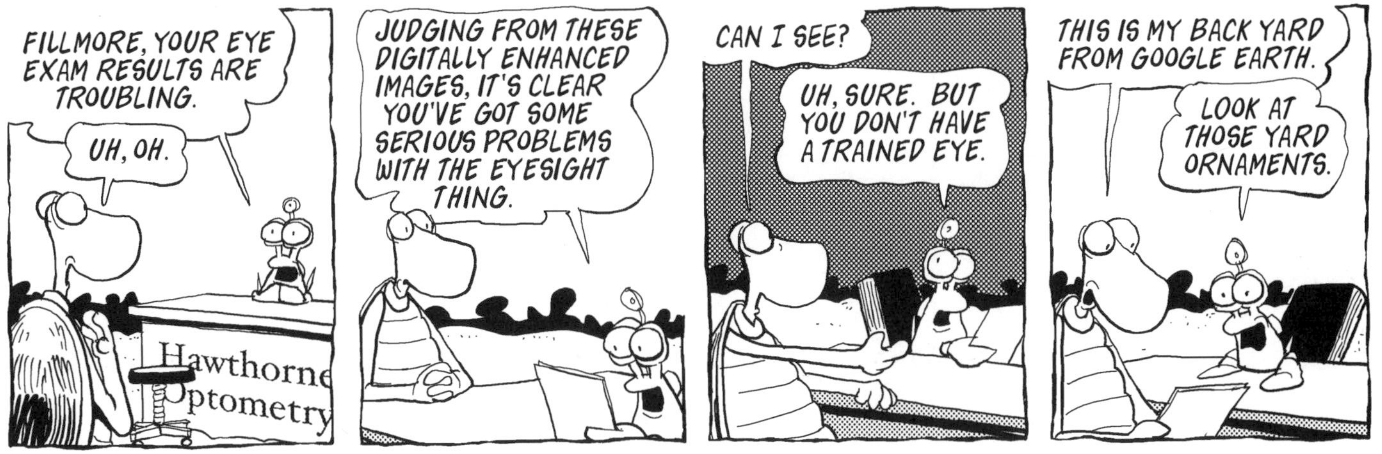
FILLMORE, YOUR EYE EXAM RESULTS ARE TROUBLING.
UH, OH.
Hawthorne Optometry
JUDGING FROM THESE DIGITALLY ENHANCED IMAGES, IT'S CLEAR YOU'VE GOT SOME SERIOUS PROBLEMS WITH THE EYESIGHT THING.
CAN I SEE?
UH, SURE. BUT YOU DON'T HAVE A TRAINED EYE.
THIS IS MY BACK YARD FROM GOOGLE EARTH.
LOOK AT THOSE YARD ORNAMENTS.

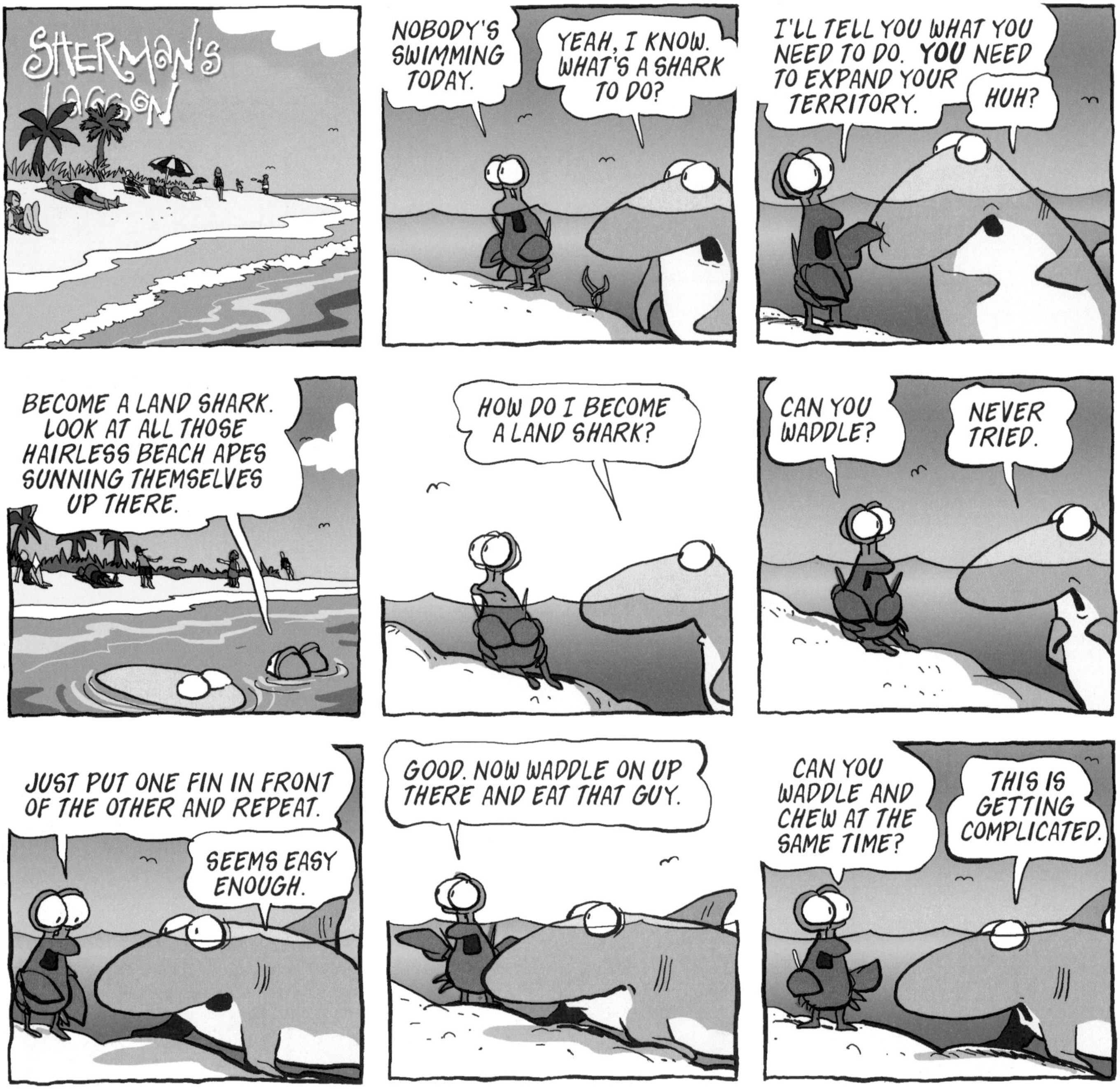
SHERMAN'S LAGOON
NOBODY'S SWIMMING TODAY.
YEAH, I KNOW. WHAT'S A SHARK TO DO?
I'LL TELL YOU WHAT YOU NEED TO DO. **YOU** NEED TO EXPAND YOUR TERRITORY.
HUH?
BECOME A LAND SHARK. LOOK AT ALL THOSE HAIRLESS BEACH APES SUNNING THEMSELVES UP THERE.
HOW DO I BECOME A LAND SHARK?
CAN YOU WADDLE?
NEVER TRIED.
JUST PUT ONE FIN IN FRONT OF THE OTHER AND REPEAT.
SEEMS EASY ENOUGH.
GOOD. NOW WADDLE ON UP THERE AND EAT THAT GUY.
CAN YOU WADDLE AND CHEW AT THE SAME TIME?
THIS IS GETTING COMPLICATED.

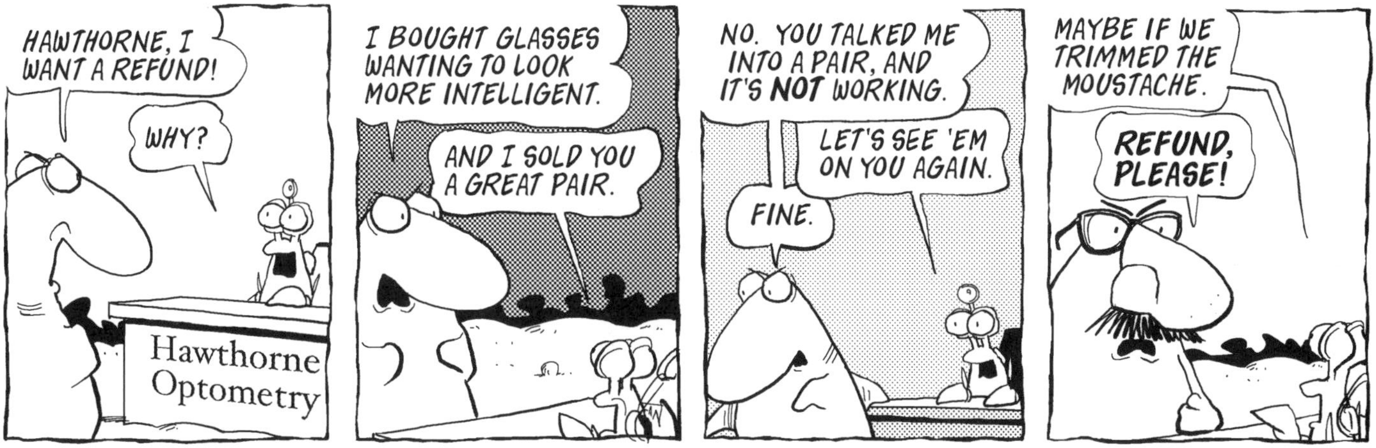
HAWTHORNE, I WANT A REFUND!
WHY?
Hawthorne Optometry
I BOUGHT GLASSES WANTING TO LOOK MORE INTELLIGENT.
AND I SOLD YOU A GREAT PAIR.
NO. YOU TALKED ME INTO A PAIR, AND IT'S **NOT** WORKING.
LET'S SEE 'EM ON YOU AGAIN.
FINE.
MAYBE IF WE TRIMMED THE MOUSTACHE.
REFUND, PLEASE!

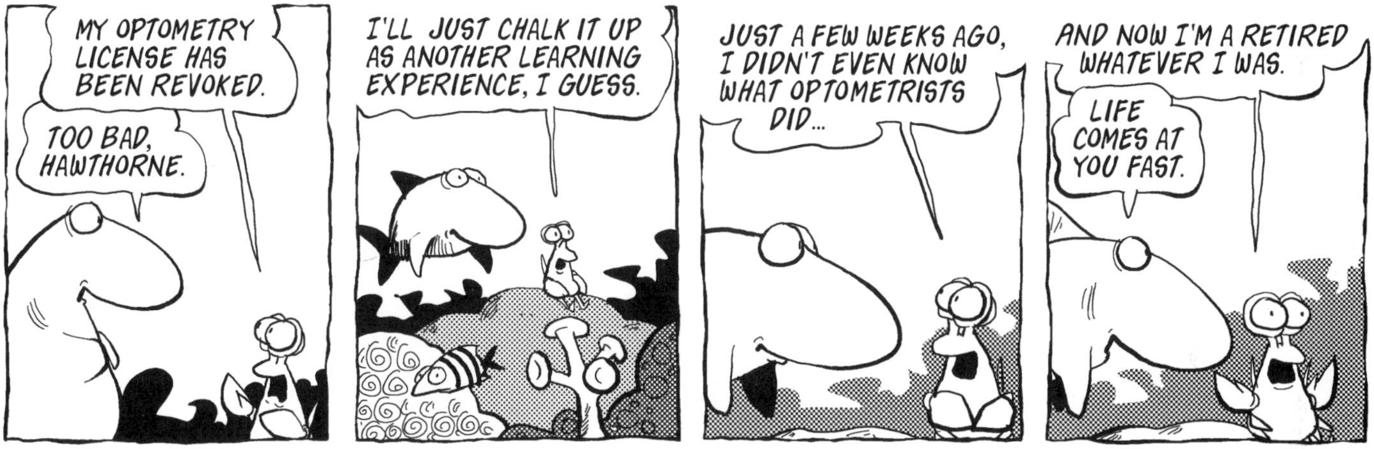
MY OPTOMETRY LICENSE HAS BEEN REVOKED.
TOO BAD, HAWTHORNE.
I'LL JUST CHALK IT UP AS ANOTHER LEARNING EXPERIENCE, I GUESS.
JUST A FEW WEEKS AGO, I DIDN'T EVEN KNOW WHAT OPTOMETRISTS DID...
AND NOW I'M A RETIRED WHATEVER I WAS.
LIFE COMES AT YOU FAST.

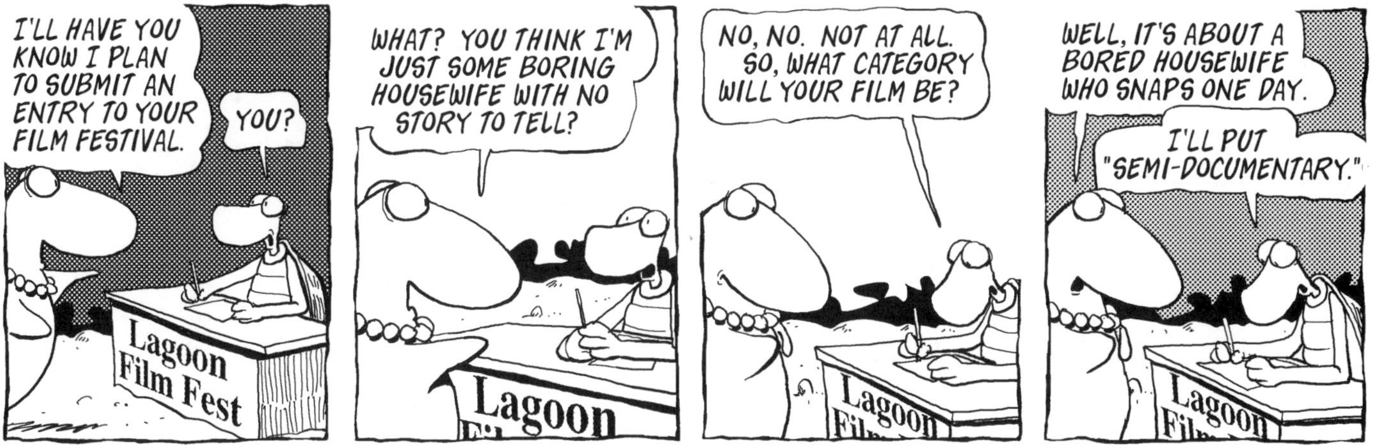
I'LL HAVE YOU KNOW I PLAN TO SUBMIT AN ENTRY TO YOUR FILM FESTIVAL.
YOU?
Lagoon Film Fest
WHAT? YOU THINK I'M JUST SOME BORING HOUSEWIFE WITH NO STORY TO TELL?
Lagoon
NO, NO. NOT AT ALL. SO, WHAT CATEGORY WILL YOUR FILM BE?
WELL, IT'S ABOUT A BORED HOUSEWIFE WHO SNAPS ONE DAY.
I'LL PUT "SEMI-DOCUMENTARY."

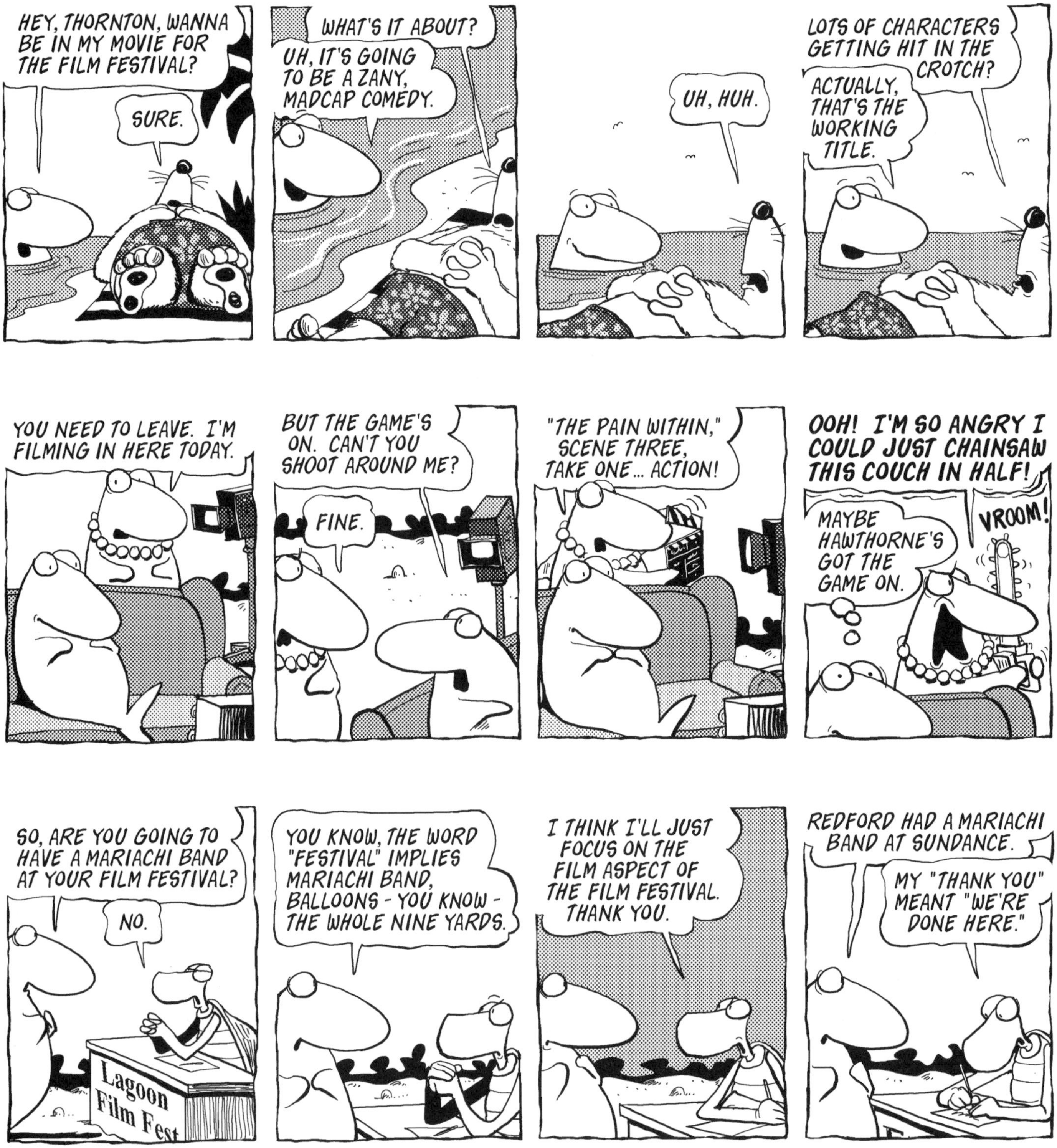
HEY, THORNTON, WANNA BE IN MY MOVIE FOR THE FILM FESTIVAL?
SURE.
WHAT'S IT ABOUT?
UH, IT'S GOING TO BE A ZANY, MADCAP COMEDY.
UH, HUH.
LOTS OF CHARACTERS GETTING HIT IN THE CROTCH?
ACTUALLY, THAT'S THE WORKING TITLE.
YOU NEED TO LEAVE. I'M FILMING IN HERE TODAY.
BUT THE GAME'S ON. CAN'T YOU SHOOT AROUND ME?
FINE.
"THE PAIN WITHIN," SCENE THREE, TAKE ONE... ACTION!
OOH! I'M SO ANGRY I COULD JUST CHAINSAW THIS COUCH IN HALF!
MAYBE HAWTHORNE'S GOT THE GAME ON.
VROOM!
SO, ARE YOU GOING TO HAVE A MARIACHI BAND AT YOUR FILM FESTIVAL?
NO.
Lagoon Film Fest
YOU KNOW, THE WORD "FESTIVAL" IMPLIES MARIACHI BAND, BALLOONS - YOU KNOW - THE WHOLE NINE YARDS.
I THINK I'LL JUST FOCUS ON THE FILM ASPECT OF THE FILM FESTIVAL. THANK YOU.
REDFORD HAD A MARIACHI BAND AT SUNDANCE.
MY "THANK YOU" MEANT "WE'RE DONE HERE."

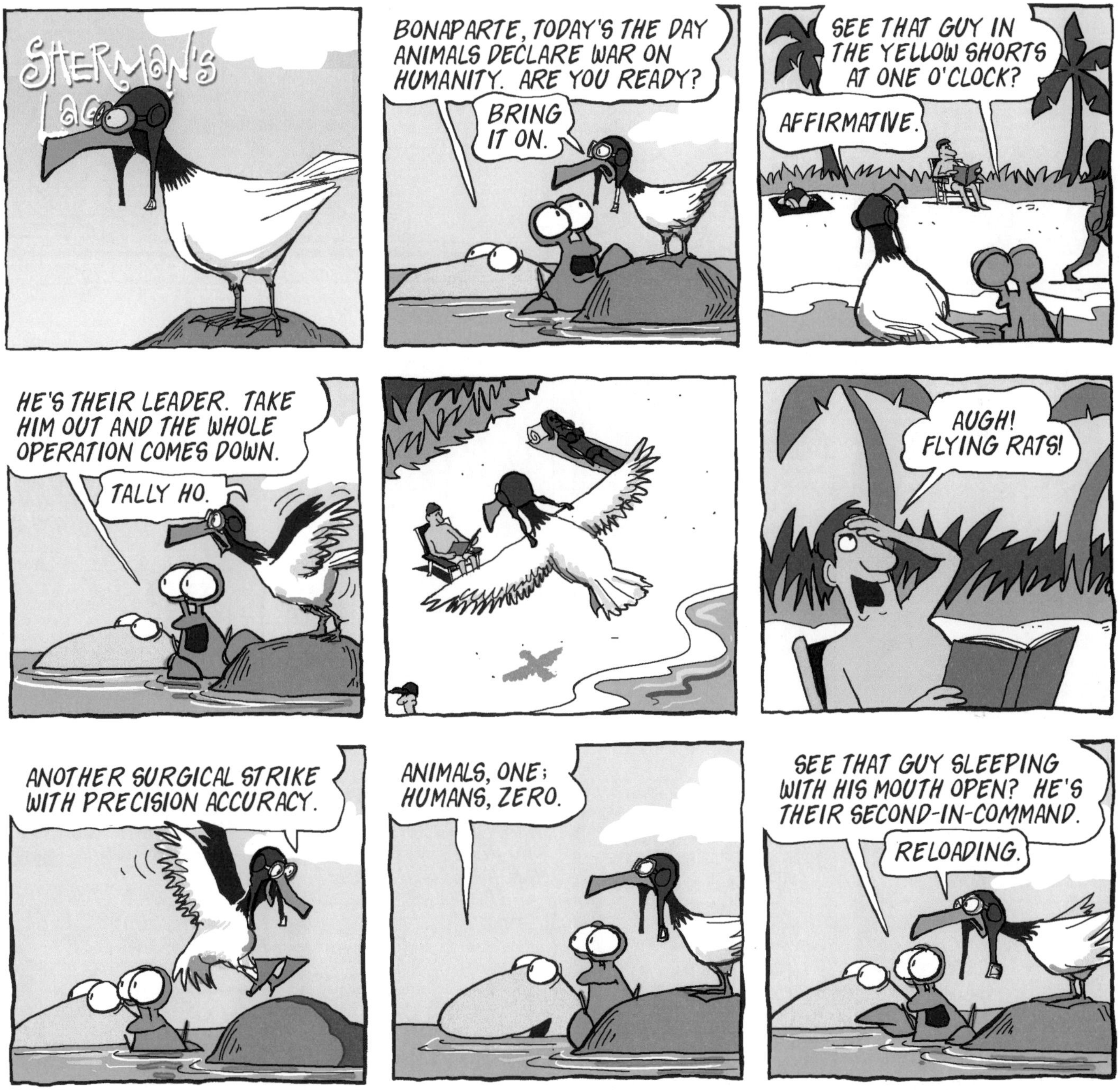
SHERMAN'S LAGOON
BONAPARTE, TODAY'S THE DAY ANIMALS DECLARE WAR ON HUMANITY. ARE YOU READY?
BRING IT ON.
SEE THAT GUY IN THE YELLOW SHORTS AT ONE O'CLOCK?
AFFIRMATIVE.
HE'S THEIR LEADER. TAKE HIM OUT AND THE WHOLE OPERATION COMES DOWN.
TALLY HO.
AUGH! FLYING RATS!
ANOTHER SURGICAL STRIKE WITH PRECISION ACCURACY.
ANIMALS, ONE; HUMANS, ZERO.
SEE THAT GUY SLEEPING WITH HIS MOUTH OPEN? HE'S THEIR SECOND-IN-COMMAND.
RELOADING.

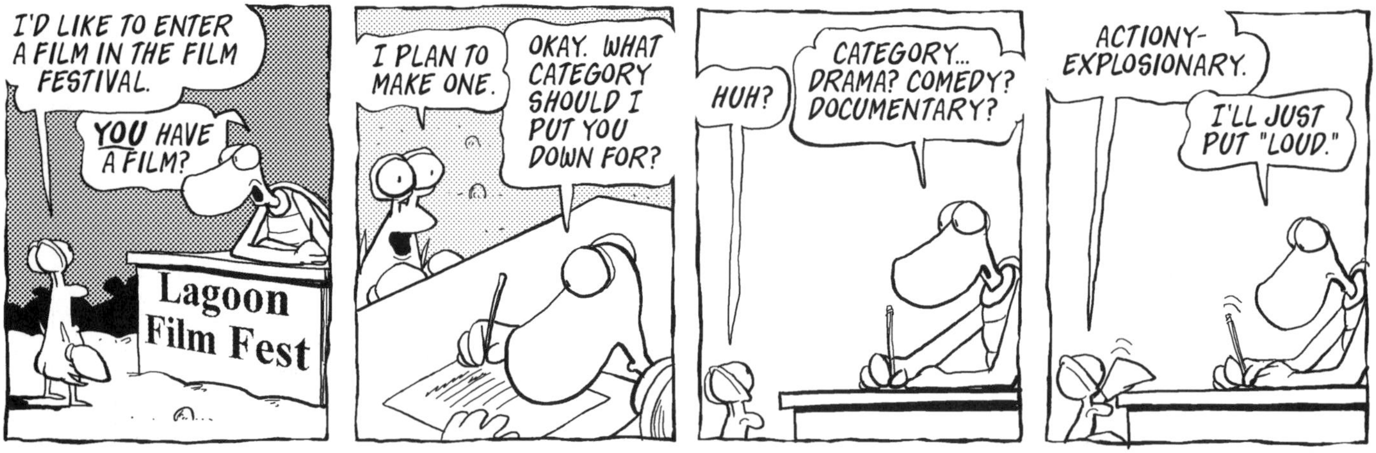
I'D LIKE TO ENTER A FILM IN THE FILM FESTIVAL.
YOU HAVE A FILM?
Lagoon Film Fest
I PLAN TO MAKE ONE.
OKAY. WHAT CATEGORY SHOULD I PUT YOU DOWN FOR?
HUH?
CATEGORY... DRAMA? COMEDY? DOCUMENTARY?
ACTIONY-EXPLOSIONARY.
I'LL JUST PUT "LOUD."

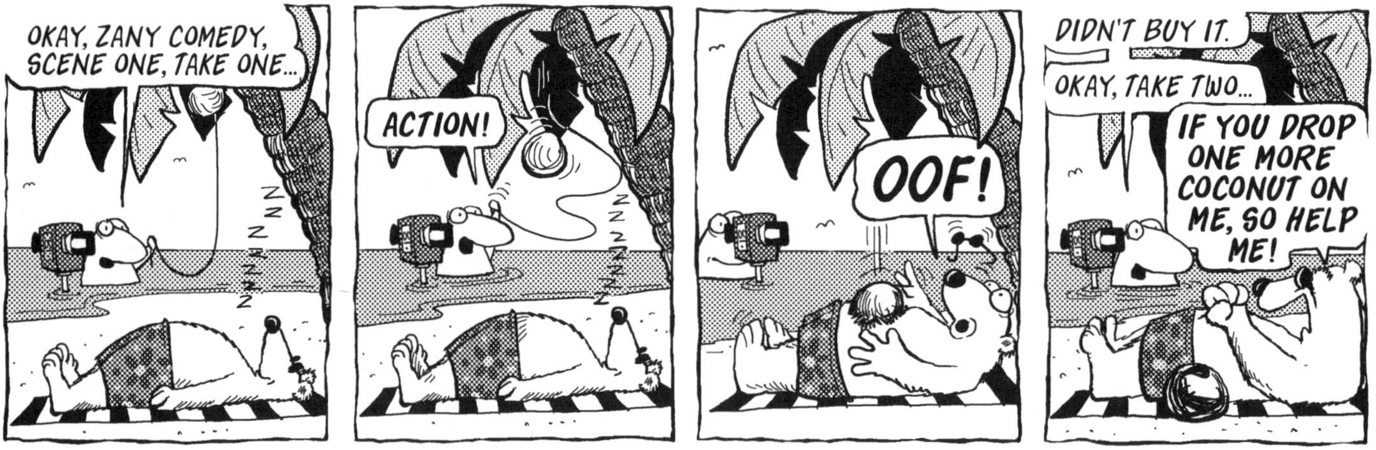
OKAY, ZANY COMEDY, SCENE ONE, TAKE ONE...
ACTION!
OOF!
DIDN'T BUY IT.
OKAY, TAKE TWO...
IF YOU DROP ONE MORE COCONUT ON ME, SO HELP ME!

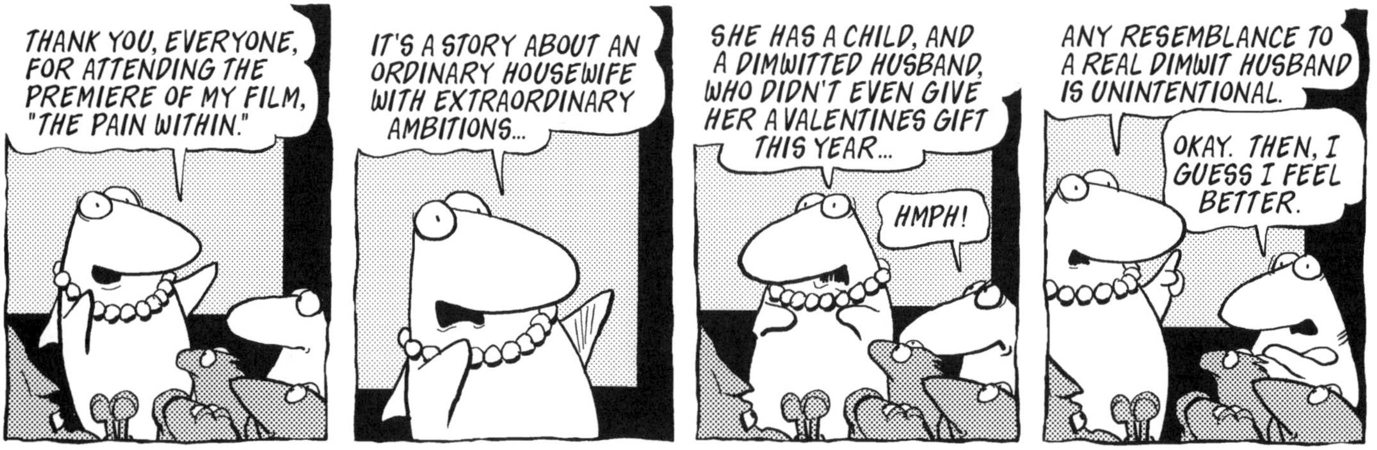
THANK YOU, EVERYONE, FOR ATTENDING THE PREMIERE OF MY FILM, "THE PAIN WITHIN."
IT'S A STORY ABOUT AN ORDINARY HOUSEWIFE WITH EXTRAORDINARY AMBITIONS...
SHE HAS A CHILD, AND A DIMWITTED HUSBAND, WHO DIDN'T EVEN GIVE HER A VALENTINES GIFT THIS YEAR...
HMPH!
ANY RESEMBLANCE TO A REAL DIMWIT HUSBAND IS UNINTENTIONAL.
OKAY. THEN, I GUESS I FEEL BETTER.

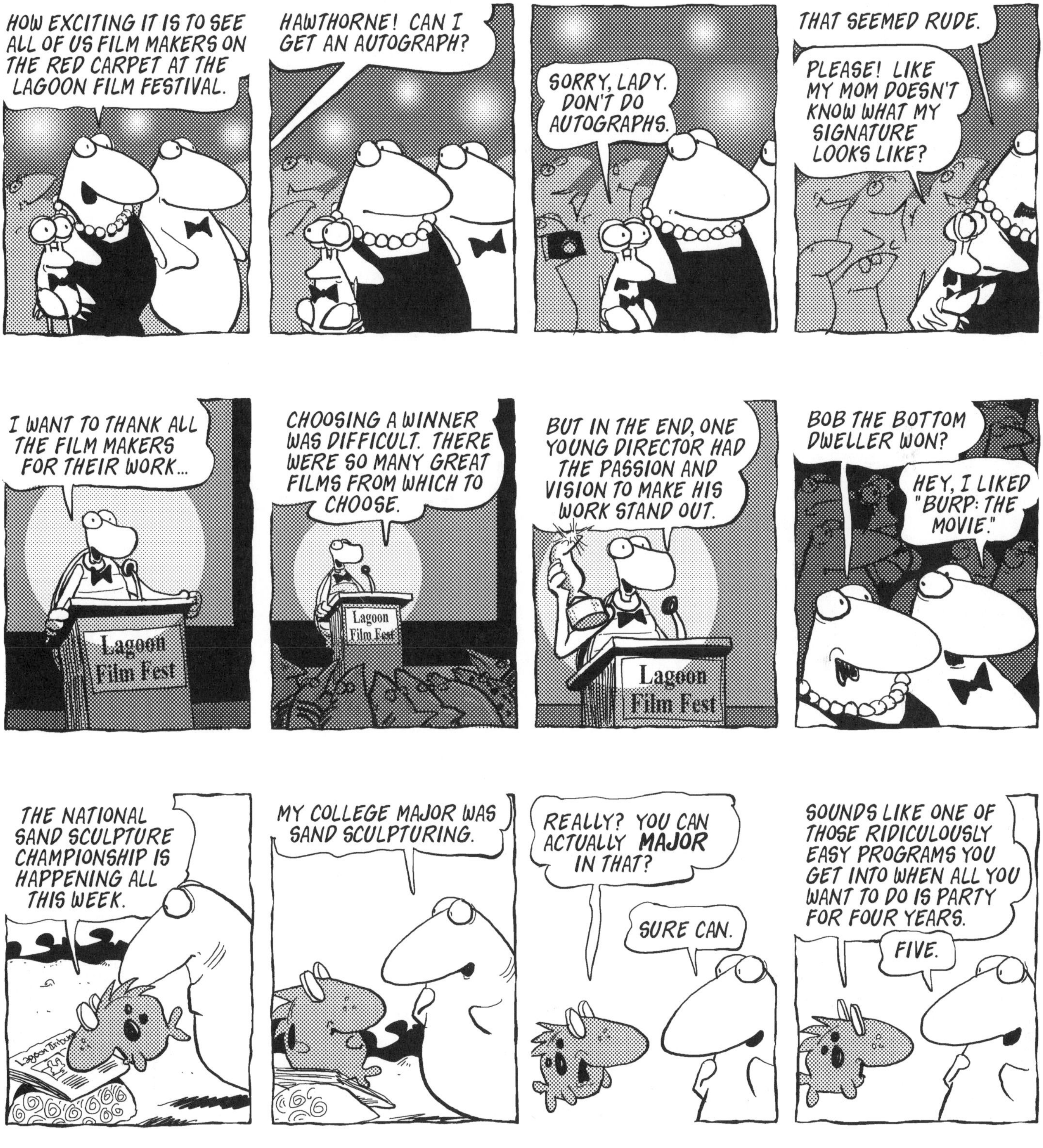
HOW EXCITING IT IS TO SEE ALL OF US FILM MAKERS ON THE RED CARPET AT THE LAGOON FILM FESTIVAL.
HAWTHORNE! CAN I GET AN AUTOGRAPH?
SORRY, LADY. DON'T DO AUTOGRAPHS.
THAT SEEMED RUDE.
PLEASE! LIKE MY MOM DOESN'T KNOW WHAT MY SIGNATURE LOOKS LIKE?
I WANT TO THANK ALL THE FILM MAKERS FOR THEIR WORK...
Lagoon Film Fest
CHOOSING A WINNER WAS DIFFICULT. THERE WERE SO MANY GREAT FILMS FROM WHICH TO CHOOSE.
Lagoon Film Fest
BUT IN THE END, ONE YOUNG DIRECTOR HAD THE PASSION AND VISION TO MAKE HIS WORK STAND OUT.
Lagoon Film Fest
BOB THE BOTTOM DWELLER WON?
HEY, I LIKED "BURP: THE MOVIE."
THE NATIONAL SAND SCULPTURE CHAMPIONSHIP IS HAPPENING ALL THIS WEEK.
MY COLLEGE MAJOR WAS SAND SCULPTURING.
REALLY? YOU CAN ACTUALLY **MAJOR** IN THAT?
SURE CAN.
SOUNDS LIKE ONE OF THOSE RIDICULOUSLY EASY PROGRAMS YOU GET INTO WHEN ALL YOU WANT TO DO IS PARTY FOR FOUR YEARS.
FIVE.

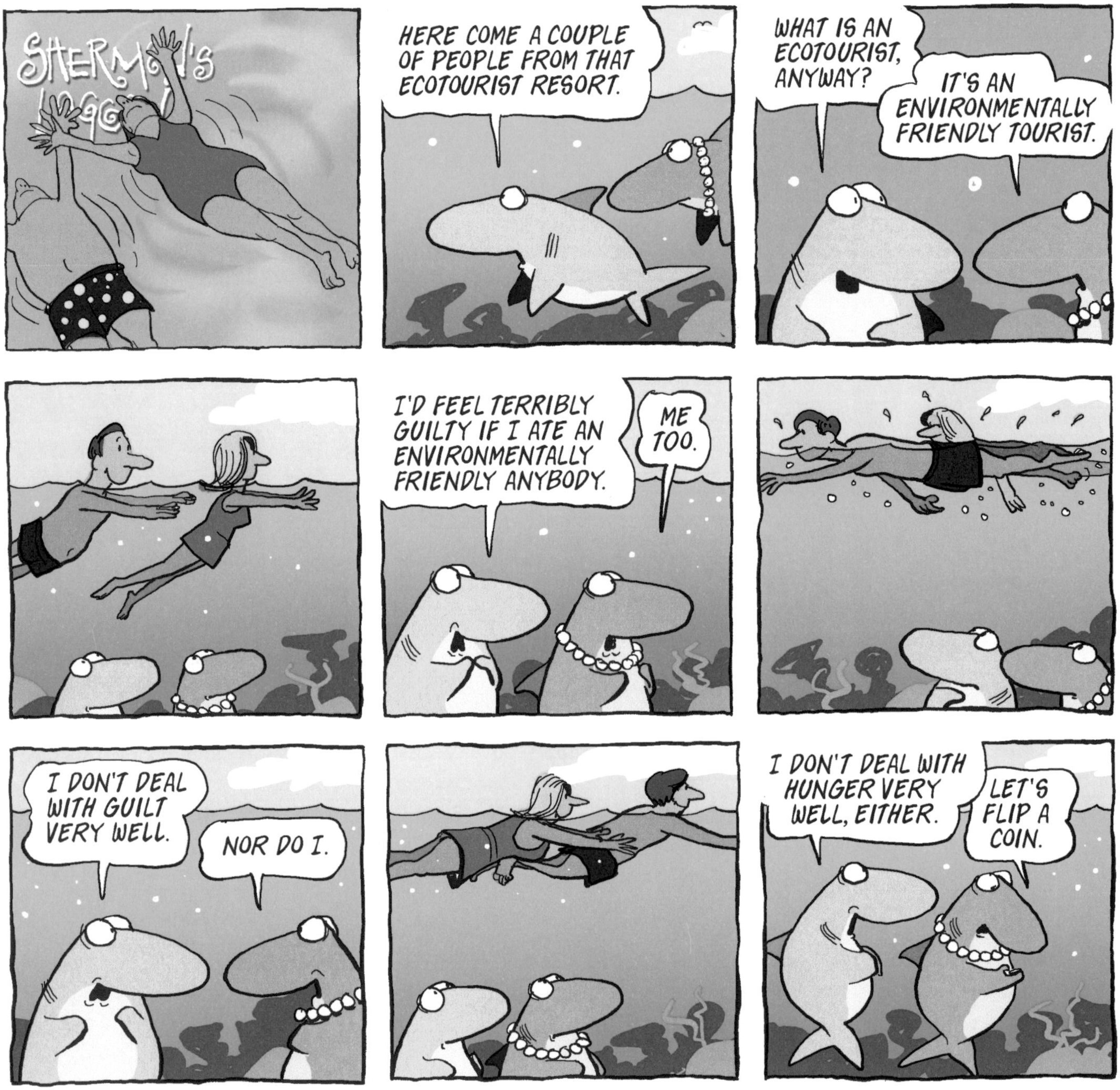
HERE COME A COUPLE OF PEOPLE FROM THAT ECOTOURIST RESORT.
WHAT IS AN ECOTOURIST, ANYWAY?
IT'S AN ENVIRONMENTALLY FRIENDLY TOURIST.
I'D FEEL TERRIBLY GUILTY IF I ATE AN ENVIRONMENTALLY FRIENDLY ANYBODY.
ME TOO.
I DON'T DEAL WITH GUILT VERY WELL.
NOR DO I.
I DON'T DEAL WITH HUNGER VERY WELL, EITHER.
LET'S FLIP A COIN.

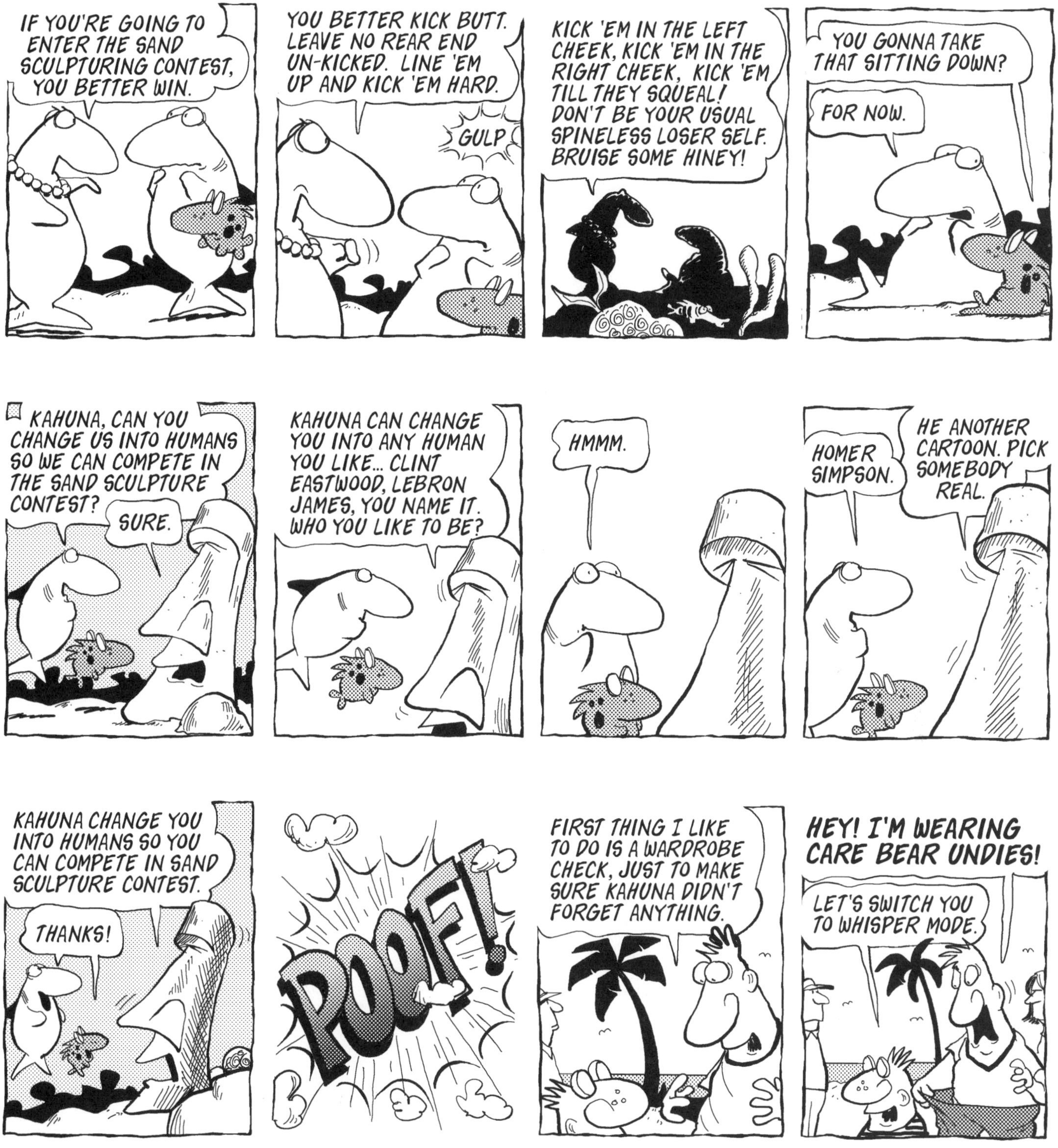
IF YOU'RE GOING TO ENTER THE SAND SCULPTURING CONTEST, YOU BETTER WIN.
YOU BETTER KICK BUTT. LEAVE NO REAR END UN-KICKED. LINE 'EM UP AND KICK 'EM HARD.
GULP
KICK 'EM IN THE LEFT CHEEK, KICK 'EM IN THE RIGHT CHEEK, KICK 'EM TILL THEY SQUEAL! DON'T BE YOUR USUAL SPINELESS LOSER SELF. BRUISE SOME HINEY!
YOU GONNA TAKE THAT SITTING DOWN?
FOR NOW.
KAHUNA, CAN YOU CHANGE US INTO HUMANS SO WE CAN COMPETE IN THE SAND SCULPTURE CONTEST?
SURE.
KAHUNA CAN CHANGE YOU INTO ANY HUMAN YOU LIKE... CLINT EASTWOOD, LEBRON JAMES, YOU NAME IT. WHO YOU LIKE TO BE?
HMMM.
HOMER SIMPSON.
HE ANOTHER CARTOON. PICK SOMEBODY REAL.
KAHUNA CHANGE YOU INTO HUMANS SO YOU CAN COMPETE IN SAND SCULPTURE CONTEST.
THANKS!
POOF!
FIRST THING I LIKE TO DO IS A WARDROBE CHECK, JUST TO MAKE SURE KAHUNA DIDN'T FORGET ANYTHING.
HEY! I'M WEARING CARE BEAR UNDIES!
LET'S SWITCH YOU TO WHISPER MODE.

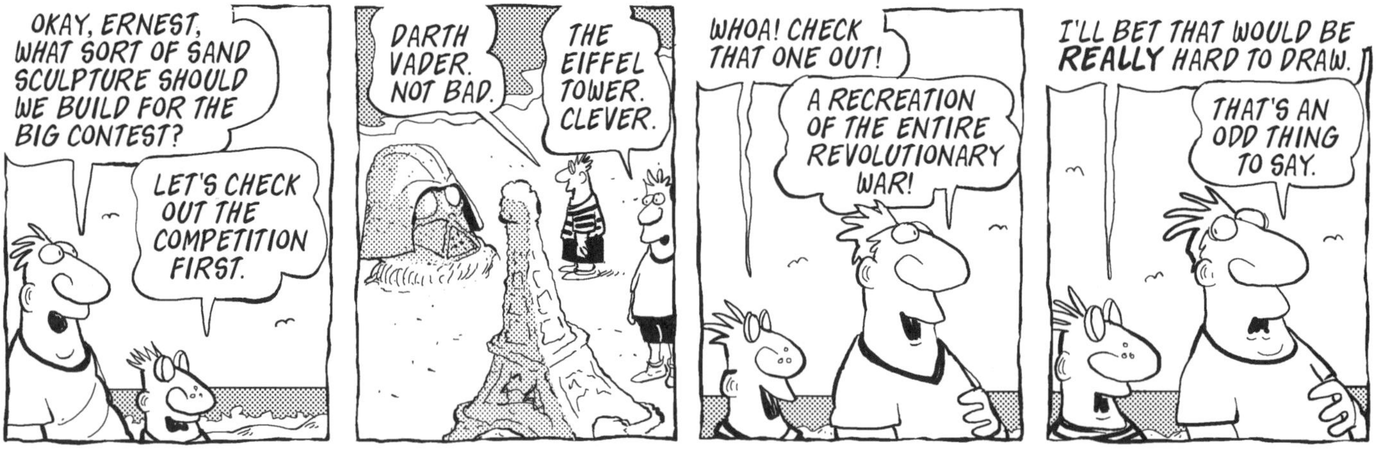
OKAY, ERNEST, WHAT SORT OF SAND SCULPTURE SHOULD WE BUILD FOR THE BIG CONTEST?
LET'S CHECK OUT THE COMPETITION FIRST.
DARTH VADER. NOT BAD.
THE EIFFEL TOWER. CLEVER.
WHOA! CHECK THAT ONE OUT!
A RECREATION OF THE ENTIRE REVOLUTIONARY WAR!
I'LL BET THAT WOULD BE **REALLY** HARD TO DRAW.
THAT'S AN ODD THING TO SAY.

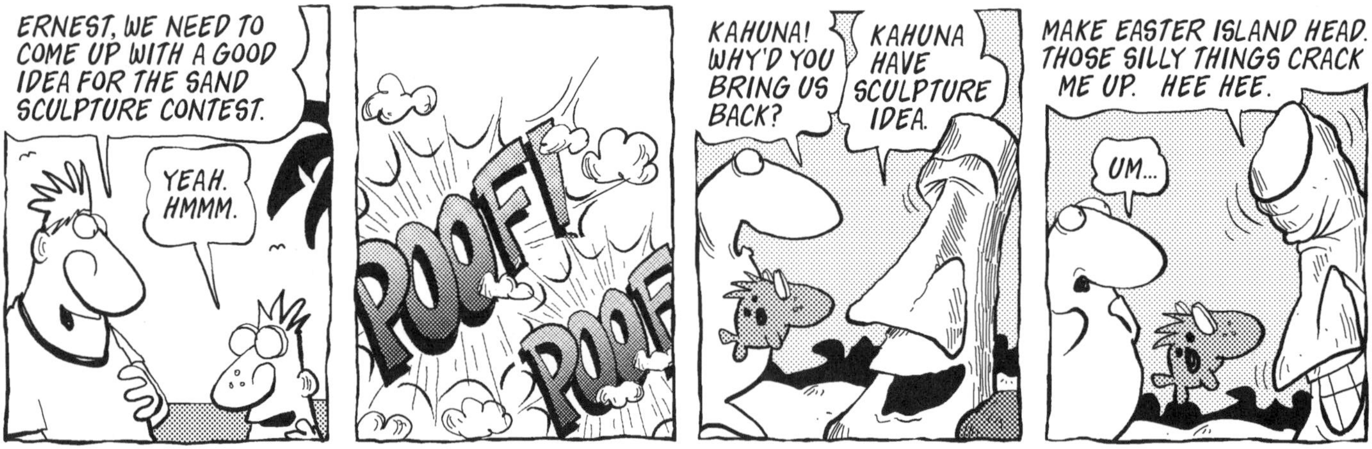
ERNEST, WE NEED TO COME UP WITH A GOOD IDEA FOR THE SAND SCULPTURE CONTEST.
YEAH. HMMM.
POOF!
POOF
KAHUNA! WHY'D YOU BRING US BACK?
KAHUNA HAVE SCULPTURE IDEA.
MAKE EASTER ISLAND HEAD. THOSE SILLY THINGS CRACK ME UP. HEE HEE.
UM...

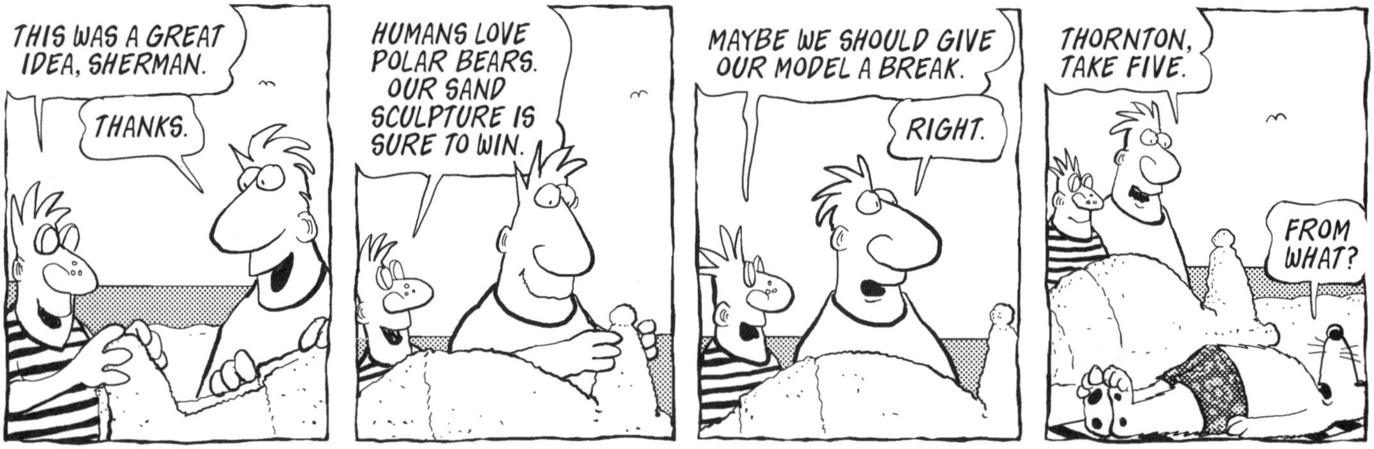
THIS WAS A GREAT IDEA, SHERMAN.
THANKS.
HUMANS LOVE POLAR BEARS. OUR SAND SCULPTURE IS SURE TO WIN.
MAYBE WE SHOULD GIVE OUR MODEL A BREAK.
RIGHT.
THORNTON, TAKE FIVE.
FROM WHAT?

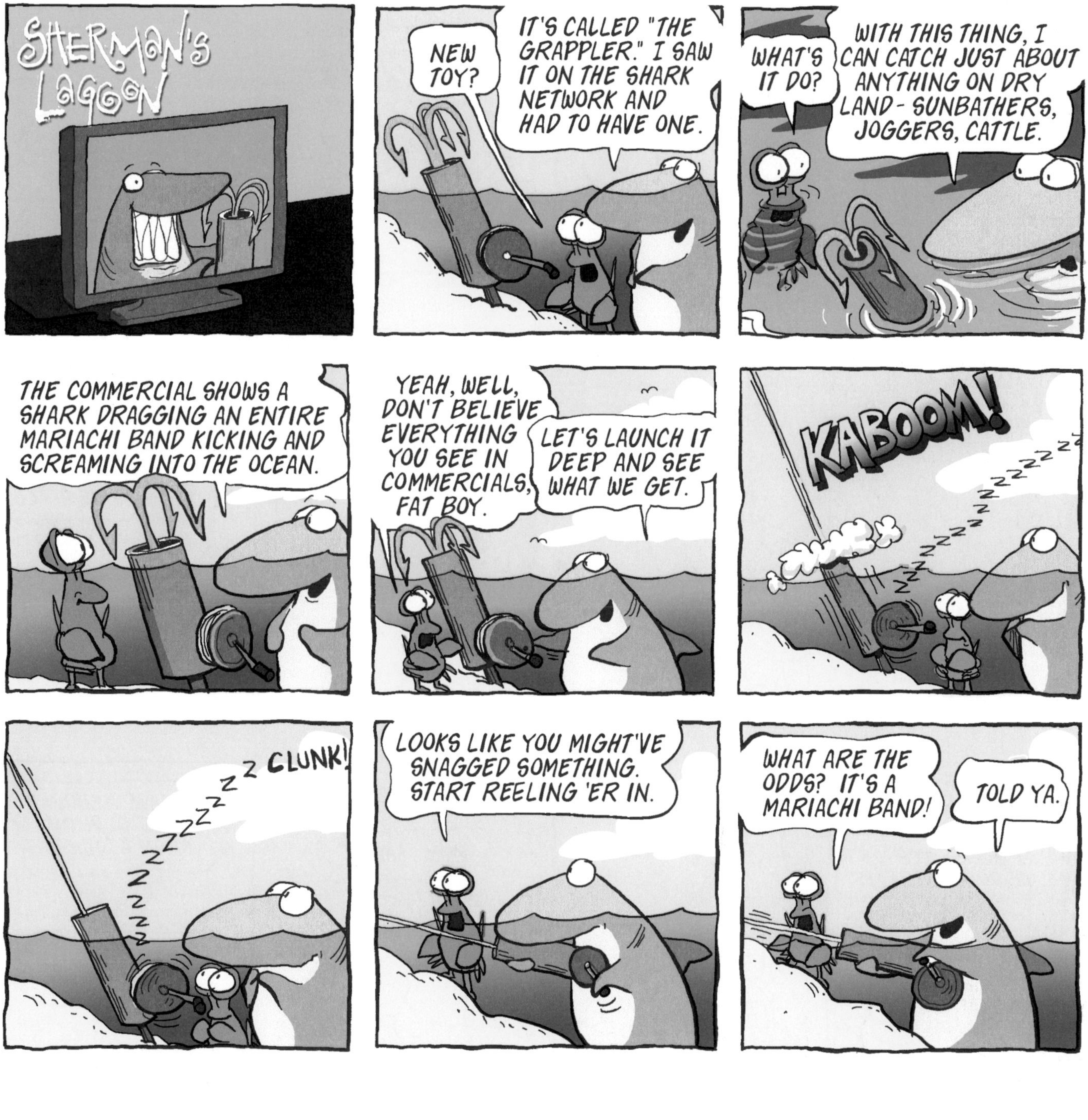
SHERMAN'S LAGOON
NEW TOY?
IT'S CALLED "THE GRAPPLER." I SAW IT ON THE SHARK NETWORK AND HAD TO HAVE ONE.
WHAT'S IT DO?
WITH THIS THING, I CAN CATCH JUST ABOUT ANYTHING ON DRY LAND - SUNBATHERS, JOGGERS, CATTLE.
THE COMMERCIAL SHOWS A SHARK DRAGGING AN ENTIRE MARIACHI BAND KICKING AND SCREAMING INTO THE OCEAN.
YEAH, WELL, DON'T BELIEVE EVERYTHING YOU SEE IN COMMERCIALS, FAT BOY.
LET'S LAUNCH IT DEEP AND SEE WHAT WE GET.
KABOOM!
CLUNK!
LOOKS LIKE YOU MIGHT'VE SNAGGED SOMETHING. START REELING 'ER IN.
WHAT ARE THE ODDS? IT'S A MARIACHI BAND!
TOLD YA.

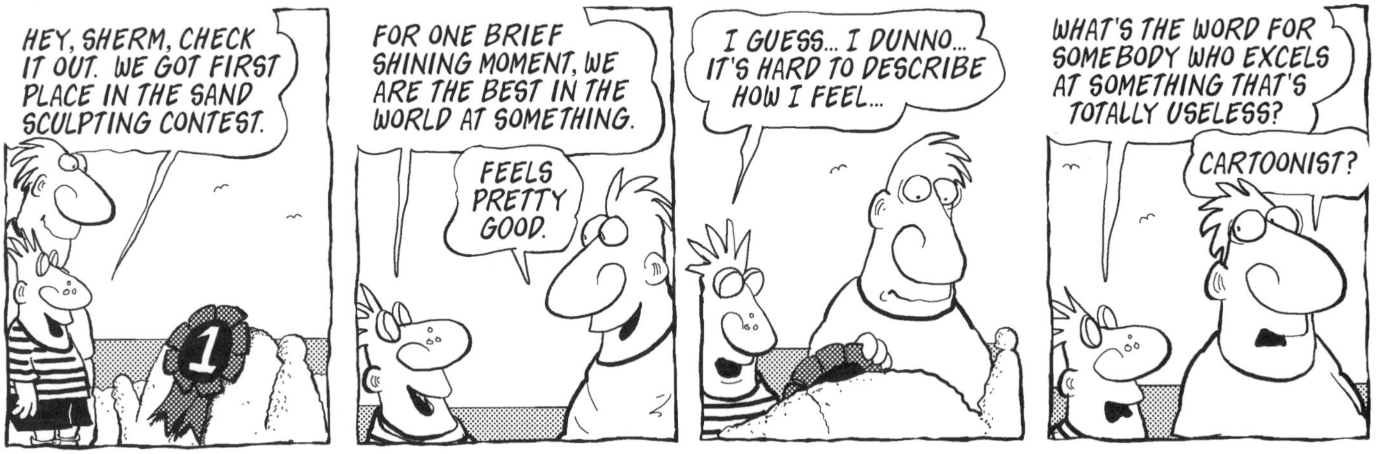
HEY, SHERM, CHECK IT OUT. WE GOT FIRST PLACE IN THE SAND SCULPTING CONTEST.
1
FOR ONE BRIEF SHINING MOMENT, WE ARE THE BEST IN THE WORLD AT SOMETHING.
FEELS PRETTY GOOD.
I GUESS... I DUNNO... IT'S HARD TO DESCRIBE HOW I FEEL...
WHAT'S THE WORD FOR SOMEBODY WHO EXCELS AT SOMETHING THAT'S TOTALLY USELESS?
CARTOONIST?

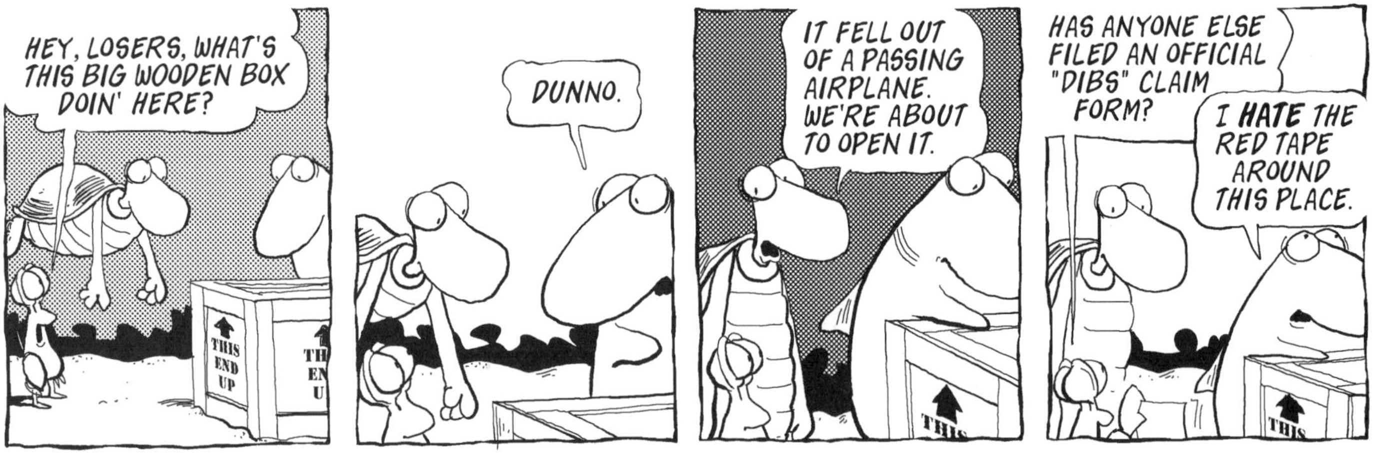
HEY, LOSERS, WHAT'S THIS BIG WOODEN BOX DOIN' HERE?
THIS END UP
DUNNO.
IT FELL OUT OF A PASSING AIRPLANE. WE'RE ABOUT TO OPEN IT.
HAS ANYONE ELSE FILED AN OFFICIAL "DIBS" CLAIM FORM?
I **HATE** THE RED TAPE AROUND THIS PLACE.

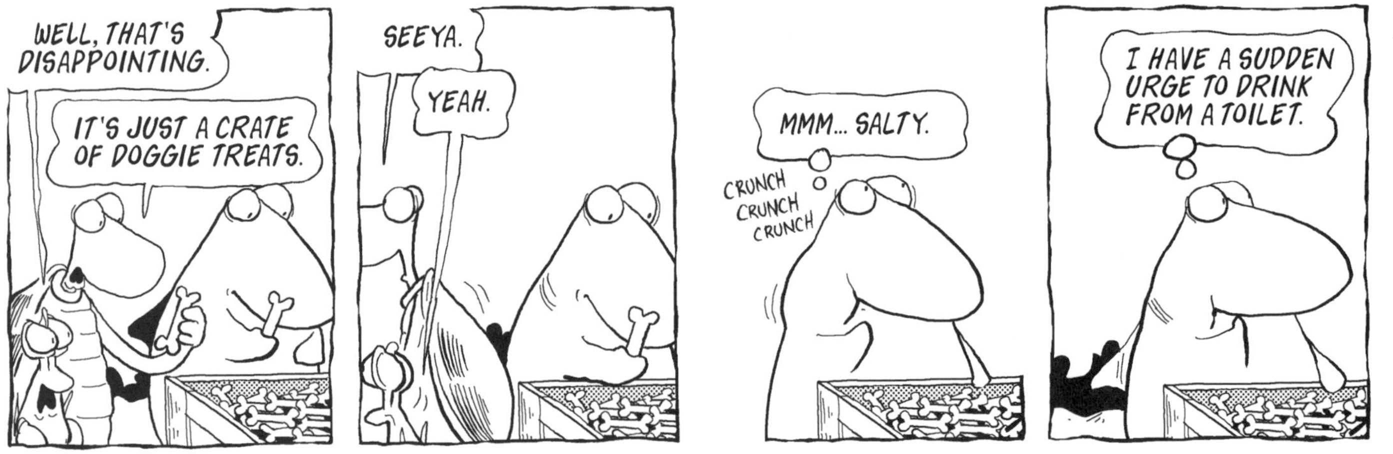
WELL, THAT'S DISAPPOINTING.
IT'S JUST A CRATE OF DOGGIE TREATS.
SEEYA.
YEAH.
MMM... SALTY.
CRUNCH CRUNCH CRUNCH
I HAVE A SUDDEN URGE TO DRINK FROM A TOILET.

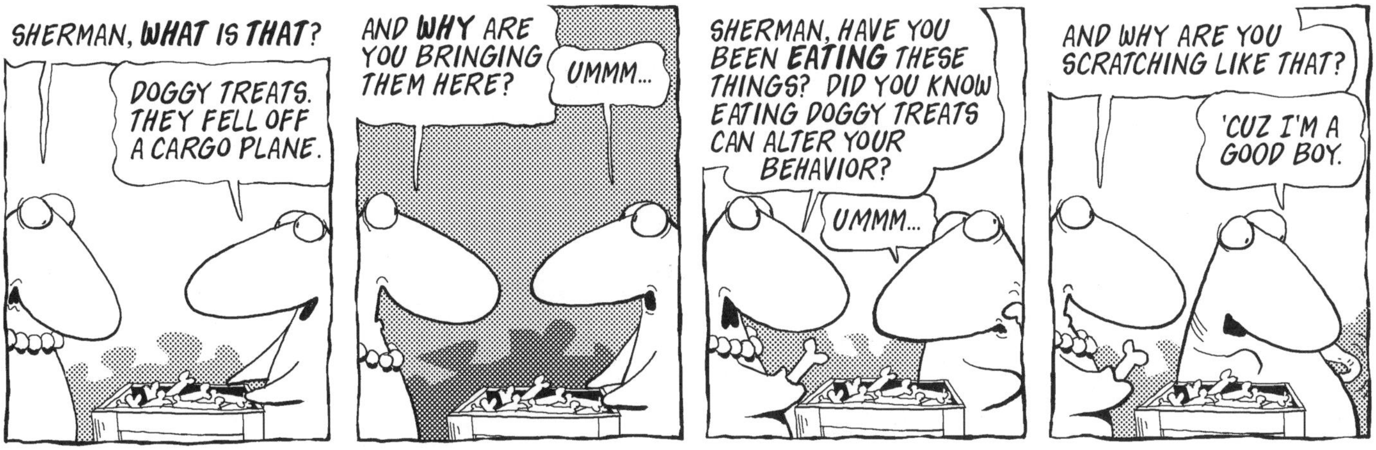
SHERMAN, WHAT IS THAT?
DOGGY TREATS. THEY FELL OFF A CARGO PLANE.
AND WHY ARE YOU BRINGING THEM HERE?
UMMM...
SHERMAN, HAVE YOU BEEN EATING THESE THINGS? DID YOU KNOW EATING DOGGY TREATS CAN ALTER YOUR BEHAVIOR?
UMMM...
AND WHY ARE YOU SCRATCHING LIKE THAT?
'CUZ I'M A GOOD BOY.

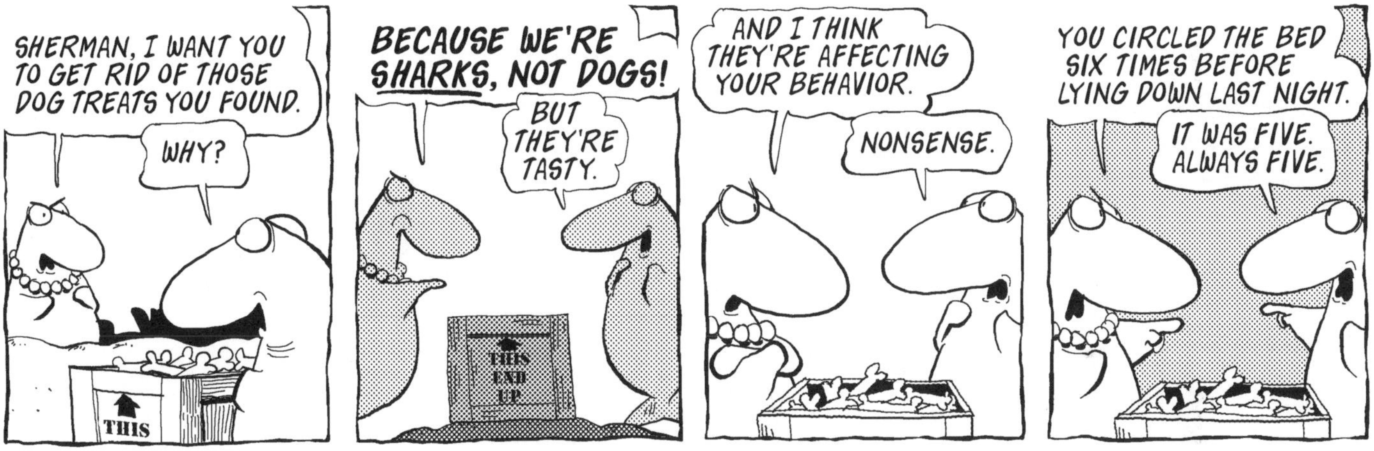
SHERMAN, I WANT YOU TO GET RID OF THOSE DOG TREATS YOU FOUND.
WHY?
THIS
BECAUSE WE'RE SHARKS, NOT DOGS!
BUT THEY'RE TASTY.
THIS END UP
AND I THINK THEY'RE AFFECTING YOUR BEHAVIOR.
NONSENSE.
YOU CIRCLED THE BED SIX TIMES BEFORE LYING DOWN LAST NIGHT.
IT WAS FIVE. ALWAYS FIVE.

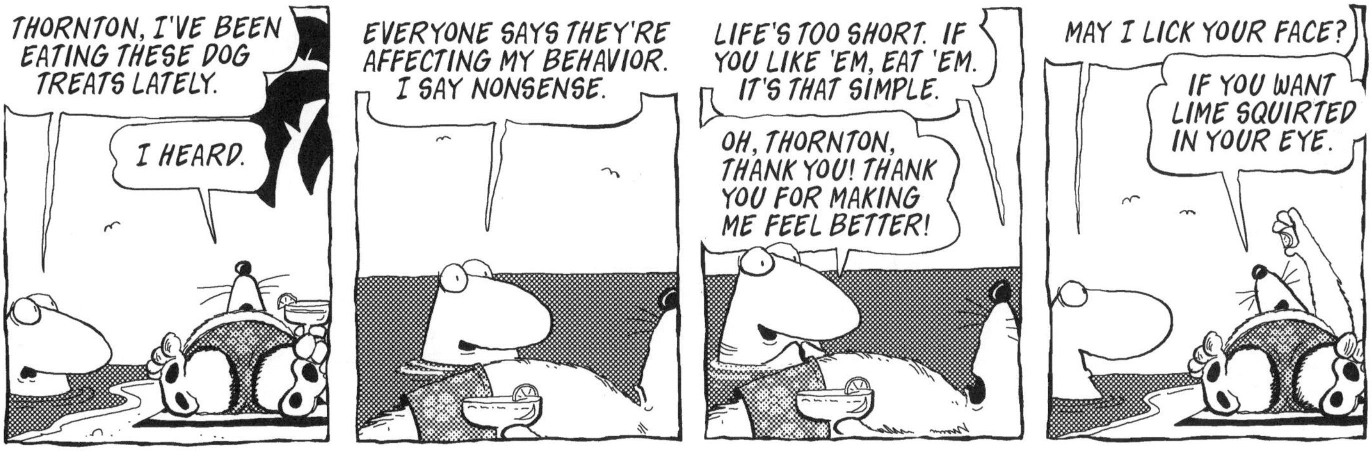
THORNTON, I'VE BEEN EATING THESE DOG TREATS LATELY.
I HEARD.
EVERYONE SAYS THEY'RE AFFECTING MY BEHAVIOR. I SAY NONSENSE.
LIFE'S TOO SHORT. IF YOU LIKE 'EM, EAT 'EM. IT'S THAT SIMPLE.
OH, THORNTON, THANK YOU! THANK YOU FOR MAKING ME FEEL BETTER!
MAY I LICK YOUR FACE?
IF YOU WANT LIME SQUIRTED IN YOUR EYE.

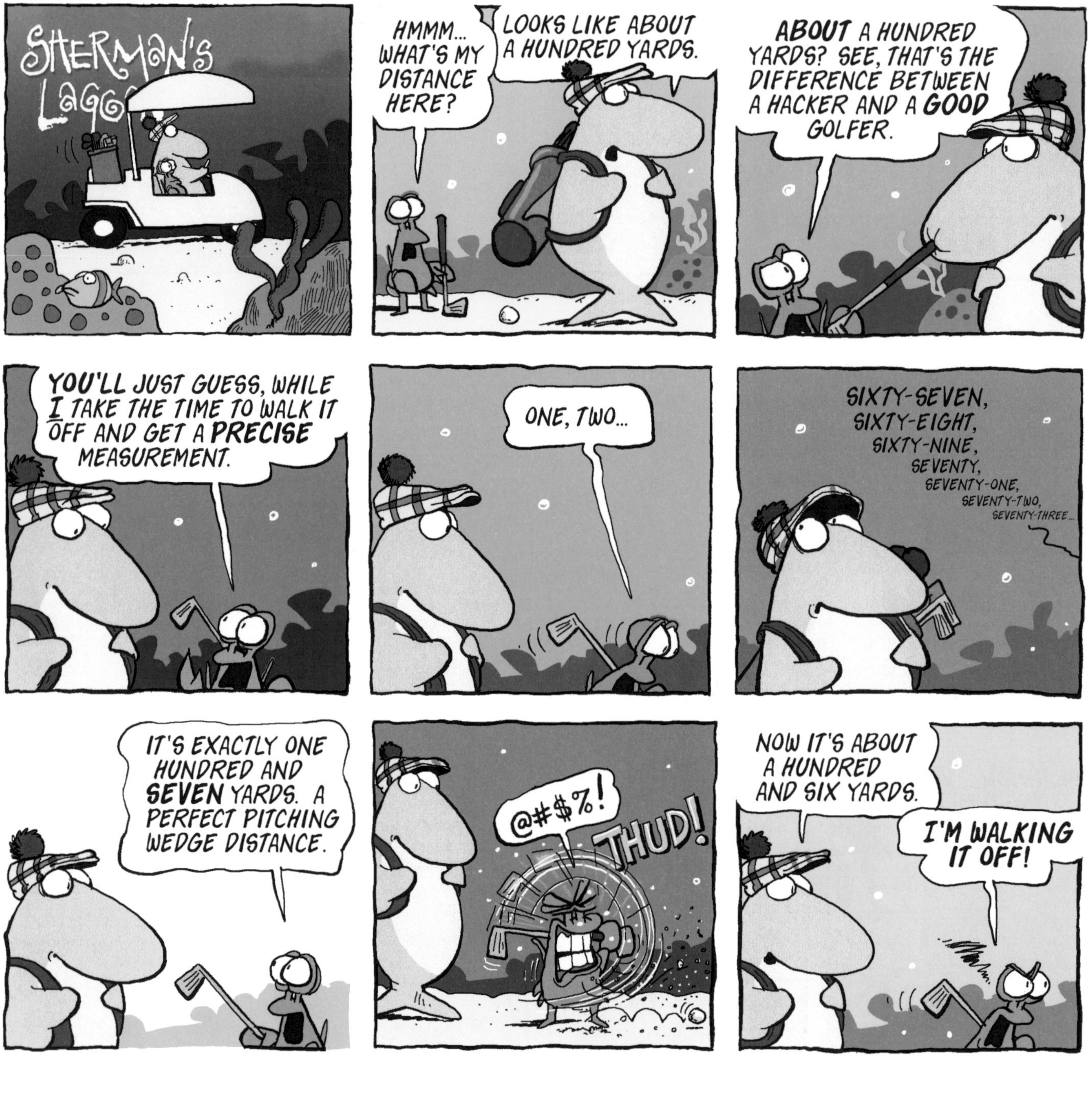
SHERMAN'S LAGO
HMMM... WHAT'S MY DISTANCE HERE?
LOOKS LIKE ABOUT A HUNDRED YARDS.
ABOUT A HUNDRED YARDS? SEE, THAT'S THE DIFFERENCE BETWEEN A HACKER AND A GOOD GOLFER.
YOU'LL JUST GUESS, WHILE I TAKE THE TIME TO WALK IT OFF AND GET A PRECISE MEASUREMENT.
ONE, TWO...
SIXTY-SEVEN, SIXTY-EIGHT, SIXTY-NINE, SEVENTY, SEVENTY-ONE, SEVENTY-TWO, SEVENTY-THREE...
IT'S EXACTLY ONE HUNDRED AND SEVEN YARDS. A PERFECT PITCHING WEDGE DISTANCE.
@#$%!
THUD!
NOW IT'S ABOUT A HUNDRED AND SIX YARDS.
I'M WALKING IT OFF!

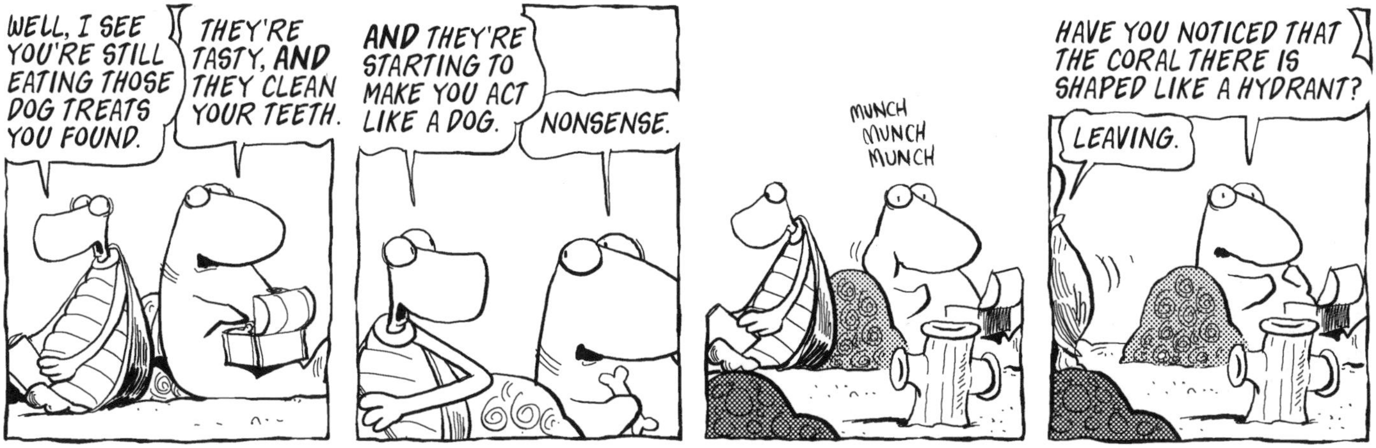
WELL, I SEE YOU'RE STILL EATING THOSE DOG TREATS YOU FOUND.
THEY'RE TASTY, AND THEY CLEAN YOUR TEETH.
AND THEY'RE STARTING TO MAKE YOU ACT LIKE A DOG.
NONSENSE.
MUNCH MUNCH MUNCH
HAVE YOU NOTICED THAT THE CORAL THERE IS SHAPED LIKE A HYDRANT?
LEAVING.

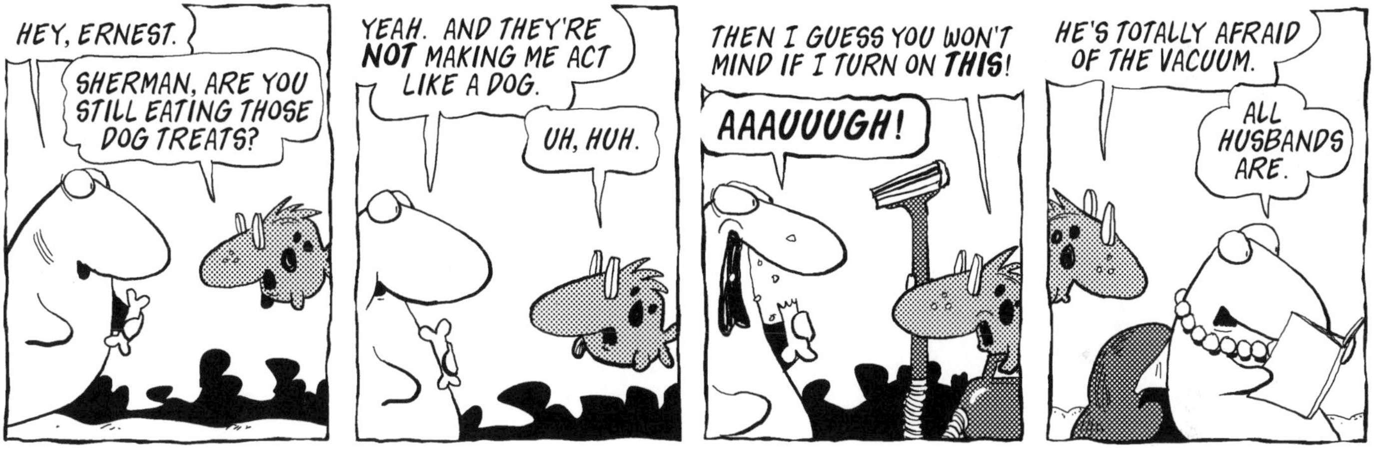
HEY, ERNEST.
SHERMAN, ARE YOU STILL EATING THOSE DOG TREATS?
YEAH. AND THEY'RE NOT MAKING ME ACT LIKE A DOG.
UH, HUH.
THEN I GUESS YOU WON'T MIND IF I TURN ON THIS!
AAAUUUGH!
HE'S TOTALLY AFRAID OF THE VACUUM.
ALL HUSBANDS ARE.

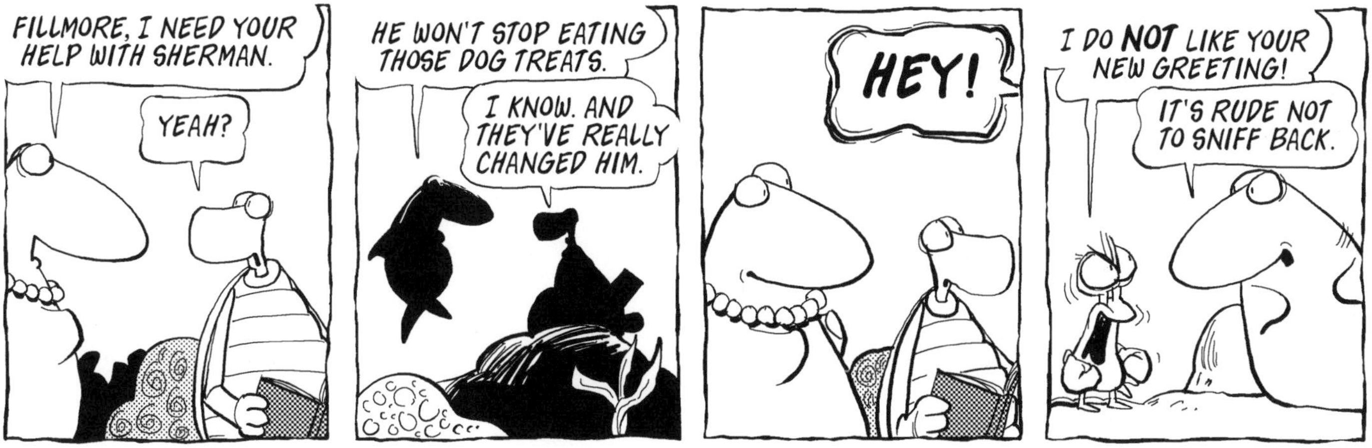
FILLMORE, I NEED YOUR HELP WITH SHERMAN.
YEAH?
HE WON'T STOP EATING THOSE DOG TREATS.
I KNOW. AND THEY'VE REALLY CHANGED HIM.
HEY!
I DO NOT LIKE YOUR NEW GREETING!
IT'S RUDE NOT TO SNIFF BACK.

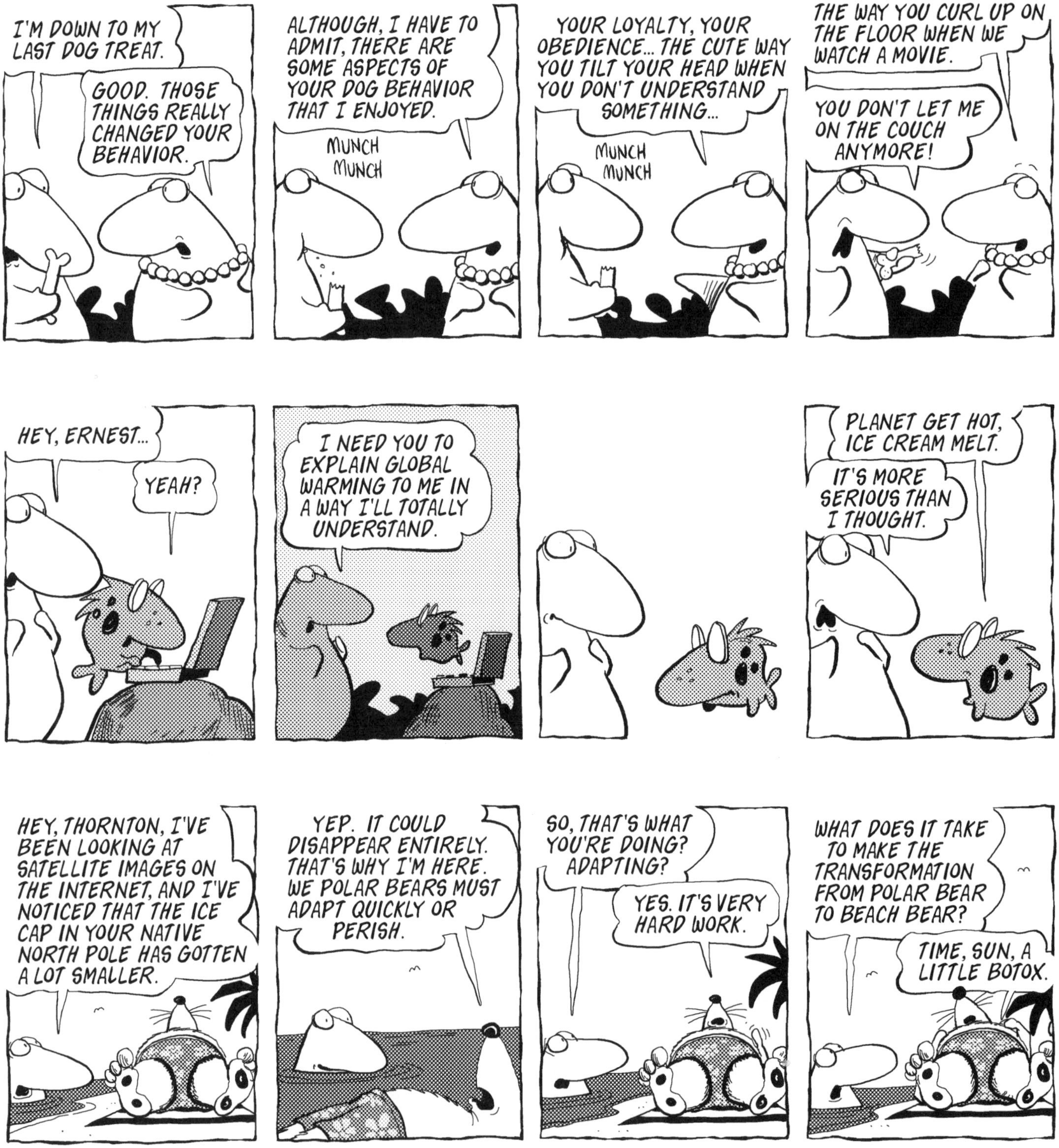
I'M DOWN TO MY LAST DOG TREAT.
GOOD. THOSE THINGS REALLY CHANGED YOUR BEHAVIOR.
ALTHOUGH, I HAVE TO ADMIT, THERE ARE SOME ASPECTS OF YOUR DOG BEHAVIOR THAT I ENJOYED.
MUNCH MUNCH
YOUR LOYALTY, YOUR OBEDIENCE... THE CUTE WAY YOU TILT YOUR HEAD WHEN YOU DON'T UNDERSTAND SOMETHING...
MUNCH MUNCH
THE WAY YOU CURL UP ON THE FLOOR WHEN WE WATCH A MOVIE.
YOU DON'T LET ME ON THE COUCH ANYMORE!
HEY, ERNEST...
YEAH?
I NEED YOU TO EXPLAIN GLOBAL WARMING TO ME IN A WAY I'LL TOTALLY UNDERSTAND.
PLANET GET HOT, ICE CREAM MELT.
IT'S MORE SERIOUS THAN I THOUGHT.
HEY, THORNTON, I'VE BEEN LOOKING AT SATELLITE IMAGES ON THE INTERNET, AND I'VE NOTICED THAT THE ICE CAP IN YOUR NATIVE NORTH POLE HAS GOTTEN A LOT SMALLER.
YEP. IT COULD DISAPPEAR ENTIRELY. THAT'S WHY I'M HERE. WE POLAR BEARS MUST ADAPT QUICKLY OR PERISH.
SO, THAT'S WHAT YOU'RE DOING? ADAPTING?
YES. IT'S VERY HARD WORK.
WHAT DOES IT TAKE TO MAKE THE TRANSFORMATION FROM POLAR BEAR TO BEACH BEAR?
TIME, SUN, A LITTLE BOTOX.

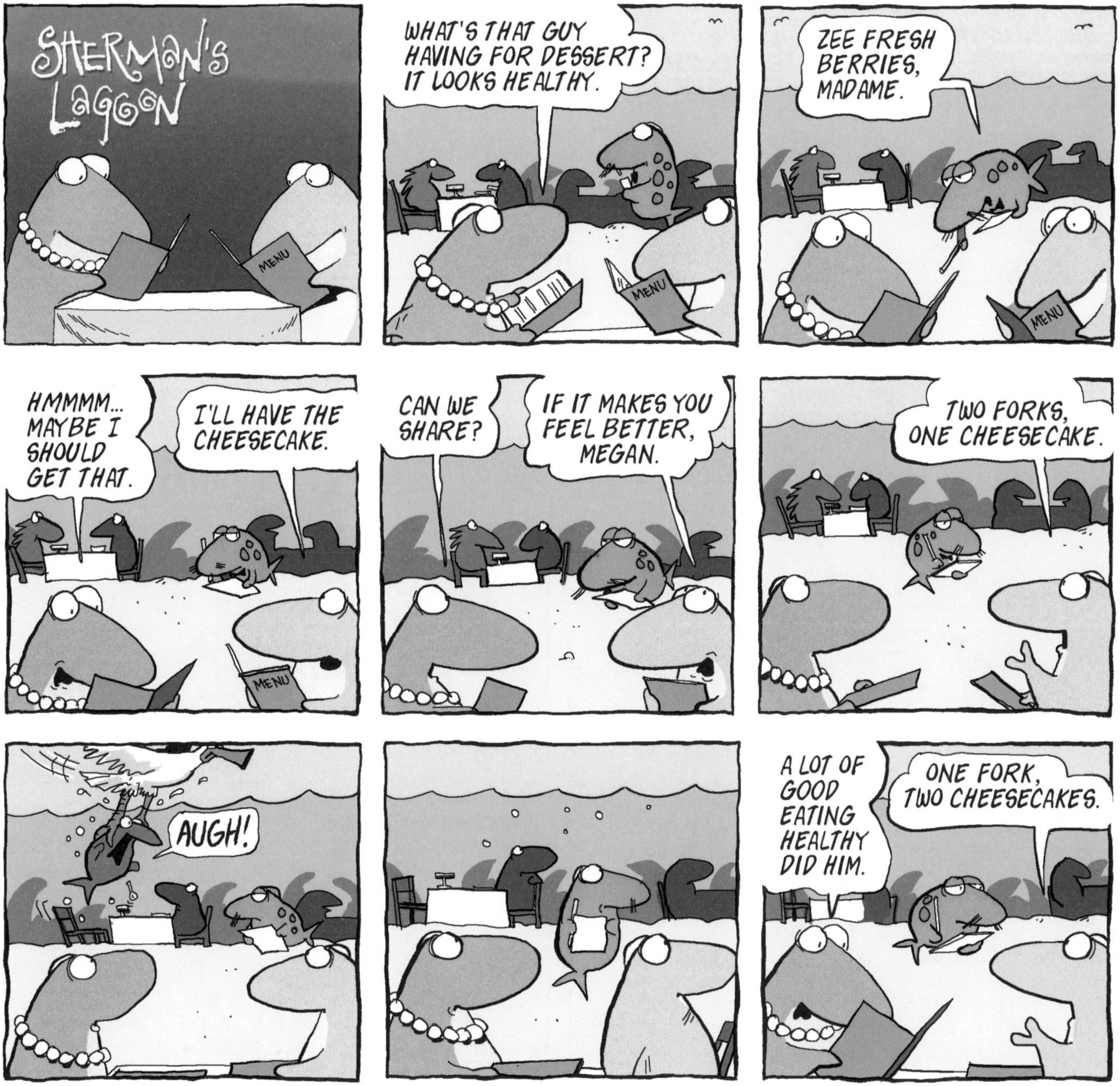
SHERMAN'S LAGOON
MENU
WHAT'S THAT GUY HAVING FOR DESSERT? IT LOOKS HEALTHY.
MENU
ZEE FRESH BERRIES, MADAME.
MENU
HMMMM... MAYBE I SHOULD GET THAT.
I'LL HAVE THE CHEESECAKE.
MENU
CAN WE SHARE?
IF IT MAKES YOU FEEL BETTER, MEGAN.
TWO FORKS, ONE CHEESECAKE.
AUGH!
A LOT OF GOOD EATING HEALTHY DID HIM.
ONE FORK, TWO CHEESECAKES.

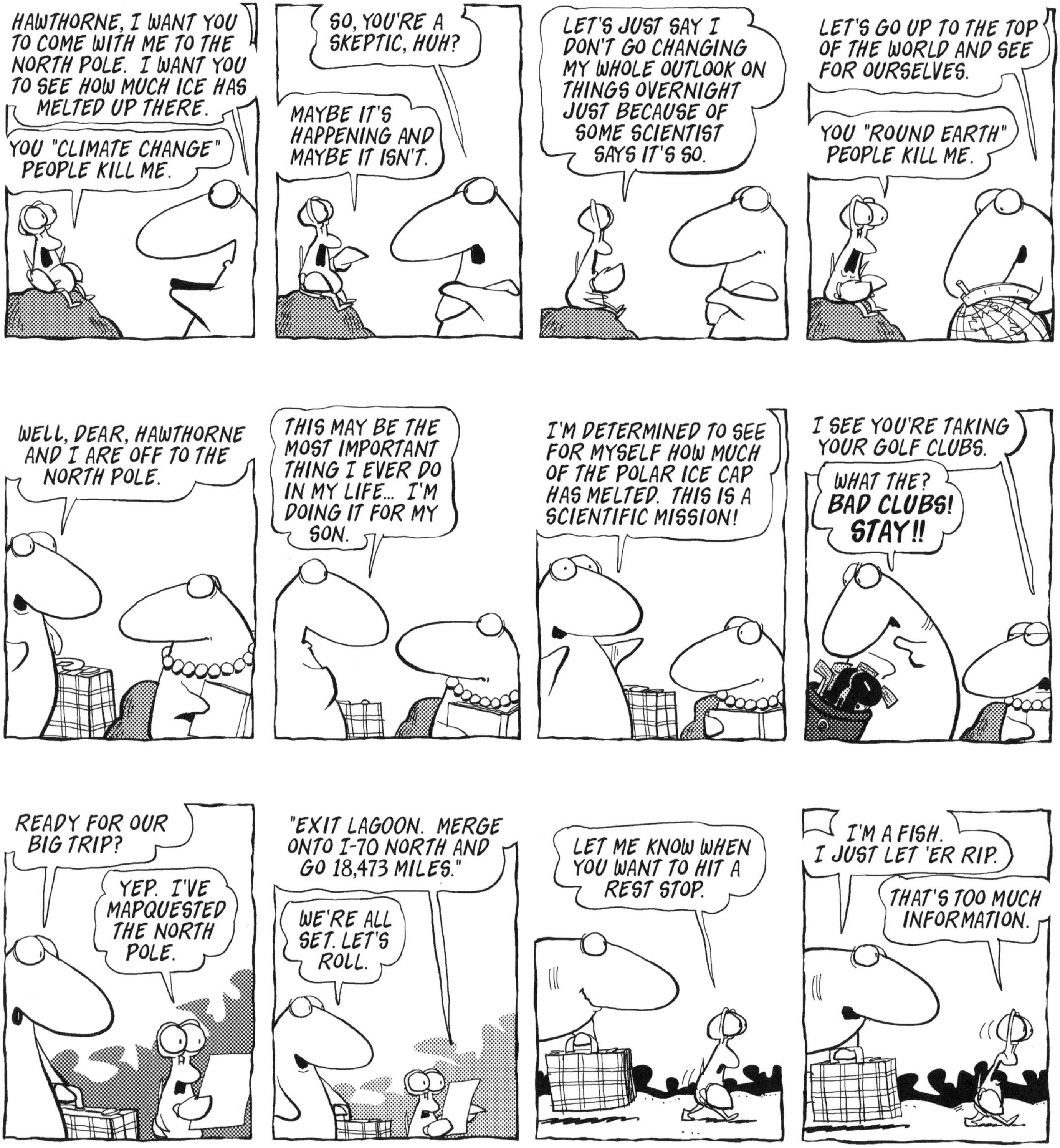
HAWTHORNE, I WANT YOU TO COME WITH ME TO THE NORTH POLE. I WANT YOU TO SEE HOW MUCH ICE HAS MELTED UP THERE.
YOU "CLIMATE CHANGE" PEOPLE KILL ME.
SO, YOU'RE A SKEPTIC, HUH?
MAYBE IT'S HAPPENING AND MAYBE IT ISN'T.
LET'S JUST SAY I DON'T GO CHANGING MY WHOLE OUTLOOK ON THINGS OVERNIGHT JUST BECAUSE OF SOME SCIENTIST SAYS IT'S SO.
LET'S GO UP TO THE TOP OF THE WORLD AND SEE FOR OURSELVES.
YOU "ROUND EARTH" PEOPLE KILL ME.
WELL, DEAR, HAWTHORNE AND I ARE OFF TO THE NORTH POLE.
THIS MAY BE THE MOST IMPORTANT THING I EVER DO IN MY LIFE... I'M DOING IT FOR MY SON.
I'M DETERMINED TO SEE FOR MYSELF HOW MUCH OF THE POLAR ICE CAP HAS MELTED. THIS IS A SCIENTIFIC MISSION!
I SEE YOU'RE TAKING YOUR GOLF CLUBS.
WHAT THE? BAD CLUBS! STAY!!
READY FOR OUR BIG TRIP?
YEP. I'VE MAPQUESTED THE NORTH POLE.
"EXIT LAGOON. MERGE ONTO I-70 NORTH AND GO 18,473 MILES."
WE'RE ALL SET. LET'S ROLL.
LET ME KNOW WHEN YOU WANT TO HIT A REST STOP.
I'M A FISH. I JUST LET 'ER RIP.
THAT'S TOO MUCH INFORMATION.

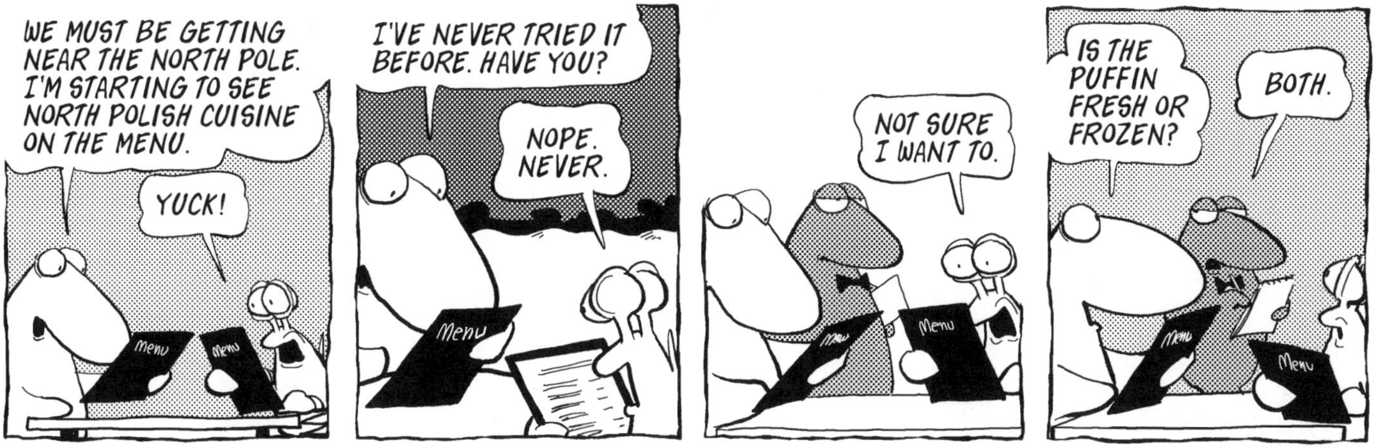
WE MUST BE GETTING NEAR THE NORTH POLE. I'M STARTING TO SEE NORTH POLISH CUISINE ON THE MENU.
YUCK!
Menu
Menu
I'VE NEVER TRIED IT BEFORE. HAVE YOU?
NOPE. NEVER.
Menu
NOT SURE I WANT TO.
Menu
IS THE PUFFIN FRESH OR FROZEN?
BOTH.
Menu

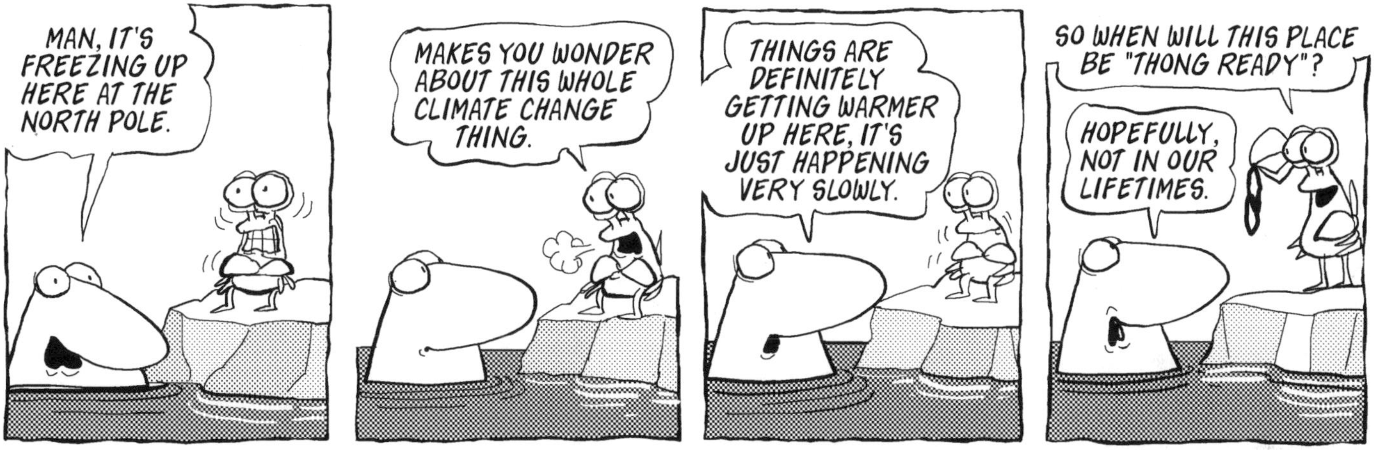
MAN, IT'S FREEZING UP HERE AT THE NORTH POLE.
MAKES YOU WONDER ABOUT THIS WHOLE CLIMATE CHANGE THING.
THINGS ARE DEFINITELY GETTING WARMER UP HERE, IT'S JUST HAPPENING VERY SLOWLY.
SO WHEN WILL THIS PLACE BE "THONG READY"?
HOPEFULLY, NOT IN OUR LIFETIMES.

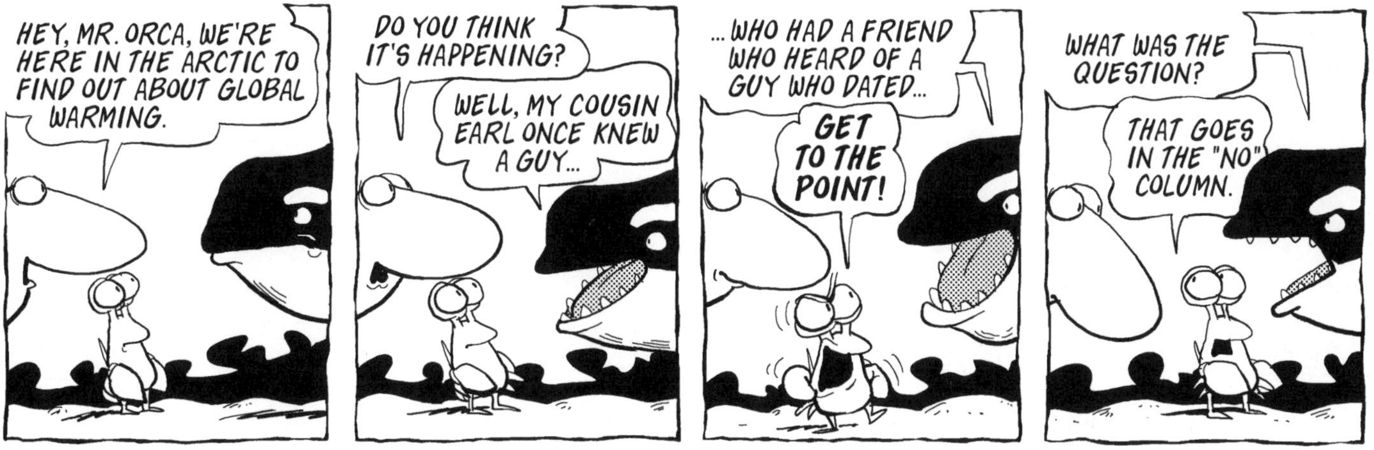
HEY, MR. ORCA, WE'RE HERE IN THE ARCTIC TO FIND OUT ABOUT GLOBAL WARMING.
DO YOU THINK IT'S HAPPENING?
WELL, MY COUSIN EARL ONCE KNEW A GUY...
...WHO HAD A FRIEND WHO HEARD OF A GUY WHO DATED...
GET TO THE POINT!
WHAT WAS THE QUESTION?
THAT GOES IN THE "NO" COLUMN.

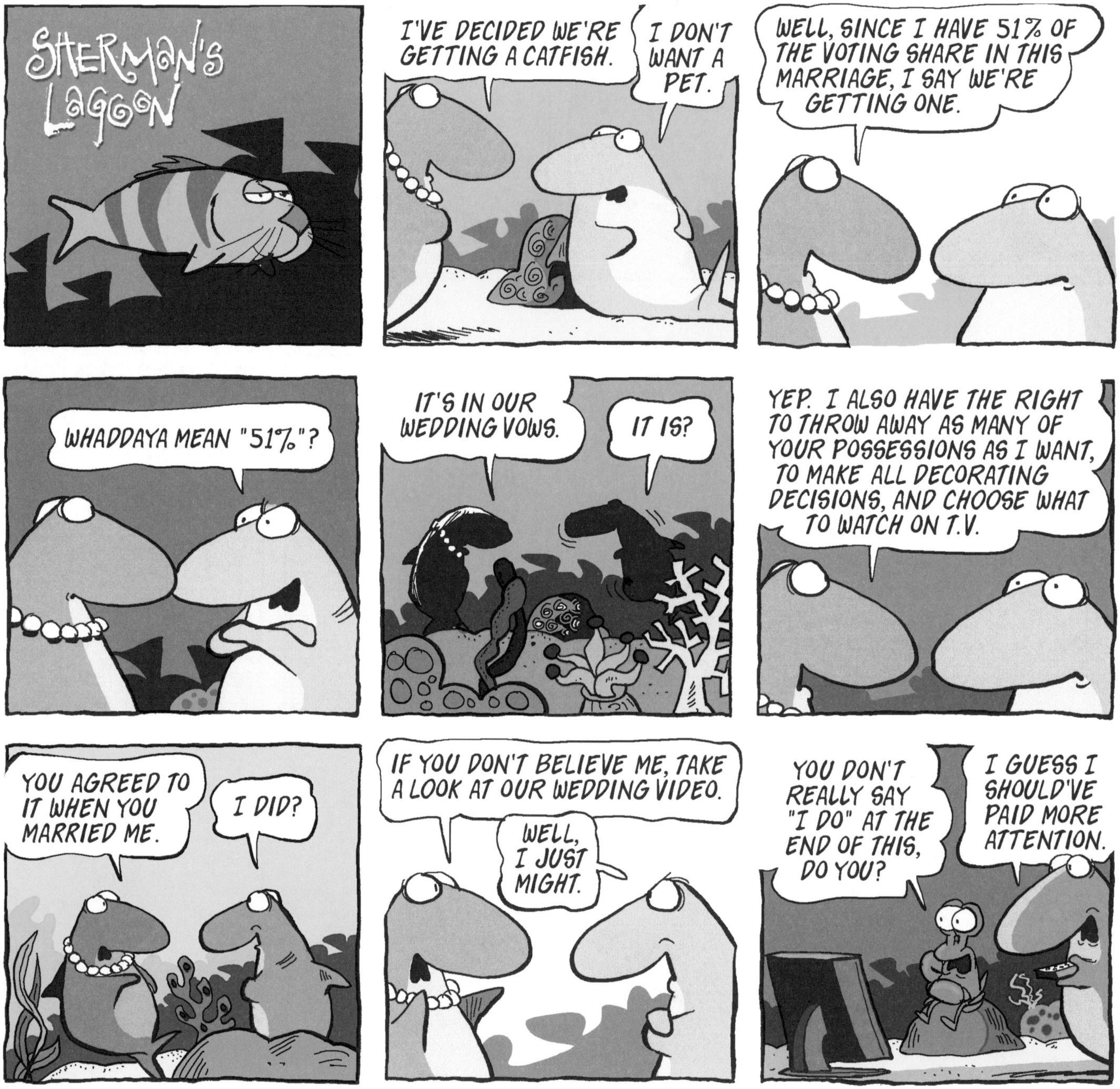
SHERMAN'S LAGOON
I'VE DECIDED WE'RE GETTING A CATFISH.
I DON'T WANT A PET.
WELL, SINCE I HAVE 51% OF THE VOTING SHARE IN THIS MARRIAGE, I SAY WE'RE GETTING ONE.
WHADDAYA MEAN "51%"?
IT'S IN OUR WEDDING VOWS.
IT IS?
YEP. I ALSO HAVE THE RIGHT TO THROW AWAY AS MANY OF YOUR POSSESSIONS AS I WANT, TO MAKE ALL DECORATING DECISIONS, AND CHOOSE WHAT TO WATCH ON T.V.
YOU AGREED TO IT WHEN YOU MARRIED ME.
I DID?
IF YOU DON'T BELIEVE ME, TAKE A LOOK AT OUR WEDDING VIDEO.
WELL, I JUST MIGHT.
YOU DON'T REALLY SAY "I DO" AT THE END OF THIS, DO YOU?
I GUESS I SHOULD'VE PAID MORE ATTENTION.

Panel 1: HELLO, MR. POLAR BEAR. HOW'S THINGS UP HERE IN THE NORTH POLE?

WET.

Panel 2: ALL THE ICE IS MELTING. THERE'S WATER EVERYWHERE. I'M RUNNING OUT OF SPACE TO ROAM.

Panel 3: SOUNDS LIKE YOU NEED TO EVOLVE INTO A SHARK.

GOOD IDEA. WHY DIDN'T I THINK OF THAT?

Panel 4: I'LL QUICKLY DEVELOP FINS AND A MUCH SMALLER BRAIN... COULD YOU GIVE ME A TOW?

SURE.

Panel 5: IT'S TIME TO GET BACK HOME NOW. I HOPE THIS LITTLE TRIP TO THE NORTH POLE HAS CHANGED YOUR VIEWS ON GLOBAL WARMING, HAWTHORNE.

Panel 6: YOU'RE RIGHT, SHERMAN. THIS PLACE HAS CHANGED.

THAT HAS A NICE RING TO IT. SAY IT AGAIN.

Panel 7: YOU'RE RIGHT, SHERMAN.

OKAY, I'M CLOSING MY EYES, AND I WANT YOU TO SAY IT ONCE MORE.

Panel 8: THIS TIME IN A HIGH-PITCHED VOICE, LIKE MY WIFE'S.

FEEL THE WRATH OF MY CLAW.

Panel 9: YOU'RE OPENING A TATTOO PARLOR?

Tattoos & Piercings

Panel 10: BODY ART IS A WONDERFUL WAY TO EXPRESS YOURSELF. GIVE IT A TRY.

Panel 11: HOW COME YOU DON'T HAVE ANY TATTOOS?

I WOULD, BUT, ALAS, MY BODY IS PERFECT THE WAY IT IS.

Tattoos & Piercings

Panel 12: YOU BOTOX YOUR CLAWS.

JUST DURING MATING SEASON!

Tattoos & Piercings

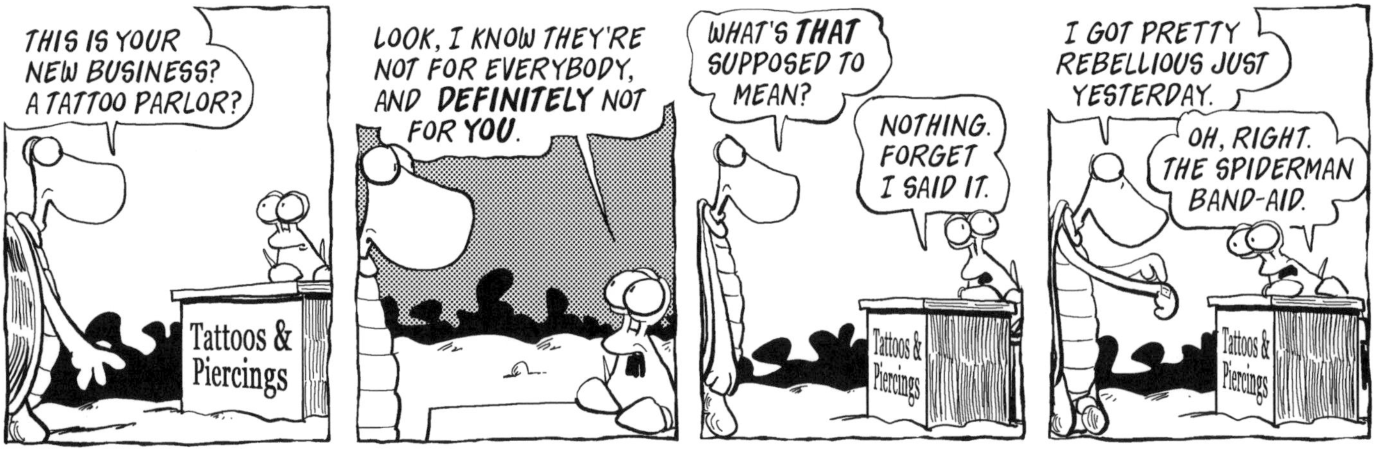
THIS IS YOUR NEW BUSINESS? A TATTOO PARLOR?
Tattoos & Piercings
LOOK, I KNOW THEY'RE NOT FOR EVERYBODY, AND **DEFINITELY** NOT FOR **YOU**.
WHAT'S **THAT** SUPPOSED TO MEAN?
NOTHING. FORGET I SAID IT.
Tattoos & Piercings
I GOT PRETTY REBELLIOUS JUST YESTERDAY.
OH, RIGHT. THE SPIDERMAN BAND-AID.
Tattoos & Piercings

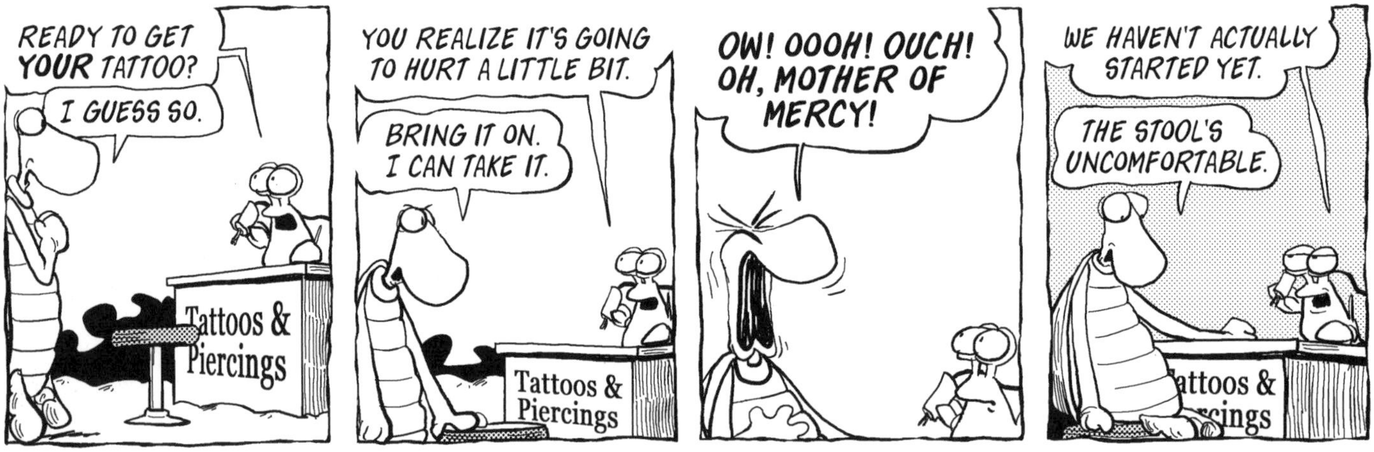
READY TO GET **YOUR** TATTOO?
I GUESS SO.
Tattoos & Piercings
YOU REALIZE IT'S GOING TO HURT A LITTLE BIT.
BRING IT ON. I CAN TAKE IT.
Tattoos & Piercings
OW! OOOH! OUCH! OH, MOTHER OF MERCY!
WE HAVEN'T ACTUALLY STARTED YET.
THE STOOL'S UNCOMFORTABLE.

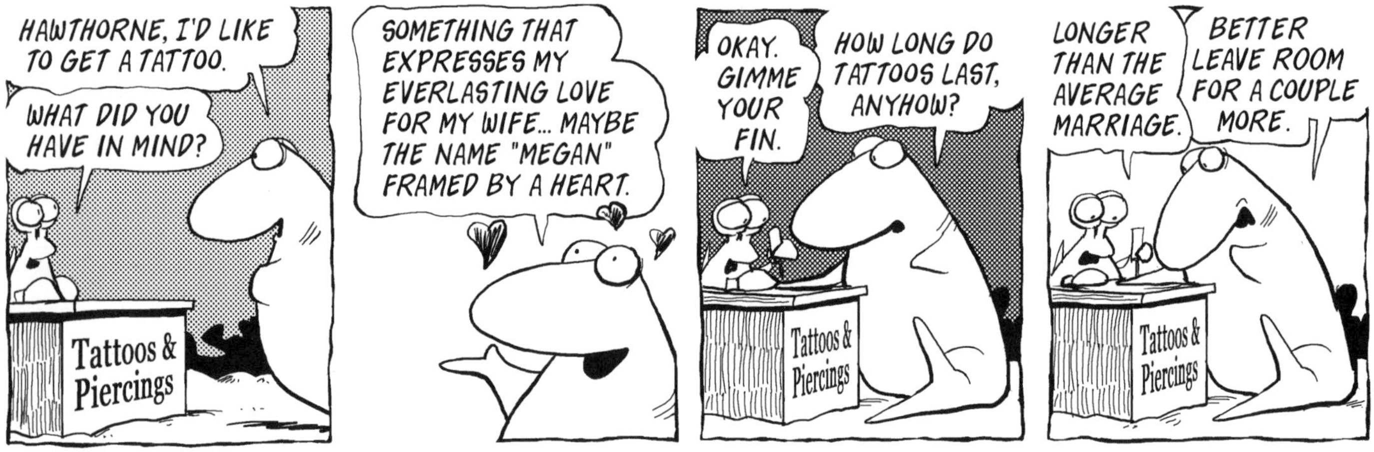
HAWTHORNE, I'D LIKE TO GET A TATTOO.
WHAT DID YOU HAVE IN MIND?
Tattoos & Piercings
SOMETHING THAT EXPRESSES MY EVERLASTING LOVE FOR MY WIFE... MAYBE THE NAME "MEGAN" FRAMED BY A HEART.
OKAY. GIMME YOUR FIN.
HOW LONG DO TATTOOS LAST, ANYHOW?
Tattoos & Piercings
LONGER THAN THE AVERAGE MARRIAGE.
BETTER LEAVE ROOM FOR A COUPLE MORE.
Tattoos & Piercings

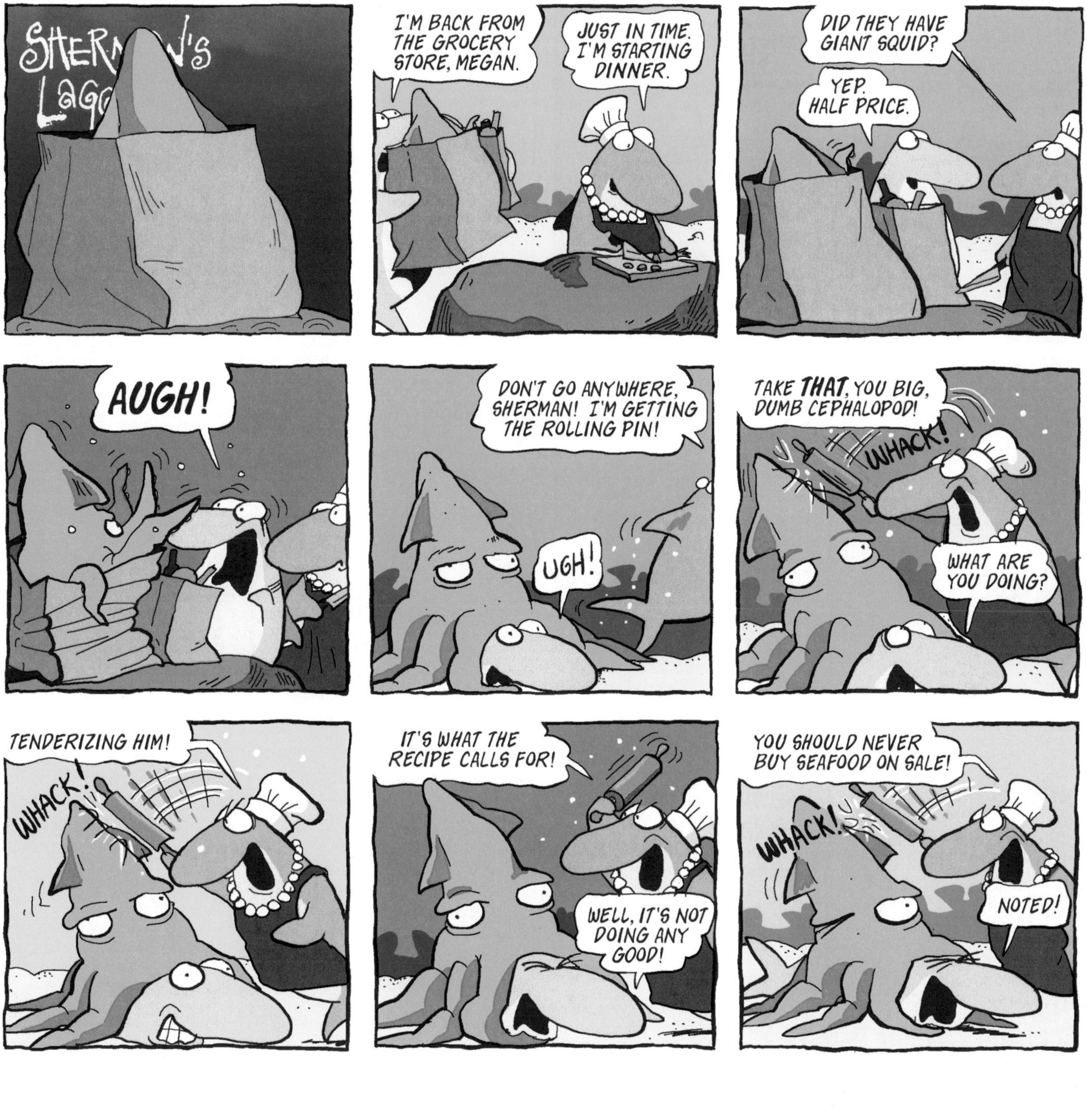
SHERMAN'S LAGOON
I'M BACK FROM THE GROCERY STORE, MEGAN.
JUST IN TIME. I'M STARTING DINNER.
DID THEY HAVE GIANT SQUID?
YEP. HALF PRICE.
AUGH!
DON'T GO ANYWHERE, SHERMAN! I'M GETTING THE ROLLING PIN!
UGH!
TAKE THAT, YOU BIG, DUMB CEPHALOPOD!
WHACK!
WHAT ARE YOU DOING?
TENDERIZING HIM!
WHACK!
IT'S WHAT THE RECIPE CALLS FOR!
WELL, IT'S NOT DOING ANY GOOD!
YOU SHOULD NEVER BUY SEAFOOD ON SALE!
WHACK!
NOTED!

Panel 1:
HAWTHORNE, DO YOU ALSO DO TATTOO REMOVALS?

PROBLEM WITH YOUR TATTOO?

Tattoos & Piercings

Panel 2:
MEGAN DOESN'T LIKE IT. SHE SAYS IT MAKES HER FEEL LIKE SOME BIKER CHICK.

TOO BAD... OH, WELL. HAVE A SEAT.

Panel 3:
I'LL JUST NEED TO GRAB MY HIGH-TECH SURGICAL DEVICE THAT REMOVES TATTOOS.

Tattoos & Piercings

Panel 4:
SAY, WHERE DO YOU KEEP YOUR BELT SANDER?

BY THE JIGSAW. WHY?

Tattoos & Piercings

Panel 5:
I'VE BEEN THINKING THAT MAYBE I SHOULD GET A LITTLE BODY EMBELLISHMENT.

Tattoos & Piercings

Panel 6:
TATTOO OR PIERCING?

PIERCING.

Panel 7:
I'D LIKE ONE OF THOSE CUTE LITTLE STUDS IN MY NOSE LIKE SCARLETT JOHANSSON.

Panel 8:
IT FEELS LIKE A PERMANENT BOOGER!

COOL! MAYBE I OUGHTA GET ONE!

Panel 9:
LOOK, SHERMAN, THE BOARD OF HEALTH IS COMING HERE TO INSPECT MY TATTOO PARLOR...

Tattoos & Piercings

Panel 10:
I NEED YOU TO SIT BEHIND THIS DESK AND ACT LIKE YOU DON'T SPEAK ENGLISH.

WHY?

Panel 11:
THEN THEY CAN'T ASK ANY QUESTIONS. THEY'LL GET ALL FLUSTERED AND LEAVE.

NOW WHY WOULD WE WANT THEM TO DO THAT?

Panel 12:
ACTUALLY, THIS IS BETTER. GO WITH THE STUPID ROUTINE.

MAKE UP YOUR MIND.

THE HEALTH DEPARTMENT SHUT US DOWN!? YOU WERE SUPPOSED TO PLAY DUMB WITH THEM!

I DID!

CLOSED By Order of The Health Department

Tattt Piercings

I PRETENDED THAT I COULDN'T SPEAK ENGLISH, SO THEY ASKED ME WHAT LANGUAGE I DID SPEAK...

SO I SAID I DIDN'T SPEAK ANY LANGUAGE. THEN THEY ASKED "WHAT LANGUAGE ARE WE SPEAKING NOW?" SO I SAID "ENGLISH." THAT'S WHEN THEY GOT SUSPICIOUS.

SO, YOU SEE, I TRIED TO PLAY DUMB.

BUT THE REAL DUMB TOOK OVER.

SO YOU ARRANGED A LITTLE SURPRISE VACATION FOR US, HUH? WHERE?

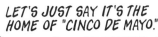

LET'S JUST SAY IT'S THE HOME OF "CINCO DE MAYO."

CHEVY'S?

MEXICO.

Mexico

MEGAN AND I ARE GOING TO ACAPULCO FOR A LITTLE ROMANTIC GETAWAY.

FUN.

HOW'S YOUR SPANISH?

WHY? WE'RE GOING TO MEXICO, NOT SPAIN.

RIGHT. BUT IN MEXICO THEY SPEAK SPANISH, TOO.

CONFUSING.

MAYBE WE SHOULD JUST GO TO CALIFORNIA.

AGAIN, SPANISH.

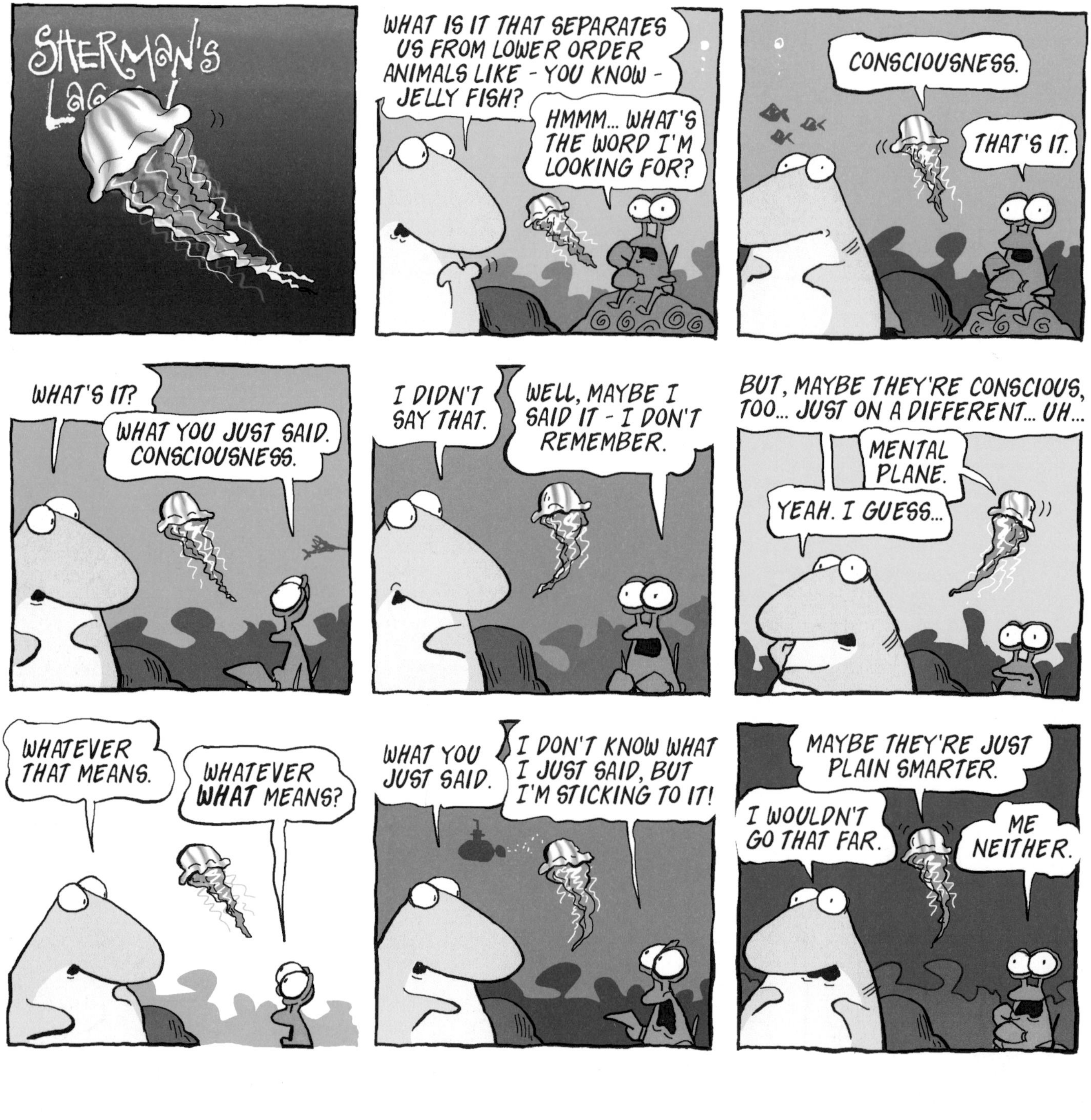
SHERMAN'S LAGOON
WHAT IS IT THAT SEPARATES US FROM LOWER ORDER ANIMALS LIKE - YOU KNOW - JELLY FISH?
HMMM... WHAT'S THE WORD I'M LOOKING FOR?
CONSCIOUSNESS.
THAT'S IT.
WHAT'S IT?
WHAT YOU JUST SAID. CONSCIOUSNESS.
I DIDN'T SAY THAT.
WELL, MAYBE I SAID IT - I DON'T REMEMBER.
BUT, MAYBE THEY'RE CONSCIOUS, TOO... JUST ON A DIFFERENT... UH...
MENTAL PLANE.
YEAH. I GUESS...
WHATEVER THAT MEANS.
WHATEVER WHAT MEANS?
WHAT YOU JUST SAID.
I DON'T KNOW WHAT I JUST SAID, BUT I'M STICKING TO IT!
MAYBE THEY'RE JUST PLAIN SMARTER.
I WOULDN'T GO THAT FAR.
ME NEITHER.

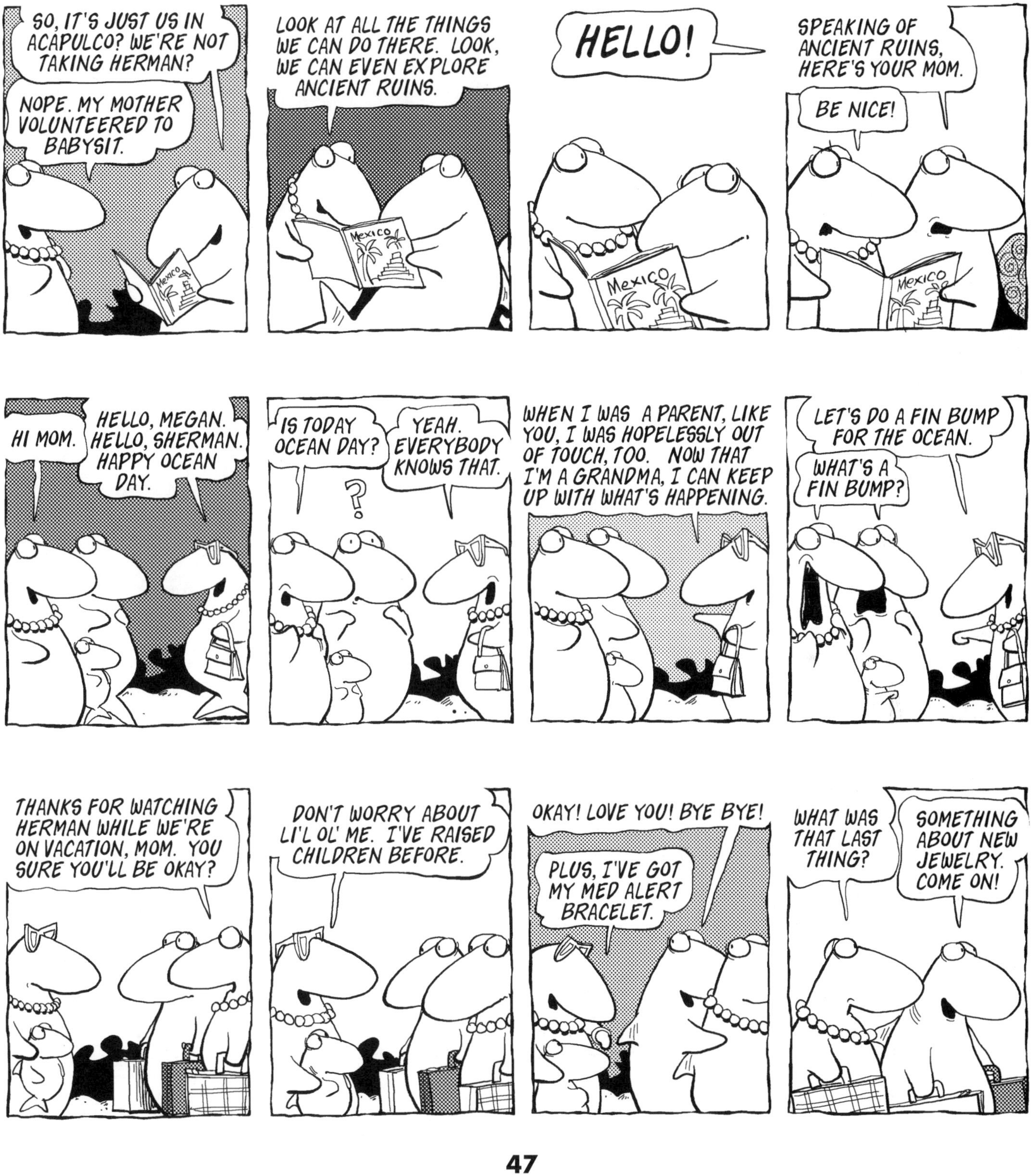
SO, IT'S JUST US IN ACAPULCO? WE'RE NOT TAKING HERMAN?
NOPE. MY MOTHER VOLUNTEERED TO BABYSIT.
Mexico
LOOK AT ALL THE THINGS WE CAN DO THERE. LOOK, WE CAN EVEN EXPLORE ANCIENT RUINS.
Mexico
HELLO!
Mexico
SPEAKING OF ANCIENT RUINS, HERE'S YOUR MOM.
BE NICE!
Mexico
HI MOM.
HELLO, MEGAN. HELLO, SHERMAN. HAPPY OCEAN DAY.
IS TODAY OCEAN DAY?
YEAH. EVERYBODY KNOWS THAT.
?
WHEN I WAS A PARENT, LIKE YOU, I WAS HOPELESSLY OUT OF TOUCH, TOO. NOW THAT I'M A GRANDMA, I CAN KEEP UP WITH WHAT'S HAPPENING.
LET'S DO A FIN BUMP FOR THE OCEAN.
WHAT'S A FIN BUMP?
THANKS FOR WATCHING HERMAN WHILE WE'RE ON VACATION, MOM. YOU SURE YOU'LL BE OKAY?
DON'T WORRY ABOUT LI'L OL' ME. I'VE RAISED CHILDREN BEFORE.
OKAY! LOVE YOU! BYE BYE!
PLUS, I'VE GOT MY MED ALERT BRACELET.
WHAT WAS THAT LAST THING?
SOMETHING ABOUT NEW JEWELRY. COME ON!

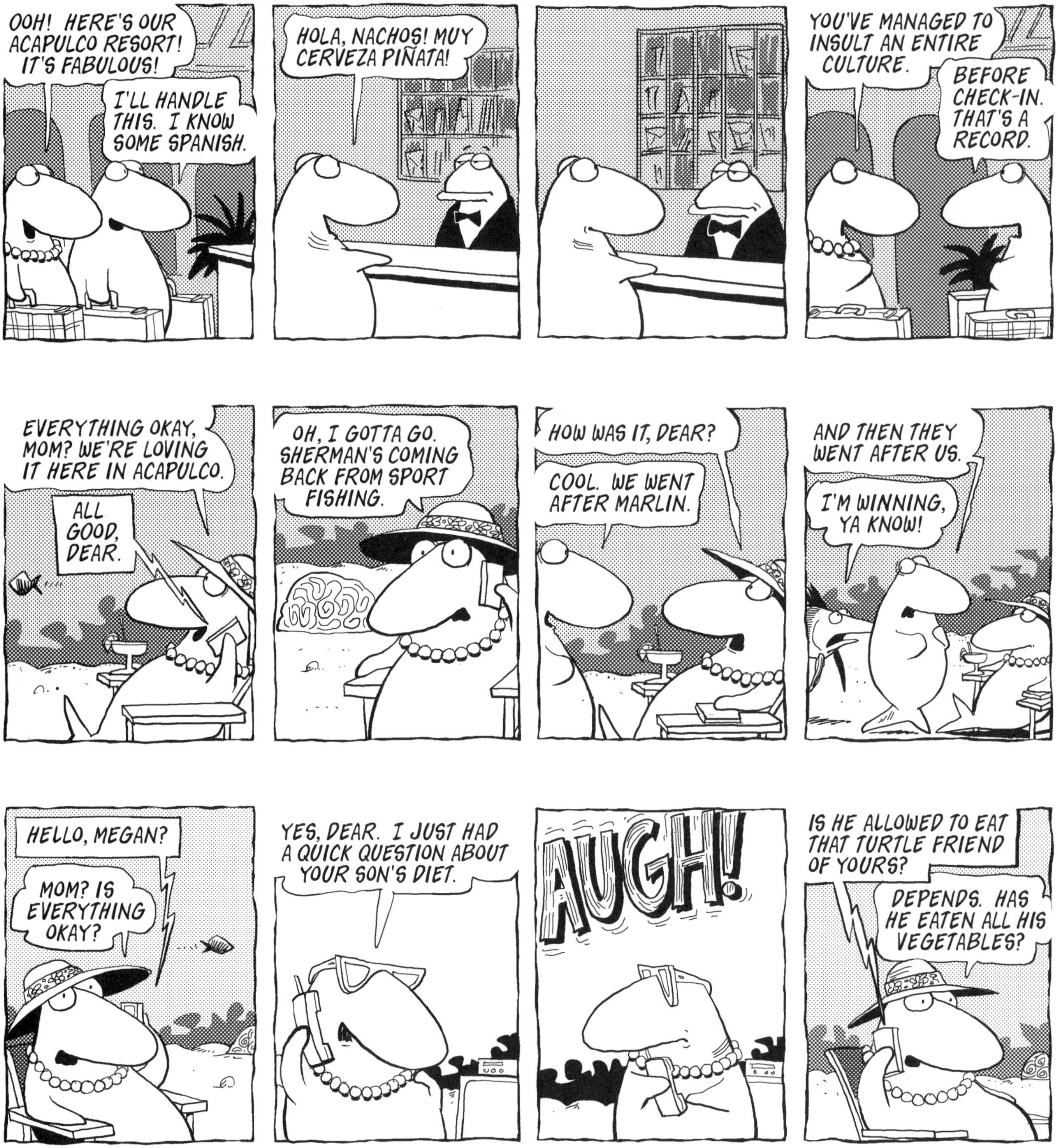
OOH! HERE'S OUR ACAPULCO RESORT! IT'S FABULOUS!
I'LL HANDLE THIS. I KNOW SOME SPANISH.
HOLA, NACHOS! MUY CERVEZA PIÑATA!
YOU'VE MANAGED TO INSULT AN ENTIRE CULTURE.
BEFORE CHECK-IN. THAT'S A RECORD.
EVERYTHING OKAY, MOM? WE'RE LOVING IT HERE IN ACAPULCO.
ALL GOOD, DEAR.
OH, I GOTTA GO. SHERMAN'S COMING BACK FROM SPORT FISHING.
HOW WAS IT, DEAR?
COOL. WE WENT AFTER MARLIN.
AND THEN THEY WENT AFTER US.
I'M WINNING, YA KNOW!
HELLO, MEGAN?
MOM? IS EVERYTHING OKAY?
YES, DEAR. I JUST HAD A QUICK QUESTION ABOUT YOUR SON'S DIET.
AUGH!
IS HE ALLOWED TO EAT THAT TURTLE FRIEND OF YOURS?
DEPENDS. HAS HE EATEN ALL HIS VEGETABLES?

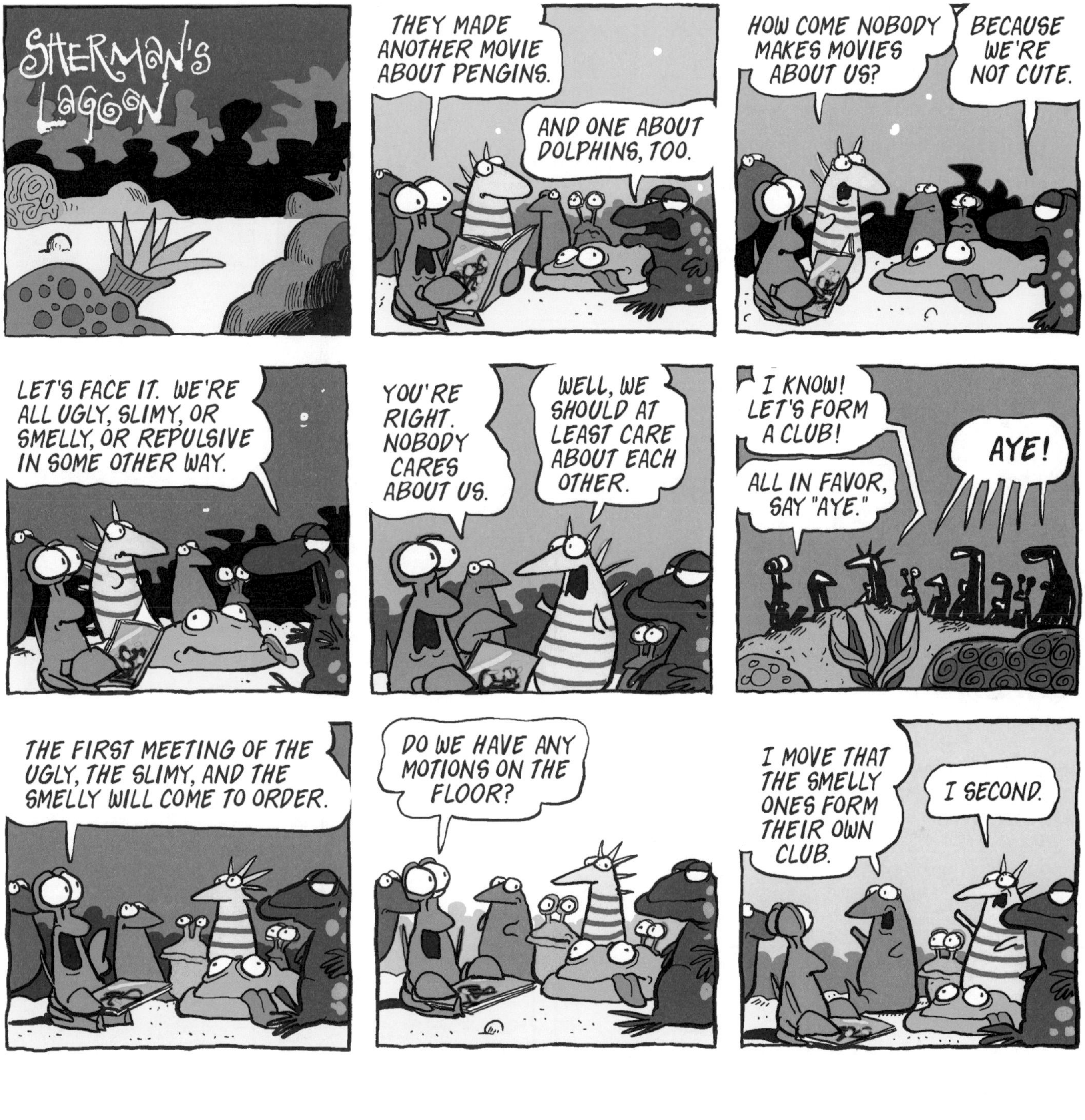
SHERMAN'S LAGOON
THEY MADE ANOTHER MOVIE ABOUT PENGINS.
AND ONE ABOUT DOLPHINS, TOO.
HOW COME NOBODY MAKES MOVIES ABOUT US?
BECAUSE WE'RE NOT CUTE.
LET'S FACE IT. WE'RE ALL UGLY, SLIMY, OR SMELLY, OR REPULSIVE IN SOME OTHER WAY.
YOU'RE RIGHT. NOBODY CARES ABOUT US.
WELL, WE SHOULD AT LEAST CARE ABOUT EACH OTHER.
I KNOW! LET'S FORM A CLUB!
ALL IN FAVOR, SAY "AYE."
AYE!
THE FIRST MEETING OF THE UGLY, THE SLIMY, AND THE SMELLY WILL COME TO ORDER.
DO WE HAVE ANY MOTIONS ON THE FLOOR?
I MOVE THAT THE SMELLY ONES FORM THEIR OWN CLUB.
I SECOND.

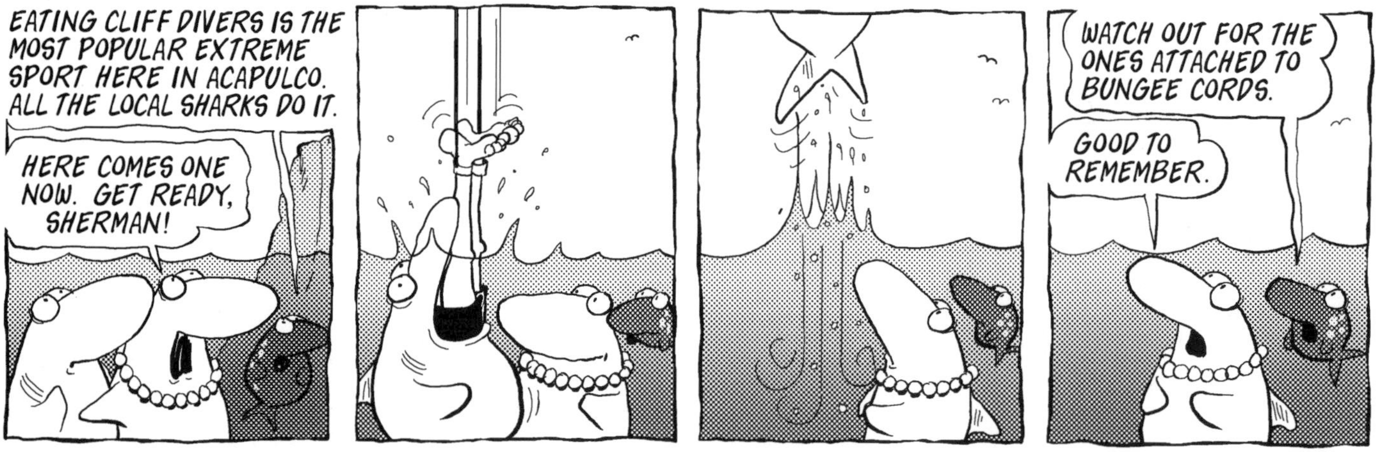
EATING CLIFF DIVERS IS THE MOST POPULAR EXTREME SPORT HERE IN ACAPULCO. ALL THE LOCAL SHARKS DO IT.
HERE COMES ONE NOW. GET READY, SHERMAN!
WATCH OUT FOR THE ONES ATTACHED TO BUNGEE CORDS.
GOOD TO REMEMBER.

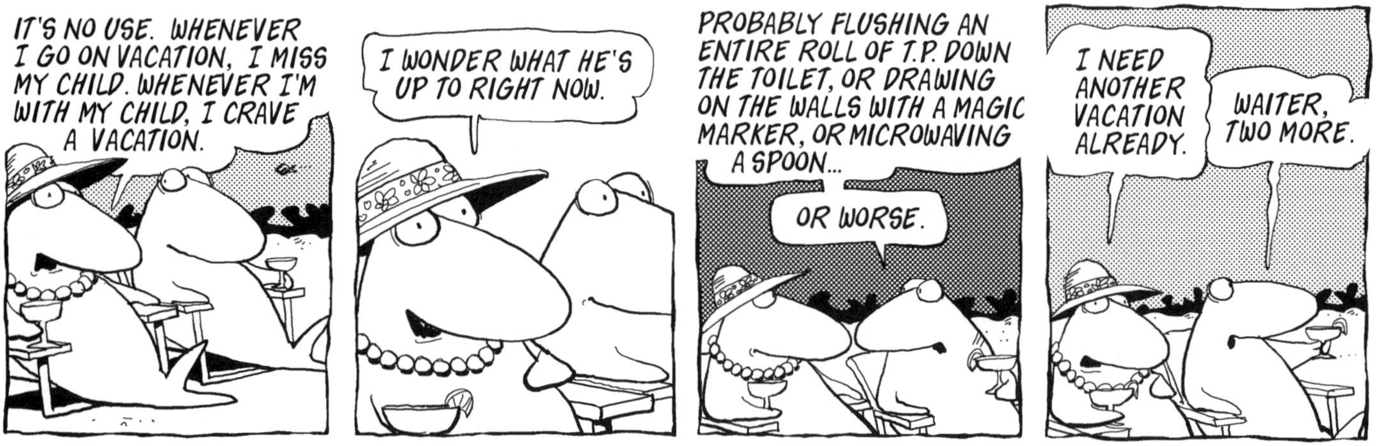
IT'S NO USE. WHENEVER I GO ON VACATION, I MISS MY CHILD. WHENEVER I'M WITH MY CHILD, I CRAVE A VACATION.
I WONDER WHAT HE'S UP TO RIGHT NOW.
PROBABLY FLUSHING AN ENTIRE ROLL OF T.P. DOWN THE TOILET, OR DRAWING ON THE WALLS WITH A MAGIC MARKER, OR MICROWAVING A SPOON...
OR WORSE.
I NEED ANOTHER VACATION ALREADY.
WAITER, TWO MORE.

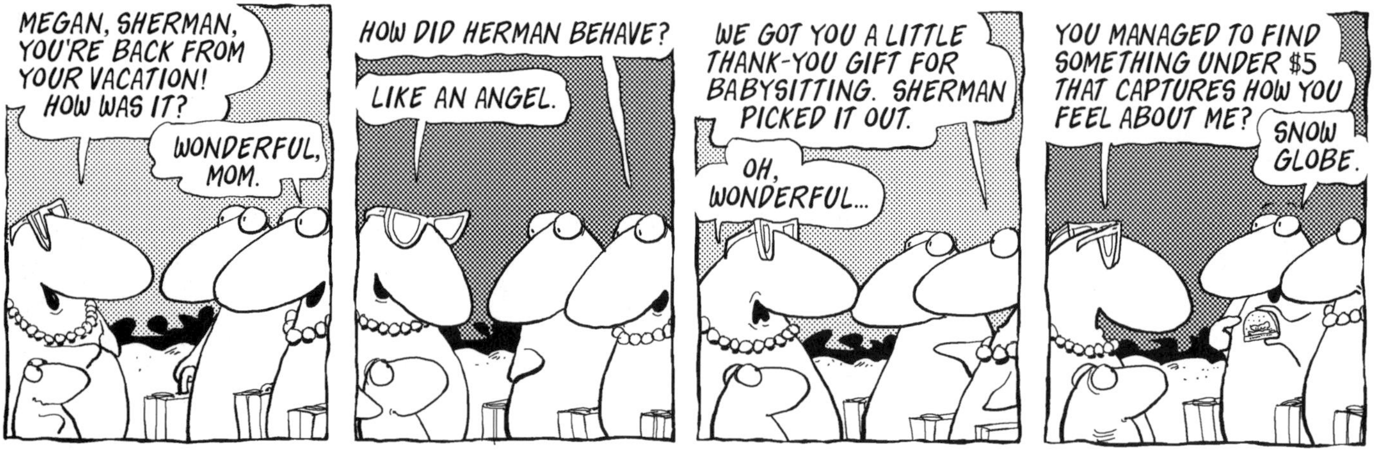
MEGAN, SHERMAN, YOU'RE BACK FROM YOUR VACATION! HOW WAS IT?
WONDERFUL, MOM.
HOW DID HERMAN BEHAVE?
LIKE AN ANGEL.
WE GOT YOU A LITTLE THANK-YOU GIFT FOR BABYSITTING. SHERMAN PICKED IT OUT.
OH, WONDERFUL...
YOU MANAGED TO FIND SOMETHING UNDER $5 THAT CAPTURES HOW YOU FEEL ABOUT ME?
SNOW GLOBE.

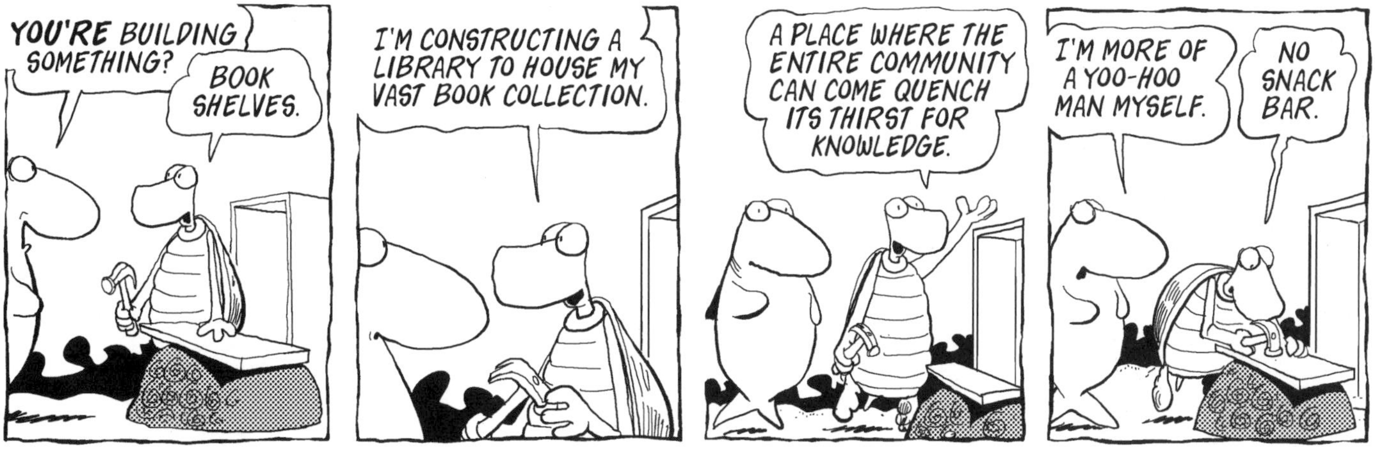
YOU'RE BUILDING SOMETHING?
BOOK SHELVES.
I'M CONSTRUCTING A LIBRARY TO HOUSE MY VAST BOOK COLLECTION.
A PLACE WHERE THE ENTIRE COMMUNITY CAN COME QUENCH ITS THIRST FOR KNOWLEDGE.
I'M MORE OF A YOO-HOO MAN MYSELF.
NO SNACK BAR.

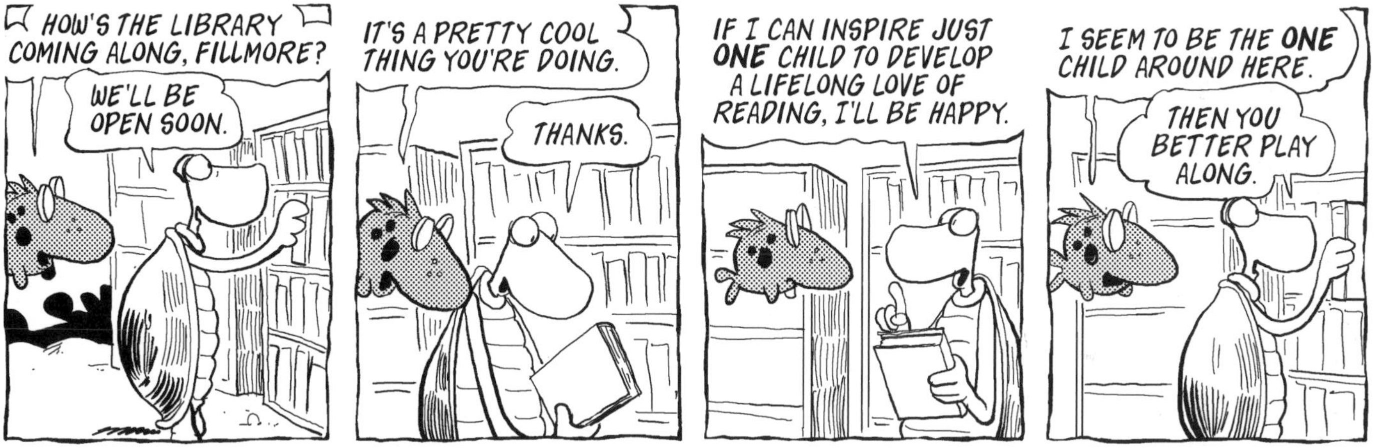
HOW'S THE LIBRARY COMING ALONG, FILLMORE?
WE'LL BE OPEN SOON.
IT'S A PRETTY COOL THING YOU'RE DOING.
THANKS.
IF I CAN INSPIRE JUST ONE CHILD TO DEVELOP A LIFELONG LOVE OF READING, I'LL BE HAPPY.
I SEEM TO BE THE ONE CHILD AROUND HERE.
THEN YOU BETTER PLAY ALONG.

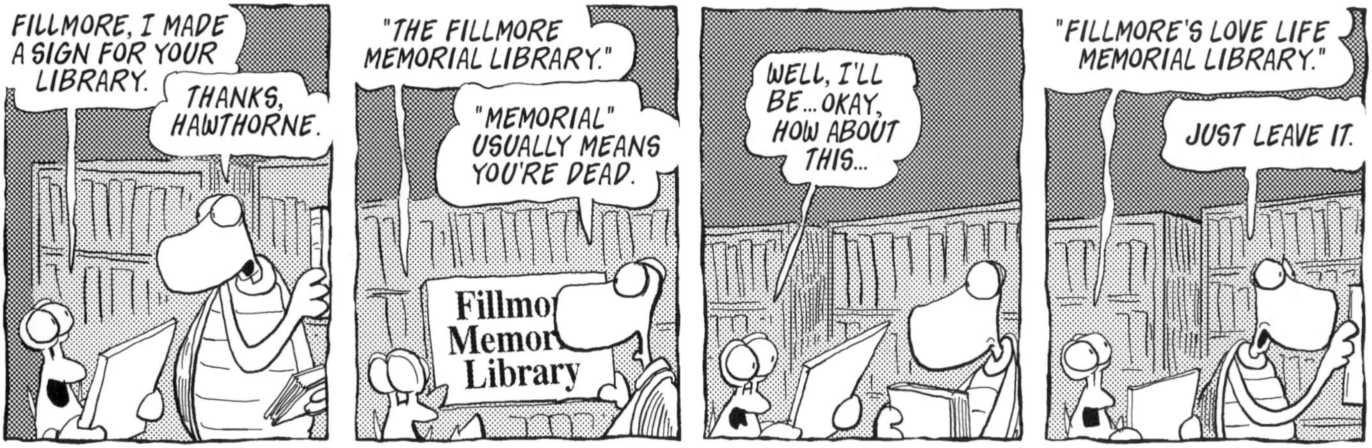
FILLMORE, I MADE A SIGN FOR YOUR LIBRARY.
THANKS, HAWTHORNE.
"THE FILLMORE MEMORIAL LIBRARY."
"MEMORIAL" USUALLY MEANS YOU'RE DEAD.
Fillmo
Memor
Library
WELL, I'LL BE... OKAY, HOW ABOUT THIS...
"FILLMORE'S LOVE LIFE MEMORIAL LIBRARY."
JUST LEAVE IT.

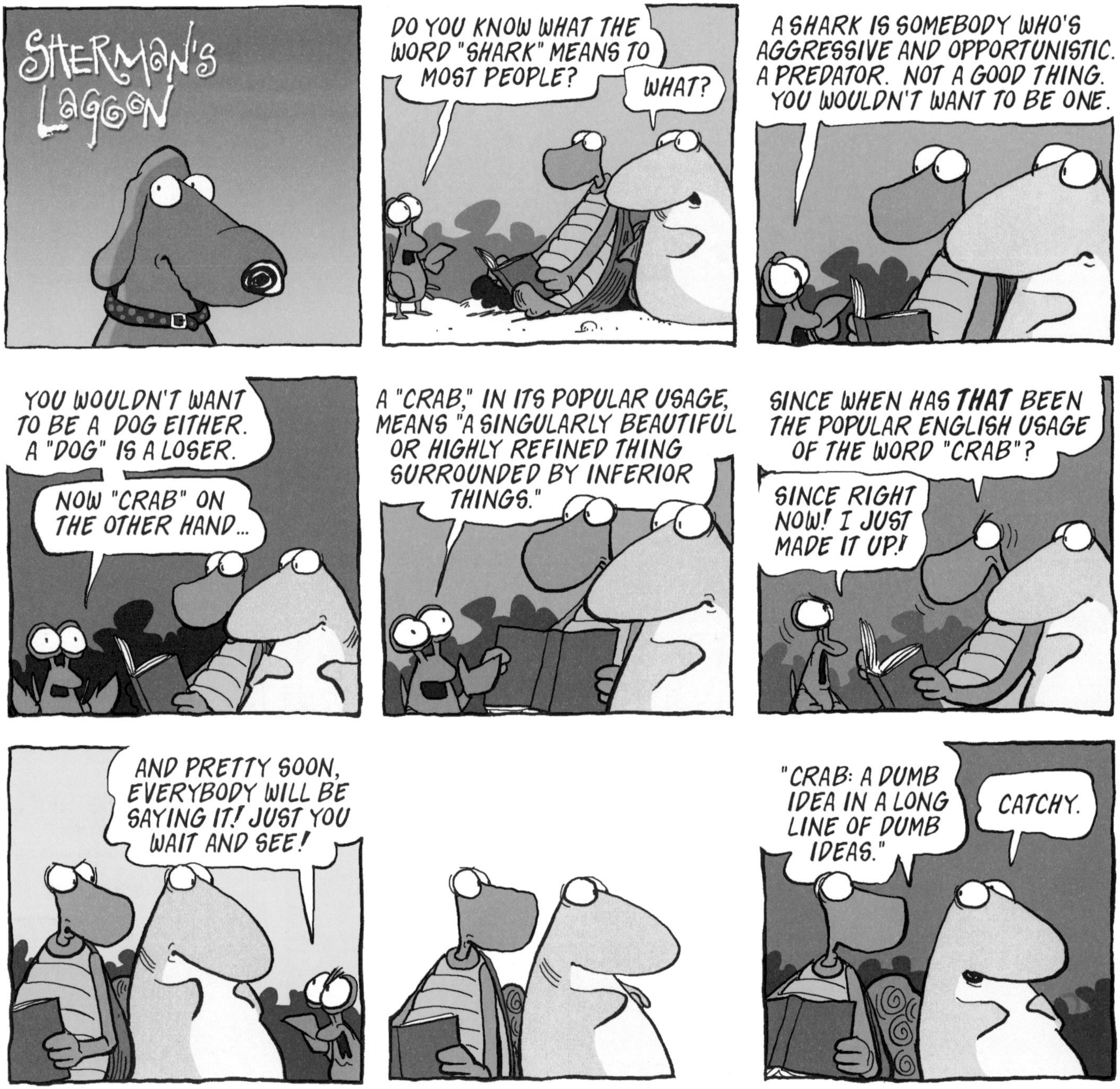
SHERMAN'S LAGOON
DO YOU KNOW WHAT THE WORD "SHARK" MEANS TO MOST PEOPLE?
WHAT?
A SHARK IS SOMEBODY WHO'S AGGRESSIVE AND OPPORTUNISTIC. A PREDATOR. NOT A GOOD THING. YOU WOULDN'T WANT TO BE ONE.
YOU WOULDN'T WANT TO BE A DOG EITHER. A "DOG" IS A LOSER.
NOW "CRAB" ON THE OTHER HAND...
A "CRAB," IN ITS POPULAR USAGE, MEANS "A SINGULARLY BEAUTIFUL OR HIGHLY REFINED THING SURROUNDED BY INFERIOR THINGS."
SINCE WHEN HAS **THAT** BEEN THE POPULAR ENGLISH USAGE OF THE WORD "CRAB"?
SINCE RIGHT NOW! I JUST MADE IT UP!
AND PRETTY SOON, EVERYBODY WILL BE SAYING IT! JUST YOU WAIT AND SEE!
"CRAB: A DUMB IDEA IN A LONG LINE OF DUMB IDEAS."
CATCHY.

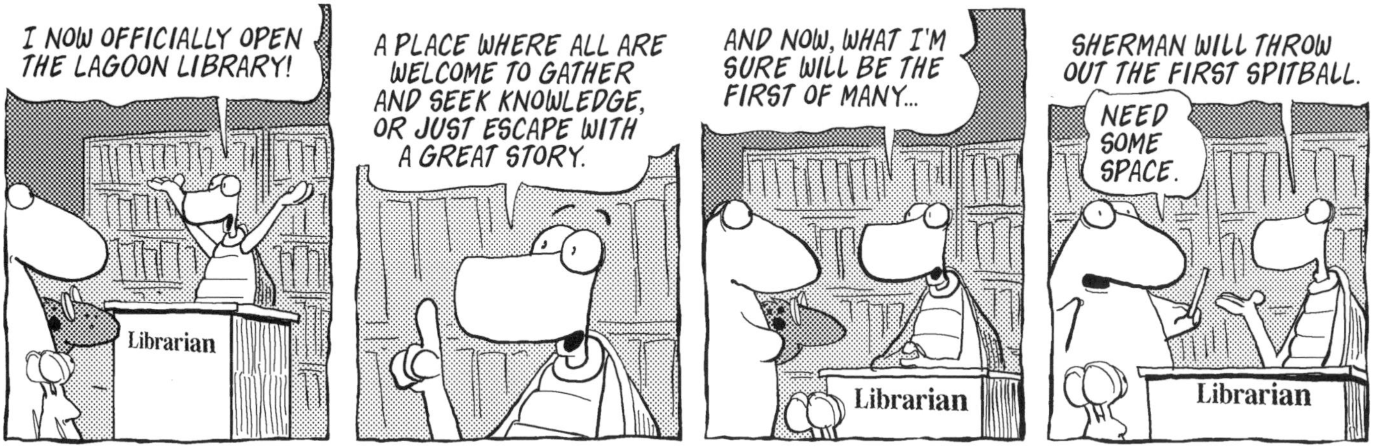
I NOW OFFICIALLY OPEN THE LAGOON LIBRARY!
Librarian
A PLACE WHERE ALL ARE WELCOME TO GATHER AND SEEK KNOWLEDGE, OR JUST ESCAPE WITH A GREAT STORY.
AND NOW, WHAT I'M SURE WILL BE THE FIRST OF MANY...
Librarian
SHERMAN WILL THROW OUT THE FIRST SPITBALL.
NEED SOME SPACE.
Librarian

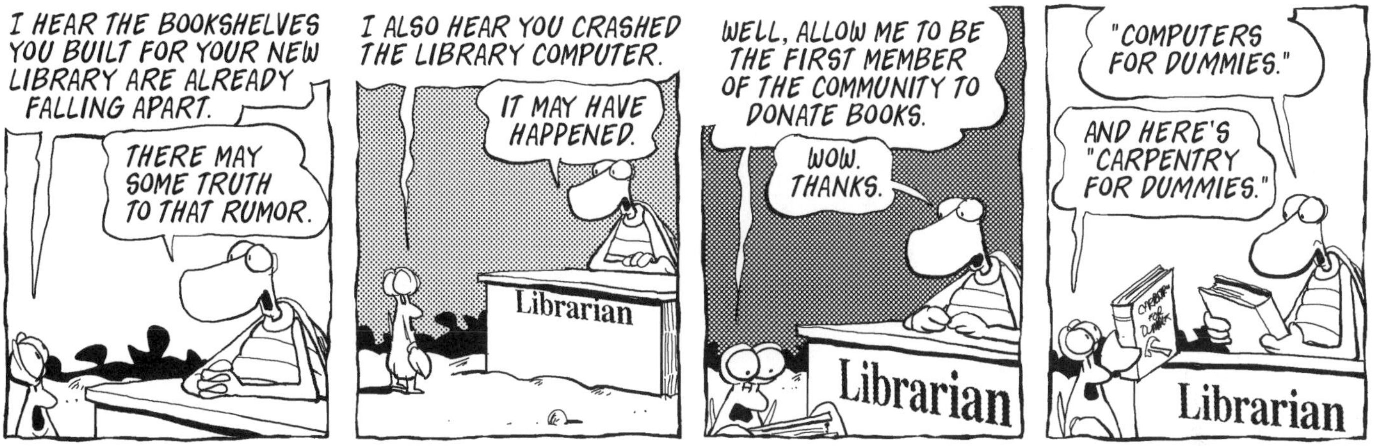
I HEAR THE BOOKSHELVES YOU BUILT FOR YOUR NEW LIBRARY ARE ALREADY FALLING APART.
THERE MAY SOME TRUTH TO THAT RUMOR.
I ALSO HEAR YOU CRASHED THE LIBRARY COMPUTER.
IT MAY HAVE HAPPENED.
Librarian
WELL, ALLOW ME TO BE THE FIRST MEMBER OF THE COMMUNITY TO DONATE BOOKS.
WOW. THANKS.
Librarian
"COMPUTERS FOR DUMMIES."
AND HERE'S "CARPENTRY FOR DUMMIES."
Librarian

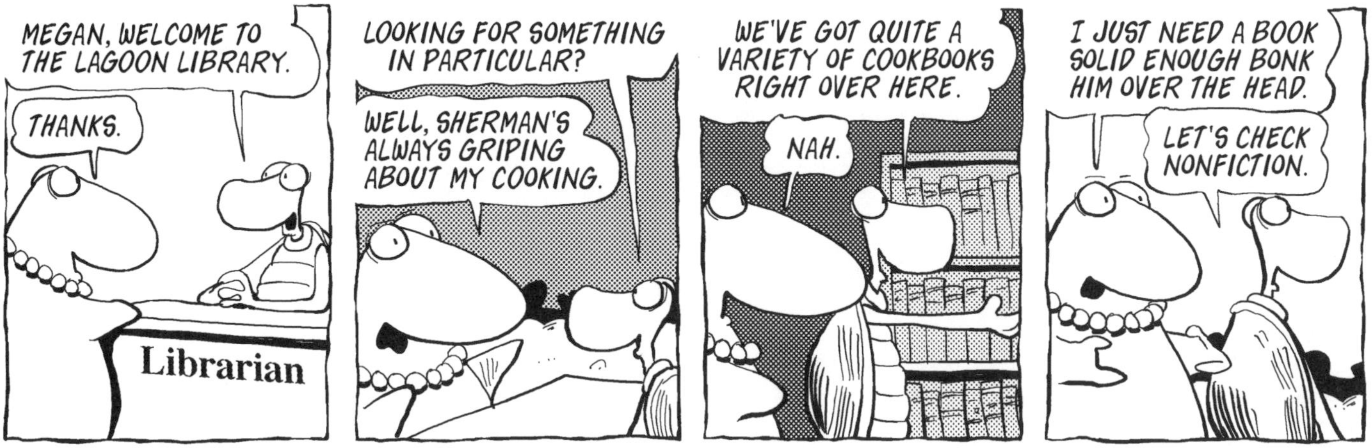
MEGAN, WELCOME TO THE LAGOON LIBRARY.
THANKS.
Librarian
LOOKING FOR SOMETHING IN PARTICULAR?
WELL, SHERMAN'S ALWAYS GRIPING ABOUT MY COOKING.
WE'VE GOT QUITE A VARIETY OF COOKBOOKS RIGHT OVER HERE.
NAH.
I JUST NEED A BOOK SOLID ENOUGH BONK HIM OVER THE HEAD.
LET'S CHECK NONFICTION.

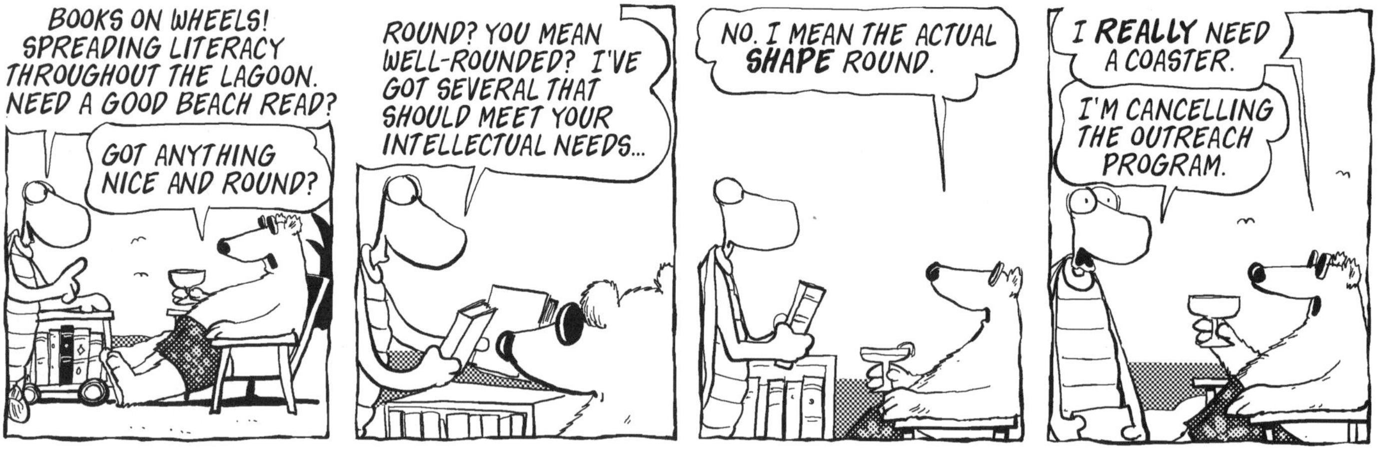
BOOKS ON WHEELS! SPREADING LITERACY THROUGHOUT THE LAGOON. NEED A GOOD BEACH READ?
GOT ANYTHING NICE AND ROUND?
ROUND? YOU MEAN WELL-ROUNDED? I'VE GOT SEVERAL THAT SHOULD MEET YOUR INTELLECTUAL NEEDS...
NO. I MEAN THE ACTUAL **SHAPE** ROUND.
I **REALLY** NEED A COASTER.
I'M CANCELLING THE OUTREACH PROGRAM.

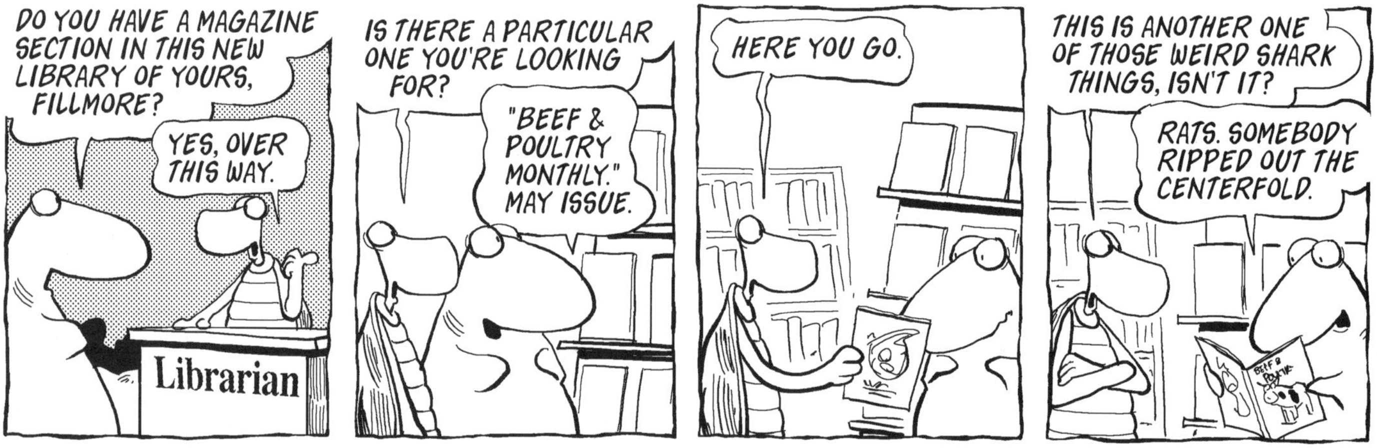
DO YOU HAVE A MAGAZINE SECTION IN THIS NEW LIBRARY OF YOURS, FILLMORE?
YES, OVER THIS WAY.
Librarian
IS THERE A PARTICULAR ONE YOU'RE LOOKING FOR?
"BEEF & POULTRY MONTHLY." MAY ISSUE.
HERE YOU GO.
THIS IS ANOTHER ONE OF THOSE WEIRD SHARK THINGS, ISN'T IT?
RATS. SOMEBODY RIPPED OUT THE CENTERFOLD.

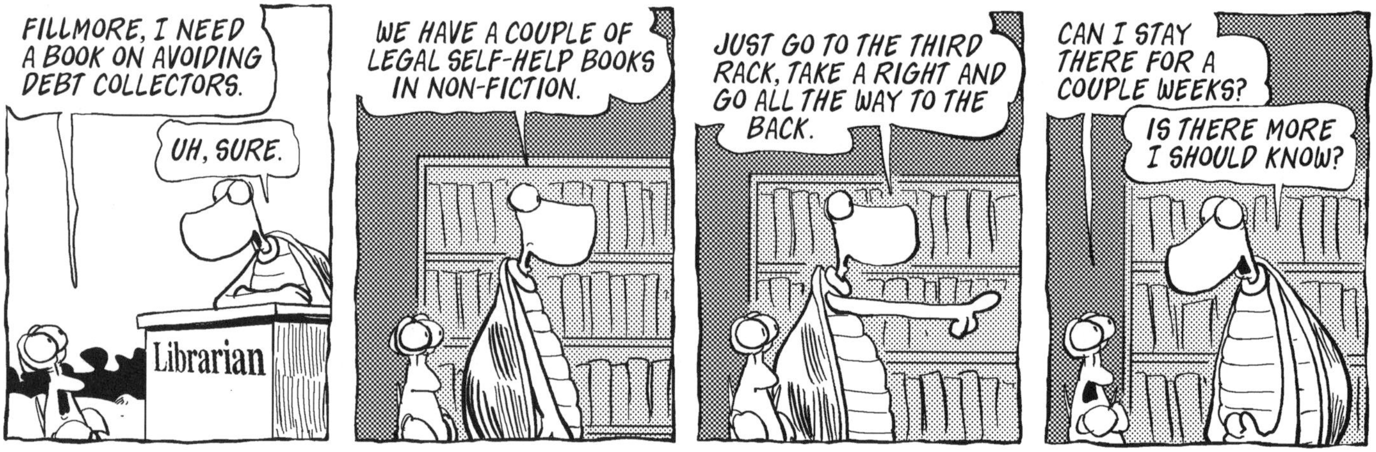
FILLMORE, I NEED A BOOK ON AVOIDING DEBT COLLECTORS.
UH, SURE.
Librarian
WE HAVE A COUPLE OF LEGAL SELF-HELP BOOKS IN NON-FICTION.
JUST GO TO THE THIRD RACK, TAKE A RIGHT AND GO ALL THE WAY TO THE BACK.
CAN I STAY THERE FOR A COUPLE WEEKS?
IS THERE MORE I SHOULD KNOW?

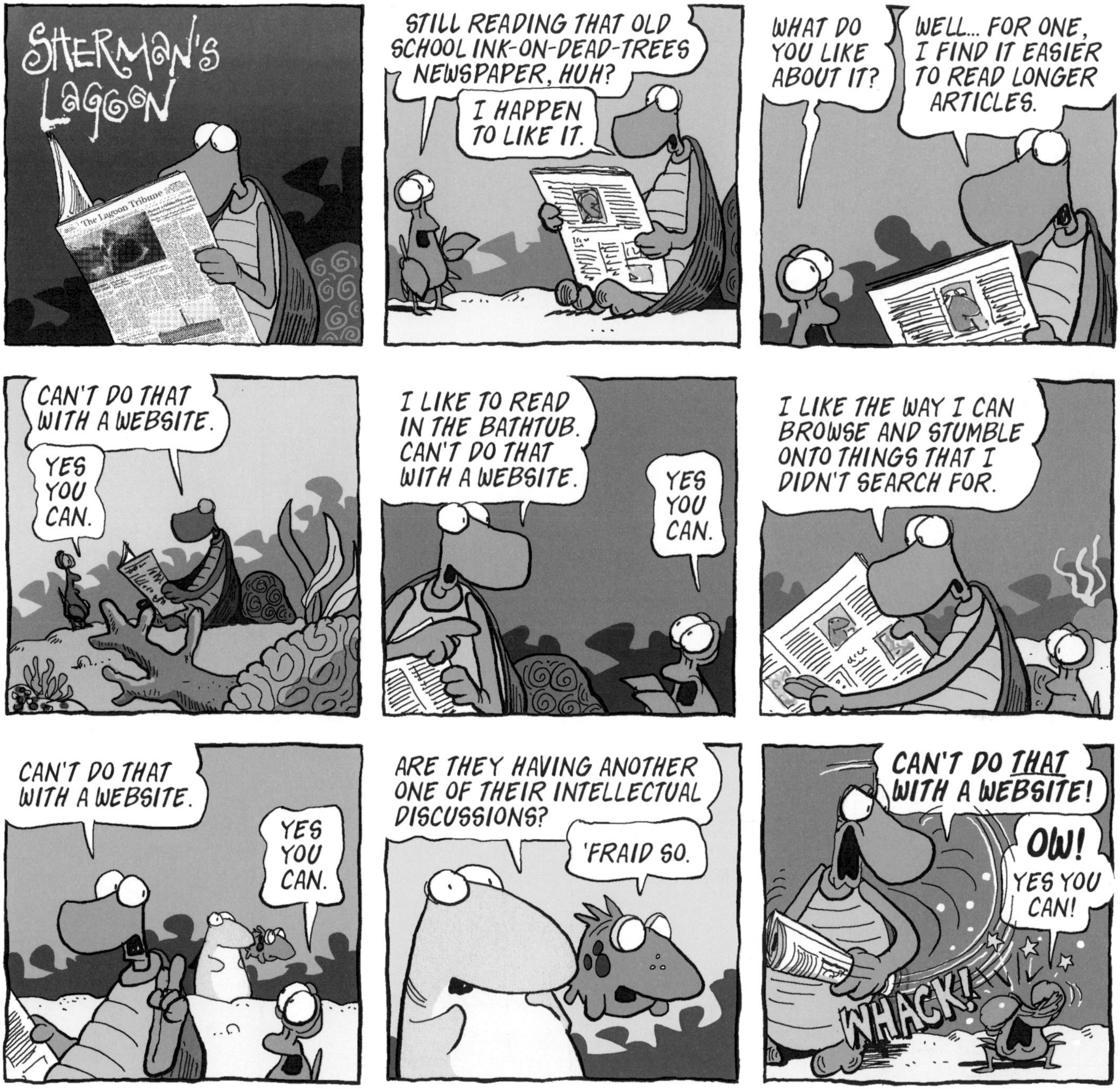
SHERMAN'S LAGOON
The Lagoon Tribune
STILL READING THAT OLD SCHOOL INK-ON-DEAD-TREES NEWSPAPER, HUH?
I HAPPEN TO LIKE IT.
WHAT DO YOU LIKE ABOUT IT?
WELL... FOR ONE, I FIND IT EASIER TO READ LONGER ARTICLES.
CAN'T DO THAT WITH A WEBSITE.
YES YOU CAN.
I LIKE TO READ IN THE BATHTUB. CAN'T DO THAT WITH A WEBSITE.
YES YOU CAN.
I LIKE THE WAY I CAN BROWSE AND STUMBLE ONTO THINGS THAT I DIDN'T SEARCH FOR.
CAN'T DO THAT WITH A WEBSITE.
YES YOU CAN.
ARE THEY HAVING ANOTHER ONE OF THEIR INTELLECTUAL DISCUSSIONS?
'FRAID SO.
CAN'T DO THAT WITH A WEBSITE!
WHACK!
OW!
YES YOU CAN!

Panel 1: FILLMORE, WHY AREN'T YOU WORKING AT YOUR LIBRARY TODAY? / I HIRED A FULLTIME LIBRARIAN.

Panel 2: I'VE DECIDED I CAN'T HANDLE JOBS THAT REQUIRE ME TO INTERACT WITH THE GENERAL PUBLIC.

Panel 3: I'M NOT "BUBBLY." / YOU? NOT BUBBLY?

Panel 4: WITH ALL THE BUBBLES YOU PRODUCE? / THAT DOESN'T MAKE ME BUBBLY.

Panel 5: LOOKS LIKE THE ANNUAL 5K CHARITY BEACH RUN IS COMING UP IN A FEW DAYS.

Panel 6: I TRIED THAT ONCE.

Panel 7: IT JUST CAUSES TOO MUCH PAIN. I ACTUALLY GET BLISTERS WHEN I DO IT.

Panel 8: RUNNING? / CHARITY.

Panel 9: I'M GONNA DO THE 5K RACE THIS YEAR. / THAT TAKES PLACE ON LAND. YOU'RE A FISH.

Panel 10: I CAN HOLD MY BREATH LONG ENOUGH TO HIT THE BEACH FOR A COUPLE MINUTES.

Panel 11: OF COURSE, THIS MEANS I'LL HAVE TO GO INTO MY ATHLETIC TRAINING MODE.

Panel 12: NO TWINKIES FOR DINNER? / WELL, NOT **DURING** DINNER.

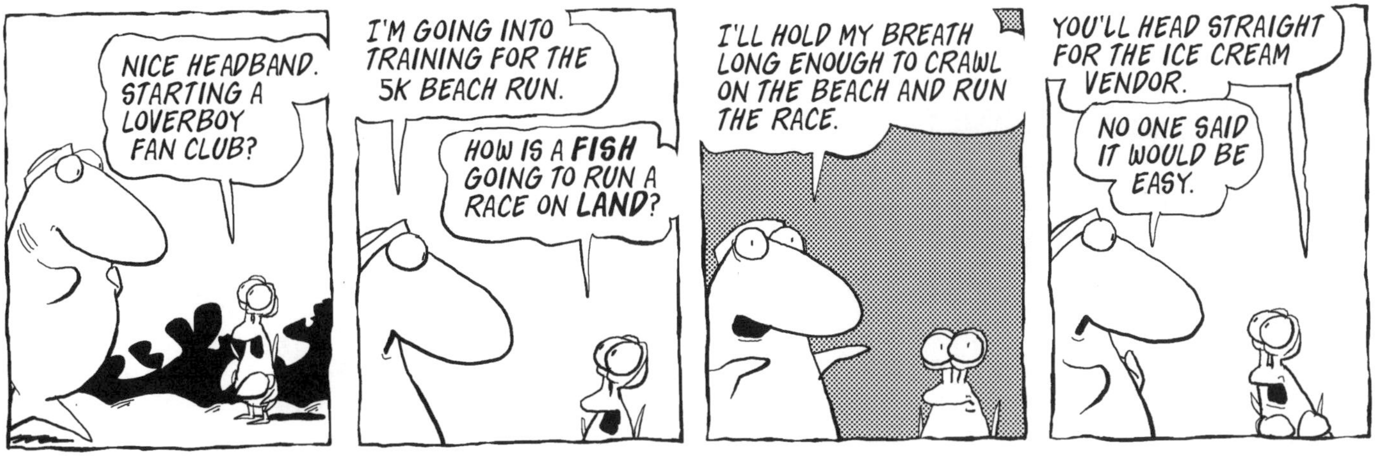
NICE HEADBAND. STARTING A LOVERBOY FAN CLUB?
I'M GOING INTO TRAINING FOR THE 5K BEACH RUN.
HOW IS A **FISH** GOING TO RUN A RACE ON **LAND**?
I'LL HOLD MY BREATH LONG ENOUGH TO CRAWL ON THE BEACH AND RUN THE RACE.
YOU'LL HEAD STRAIGHT FOR THE ICE CREAM VENDOR.
NO ONE SAID IT WOULD BE EASY.

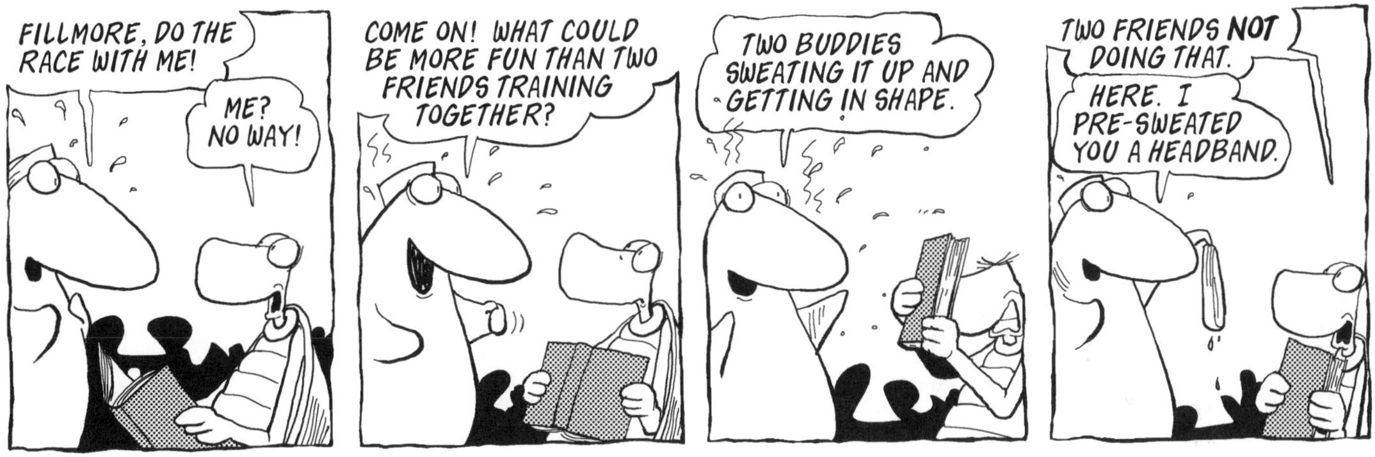
FILLMORE, DO THE RACE WITH ME!
ME? NO WAY!
COME ON! WHAT COULD BE MORE FUN THAN TWO FRIENDS TRAINING TOGETHER?
TWO BUDDIES SWEATING IT UP AND GETTING IN SHAPE.
TWO FRIENDS **NOT** DOING THAT.
HERE. I PRE-SWEATED YOU A HEADBAND.

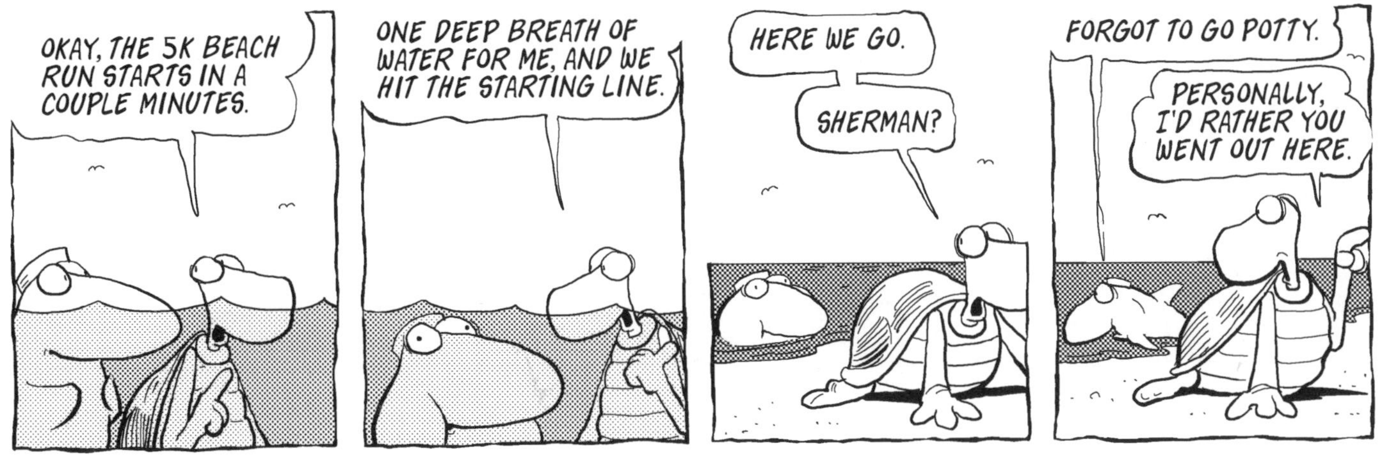
OKAY, THE 5K BEACH RUN STARTS IN A COUPLE MINUTES.
ONE DEEP BREATH OF WATER FOR ME, AND WE HIT THE STARTING LINE.
HERE WE GO.
SHERMAN?
FORGOT TO GO POTTY.
PERSONALLY, I'D RATHER YOU WENT OUT HERE.

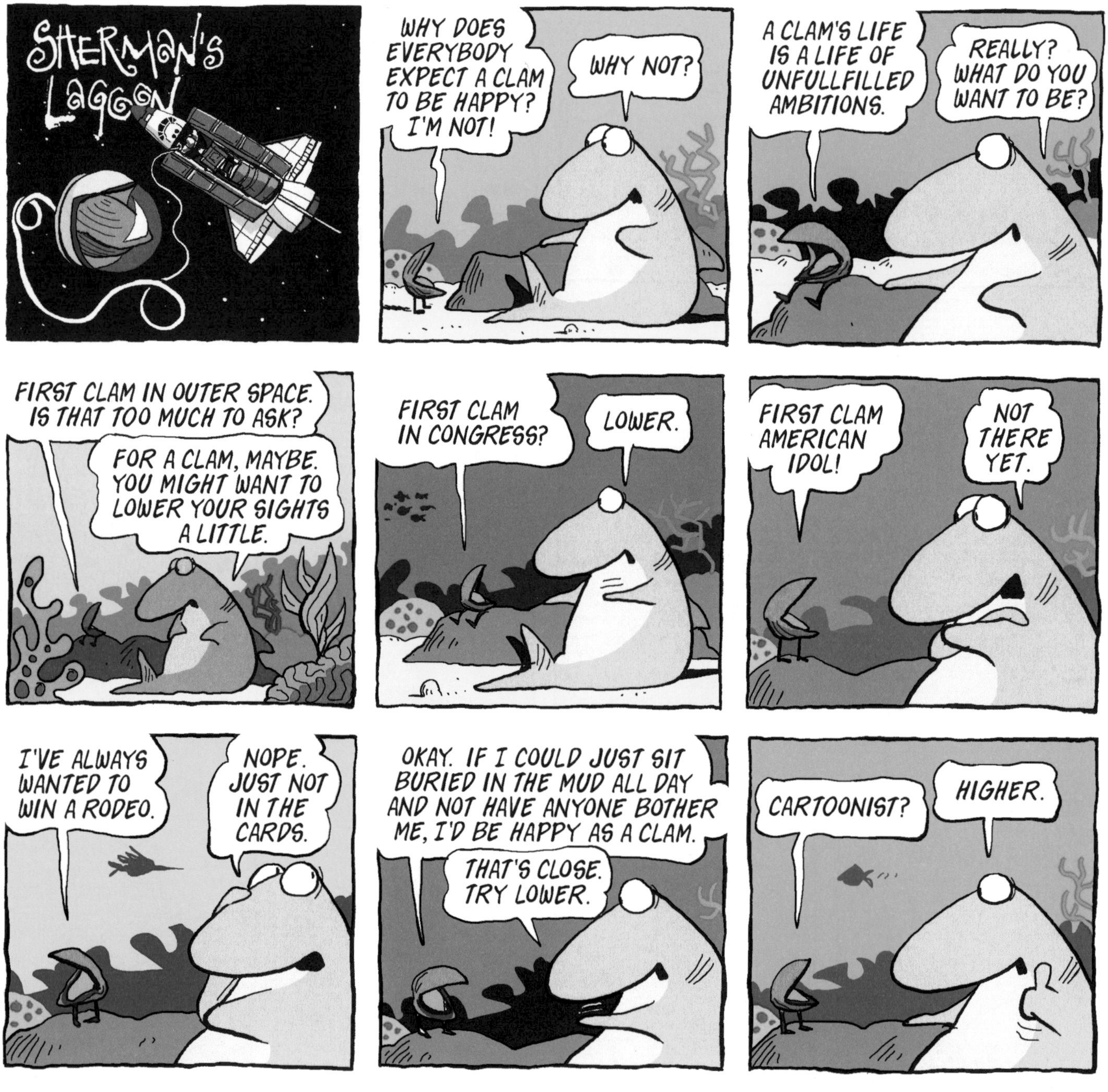
SHERMAN'S LAGOON
WHY DOES EVERYBODY EXPECT A CLAM TO BE HAPPY? I'M NOT!
WHY NOT?
A CLAM'S LIFE IS A LIFE OF UNFULLFILLED AMBITIONS.
REALLY? WHAT DO YOU WANT TO BE?
FIRST CLAM IN OUTER SPACE. IS THAT TOO MUCH TO ASK?
FOR A CLAM, MAYBE. YOU MIGHT WANT TO LOWER YOUR SIGHTS A LITTLE.
FIRST CLAM IN CONGRESS?
LOWER.
FIRST CLAM AMERICAN IDOL!
NOT THERE YET.
I'VE ALWAYS WANTED TO WIN A RODEO.
NOPE. JUST NOT IN THE CARDS.
OKAY. IF I COULD JUST SIT BURIED IN THE MUD ALL DAY AND NOT HAVE ANYONE BOTHER ME, I'D BE HAPPY AS A CLAM.
THAT'S CLOSE. TRY LOWER.
CARTOONIST?
HIGHER.

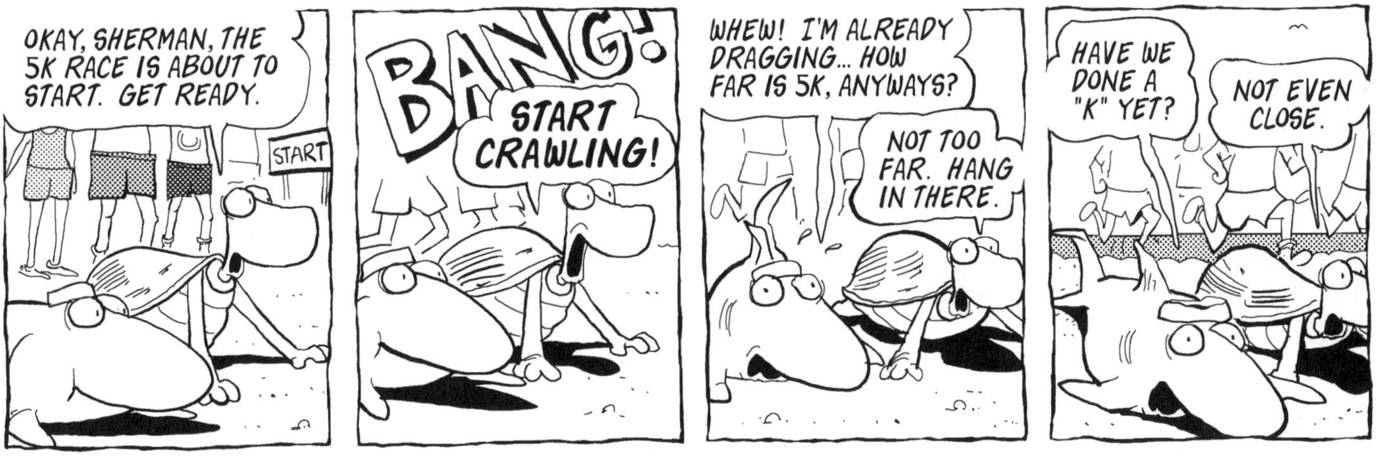
OKAY, SHERMAN, THE 5K RACE IS ABOUT TO START. GET READY.
START
BANG!
START CRAWLING!
WHEW! I'M ALREADY DRAGGING... HOW FAR IS 5K, ANYWAYS?
NOT TOO FAR. HANG IN THERE.
HAVE WE DONE A "K" YET?
NOT EVEN CLOSE.

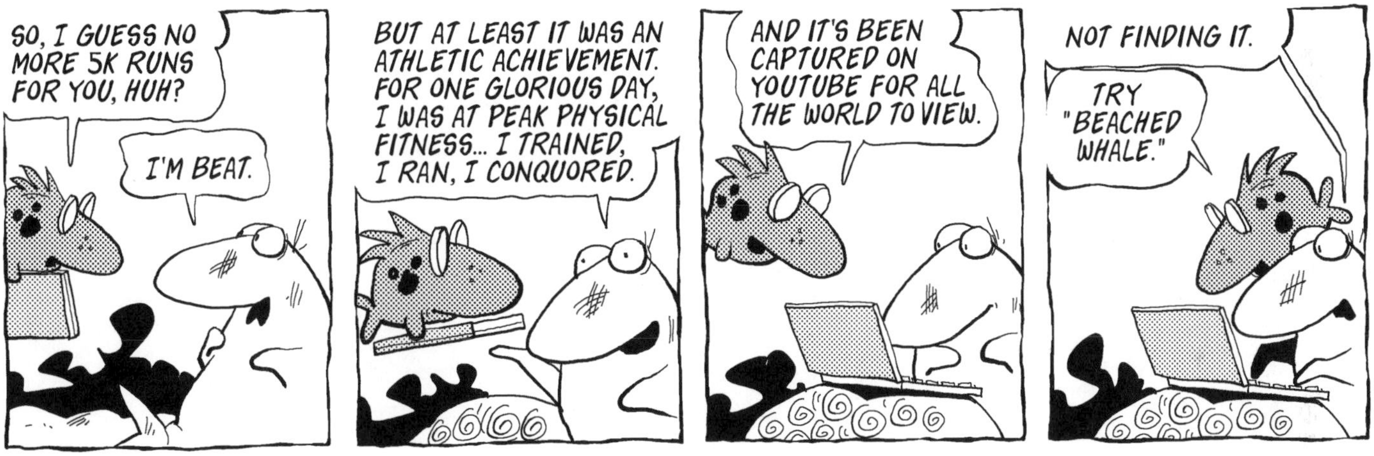
SO, I GUESS NO MORE 5K RUNS FOR YOU, HUH?
I'M BEAT.
BUT AT LEAST IT WAS AN ATHLETIC ACHIEVEMENT. FOR ONE GLORIOUS DAY, I WAS AT PEAK PHYSICAL FITNESS... I TRAINED, I RAN, I CONQUORED.
AND IT'S BEEN CAPTURED ON YOUTUBE FOR ALL THE WORLD TO VIEW.
NOT FINDING IT.
TRY "BEACHED WHALE."

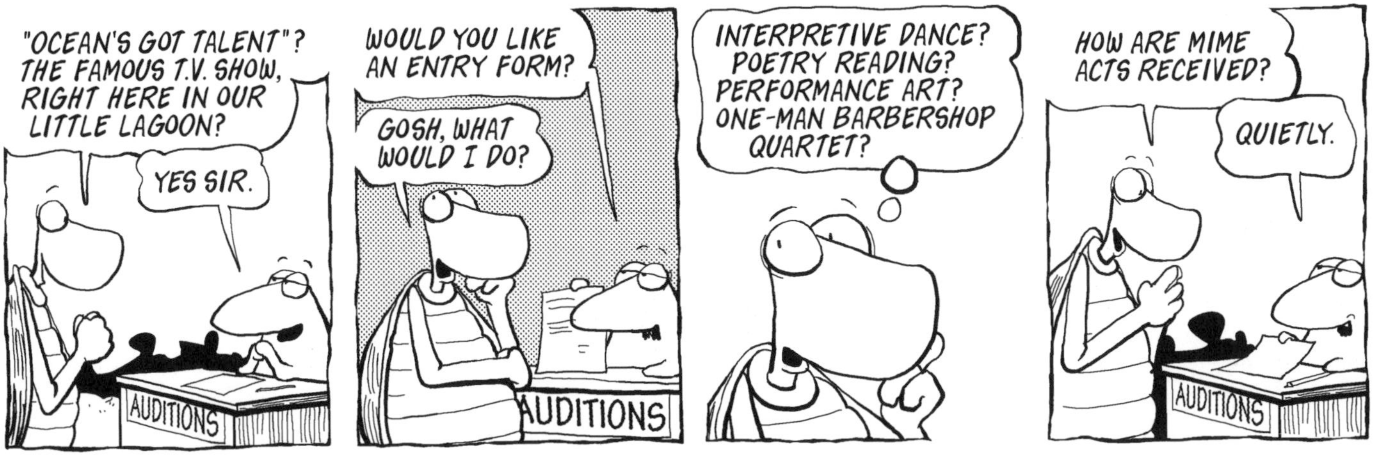
"OCEAN'S GOT TALENT"? THE FAMOUS T.V. SHOW, RIGHT HERE IN OUR LITTLE LAGOON?
YES SIR.
AUDITIONS
WOULD YOU LIKE AN ENTRY FORM?
GOSH, WHAT WOULD I DO?
AUDITIONS
INTERPRETIVE DANCE? POETRY READING? PERFORMANCE ART? ONE-MAN BARBERSHOP QUARTET?
HOW ARE MIME ACTS RECEIVED?
QUIETLY.
AUDITIONS

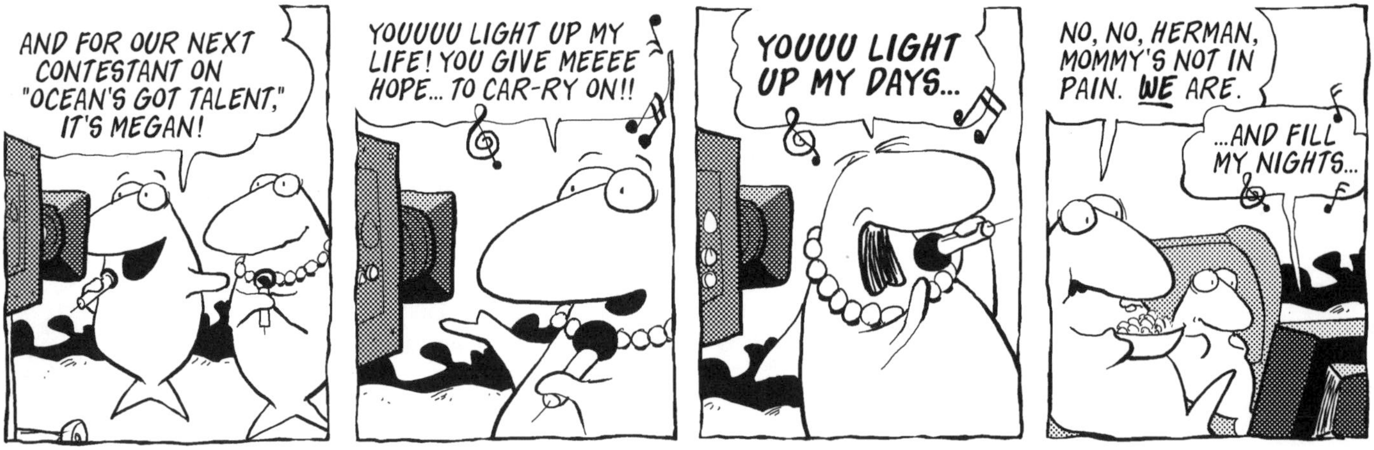
AND FOR OUR NEXT CONTESTANT ON "OCEAN'S GOT TALENT," IT'S MEGAN!
YOUUUU LIGHT UP MY LIFE! YOU GIVE MEEEE HOPE... TO CAR-RY ON!!
YOUUU LIGHT UP MY DAYS...
NO, NO, HERMAN, MOMMY'S NOT IN PAIN. WE ARE.
...AND FILL MY NIGHTS...

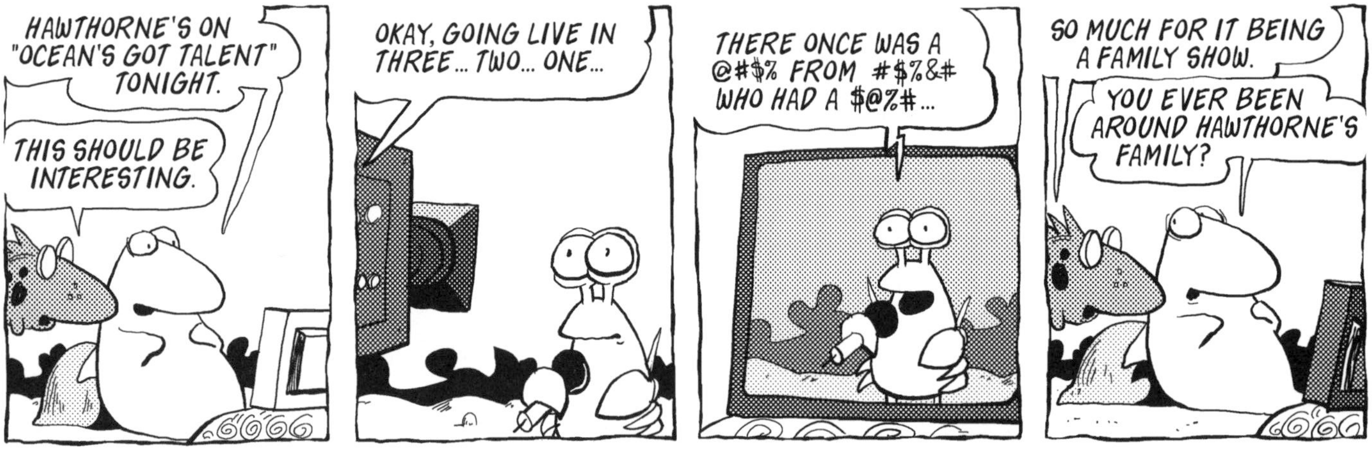
HAWTHORNE'S ON "OCEAN'S GOT TALENT" TONIGHT.
THIS SHOULD BE INTERESTING.
OKAY, GOING LIVE IN THREE... TWO... ONE...
THERE ONCE WAS A @#$% FROM #$%&# WHO HAD A $@%#...
SO MUCH FOR IT BEING A FAMILY SHOW.
YOU EVER BEEN AROUND HAWTHORNE'S FAMILY?

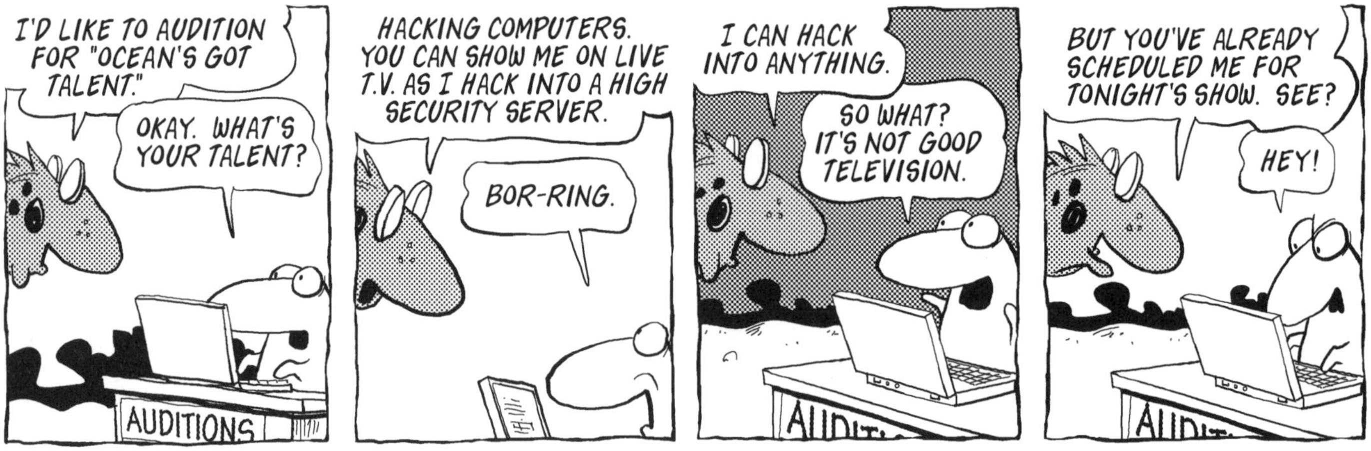
I'D LIKE TO AUDITION FOR "OCEAN'S GOT TALENT."
OKAY. WHAT'S YOUR TALENT?
AUDITIONS
HACKING COMPUTERS. YOU CAN SHOW ME ON LIVE T.V. AS I HACK INTO A HIGH SECURITY SERVER.
BOR-RING.
I CAN HACK INTO ANYTHING.
SO WHAT? IT'S NOT GOOD TELEVISION.
BUT YOU'VE ALREADY SCHEDULED ME FOR TONIGHT'S SHOW. SEE?
HEY!

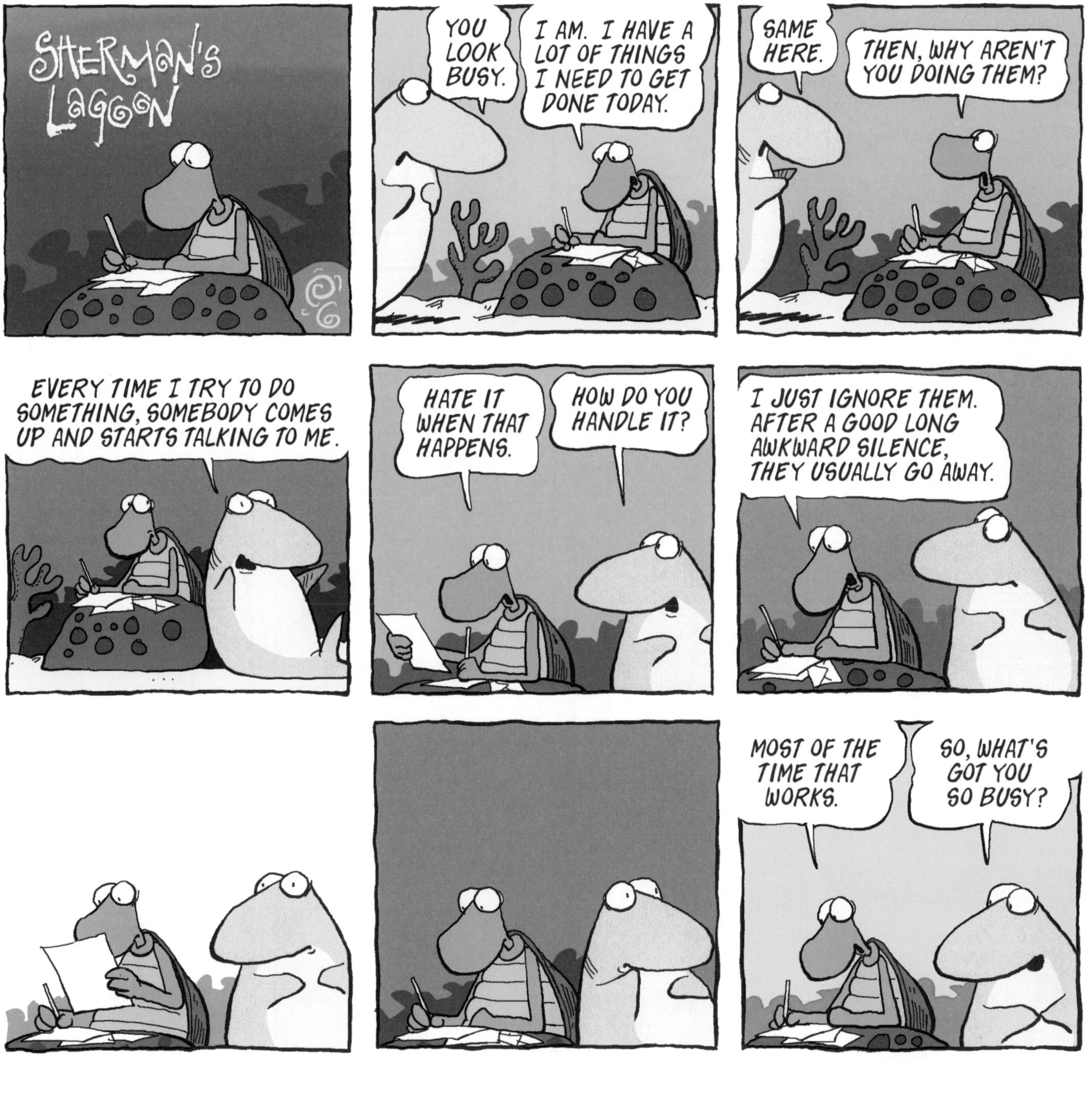
SHERMAN'S LAGOON
YOU LOOK BUSY.
I AM. I HAVE A LOT OF THINGS I NEED TO GET DONE TODAY.
SAME HERE.
THEN, WHY AREN'T YOU DOING THEM?
EVERY TIME I TRY TO DO SOMETHING, SOMEBODY COMES UP AND STARTS TALKING TO ME.
HATE IT WHEN THAT HAPPENS.
HOW DO YOU HANDLE IT?
I JUST IGNORE THEM. AFTER A GOOD LONG AWKWARD SILENCE, THEY USUALLY GO AWAY.
MOST OF THE TIME THAT WORKS.
SO, WHAT'S GOT YOU SO BUSY?

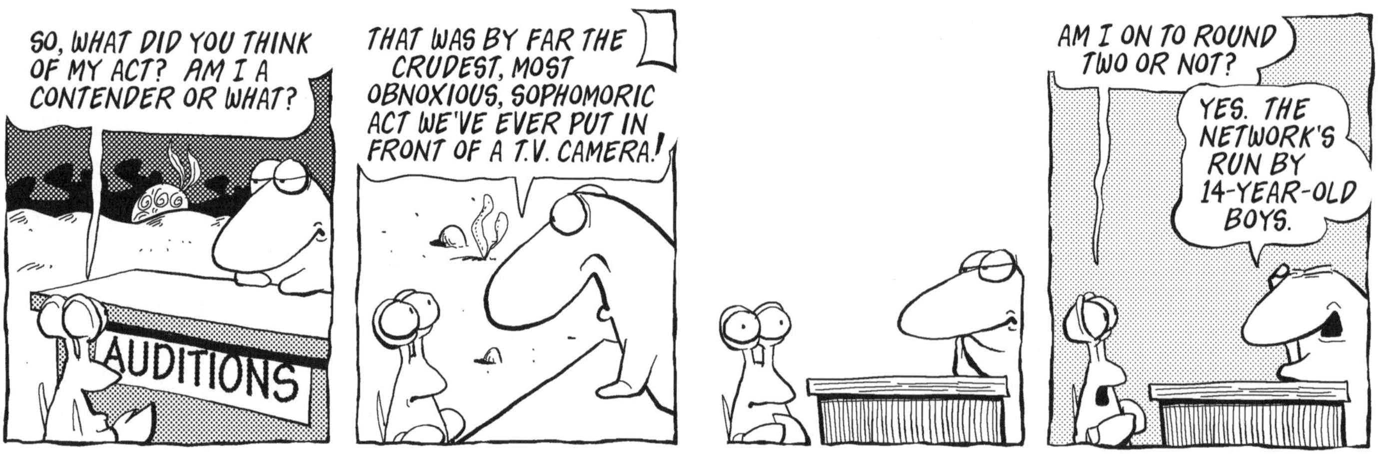
SO, WHAT DID YOU THINK OF MY ACT? AM I A CONTENDER OR WHAT?
AUDITIONS
THAT WAS BY FAR THE CRUDEST, MOST OBNOXIOUS, SOPHOMORIC ACT WE'VE EVER PUT IN FRONT OF A T.V. CAMERA!
AM I ON TO ROUND TWO OR NOT?
YES. THE NETWORK'S RUN BY 14-YEAR-OLD BOYS.

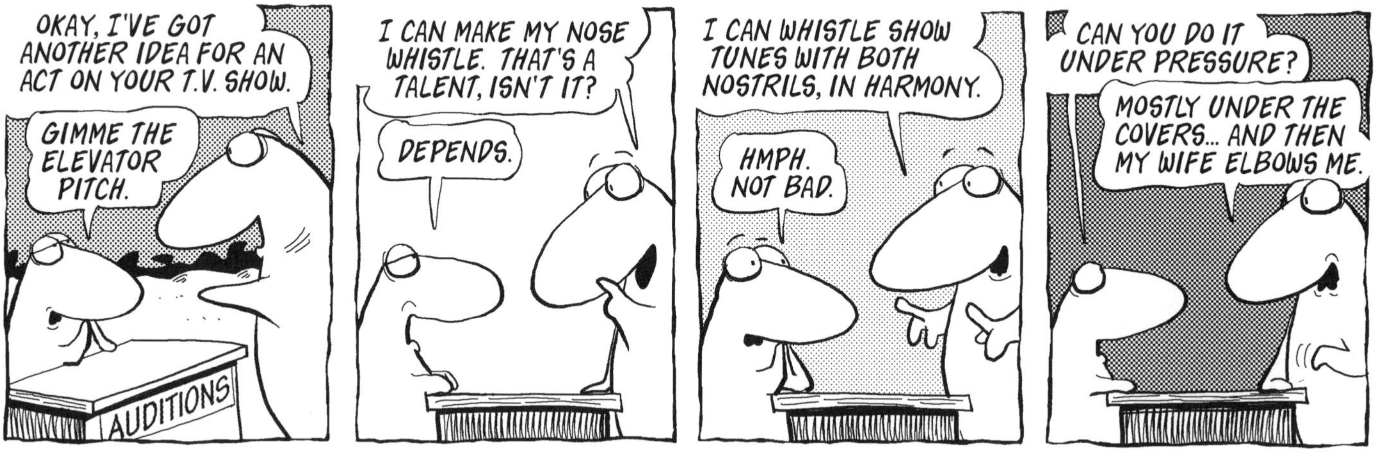
OKAY, I'VE GOT ANOTHER IDEA FOR AN ACT ON YOUR T.V. SHOW.
GIMME THE ELEVATOR PITCH.
AUDITIONS
I CAN MAKE MY NOSE WHISTLE. THAT'S A TALENT, ISN'T IT?
DEPENDS.
I CAN WHISTLE SHOW TUNES WITH BOTH NOSTRILS, IN HARMONY.
HMPH. NOT BAD.
CAN YOU DO IT UNDER PRESSURE?
MOSTLY UNDER THE COVERS... AND THEN MY WIFE ELBOWS ME.

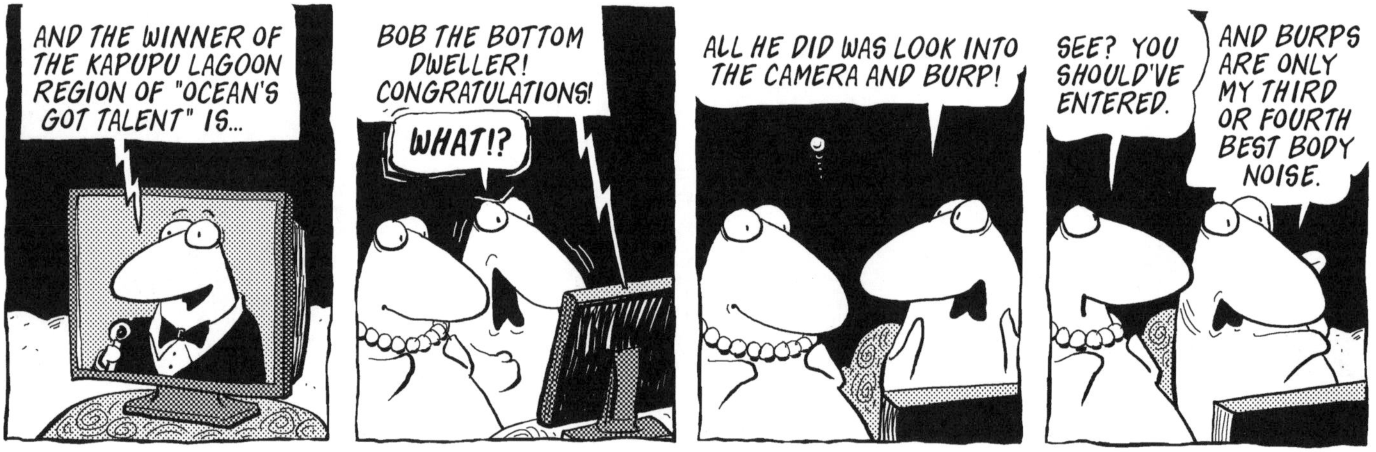
AND THE WINNER OF THE KAPUPU LAGOON REGION OF "OCEAN'S GOT TALENT" IS...
BOB THE BOTTOM DWELLER! CONGRATULATIONS!
WHAT!?
ALL HE DID WAS LOOK INTO THE CAMERA AND BURP!
SEE? YOU SHOULD'VE ENTERED.
AND BURPS ARE ONLY MY THIRD OR FOURTH BEST BODY NOISE.

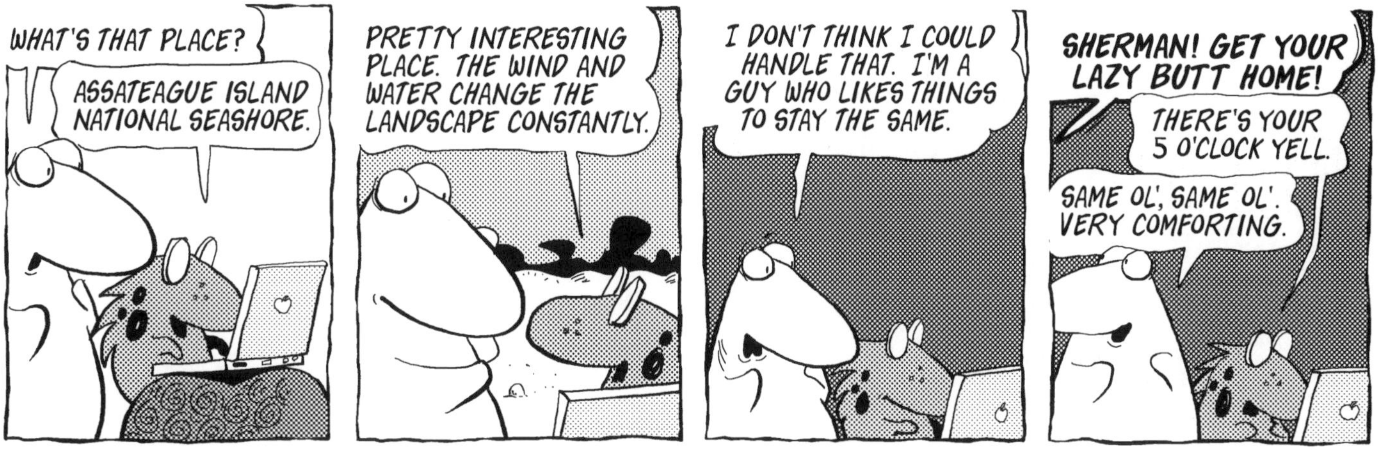
WHAT'S THAT PLACE?
ASSATEAGUE ISLAND NATIONAL SEASHORE.
PRETTY INTERESTING PLACE. THE WIND AND WATER CHANGE THE LANDSCAPE CONSTANTLY.
I DON'T THINK I COULD HANDLE THAT. I'M A GUY WHO LIKES THINGS TO STAY THE SAME.
SHERMAN! GET YOUR LAZY BUTT HOME!
THERE'S YOUR 5 O'CLOCK YELL.
SAME OL', SAME OL'. VERY COMFORTING.

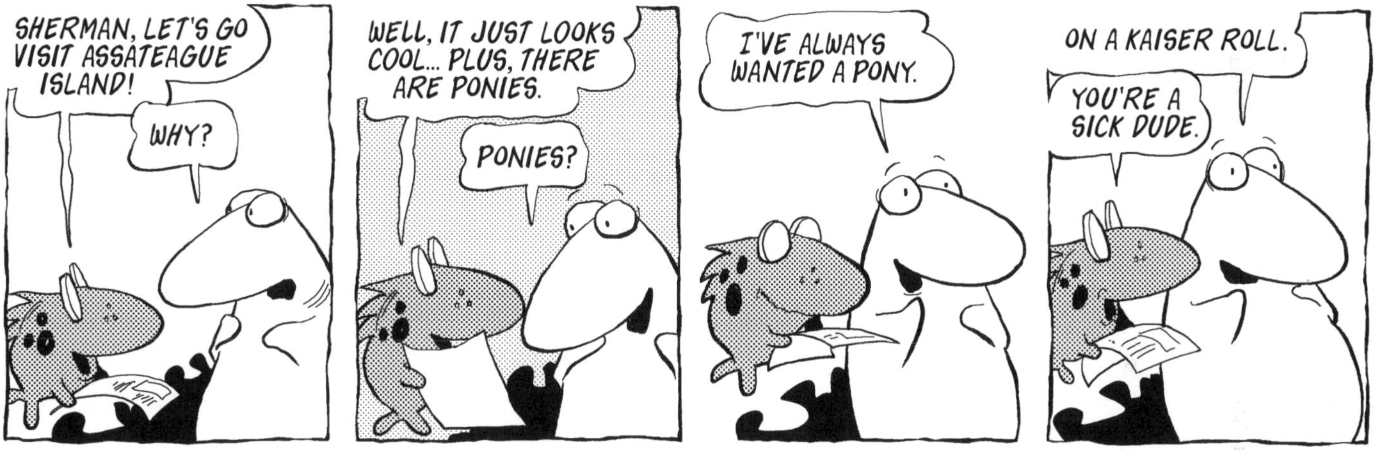
SHERMAN, LET'S GO VISIT ASSATEAGUE ISLAND!
WHY?
WELL, IT JUST LOOKS COOL... PLUS, THERE ARE PONIES.
PONIES?
I'VE ALWAYS WANTED A PONY.
ON A KAISER ROLL.
YOU'RE A SICK DUDE.

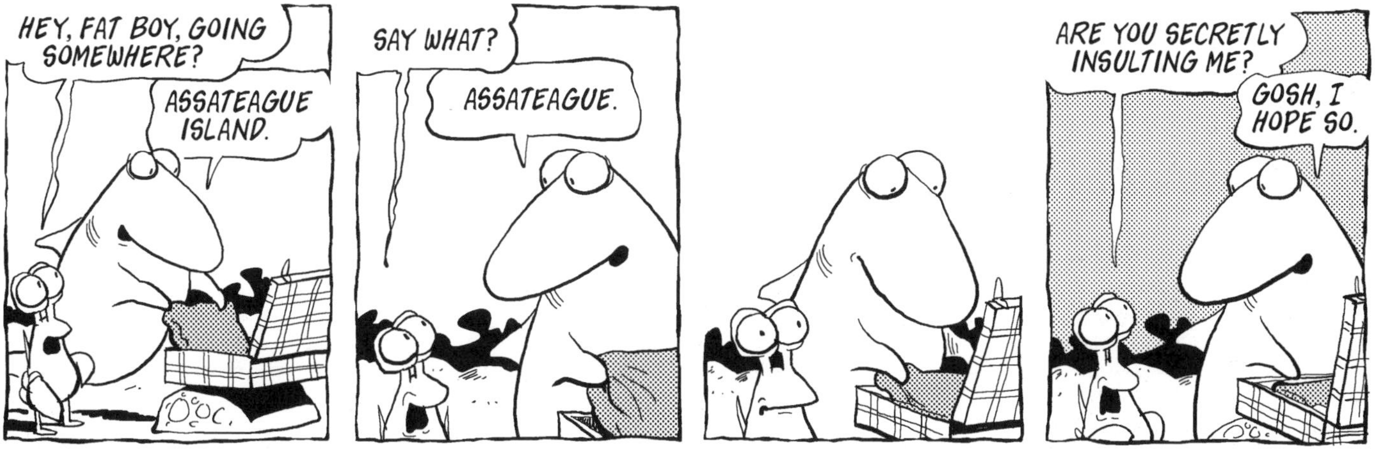
HEY, FAT BOY, GOING SOMEWHERE?
ASSATEAGUE ISLAND.
SAY WHAT?
ASSATEAGUE.
ARE YOU SECRETLY INSULTING ME?
GOSH, I HOPE SO.

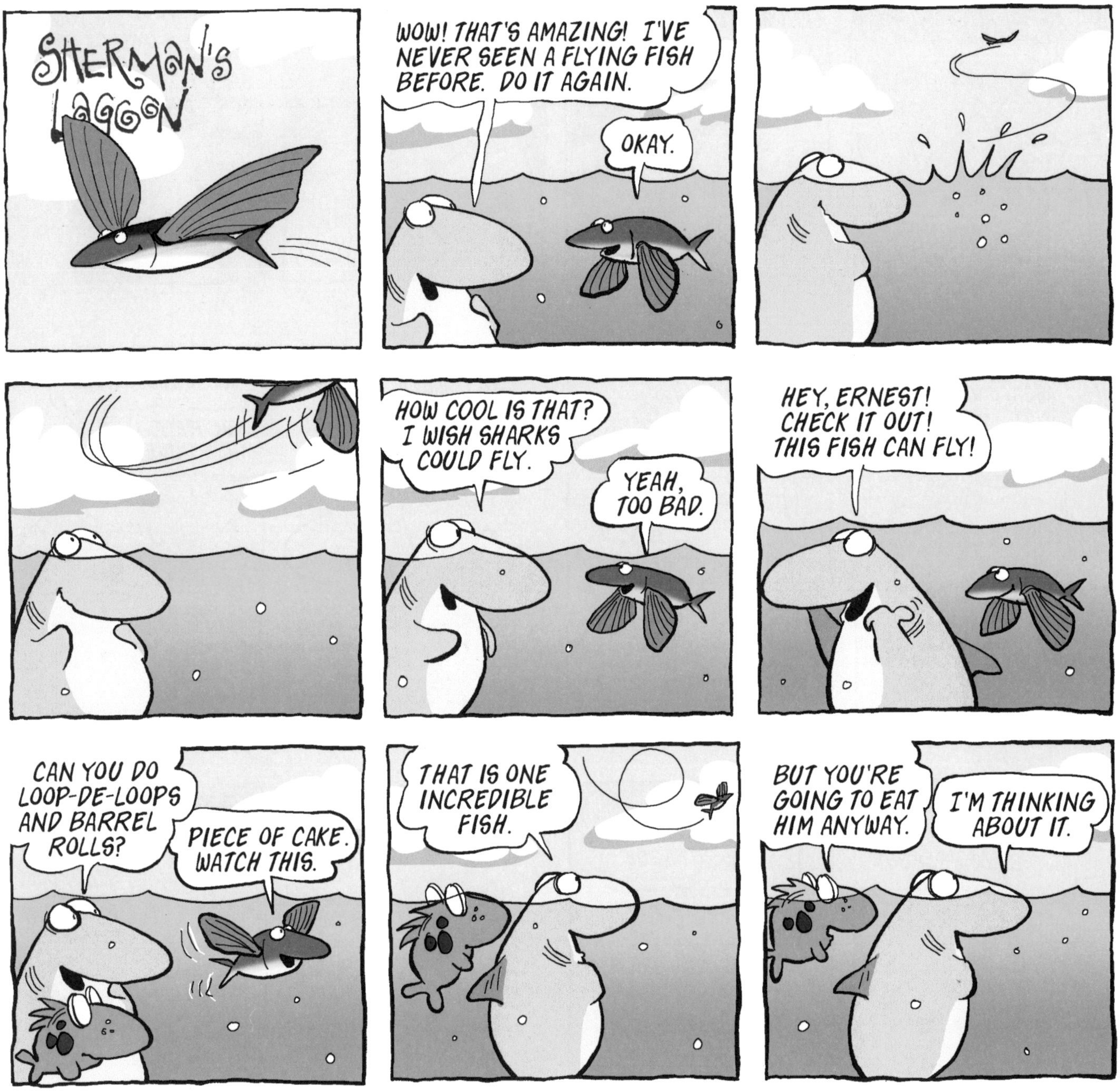
Sherman's Lagoon
WOW! THAT'S AMAZING! I'VE NEVER SEEN A FLYING FISH BEFORE. DO IT AGAIN.
OKAY.
HOW COOL IS THAT? I WISH SHARKS COULD FLY.
YEAH, TOO BAD.
HEY, ERNEST! CHECK IT OUT! THIS FISH CAN FLY!
CAN YOU DO LOOP-DE-LOOPS AND BARREL ROLLS?
PIECE OF CAKE. WATCH THIS.
THAT IS ONE INCREDIBLE FISH.
BUT YOU'RE GOING TO EAT HIM ANYWAY.
I'M THINKING ABOUT IT.

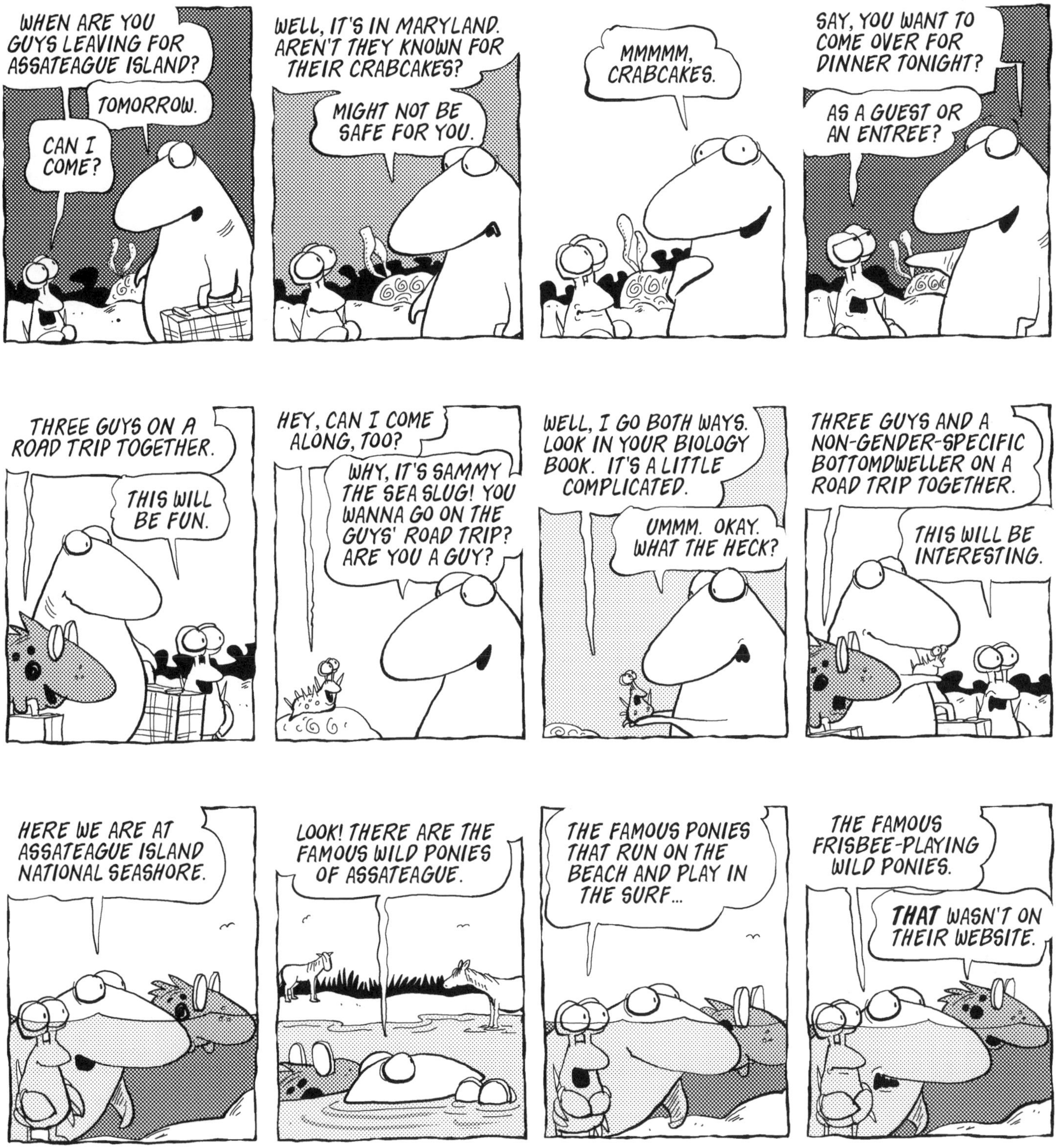
WHEN ARE YOU GUYS LEAVING FOR ASSATEAGUE ISLAND?
TOMORROW.
CAN I COME?
WELL, IT'S IN MARYLAND. AREN'T THEY KNOWN FOR THEIR CRABCAKES?
MIGHT NOT BE SAFE FOR YOU.
MMMMM, CRABCAKES.
SAY, YOU WANT TO COME OVER FOR DINNER TONIGHT?
AS A GUEST OR AN ENTREE?
THREE GUYS ON A ROAD TRIP TOGETHER.
THIS WILL BE FUN.
HEY, CAN I COME ALONG, TOO?
WHY, IT'S SAMMY THE SEA SLUG! YOU WANNA GO ON THE GUYS' ROAD TRIP? ARE YOU A GUY?
WELL, I GO BOTH WAYS. LOOK IN YOUR BIOLOGY BOOK. IT'S A LITTLE COMPLICATED.
UMMM. OKAY. WHAT THE HECK?
THREE GUYS AND A NON-GENDER-SPECIFIC BOTTOMDWELLER ON A ROAD TRIP TOGETHER.
THIS WILL BE INTERESTING.
HERE WE ARE AT ASSATEAGUE ISLAND NATIONAL SEASHORE.
LOOK! THERE ARE THE FAMOUS WILD PONIES OF ASSATEAGUE.
THE FAMOUS PONIES THAT RUN ON THE BEACH AND PLAY IN THE SURF...
THE FAMOUS FRISBEE-PLAYING WILD PONIES.
THAT WASN'T ON THEIR WEBSITE.

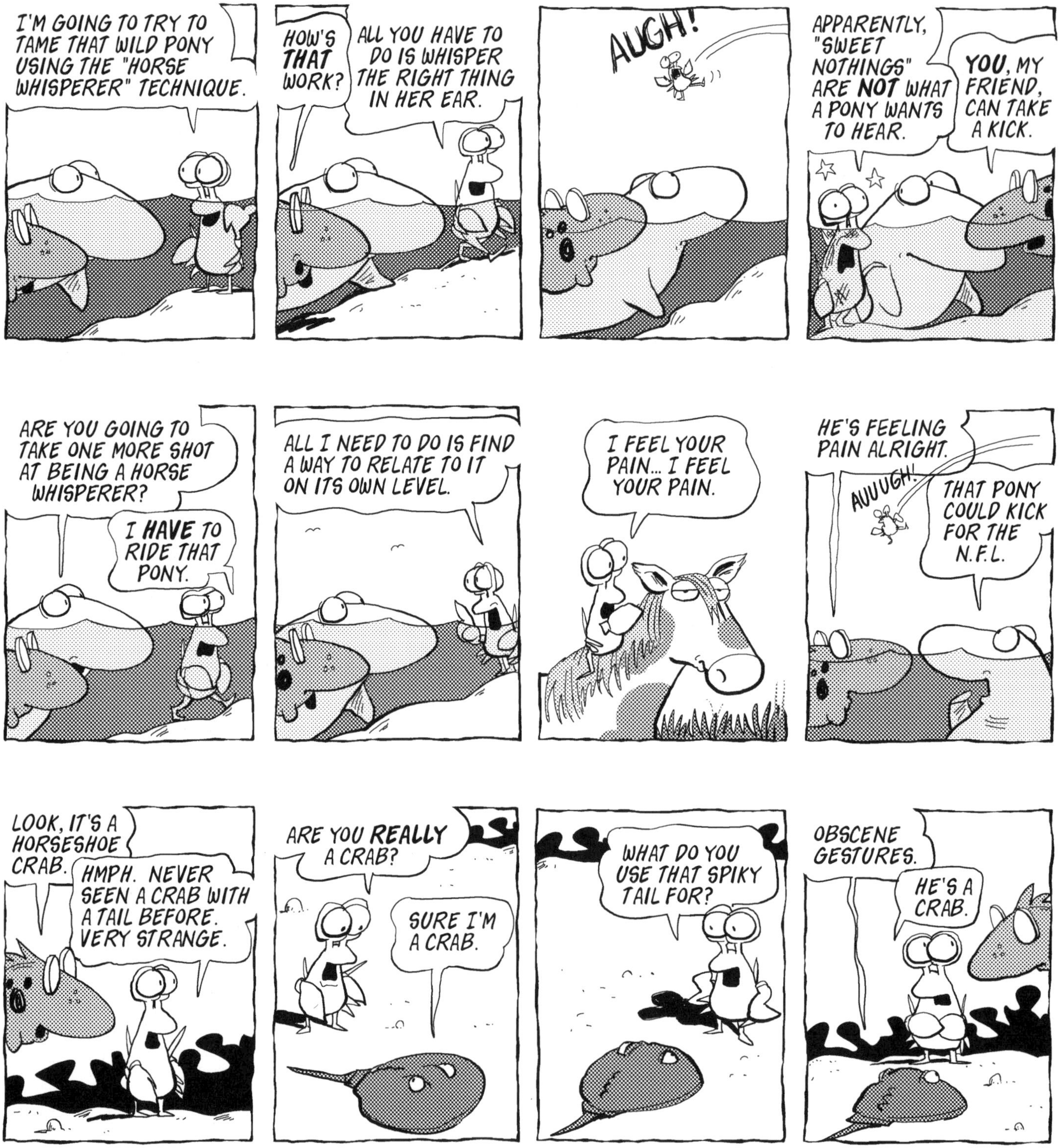
I'M GOING TO TRY TO TAME THAT WILD PONY USING THE "HORSE WHISPERER" TECHNIQUE.
HOW'S THAT WORK?
ALL YOU HAVE TO DO IS WHISPER THE RIGHT THING IN HER EAR.
AUGH!
APPARENTLY, "SWEET NOTHINGS" ARE NOT WHAT A PONY WANTS TO HEAR.
YOU, MY FRIEND, CAN TAKE A KICK.
ARE YOU GOING TO TAKE ONE MORE SHOT AT BEING A HORSE WHISPERER?
I HAVE TO RIDE THAT PONY.
ALL I NEED TO DO IS FIND A WAY TO RELATE TO IT ON ITS OWN LEVEL.
I FEEL YOUR PAIN... I FEEL YOUR PAIN.
HE'S FEELING PAIN ALRIGHT.
AUUUGH!
THAT PONY COULD KICK FOR THE N.F.L.
LOOK, IT'S A HORSESHOE CRAB.
HMPH. NEVER SEEN A CRAB WITH A TAIL BEFORE. VERY STRANGE.
ARE YOU REALLY A CRAB?
SURE I'M A CRAB.
WHAT DO YOU USE THAT SPIKY TAIL FOR?
OBSCENE GESTURES.
HE'S A CRAB.

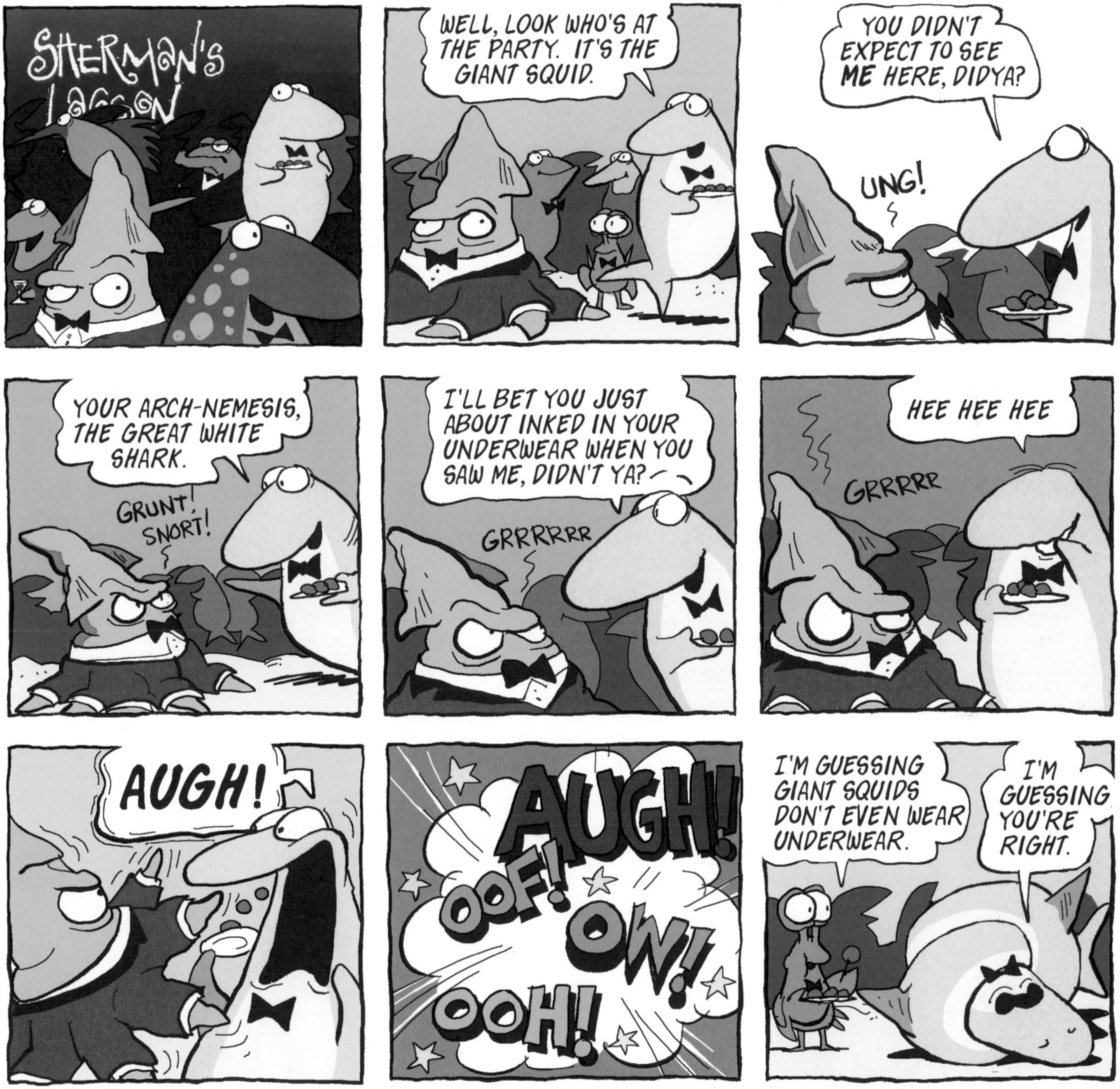
SHERMAN'S LAGOON
WELL, LOOK WHO'S AT THE PARTY. IT'S THE GIANT SQUID.
YOU DIDN'T EXPECT TO SEE ME HERE, DIDYA?
UNG!
YOUR ARCH-NEMESIS, THE GREAT WHITE SHARK.
GRUNT! SNORT!
I'LL BET YOU JUST ABOUT INKED IN YOUR UNDERWEAR WHEN YOU SAW ME, DIDN'T YA?
GRRRRRR
HEE HEE HEE
GRRRRR
AUGH!
AUGH!
OOF!
OW!
OOH!
I'M GUESSING GIANT SQUIDS DON'T EVEN WEAR UNDERWEAR.
I'M GUESSING YOU'RE RIGHT.

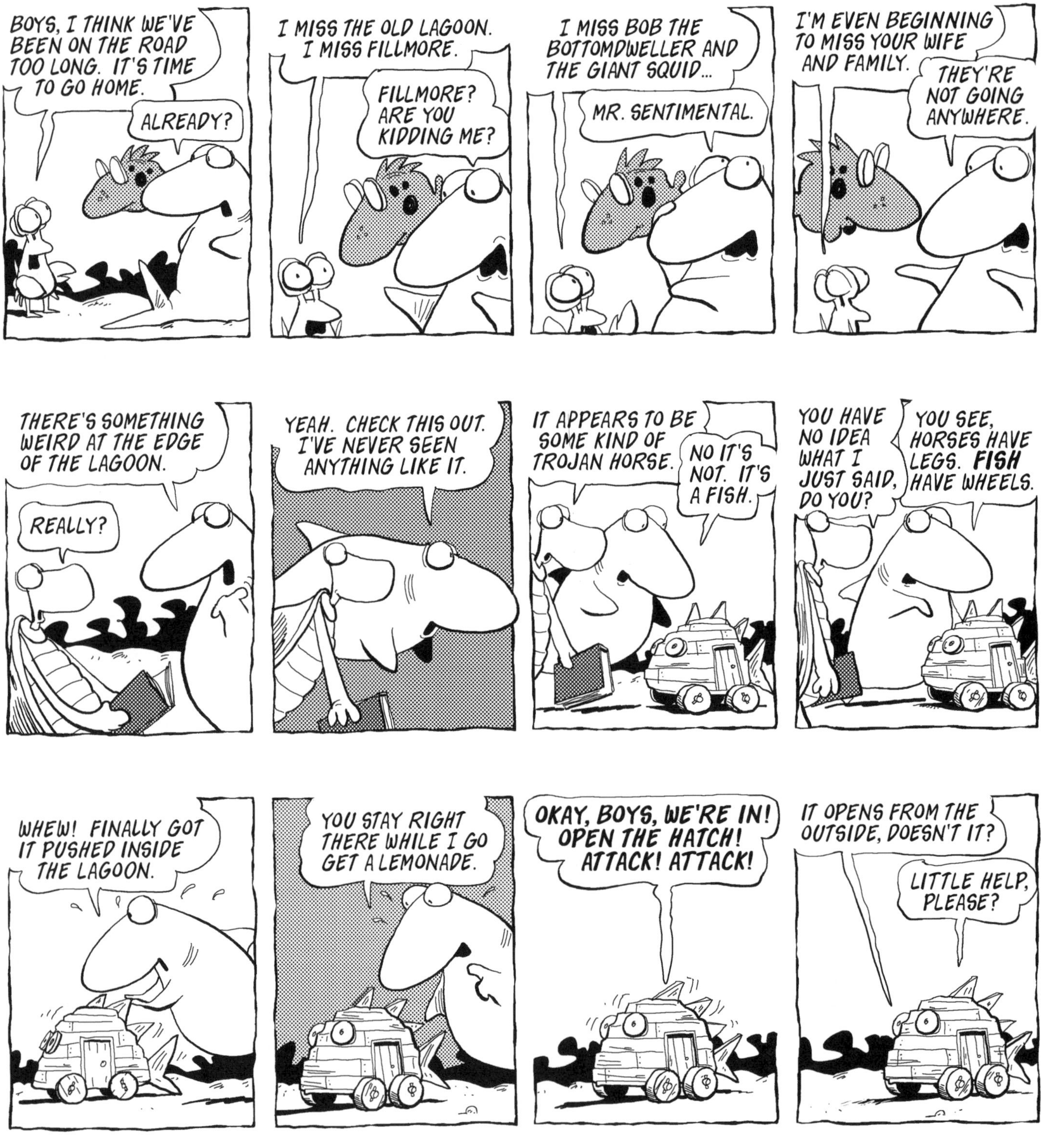
BOYS, I THINK WE'VE BEEN ON THE ROAD TOO LONG. IT'S TIME TO GO HOME.
ALREADY?
I MISS THE OLD LAGOON. I MISS FILLMORE.
FILLMORE? ARE YOU KIDDING ME?
I MISS BOB THE BOTTOMDWELLER AND THE GIANT SQUID...
MR. SENTIMENTAL.
I'M EVEN BEGINNING TO MISS YOUR WIFE AND FAMILY.
THEY'RE NOT GOING ANYWHERE.
THERE'S SOMETHING WEIRD AT THE EDGE OF THE LAGOON.
REALLY?
YEAH. CHECK THIS OUT. I'VE NEVER SEEN ANYTHING LIKE IT.
IT APPEARS TO BE SOME KIND OF TROJAN HORSE.
NO IT'S NOT. IT'S A FISH.
YOU HAVE NO IDEA WHAT I JUST SAID, DO YOU?
YOU SEE, HORSES HAVE LEGS. **FISH** HAVE WHEELS.
WHEW! FINALLY GOT IT PUSHED INSIDE THE LAGOON.
YOU STAY RIGHT THERE WHILE I GO GET A LEMONADE.
OKAY, BOYS, WE'RE IN! OPEN THE HATCH! ATTACK! ATTACK!
IT OPENS FROM THE OUTSIDE, DOESN'T IT?
LITTLE HELP, PLEASE?

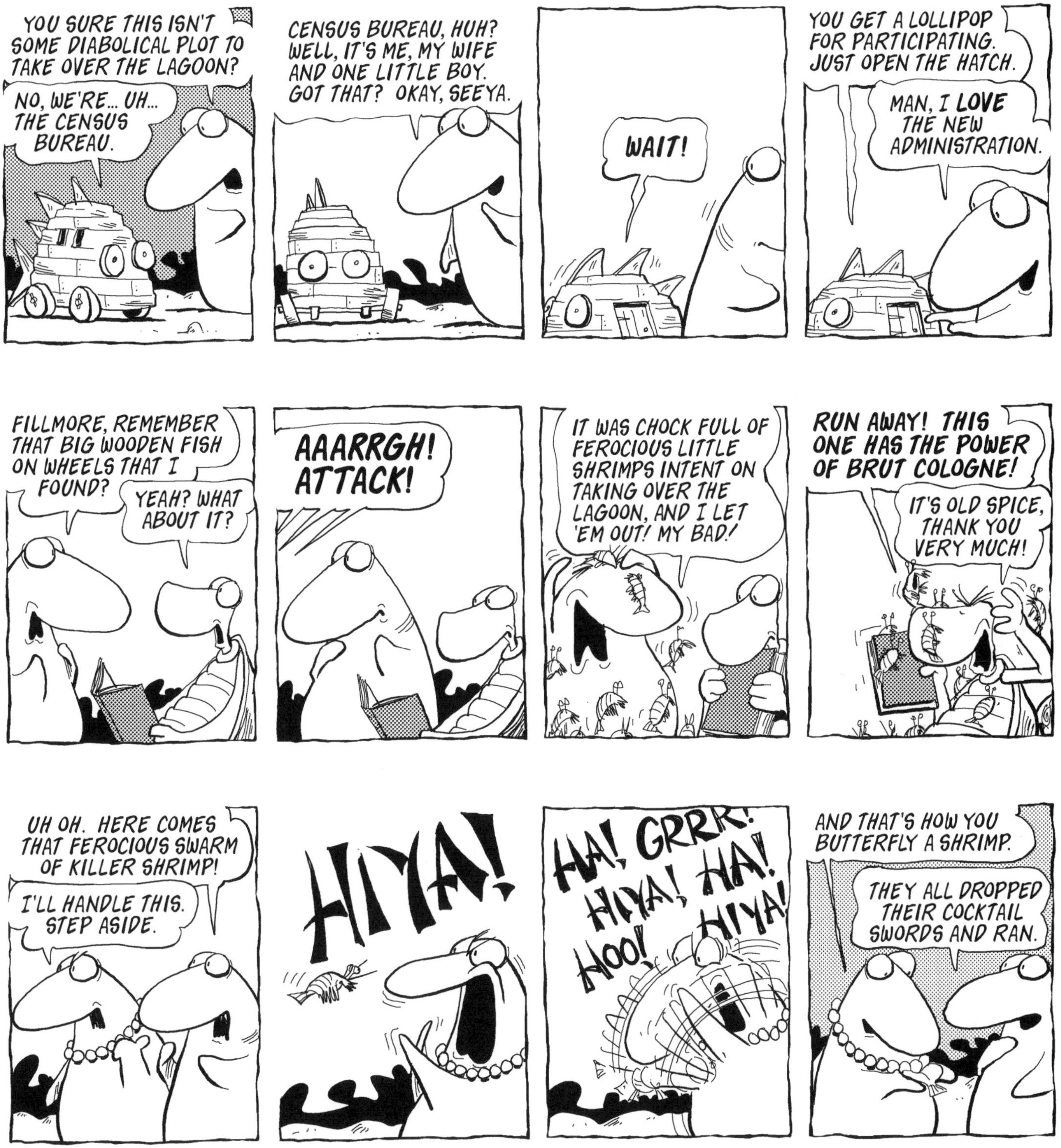
YOU SURE THIS ISN'T SOME DIABOLICAL PLOT TO TAKE OVER THE LAGOON?
NO, WE'RE... UH... THE CENSUS BUREAU.
CENSUS BUREAU, HUH? WELL, IT'S ME, MY WIFE AND ONE LITTLE BOY. GOT THAT? OKAY, SEEYA.
WAIT!
YOU GET A LOLLIPOP FOR PARTICIPATING. JUST OPEN THE HATCH.
MAN, I **LOVE** THE NEW ADMINISTRATION.
FILLMORE, REMEMBER THAT BIG WOODEN FISH ON WHEELS THAT I FOUND?
YEAH? WHAT ABOUT IT?
AAARRGH! ATTACK!
IT WAS CHOCK FULL OF FEROCIOUS LITTLE SHRIMPS INTENT ON TAKING OVER THE LAGOON, AND I LET 'EM OUT! MY BAD!
RUN AWAY! THIS ONE HAS THE POWER OF BRUT COLOGNE!
IT'S OLD SPICE, THANK YOU VERY MUCH!
UH OH. HERE COMES THAT FEROCIOUS SWARM OF KILLER SHRIMP!
I'LL HANDLE THIS. STEP ASIDE.
HIYA!
HA! GRRR! HIYA! HA! HOO! HIYA!
AND THAT'S HOW YOU BUTTERFLY A SHRIMP.
THEY ALL DROPPED THEIR COCKTAIL SWORDS AND RAN.

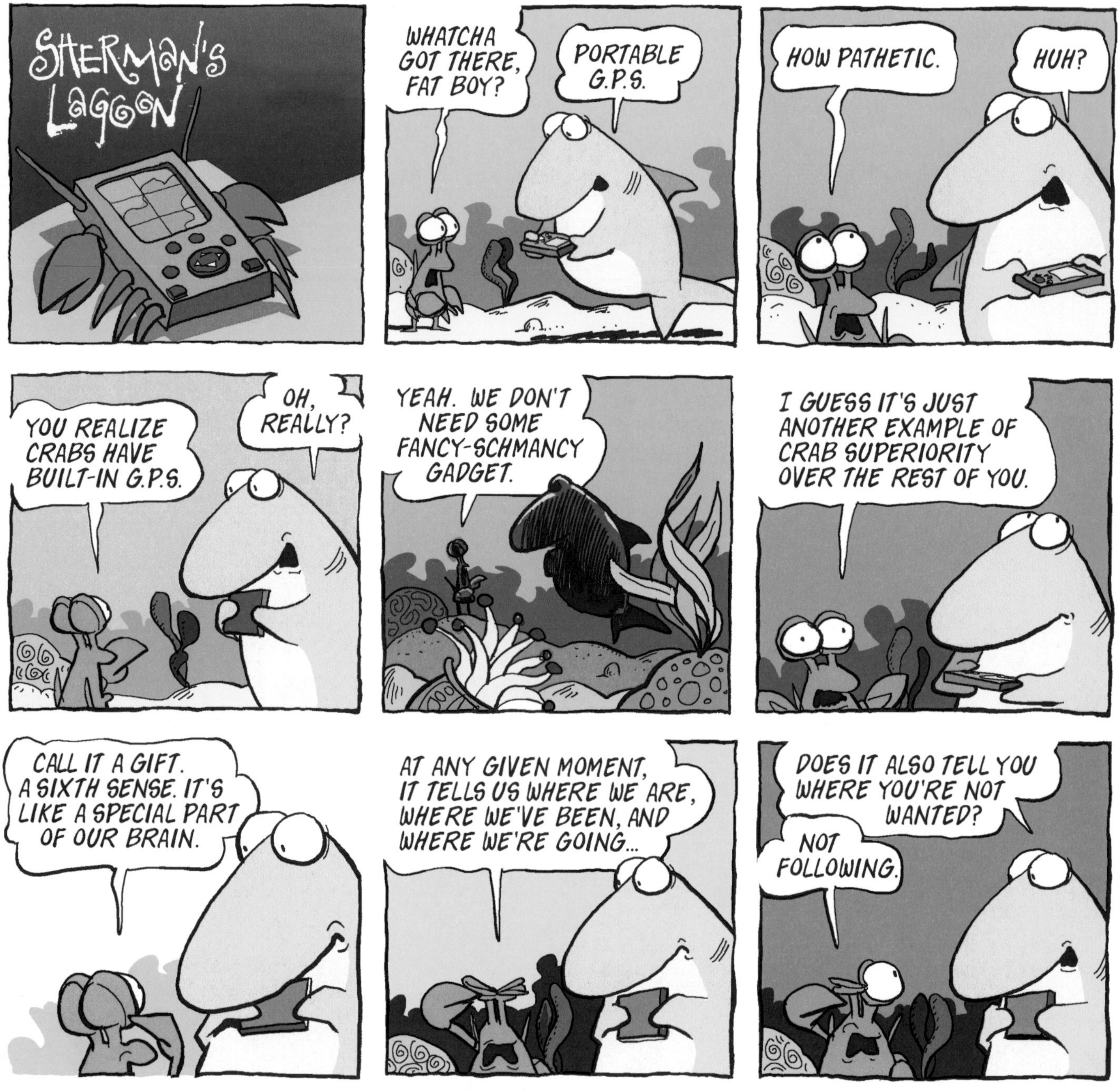
SHERMAN'S LAGOON
WHATCHA GOT THERE, FAT BOY?
PORTABLE G.P.S.
HOW PATHETIC.
HUH?
YOU REALIZE CRABS HAVE BUILT-IN G.P.S.
OH, REALLY?
YEAH. WE DON'T NEED SOME FANCY-SCHMANCY GADGET.
I GUESS IT'S JUST ANOTHER EXAMPLE OF CRAB SUPERIORITY OVER THE REST OF YOU.
CALL IT A GIFT. A SIXTH SENSE. IT'S LIKE A SPECIAL PART OF OUR BRAIN.
AT ANY GIVEN MOMENT, IT TELLS US WHERE WE ARE, WHERE WE'VE BEEN, AND WHERE WE'RE GOING...
DOES IT ALSO TELL YOU WHERE YOU'RE NOT WANTED?
NOT FOLLOWING.

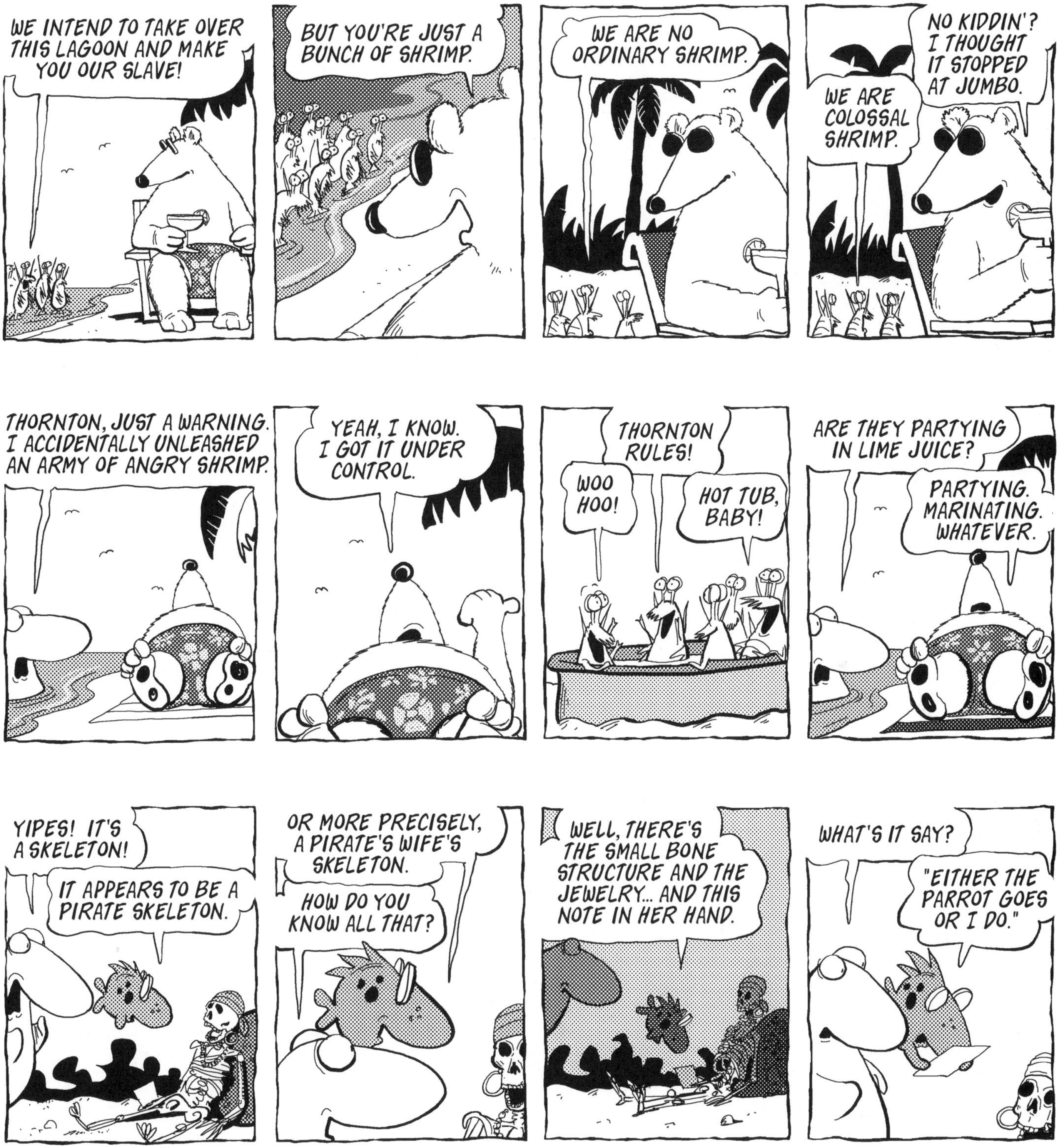
WE INTEND TO TAKE OVER THIS LAGOON AND MAKE YOU OUR SLAVE!
BUT YOU'RE JUST A BUNCH OF SHRIMP.
WE ARE NO ORDINARY SHRIMP.
WE ARE COLOSSAL SHRIMP.
NO KIDDIN'? I THOUGHT IT STOPPED AT JUMBO.
THORNTON, JUST A WARNING. I ACCIDENTALLY UNLEASHED AN ARMY OF ANGRY SHRIMP.
YEAH, I KNOW. I GOT IT UNDER CONTROL.
THORNTON RULES!
WOO HOO!
HOT TUB, BABY!
ARE THEY PARTYING IN LIME JUICE?
PARTYING. MARINATING. WHATEVER.
YIPES! IT'S A SKELETON!
IT APPEARS TO BE A PIRATE SKELETON.
OR MORE PRECISELY, A PIRATE'S WIFE'S SKELETON.
HOW DO YOU KNOW ALL THAT?
WELL, THERE'S THE SMALL BONE STRUCTURE AND THE JEWELRY... AND THIS NOTE IN HER HAND.
WHAT'S IT SAY?
"EITHER THE PARROT GOES OR I DO."

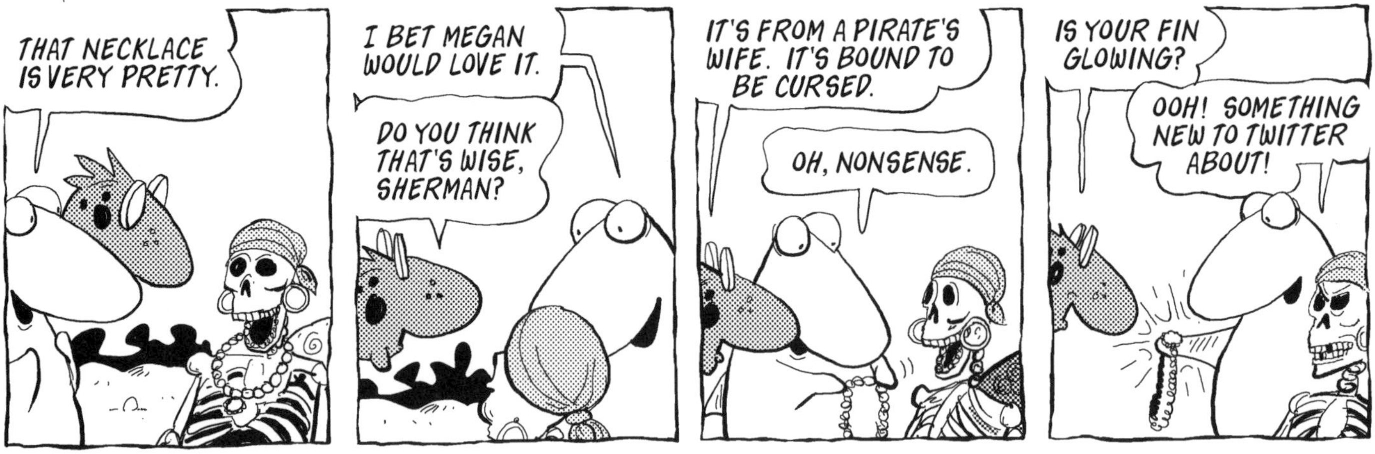
THAT NECKLACE IS VERY PRETTY.
I BET MEGAN WOULD LOVE IT.
DO YOU THINK THAT'S WISE, SHERMAN?
IT'S FROM A PIRATE'S WIFE. IT'S BOUND TO BE CURSED.
OH, NONSENSE.
IS YOUR FIN GLOWING?
OOH! SOMETHING NEW TO TWITTER ABOUT!

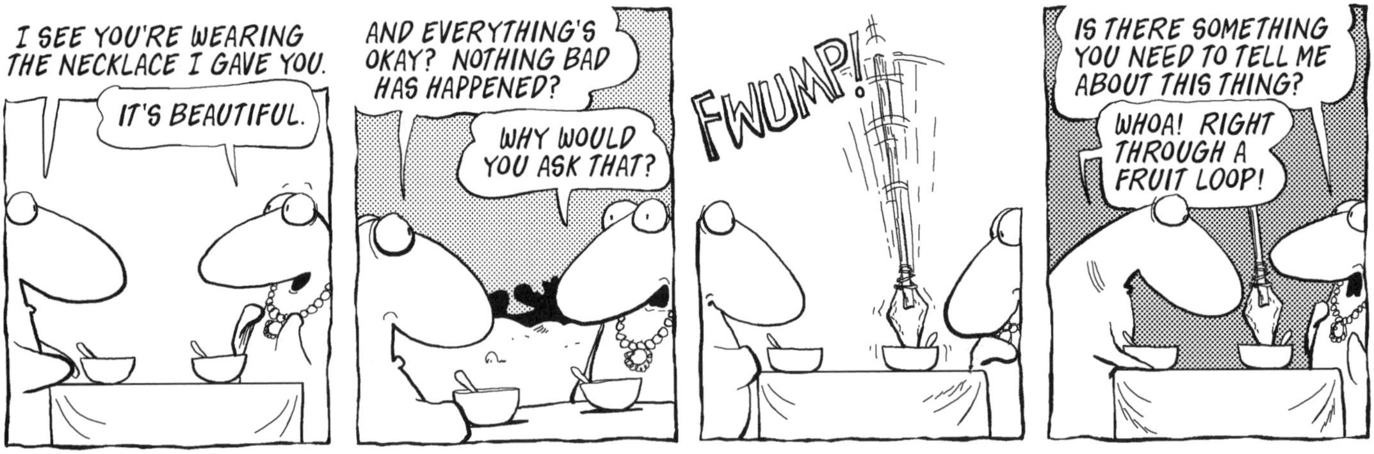
I SEE YOU'RE WEARING THE NECKLACE I GAVE YOU.
IT'S BEAUTIFUL.
AND EVERYTHING'S OKAY? NOTHING BAD HAS HAPPENED?
WHY WOULD YOU ASK THAT?
FWUMP!
IS THERE SOMETHING YOU NEED TO TELL ME ABOUT THIS THING?
WHOA! RIGHT THROUGH A FRUIT LOOP!

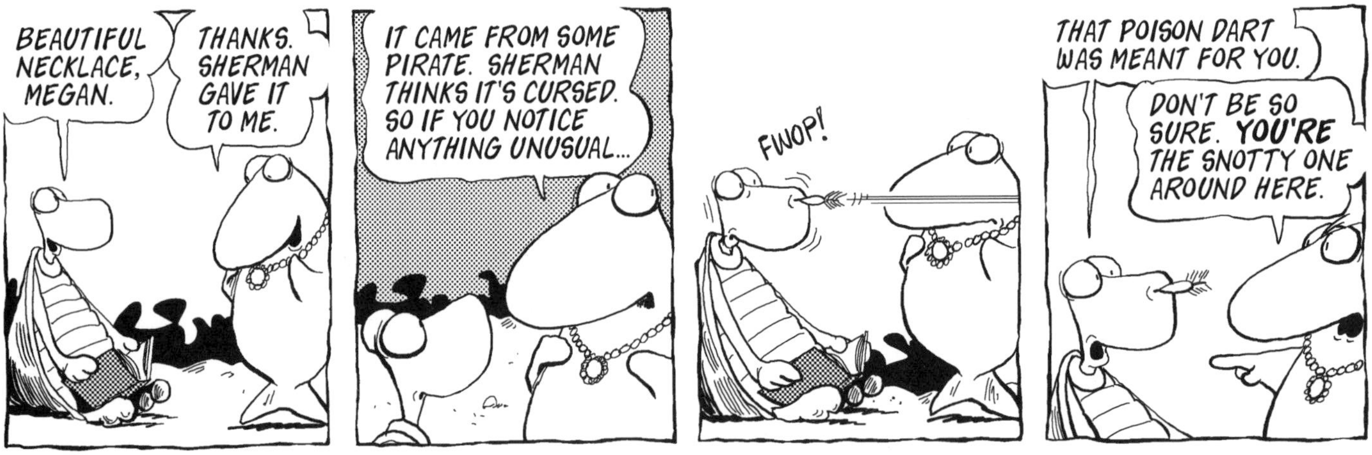
BEAUTIFUL NECKLACE, MEGAN.
THANKS. SHERMAN GAVE IT TO ME.
IT CAME FROM SOME PIRATE. SHERMAN THINKS IT'S CURSED. SO IF YOU NOTICE ANYTHING UNUSUAL...
FWOP!
THAT POISON DART WAS MEANT FOR YOU.
DON'T BE SO SURE. YOU'RE THE SNOTTY ONE AROUND HERE.

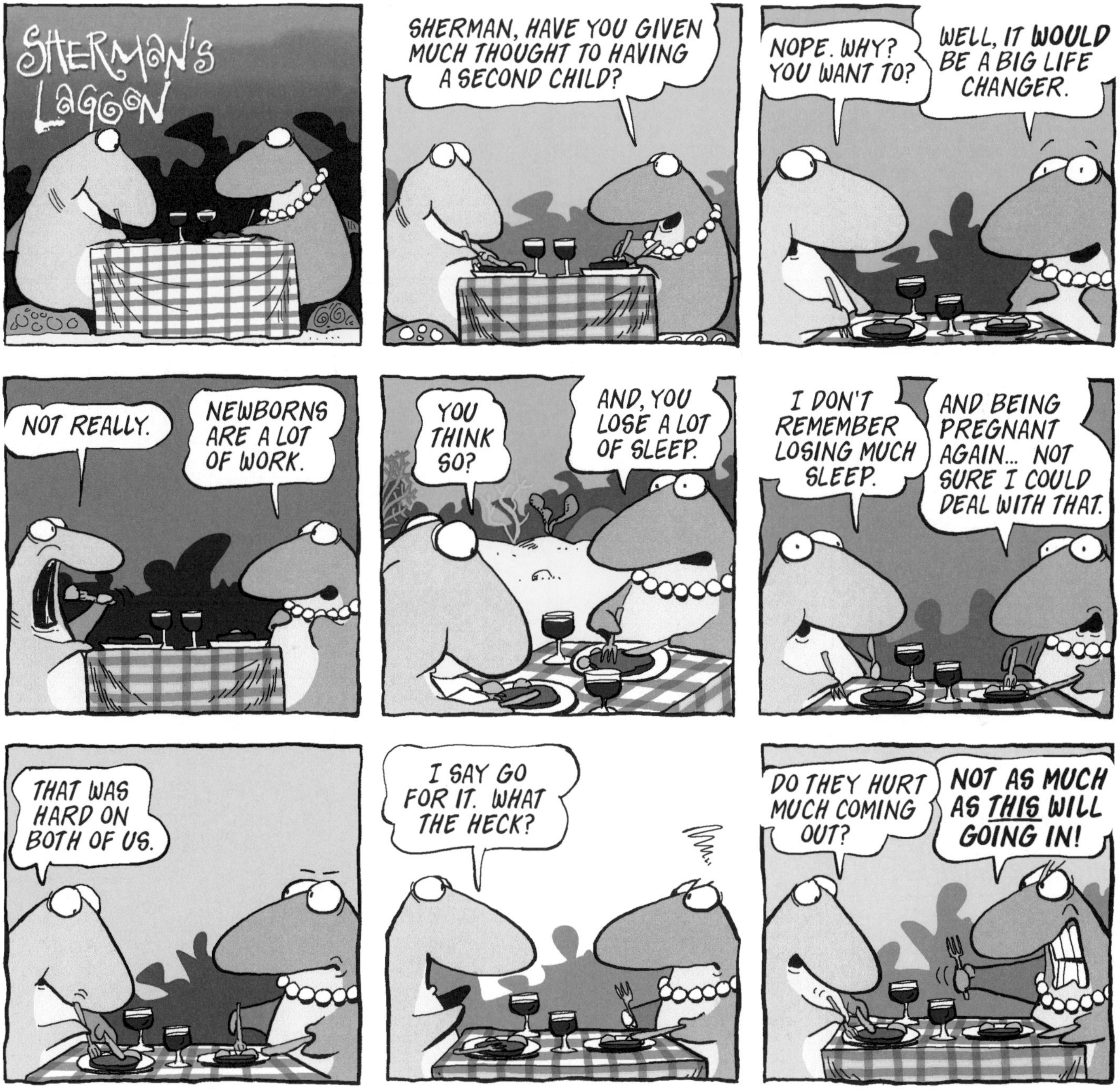
SHERMAN'S LAGOON
SHERMAN, HAVE YOU GIVEN MUCH THOUGHT TO HAVING A SECOND CHILD?
NOPE. WHY? YOU WANT TO?
WELL, IT **WOULD** BE A BIG LIFE CHANGER.
NOT REALLY.
NEWBORNS ARE A LOT OF WORK.
YOU THINK SO?
AND, YOU LOSE A LOT OF SLEEP.
I DON'T REMEMBER LOSING MUCH SLEEP.
AND BEING PREGNANT AGAIN... NOT SURE I COULD DEAL WITH THAT.
THAT WAS HARD ON BOTH OF US.
I SAY GO FOR IT. WHAT THE HECK?
DO THEY HURT MUCH COMING OUT?
NOT AS MUCH AS THIS WILL GOING IN!

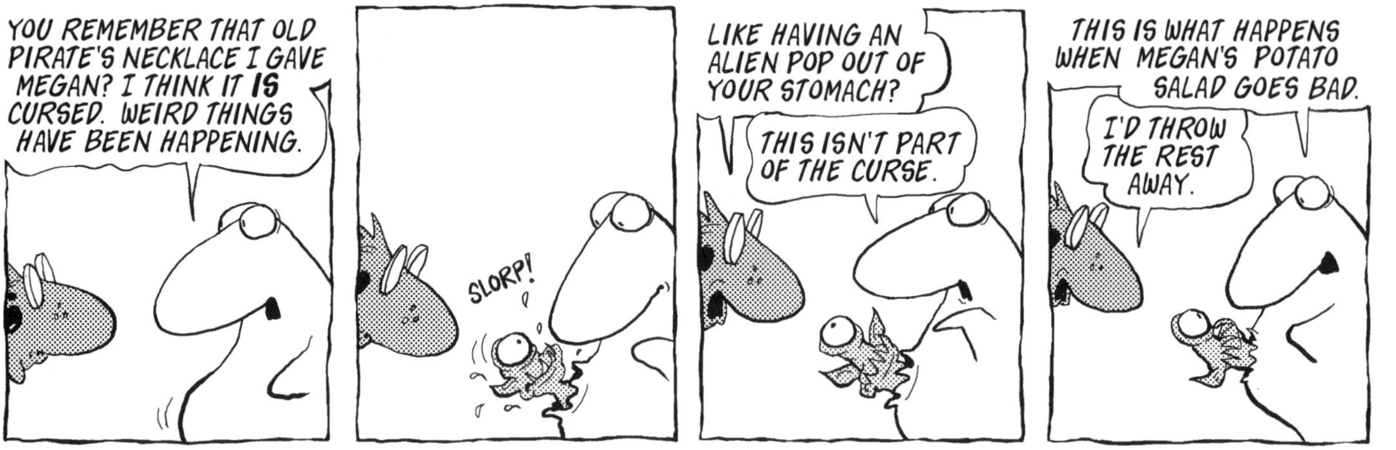
YOU REMEMBER THAT OLD PIRATE'S NECKLACE I GAVE MEGAN? I THINK IT **IS** CURSED. WEIRD THINGS HAVE BEEN HAPPENING.
SLORP!
LIKE HAVING AN ALIEN POP OUT OF YOUR STOMACH?
THIS ISN'T PART OF THE CURSE.
THIS IS WHAT HAPPENS WHEN MEGAN'S POTATO SALAD GOES BAD.
I'D THROW THE REST AWAY.

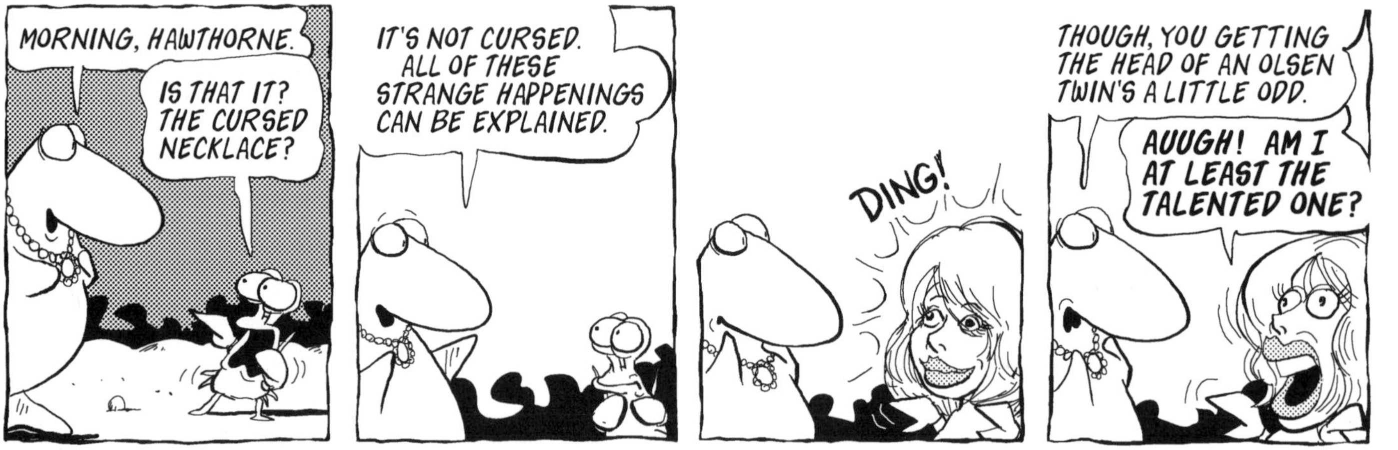
MORNING, HAWTHORNE.
IS THAT IT? THE CURSED NECKLACE?
IT'S NOT CURSED. ALL OF THESE STRANGE HAPPENINGS CAN BE EXPLAINED.
DING!
THOUGH, YOU GETTING THE HEAD OF AN OLSEN TWIN'S A LITTLE ODD.
AUUGH! AM I AT LEAST THE TALENTED ONE?

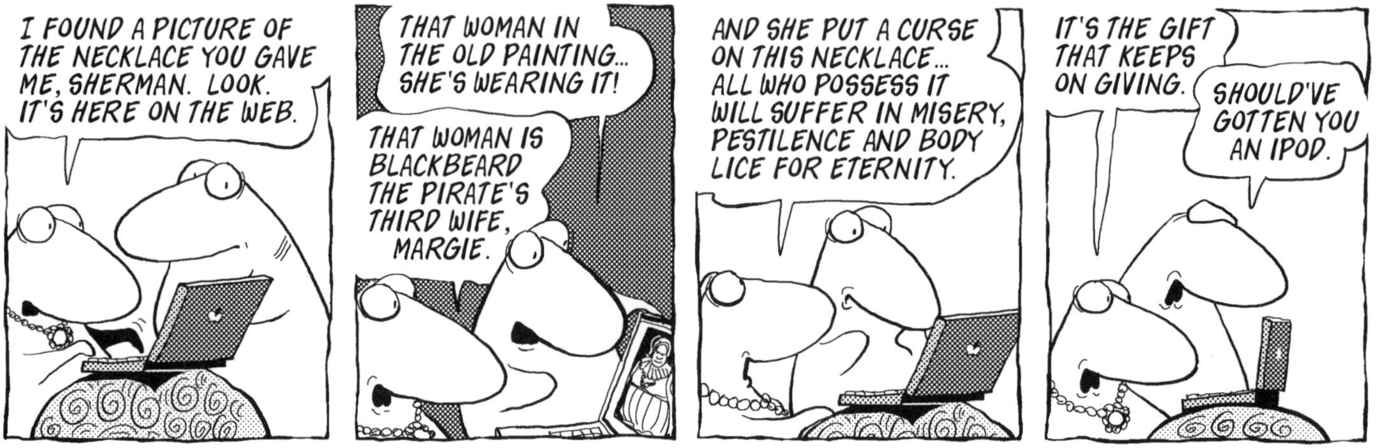
I FOUND A PICTURE OF THE NECKLACE YOU GAVE ME, SHERMAN. LOOK. IT'S HERE ON THE WEB.
THAT WOMAN IN THE OLD PAINTING... SHE'S WEARING IT!
THAT WOMAN IS BLACKBEARD THE PIRATE'S THIRD WIFE, MARGIE.
AND SHE PUT A CURSE ON THIS NECKLACE... ALL WHO POSSESS IT WILL SUFFER IN MISERY, PESTILENCE AND BODY LICE FOR ETERNITY.
IT'S THE GIFT THAT KEEPS ON GIVING.
SHOULD'VE GOTTEN YOU AN IPOD.

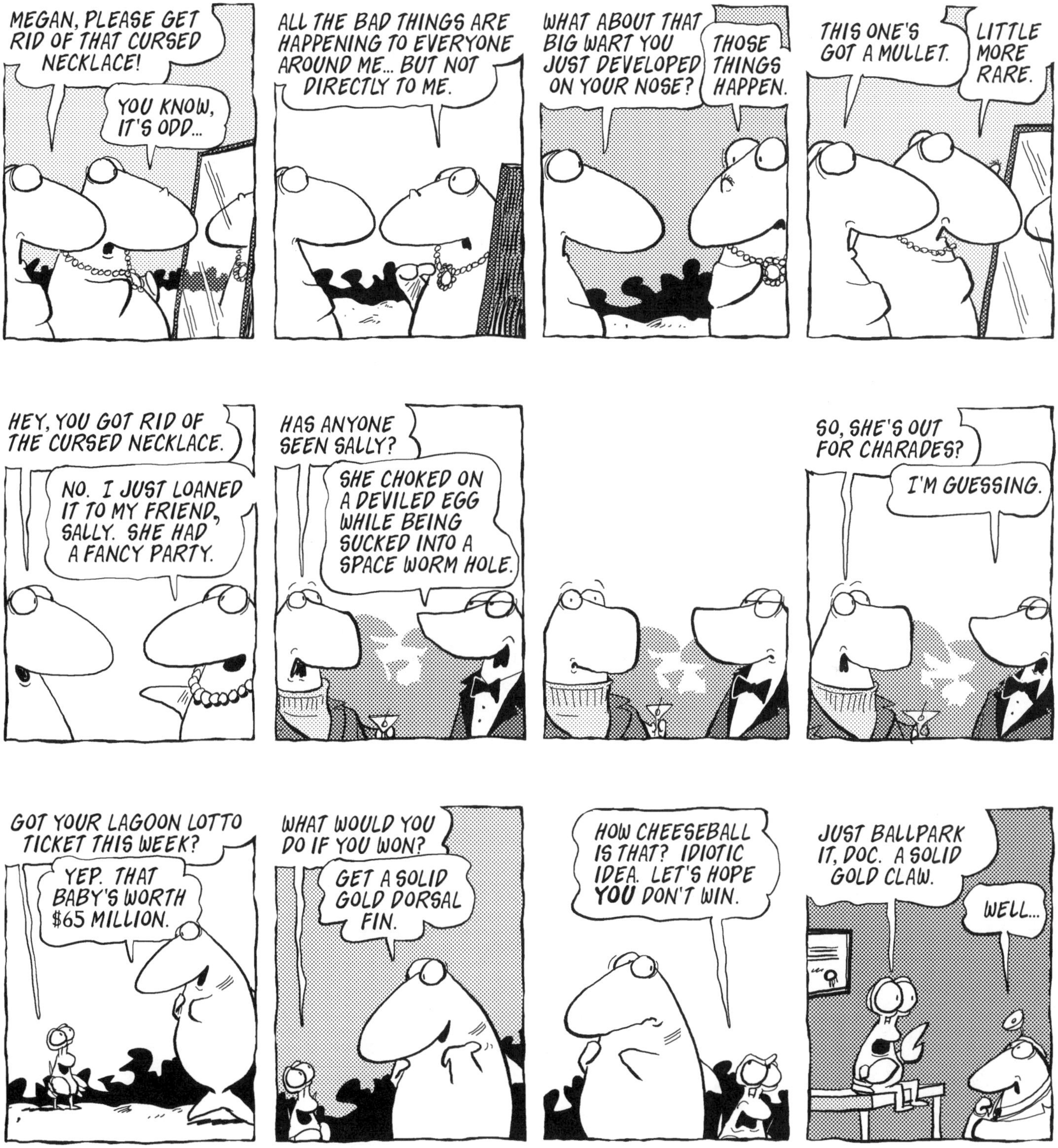
MEGAN, PLEASE GET RID OF THAT CURSED NECKLACE!
YOU KNOW, IT'S ODD...
ALL THE BAD THINGS ARE HAPPENING TO EVERYONE AROUND ME... BUT NOT DIRECTLY TO ME.
WHAT ABOUT THAT BIG WART YOU JUST DEVELOPED ON YOUR NOSE?
THOSE THINGS HAPPEN.
THIS ONE'S GOT A MULLET.
LITTLE MORE RARE.
HEY, YOU GOT RID OF THE CURSED NECKLACE.
NO. I JUST LOANED IT TO MY FRIEND, SALLY. SHE HAD A FANCY PARTY.
HAS ANYONE SEEN SALLY?
SHE CHOKED ON A DEVILED EGG WHILE BEING SUCKED INTO A SPACE WORM HOLE.
SO, SHE'S OUT FOR CHARADES?
I'M GUESSING.
GOT YOUR LAGOON LOTTO TICKET THIS WEEK?
YEP. THAT BABY'S WORTH $65 MILLION.
WHAT WOULD YOU DO IF YOU WON?
GET A SOLID GOLD DORSAL FIN.
HOW CHEESEBALL IS THAT? IDIOTIC IDEA. LET'S HOPE YOU DON'T WIN.
JUST BALLPARK IT, DOC. A SOLID GOLD CLAW.
WELL...

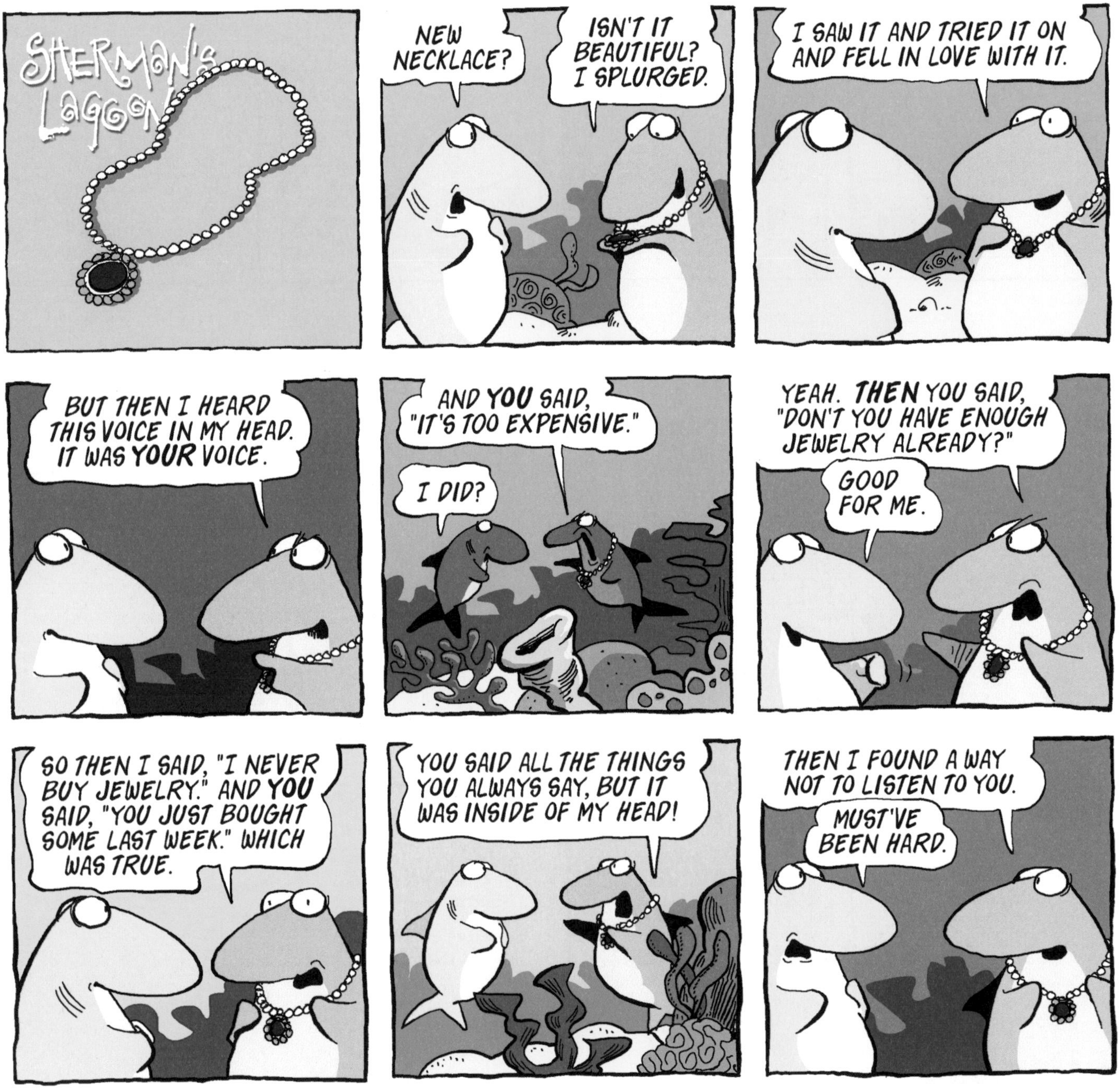
Sherman's Lagoon
NEW NECKLACE?
ISN'T IT BEAUTIFUL? I SPLURGED.
I SAW IT AND TRIED IT ON AND FELL IN LOVE WITH IT.
BUT THEN I HEARD THIS VOICE IN MY HEAD. IT WAS YOUR VOICE.
AND YOU SAID, "IT'S TOO EXPENSIVE."
I DID?
YEAH. THEN YOU SAID, "DON'T YOU HAVE ENOUGH JEWELRY ALREADY?"
GOOD FOR ME.
SO THEN I SAID, "I NEVER BUY JEWELRY." AND YOU SAID, "YOU JUST BOUGHT SOME LAST WEEK." WHICH WAS TRUE.
YOU SAID ALL THE THINGS YOU ALWAYS SAY, BUT IT WAS INSIDE OF MY HEAD!
THEN I FOUND A WAY NOT TO LISTEN TO YOU.
MUST'VE BEEN HARD.

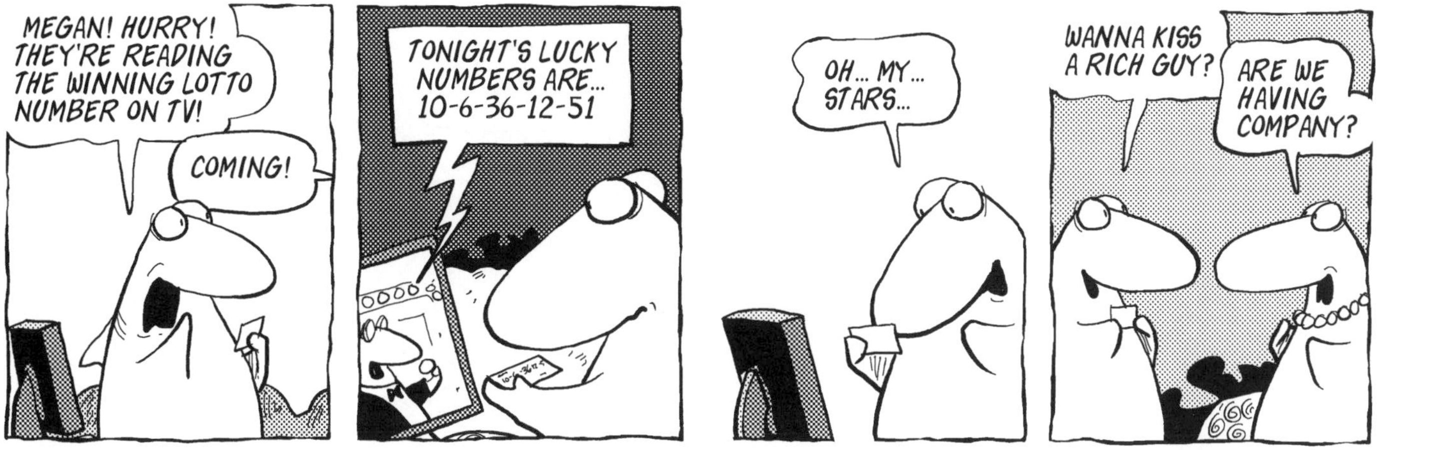
MEGAN! HURRY! THEY'RE READING THE WINNING LOTTO NUMBER ON TV!
COMING!
TONIGHT'S LUCKY NUMBERS ARE... 10-6-36-12-51
OH... MY... STARS...
WANNA KISS A RICH GUY?
ARE WE HAVING COMPANY?

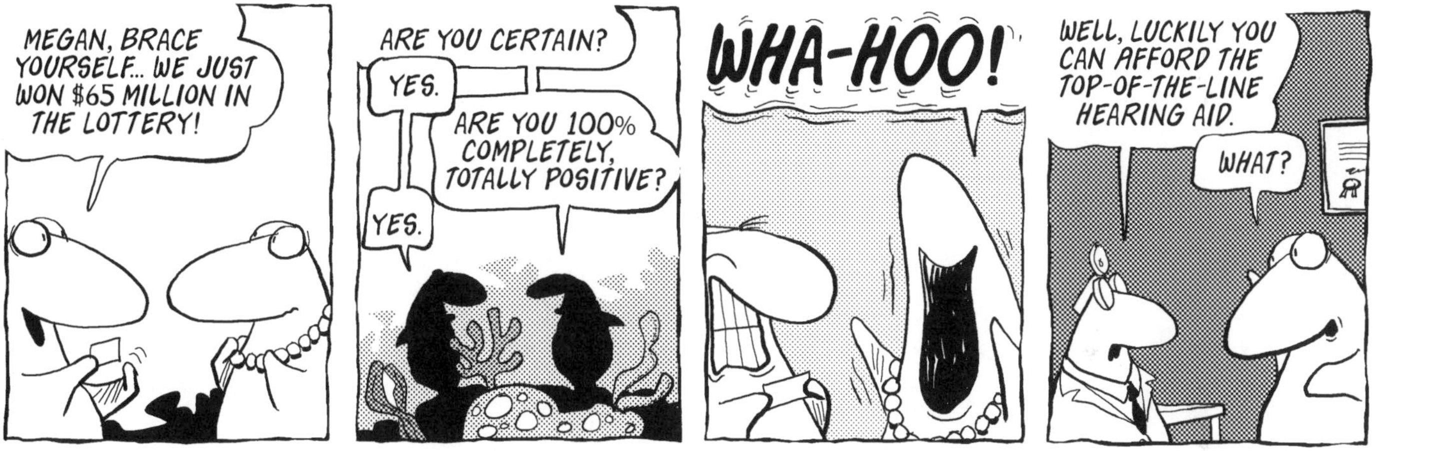
MEGAN, BRACE YOURSELF... WE JUST WON $65 MILLION IN THE LOTTERY!
ARE YOU CERTAIN?
YES.
ARE YOU 100% COMPLETELY, TOTALLY POSITIVE?
YES.
WHA-HOO!
WELL, LUCKILY YOU CAN AFFORD THE TOP-OF-THE-LINE HEARING AID.
WHAT?

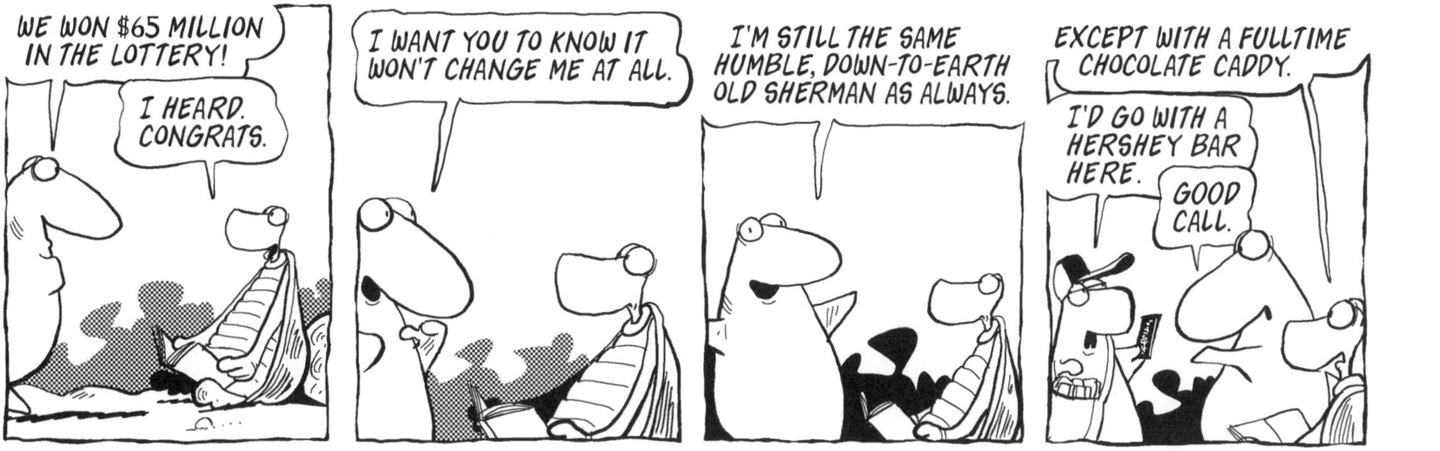
WE WON $65 MILLION IN THE LOTTERY!
I HEARD. CONGRATS.
I WANT YOU TO KNOW IT WON'T CHANGE ME AT ALL.
I'M STILL THE SAME HUMBLE, DOWN-TO-EARTH OLD SHERMAN AS ALWAYS.
EXCEPT WITH A FULLTIME CHOCOLATE CADDY.
I'D GO WITH A HERSHEY BAR HERE.
GOOD CALL.

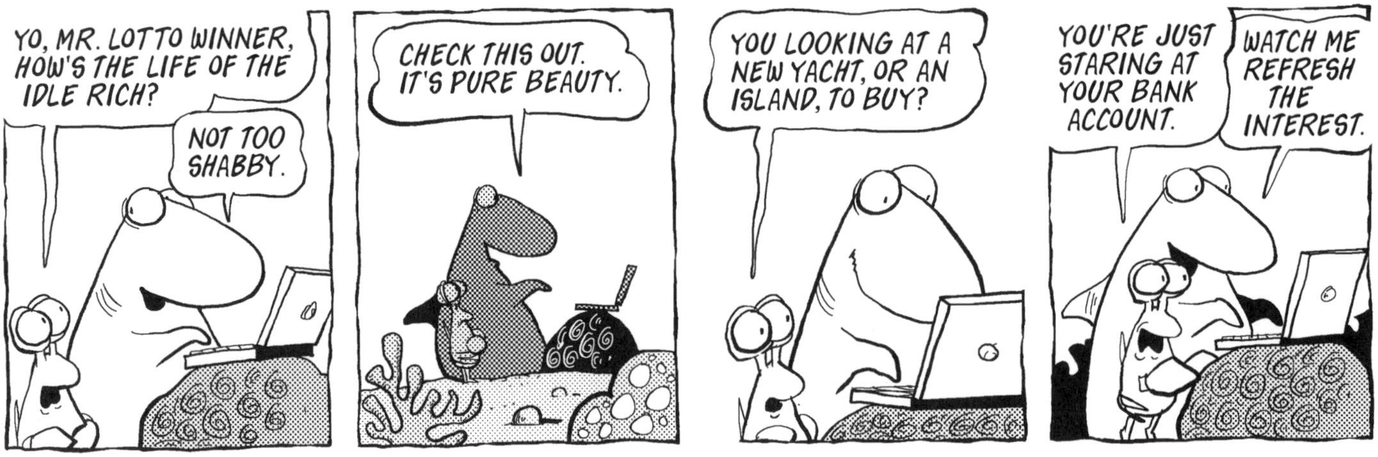
YO, MR. LOTTO WINNER, HOW'S THE LIFE OF THE IDLE RICH?
NOT TOO SHABBY.
CHECK THIS OUT. IT'S PURE BEAUTY.
YOU LOOKING AT A NEW YACHT, OR AN ISLAND, TO BUY?
YOU'RE JUST STARING AT YOUR BANK ACCOUNT.
WATCH ME REFRESH THE INTEREST.

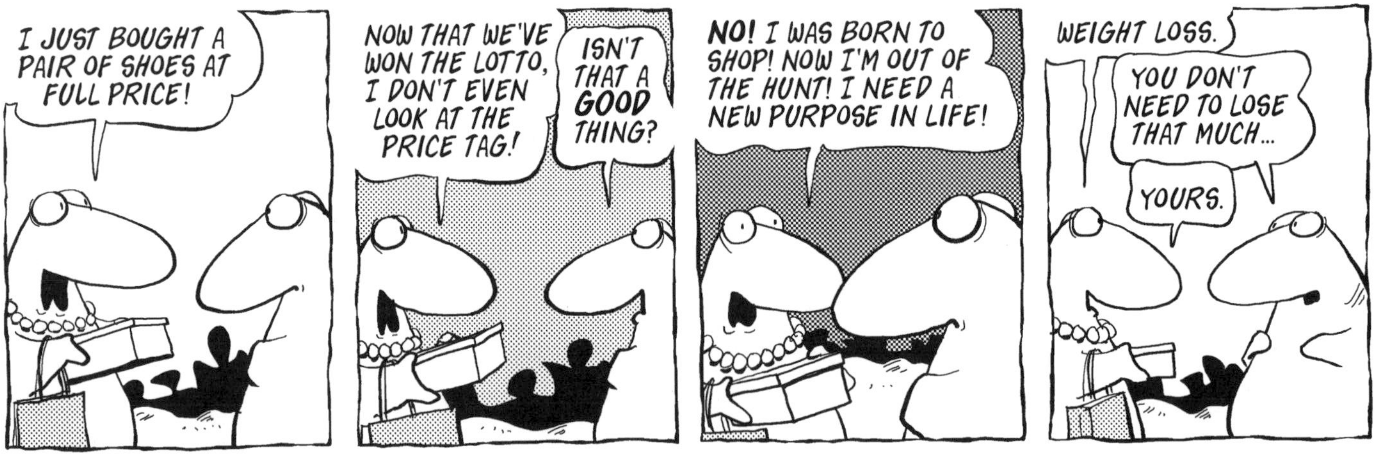
I JUST BOUGHT A PAIR OF SHOES AT FULL PRICE!
NOW THAT WE'VE WON THE LOTTO, I DON'T EVEN LOOK AT THE PRICE TAG!
ISN'T THAT A GOOD THING?
NO! I WAS BORN TO SHOP! NOW I'M OUT OF THE HUNT! I NEED A NEW PURPOSE IN LIFE!
WEIGHT LOSS.
YOU DON'T NEED TO LOSE THAT MUCH...
YOURS.

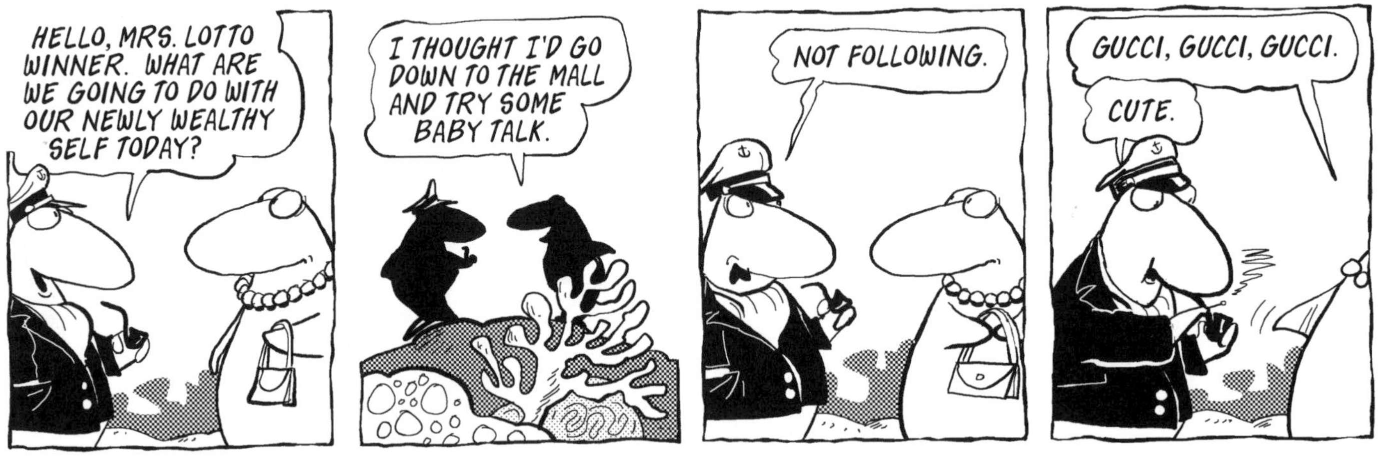
HELLO, MRS. LOTTO WINNER. WHAT ARE WE GOING TO DO WITH OUR NEWLY WEALTHY SELF TODAY?
I THOUGHT I'D GO DOWN TO THE MALL AND TRY SOME BABY TALK.
NOT FOLLOWING.
GUCCI, GUCCI, GUCCI.
CUTE.

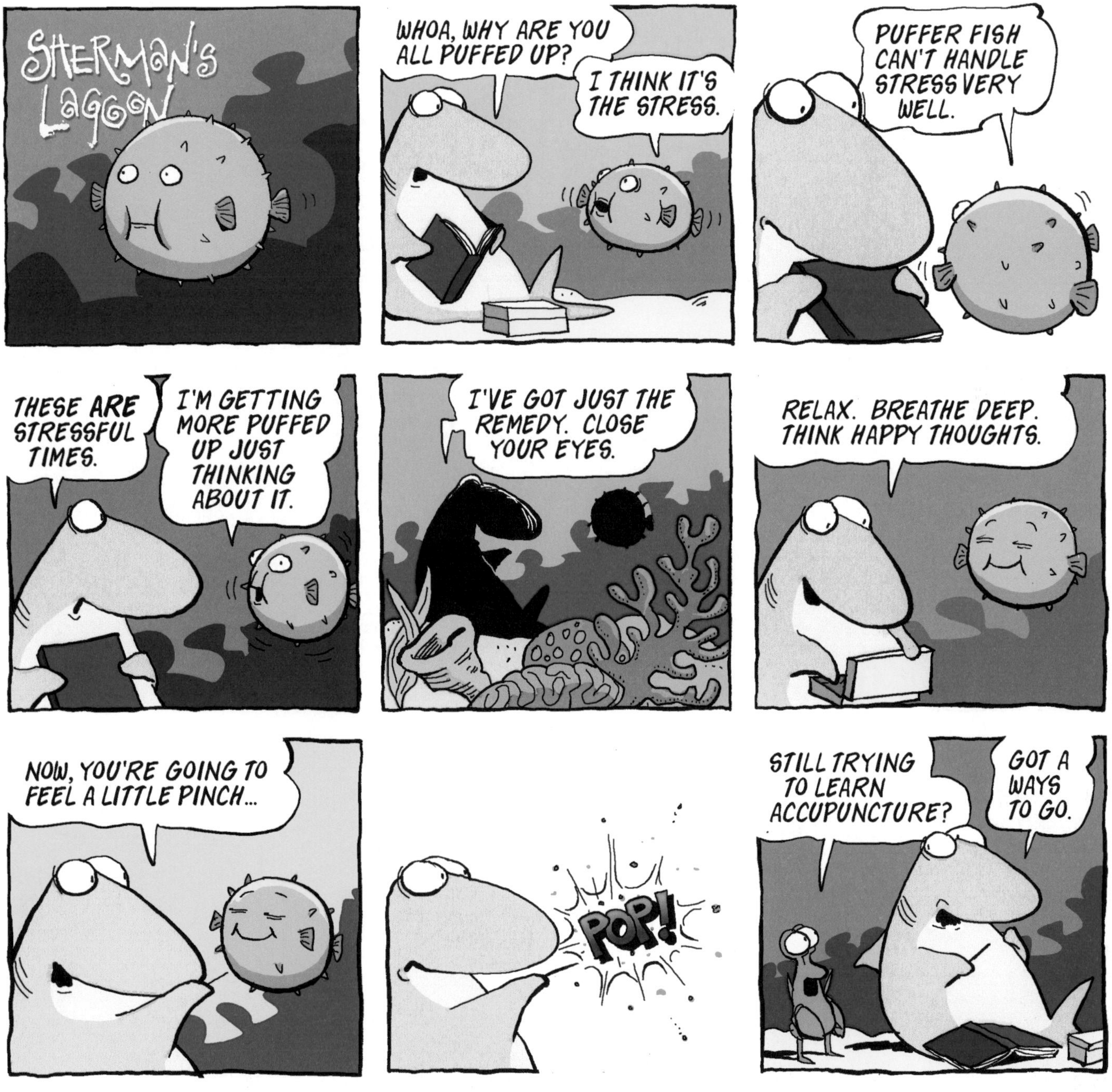
SHERMAN'S LAGOON
WHOA, WHY ARE YOU ALL PUFFED UP?
I THINK IT'S THE STRESS.
PUFFER FISH CAN'T HANDLE STRESS VERY WELL.
THESE ARE STRESSFUL TIMES.
I'M GETTING MORE PUFFED UP JUST THINKING ABOUT IT.
I'VE GOT JUST THE REMEDY. CLOSE YOUR EYES.
RELAX. BREATHE DEEP. THINK HAPPY THOUGHTS.
NOW, YOU'RE GOING TO FEEL A LITTLE PINCH...
POP!
STILL TRYING TO LEARN ACCUPUNCTURE?
GOT A WAYS TO GO.

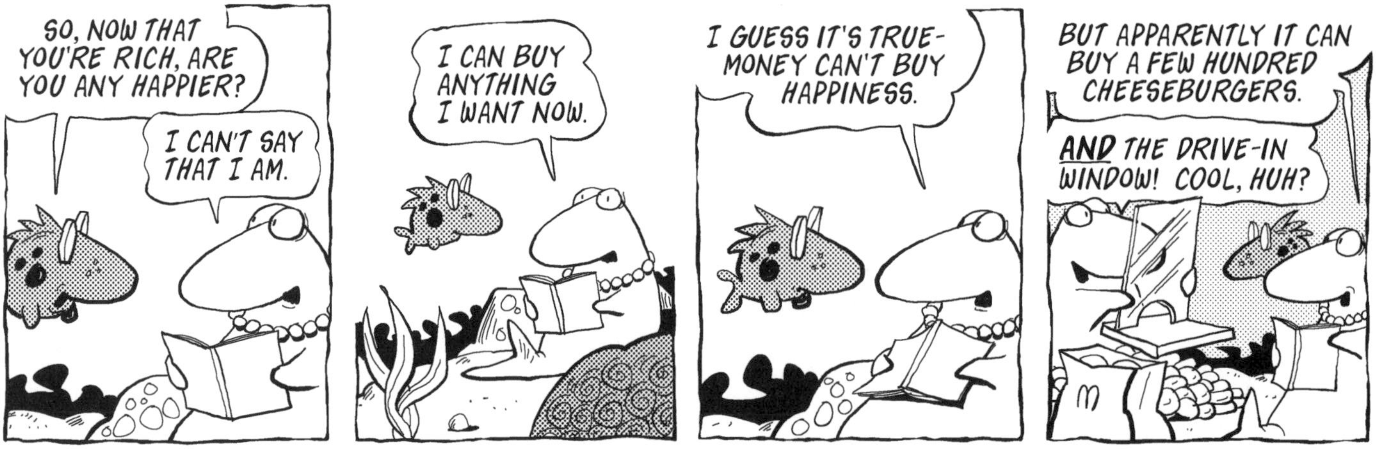
SO, NOW THAT YOU'RE RICH, ARE YOU ANY HAPPIER?
I CAN'T SAY THAT I AM.
I CAN BUY ANYTHING I WANT NOW.
I GUESS IT'S TRUE- MONEY CAN'T BUY HAPPINESS.
BUT APPARENTLY IT CAN BUY A FEW HUNDRED CHEESEBURGERS.
AND THE DRIVE-IN WINDOW! COOL, HUH?

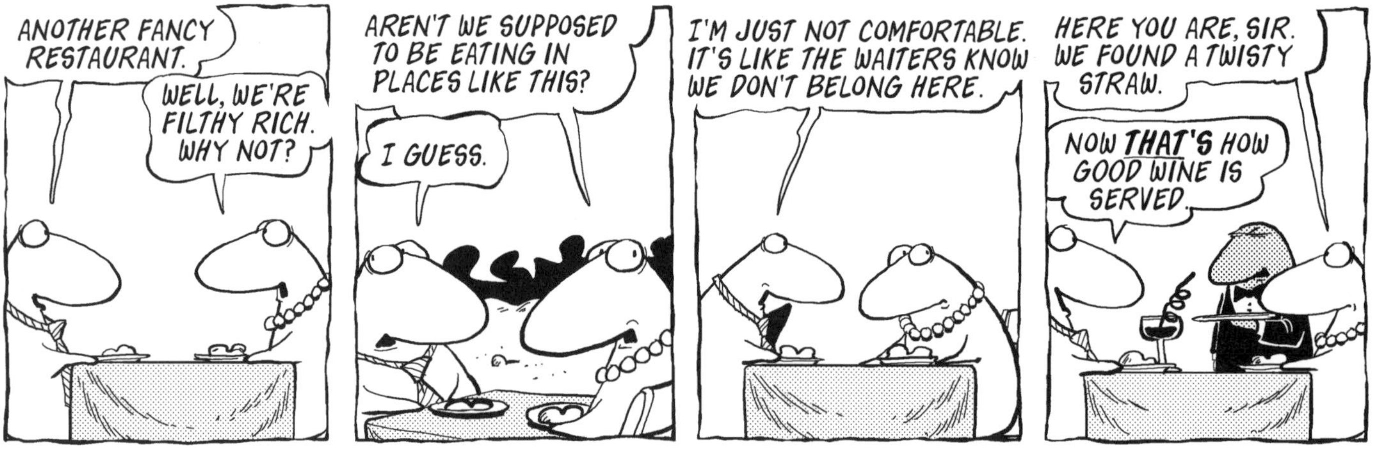
ANOTHER FANCY RESTAURANT.
WELL, WE'RE FILTHY RICH. WHY NOT?
AREN'T WE SUPPOSED TO BE EATING IN PLACES LIKE THIS?
I GUESS.
I'M JUST NOT COMFORTABLE. IT'S LIKE THE WAITERS KNOW WE DON'T BELONG HERE.
HERE YOU ARE, SIR. WE FOUND A TWISTY STRAW.
NOW THAT'S HOW GOOD WINE IS SERVED.

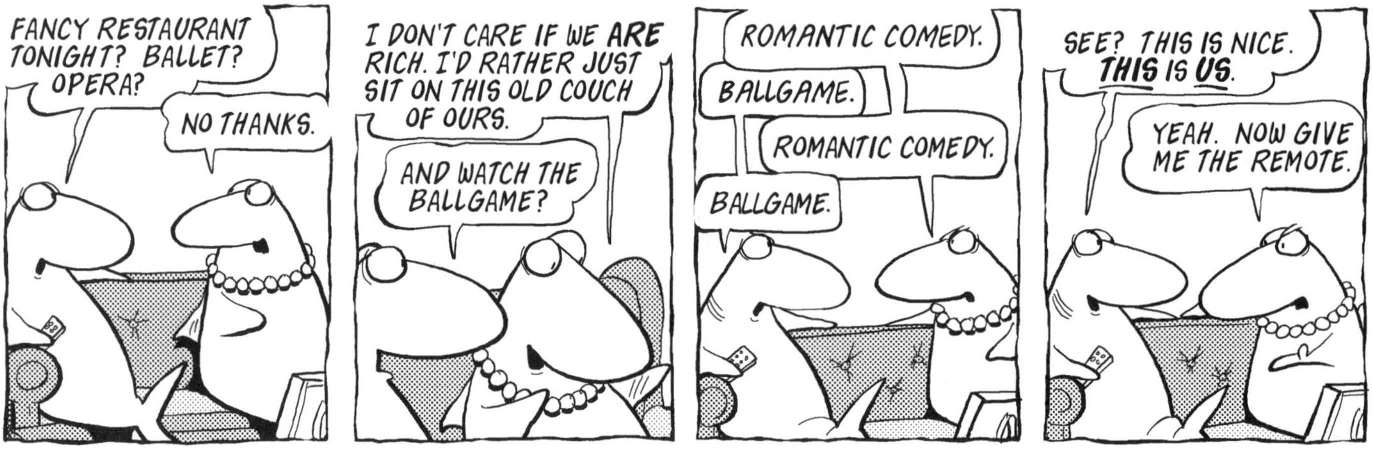
FANCY RESTAURANT TONIGHT? BALLET? OPERA?
NO THANKS.
I DON'T CARE IF WE ARE RICH. I'D RATHER JUST SIT ON THIS OLD COUCH OF OURS.
AND WATCH THE BALLGAME?
ROMANTIC COMEDY.
BALLGAME.
ROMANTIC COMEDY.
BALLGAME.
SEE? THIS IS NICE. THIS IS US.
YEAH. NOW GIVE ME THE REMOTE.

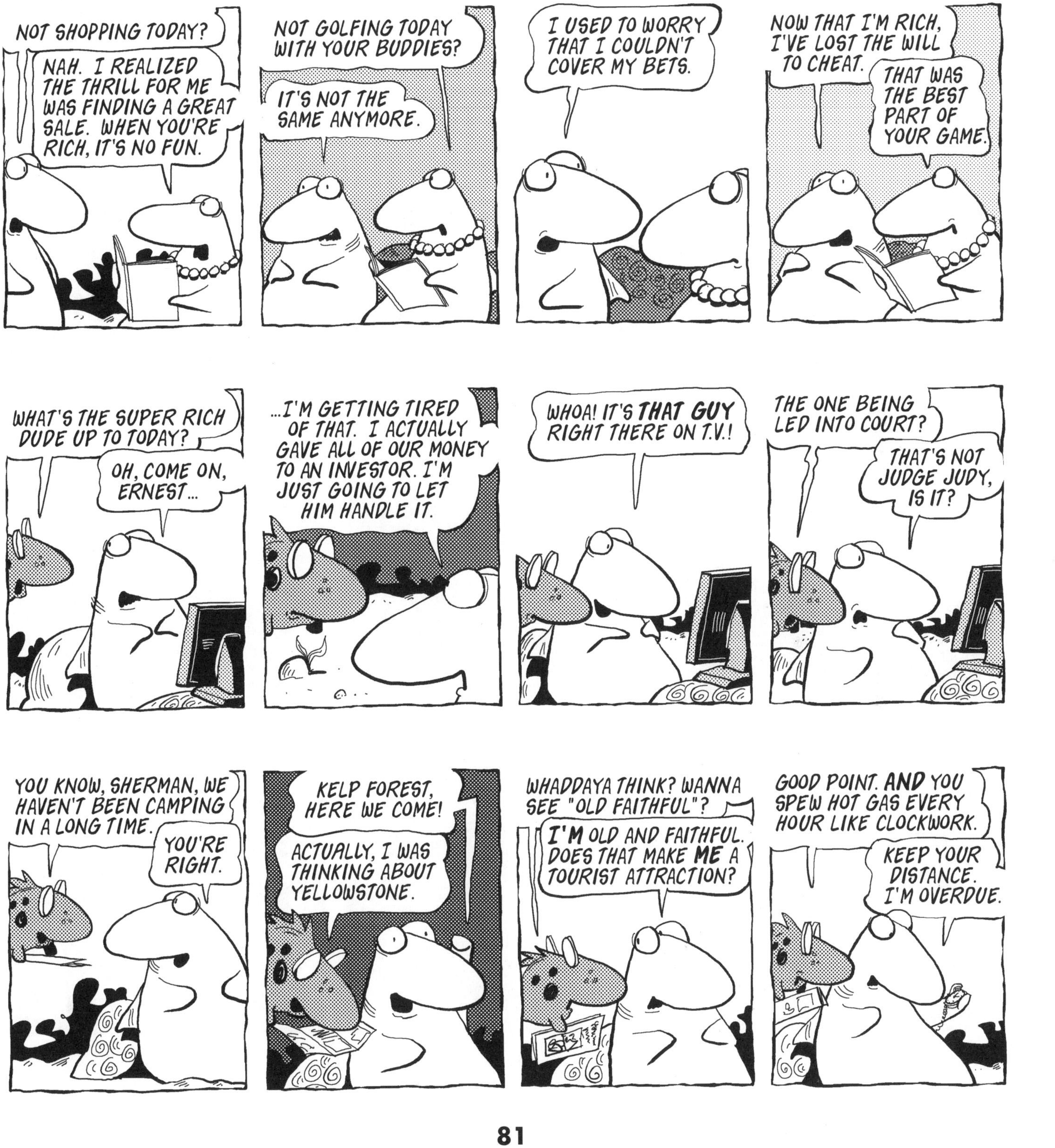
NOT SHOPPING TODAY?
NAH. I REALIZED THE THRILL FOR ME WAS FINDING A GREAT SALE. WHEN YOU'RE RICH, IT'S NO FUN.
NOT GOLFING TODAY WITH YOUR BUDDIES?
IT'S NOT THE SAME ANYMORE.
I USED TO WORRY THAT I COULDN'T COVER MY BETS.
NOW THAT I'M RICH, I'VE LOST THE WILL TO CHEAT.
THAT WAS THE BEST PART OF YOUR GAME.
WHAT'S THE SUPER RICH DUDE UP TO TODAY?
OH, COME ON, ERNEST...
...I'M GETTING TIRED OF THAT. I ACTUALLY GAVE ALL OF OUR MONEY TO AN INVESTOR. I'M JUST GOING TO LET HIM HANDLE IT.
WHOA! IT'S **THAT GUY** RIGHT THERE ON T.V.!
THE ONE BEING LED INTO COURT?
THAT'S NOT JUDGE JUDY, IS IT?
YOU KNOW, SHERMAN, WE HAVEN'T BEEN CAMPING IN A LONG TIME.
YOU'RE RIGHT.
KELP FOREST, HERE WE COME!
ACTUALLY, I WAS THINKING ABOUT YELLOWSTONE.
WHADDAYA THINK? WANNA SEE "OLD FAITHFUL"?
I'M OLD AND FAITHFUL. DOES THAT MAKE **ME** A TOURIST ATTRACTION?
GOOD POINT. **AND** YOU SPEW HOT GAS EVERY HOUR LIKE CLOCKWORK.
KEEP YOUR DISTANCE. I'M OVERDUE.

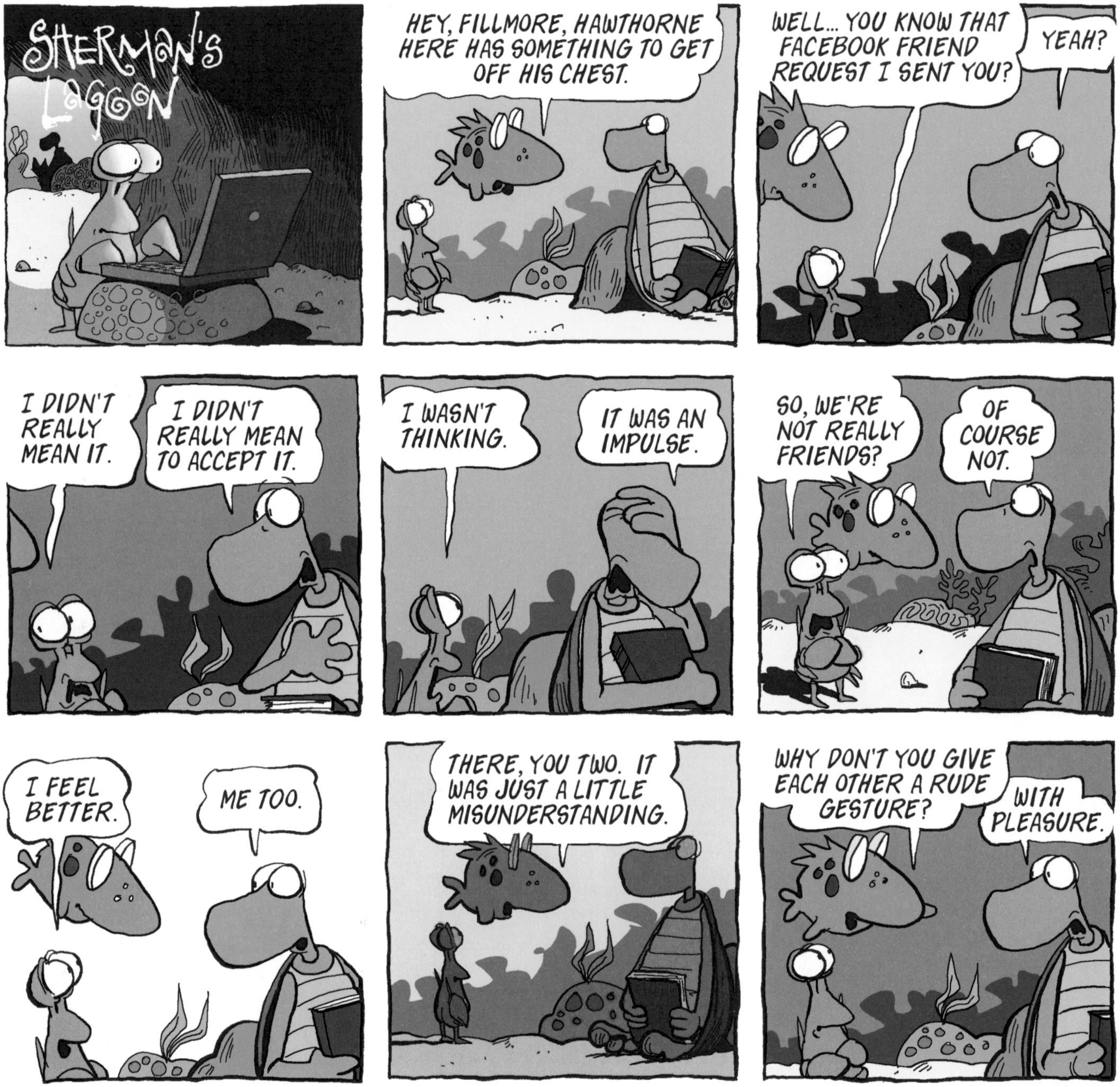
SHERMAN'S LAGOON
HEY, FILLMORE, HAWTHORNE HERE HAS SOMETHING TO GET OFF HIS CHEST.
WELL... YOU KNOW THAT FACEBOOK FRIEND REQUEST I SENT YOU?
YEAH?
I DIDN'T REALLY MEAN IT.
I DIDN'T REALLY MEAN TO ACCEPT IT.
I WASN'T THINKING.
IT WAS AN IMPULSE.
SO, WE'RE NOT REALLY FRIENDS?
OF COURSE NOT.
I FEEL BETTER.
ME TOO.
THERE, YOU TWO. IT WAS JUST A LITTLE MISUNDERSTANDING.
WHY DON'T YOU GIVE EACH OTHER A RUDE GESTURE?
WITH PLEASURE.

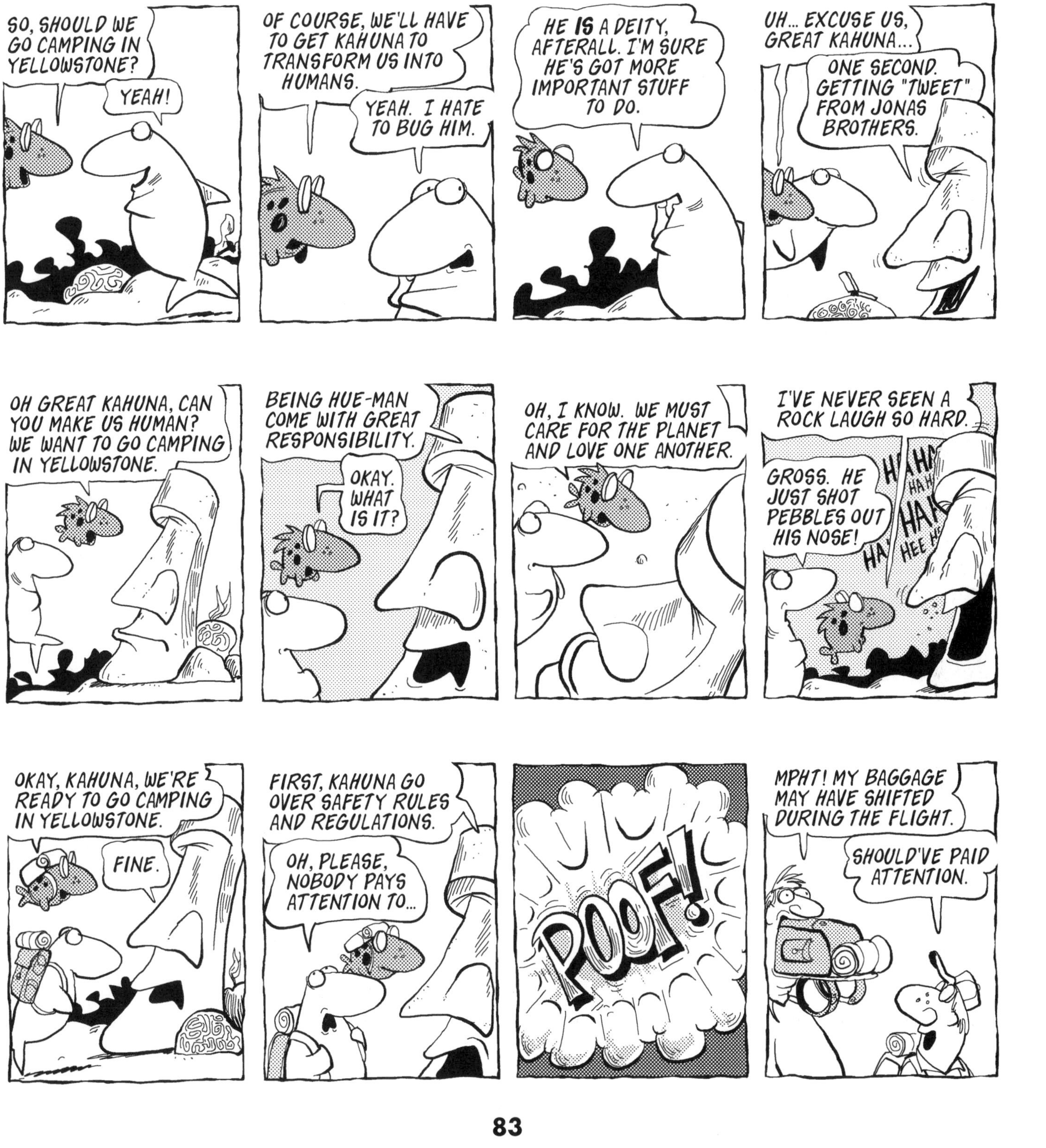

SO, SHOULD WE GO CAMPING IN YELLOWSTONE?
YEAH!
OF COURSE, WE'LL HAVE TO GET KAHUNA TO TRANSFORM US INTO HUMANS.
YEAH. I HATE TO BUG HIM.
HE **IS** A DEITY, AFTERALL. I'M SURE HE'S GOT MORE IMPORTANT STUFF TO DO.
UH... EXCUSE US, GREAT KAHUNA...
ONE SECOND. GETTING "TWEET" FROM JONAS BROTHERS.
OH GREAT KAHUNA, CAN YOU MAKE US HUMAN? WE WANT TO GO CAMPING IN YELLOWSTONE.
BEING HUE-MAN COME WITH GREAT RESPONSIBILITY.
OKAY. WHAT IS IT?
OH, I KNOW. WE MUST CARE FOR THE PLANET AND LOVE ONE ANOTHER.
I'VE NEVER SEEN A ROCK LAUGH SO HARD.
GROSS. HE JUST SHOT PEBBLES OUT HIS NOSE!
OKAY, KAHUNA, WE'RE READY TO GO CAMPING IN YELLOWSTONE.
FINE.
FIRST, KAHUNA GO OVER SAFETY RULES AND REGULATIONS.
OH, PLEASE, NOBODY PAYS ATTENTION TO...
POOF!
MPHT! MY BAGGAGE MAY HAVE SHIFTED DURING THE FLIGHT.
SHOULD'VE PAID ATTENTION.

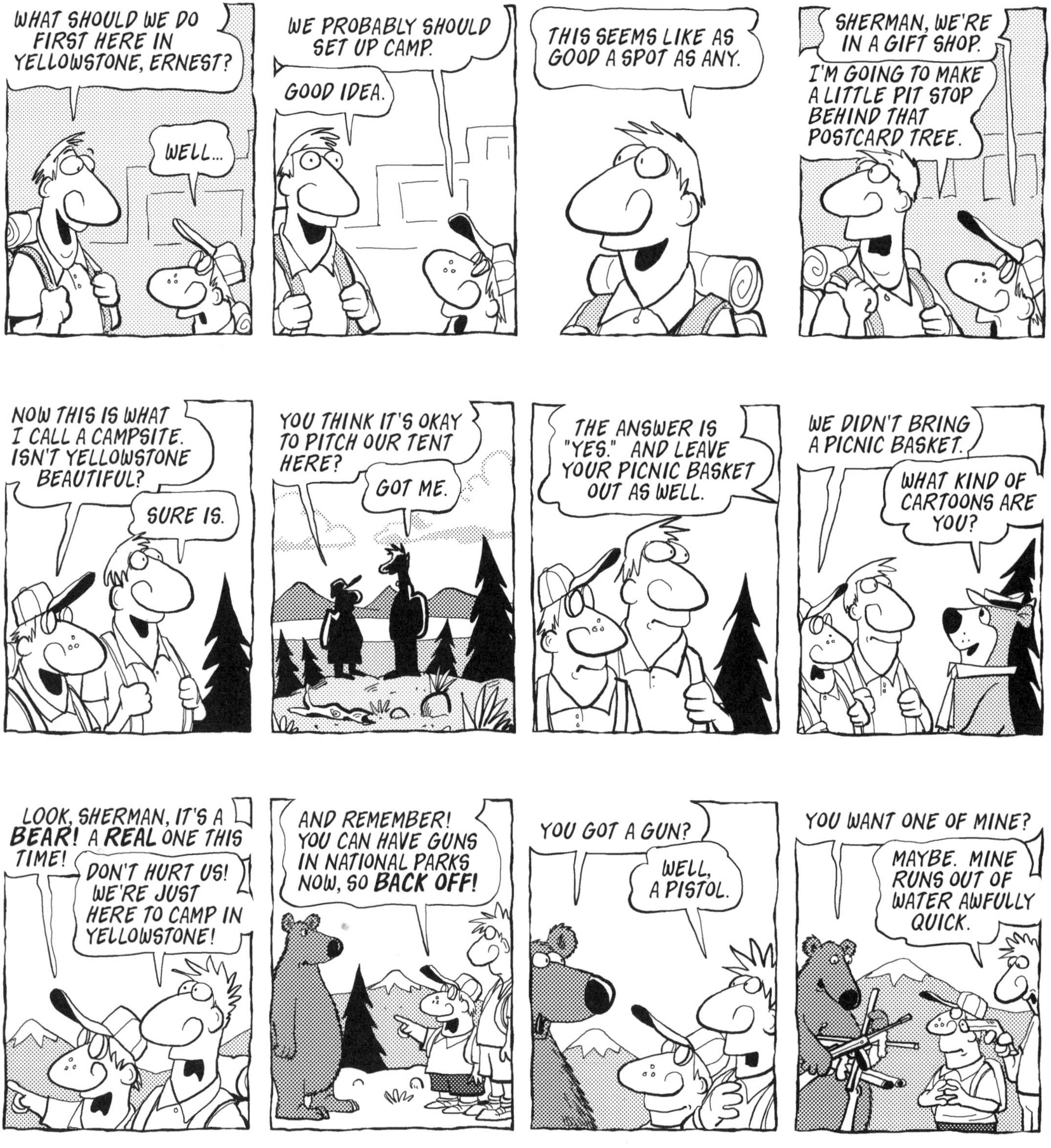
WHAT SHOULD WE DO FIRST HERE IN YELLOWSTONE, ERNEST?
WELL...
WE PROBABLY SHOULD SET UP CAMP.
GOOD IDEA.
THIS SEEMS LIKE AS GOOD A SPOT AS ANY.
SHERMAN, WE'RE IN A GIFT SHOP.
I'M GOING TO MAKE A LITTLE PIT STOP BEHIND THAT POSTCARD TREE.
NOW THIS IS WHAT I CALL A CAMPSITE. ISN'T YELLOWSTONE BEAUTIFUL?
SURE IS.
YOU THINK IT'S OKAY TO PITCH OUR TENT HERE?
GOT ME.
THE ANSWER IS "YES." AND LEAVE YOUR PICNIC BASKET OUT AS WELL.
WE DIDN'T BRING A PICNIC BASKET.
WHAT KIND OF CARTOONS ARE YOU?
LOOK, SHERMAN, IT'S A BEAR! A REAL ONE THIS TIME!
DON'T HURT US! WE'RE JUST HERE TO CAMP IN YELLOWSTONE!
AND REMEMBER! YOU CAN HAVE GUNS IN NATIONAL PARKS NOW, SO BACK OFF!
YOU GOT A GUN?
WELL, A PISTOL.
YOU WANT ONE OF MINE?
MAYBE. MINE RUNS OUT OF WATER AWFULLY QUICK.

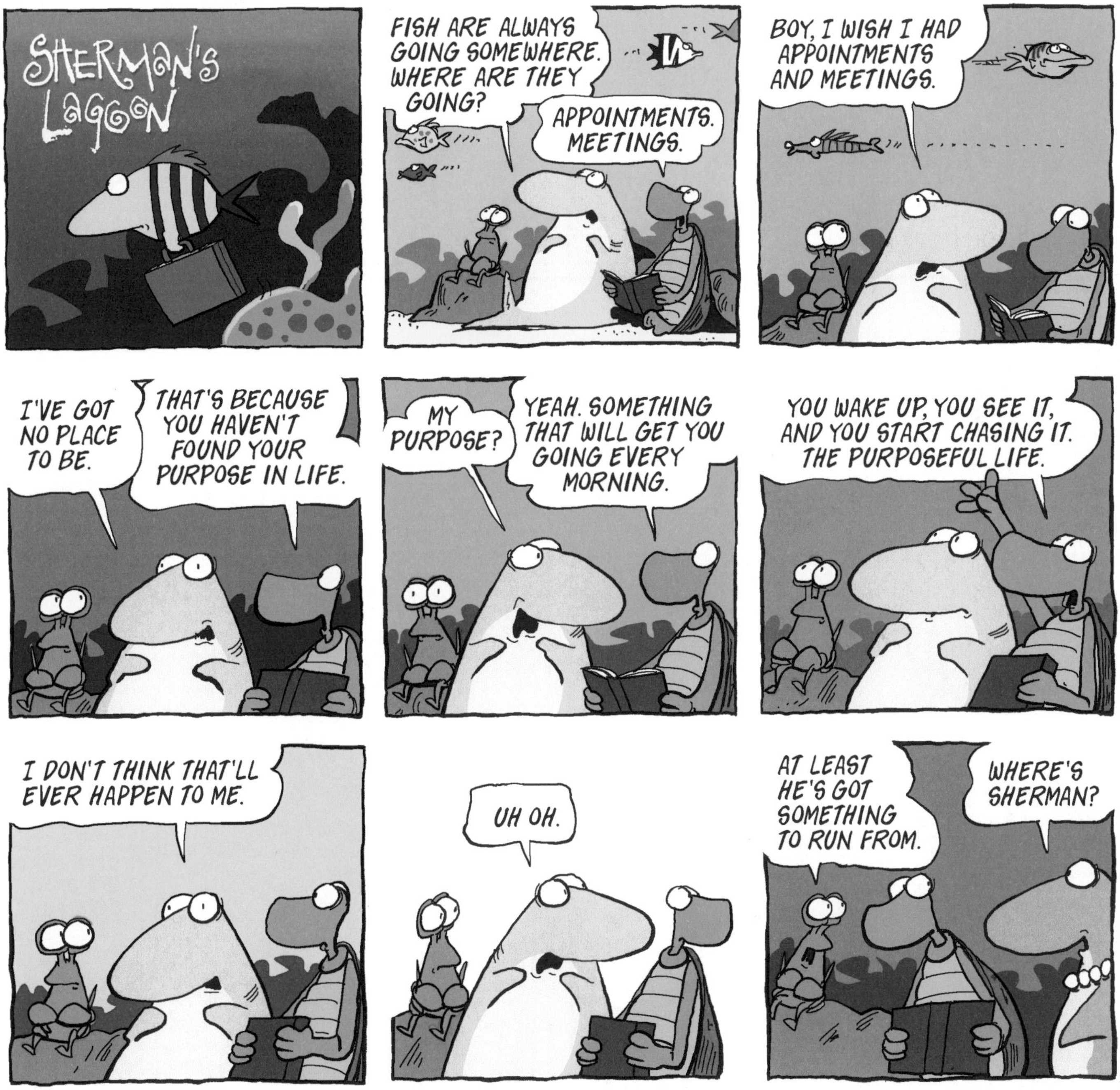
SHERMAN'S LAGOON
FISH ARE ALWAYS GOING SOMEWHERE. WHERE ARE THEY GOING?
APPOINTMENTS. MEETINGS.
BOY, I WISH I HAD APPOINTMENTS AND MEETINGS.
I'VE GOT NO PLACE TO BE.
THAT'S BECAUSE YOU HAVEN'T FOUND YOUR PURPOSE IN LIFE.
MY PURPOSE?
YEAH. SOMETHING THAT WILL GET YOU GOING EVERY MORNING.
YOU WAKE UP, YOU SEE IT, AND YOU START CHASING IT. THE PURPOSEFUL LIFE.
I DON'T THINK THAT'LL EVER HAPPEN TO ME.
UH OH.
AT LEAST HE'S GOT SOMETHING TO RUN FROM.
WHERE'S SHERMAN?

Panel 1: WOW, ISN'T YELLOWSTONE SPECTACULAR! LOOK AT THAT WATERFALL!

Panel 2: EXCUSE US. WOULD YOU MIND TAKING OUR PICTURE IN FRONT OF THE FALLS?

UH, SURE.

Panel 3: OKAY, STILL NOT IN THE FRAME... BACK IT UP... LITTLE MORE... BIT MORE...

Panel 4: AAAAAAUUUUUGHHHHHHHHHHH

UM, SO WHAT'S THE ETIQUETTE HERE? DO I GET THEIR CAMERA?

HOLD ON. THEY HIT WATER.

Panel 5: SO, WHAT'S ON TODAY'S AGENDA HERE IN YELLOWSTONE?

FISHING!

Panel 6: BUT, YOU'RE A SHARK IN YOUR OTHER LIFE! YOU EAT FISH EVERY DAY BACK IN THE LAGOON!

YES...

Panel 7: BUT NOT FRESHWATER FISH.

Panel 8: WELL, HOW IS IT?

NEEDS SALT.

Panel 9: THE YELLOWSTONE MUD PITS. INTERESTING SPECTACLE OF NATURE, ISN'T IT?

YEAH. YOU KNOW HOW IT WORKS?

Panel 10: TINY GNOMES LIVING UNDERGROUND SPIT MUD UPWARDS WHEN THEY HEAR OUR FOOTSTEPS.

Panel 11: ACTUALLY, IT'S THE GEOTHERMAL HEAT THAT CAUSES THEM TO BUBBLE, EINSTEIN.

Panel 12: DOES HE KNOW HE'S TALKING TO A GREAT WHITE SHARK?

BACK HOME, I'D HAVE EATEN HIM.

"YELLOWSTONE HAS THE HIGHEST CONCENTRATION OF ACTIVE GEYSERS IN THE WORLD."

SHERMAN, YOU SHOULD STAY ON THIS SIDE OF THE ROPES.

MEGAN SAYS STEAM IS GOOD FOR THE COMPLEXION.

WHOOOOOOO-SSH

DANG

HOW ARE MY PORES?

GONE.

POOF!

WOMAN CARNIVORE

SHERMAN, YOU'RE BACK! HOW WAS YOUR ADVENTURE IN THE WILDERNESS? I HOPE YOU HAD A GOOD TIME.

IT WAS FUN.

YOU LEFT ME ALL ALONE! THINGS GOT BAD. I HAD TO MAKE DECISIONS ALL BY MYSELF!

HOW SELFISH OF ME, MEGAN. TELL ME ABOUT IT.

WOMAN CARNIVORE

WELL... THERE WAS A SALE...

MANY A HORROR STORY HAS STARTED LIKE THIS.

LOOK! A TREASURE CHEST!

ANOTHER ONE? HOW MANY CAN THERE BE IN THIS LAGOON?

THIS IS EXCITING! LET'S SEE WHAT'S INSIDE.

MAYBE A DIAMOND TIARA FOR MEGAN.

OLD BOOKS.

JACKPOT!

I CAN STILL CATCH "DORA" IF I HURRY.

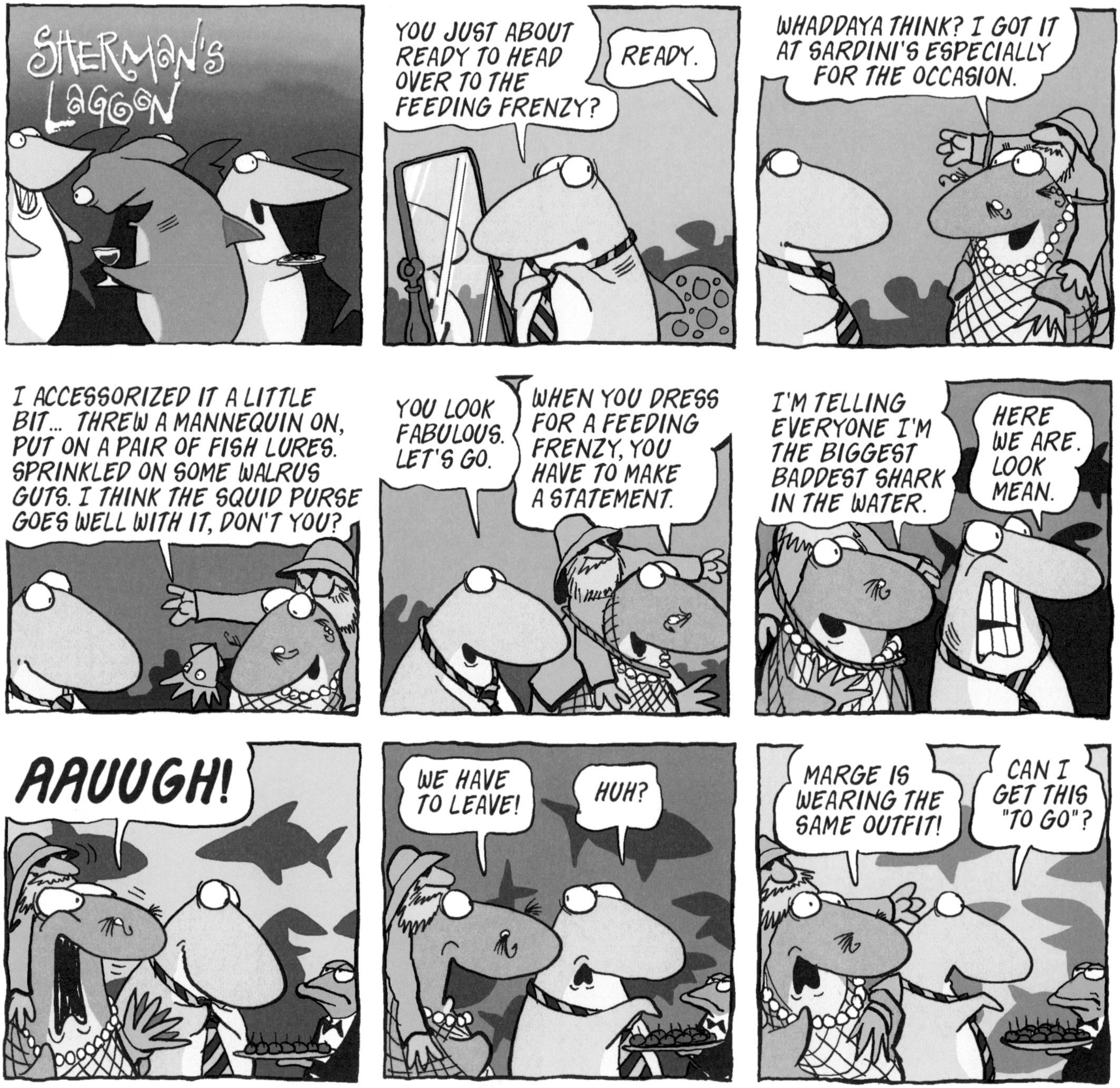
SHERMAN'S LAGOON
YOU JUST ABOUT READY TO HEAD OVER TO THE FEEDING FRENZY?
READY.
WHADDAYA THINK? I GOT IT AT SARDINI'S ESPECIALLY FOR THE OCCASION.
I ACCESSORIZED IT A LITTLE BIT... THREW A MANNEQUIN ON, PUT ON A PAIR OF FISH LURES. SPRINKLED ON SOME WALRUS GUTS. I THINK THE SQUID PURSE GOES WELL WITH IT, DON'T YOU?
YOU LOOK FABULOUS. LET'S GO.
WHEN YOU DRESS FOR A FEEDING FRENZY, YOU HAVE TO MAKE A STATEMENT.
I'M TELLING EVERYONE I'M THE BIGGEST BADDEST SHARK IN THE WATER.
HERE WE ARE. LOOK MEAN.
AAUUGH!
WE HAVE TO LEAVE!
HUH?
MARGE IS WEARING THE SAME OUTFIT!
CAN I GET THIS "TO GO"?

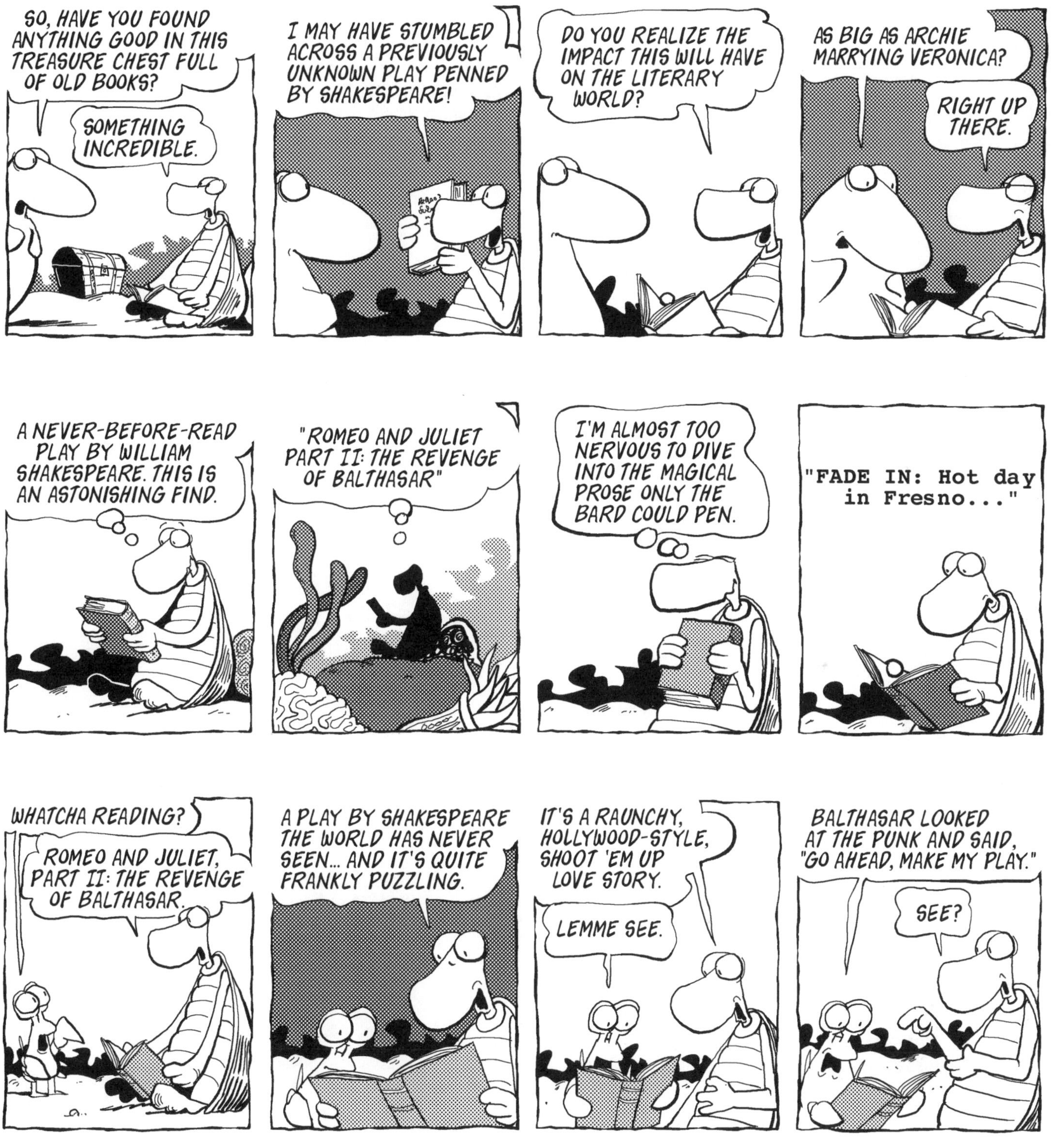
SO, HAVE YOU FOUND ANYTHING GOOD IN THIS TREASURE CHEST FULL OF OLD BOOKS?
SOMETHING INCREDIBLE.
I MAY HAVE STUMBLED ACROSS A PREVIOUSLY UNKNOWN PLAY PENNED BY SHAKESPEARE!
DO YOU REALIZE THE IMPACT THIS WILL HAVE ON THE LITERARY WORLD?
AS BIG AS ARCHIE MARRYING VERONICA?
RIGHT UP THERE.
A NEVER-BEFORE-READ PLAY BY WILLIAM SHAKESPEARE. THIS IS AN ASTONISHING FIND.
"ROMEO AND JULIET PART II: THE REVENGE OF BALTHASAR"
I'M ALMOST TOO NERVOUS TO DIVE INTO THE MAGICAL PROSE ONLY THE BARD COULD PEN.
"FADE IN: Hot day in Fresno..."
WHATCHA READING?
ROMEO AND JULIET, PART II: THE REVENGE OF BALTHASAR.
A PLAY BY SHAKESPEARE THE WORLD HAS NEVER SEEN... AND IT'S QUITE FRANKLY PUZZLING.
IT'S A RAUNCHY, HOLLYWOOD-STYLE, SHOOT 'EM UP LOVE STORY.
LEMME SEE.
BALTHASAR LOOKED AT THE PUNK AND SAID, "GO AHEAD, MAKE MY PLAY."
SEE?

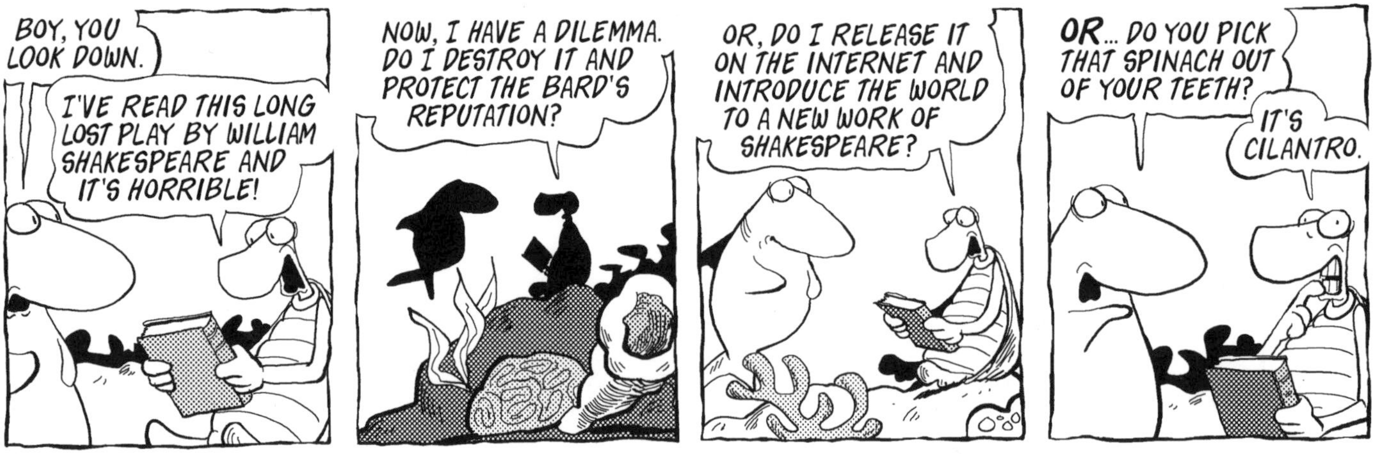
BOY, YOU LOOK DOWN.
I'VE READ THIS LONG LOST PLAY BY WILLIAM SHAKESPEARE AND IT'S HORRIBLE!
NOW, I HAVE A DILEMMA. DO I DESTROY IT AND PROTECT THE BARD'S REPUTATION?
OR, DO I RELEASE IT ON THE INTERNET AND INTRODUCE THE WORLD TO A NEW WORK OF SHAKESPEARE?
OR... DO YOU PICK THAT SPINACH OUT OF YOUR TEETH?
IT'S CILANTRO.

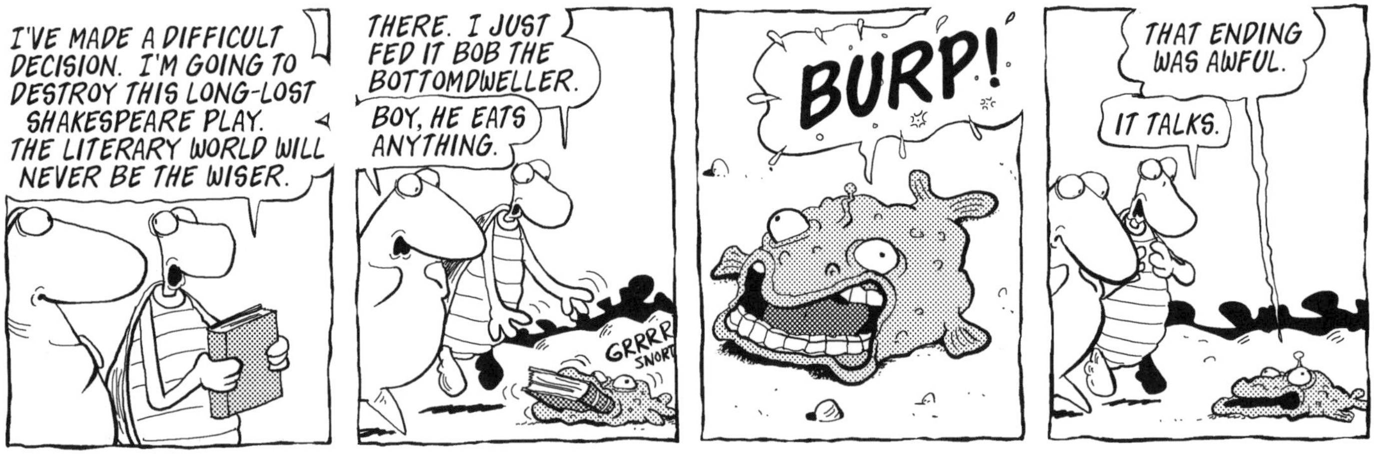
I'VE MADE A DIFFICULT DECISION. I'M GOING TO DESTROY THIS LONG-LOST SHAKESPEARE PLAY. THE LITERARY WORLD WILL NEVER BE THE WISER.
THERE. I JUST FED IT BOB THE BOTTOMDWELLER.
BOY, HE EATS ANYTHING.
GRRRR
SNORT
BURP!
THAT ENDING WAS AWFUL.
IT TALKS.

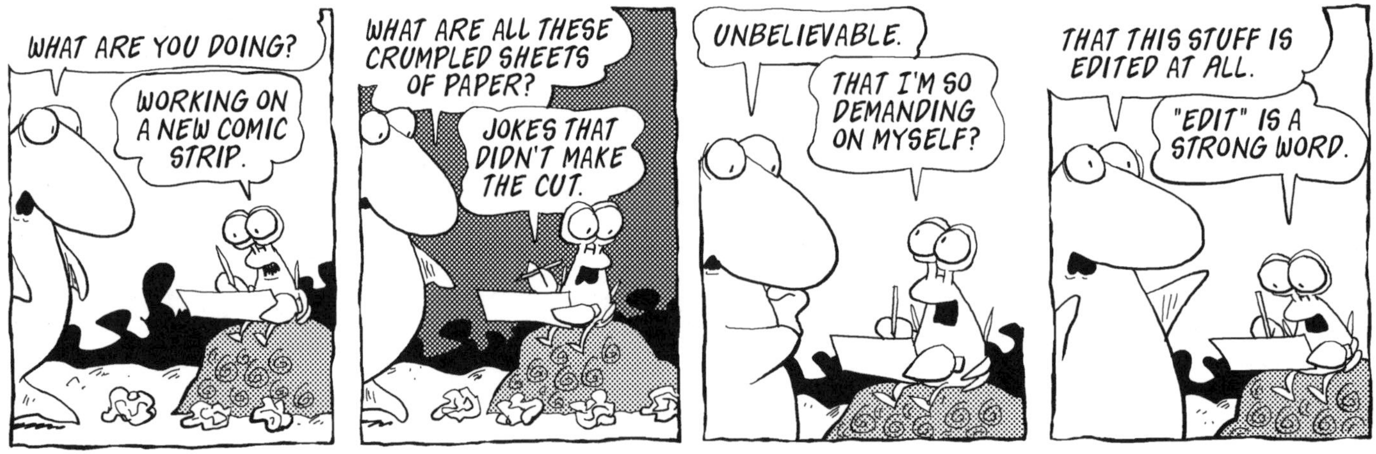
WHAT ARE YOU DOING?
WORKING ON A NEW COMIC STRIP.
WHAT ARE ALL THESE CRUMPLED SHEETS OF PAPER?
JOKES THAT DIDN'T MAKE THE CUT.
UNBELIEVABLE.
THAT I'M SO DEMANDING ON MYSELF?
THAT THIS STUFF IS EDITED AT ALL.
"EDIT" IS A STRONG WORD.

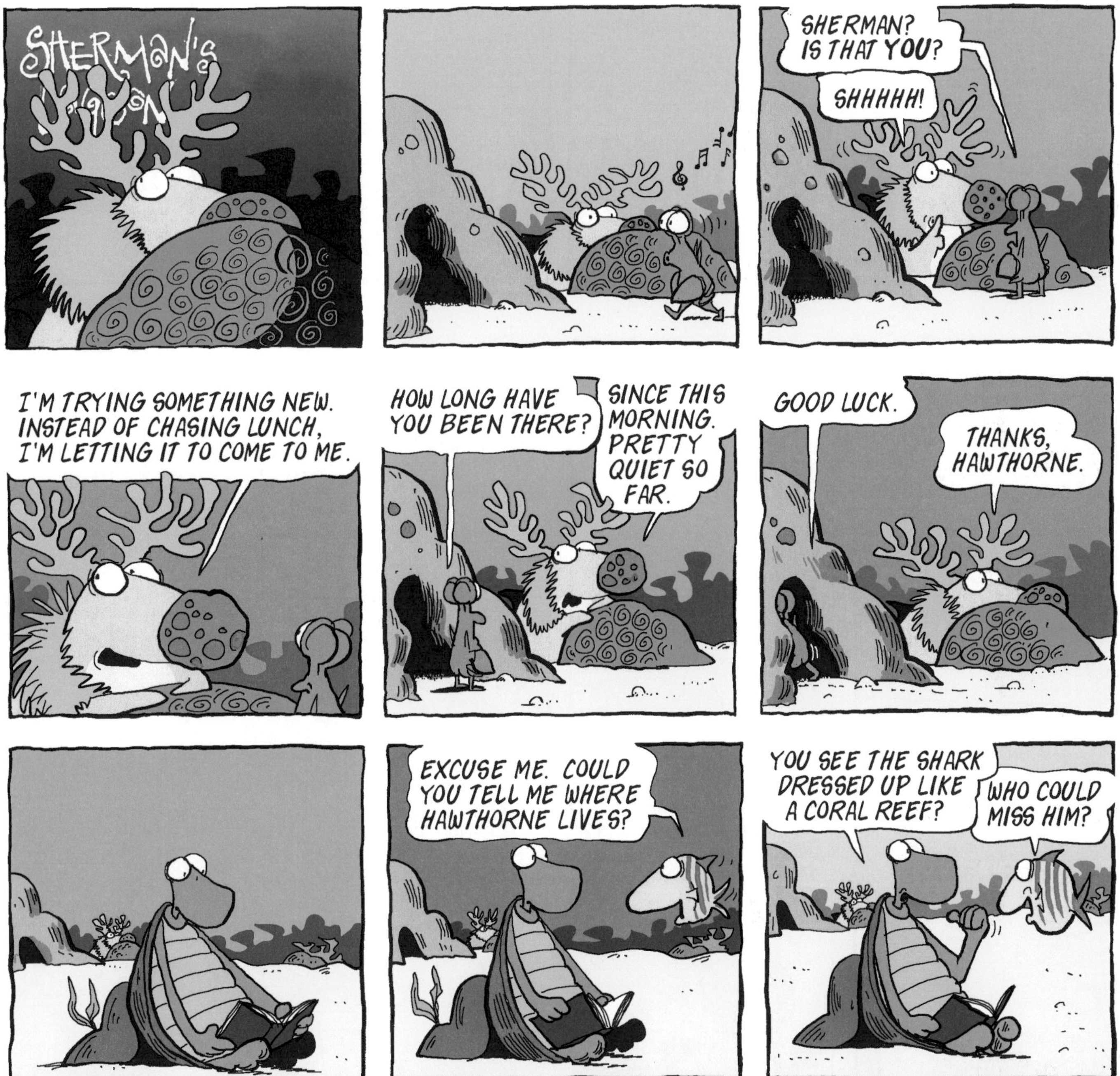
SHERMAN'S LAGOON
SHERMAN? IS THAT YOU?
SHHHHH!
I'M TRYING SOMETHING NEW. INSTEAD OF CHASING LUNCH, I'M LETTING IT TO COME TO ME.
HOW LONG HAVE YOU BEEN THERE?
SINCE THIS MORNING. PRETTY QUIET SO FAR.
GOOD LUCK.
THANKS, HAWTHORNE.
EXCUSE ME. COULD YOU TELL ME WHERE HAWTHORNE LIVES?
YOU SEE THE SHARK DRESSED UP LIKE A CORAL REEF?
WHO COULD MISS HIM?

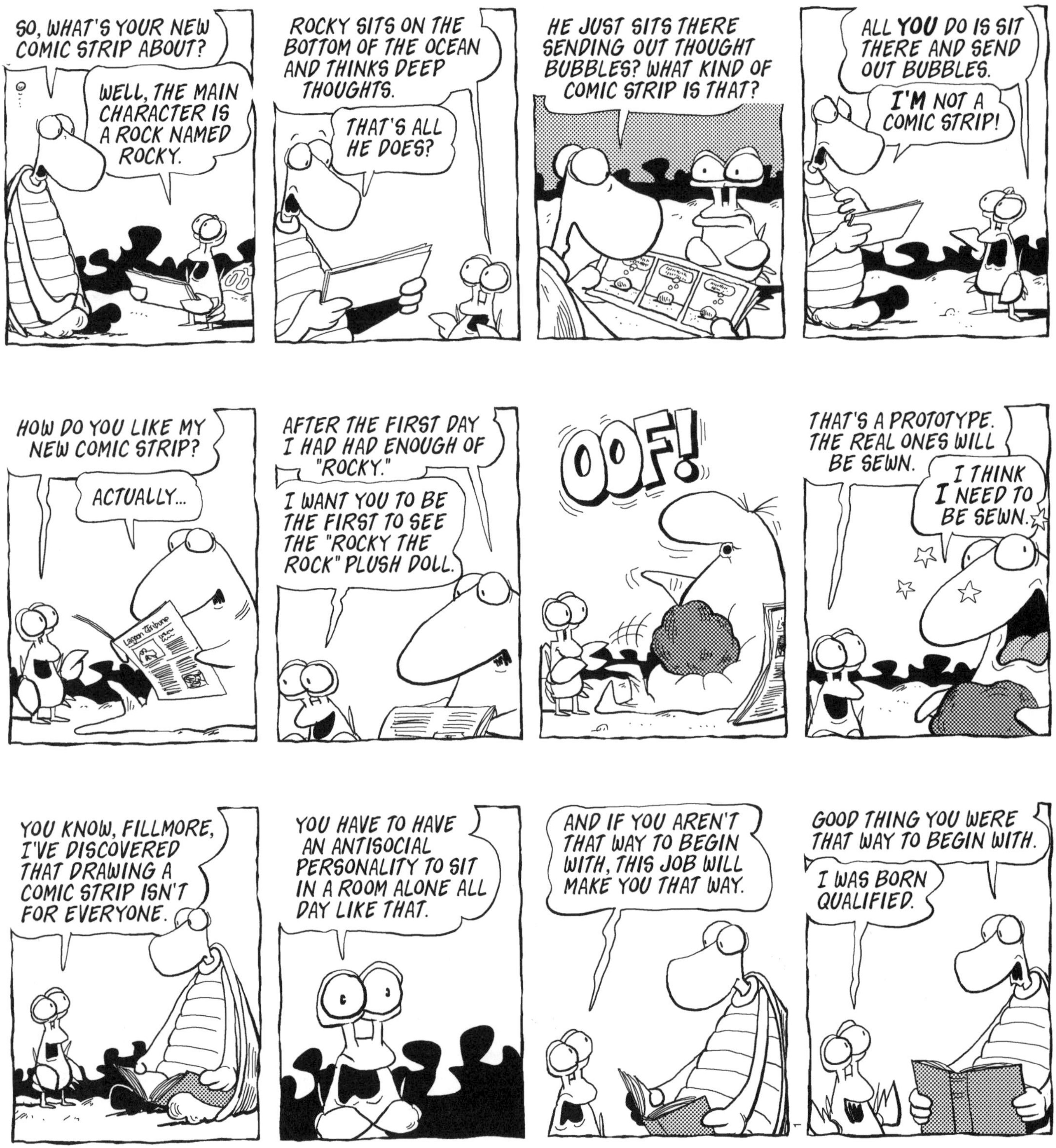
SO, WHAT'S YOUR NEW COMIC STRIP ABOUT?
WELL, THE MAIN CHARACTER IS A ROCK NAMED ROCKY.
ROCKY SITS ON THE BOTTOM OF THE OCEAN AND THINKS DEEP THOUGHTS.
THAT'S ALL HE DOES?
HE JUST SITS THERE SENDING OUT THOUGHT BUBBLES? WHAT KIND OF COMIC STRIP IS THAT?
ALL YOU DO IS SIT THERE AND SEND OUT BUBBLES.
I'M NOT A COMIC STRIP!
HOW DO YOU LIKE MY NEW COMIC STRIP?
ACTUALLY...
AFTER THE FIRST DAY I HAD HAD ENOUGH OF "ROCKY."
I WANT YOU TO BE THE FIRST TO SEE THE "ROCKY THE ROCK" PLUSH DOLL.
OOF!
THAT'S A PROTOTYPE. THE REAL ONES WILL BE SEWN.
I THINK I NEED TO BE SEWN.
YOU KNOW, FILLMORE, I'VE DISCOVERED THAT DRAWING A COMIC STRIP ISN'T FOR EVERYONE.
YOU HAVE TO HAVE AN ANTISOCIAL PERSONALITY TO SIT IN A ROOM ALONE ALL DAY LIKE THAT.
AND IF YOU AREN'T THAT WAY TO BEGIN WITH, THIS JOB WILL MAKE YOU THAT WAY.
GOOD THING YOU WERE THAT WAY TO BEGIN WITH.
I WAS BORN QUALIFIED.

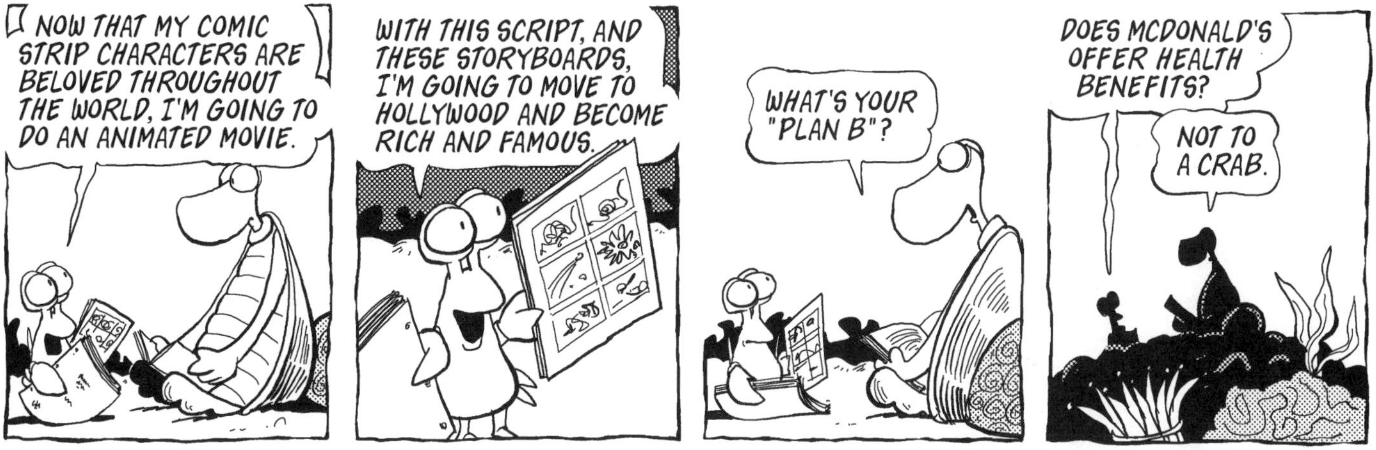
NOW THAT MY COMIC STRIP CHARACTERS ARE BELOVED THROUGHOUT THE WORLD, I'M GOING TO DO AN ANIMATED MOVIE.
WITH THIS SCRIPT, AND THESE STORYBOARDS, I'M GOING TO MOVE TO HOLLYWOOD AND BECOME RICH AND FAMOUS.
WHAT'S YOUR "PLAN B"?
DOES MCDONALD'S OFFER HEALTH BENEFITS?
NOT TO A CRAB.

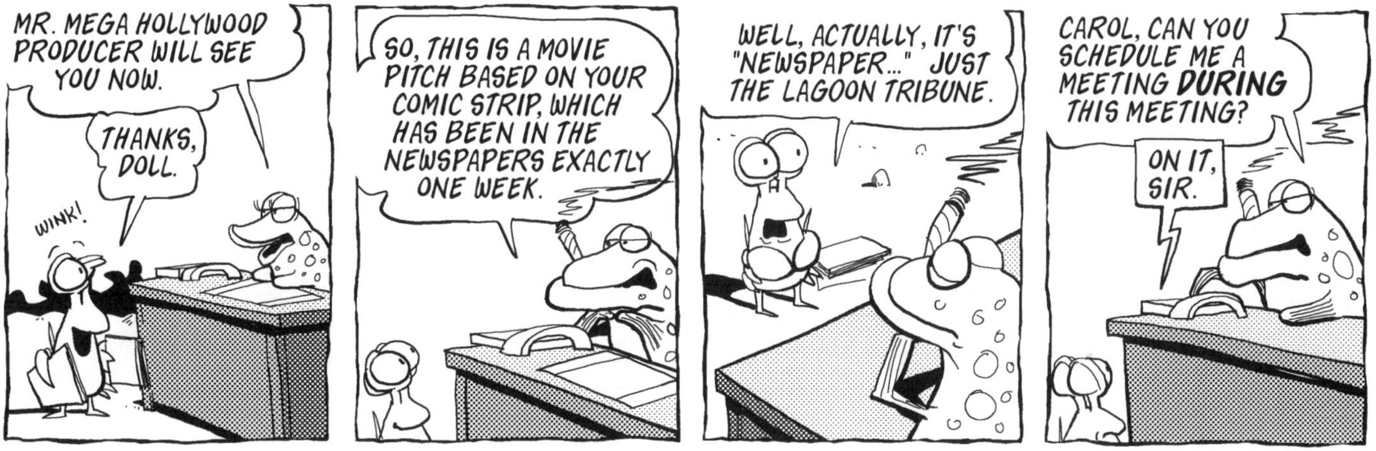
MR. MEGA HOLLYWOOD PRODUCER WILL SEE YOU NOW.
THANKS, DOLL.
WINK!
SO, THIS IS A MOVIE PITCH BASED ON YOUR COMIC STRIP, WHICH HAS BEEN IN THE NEWSPAPERS EXACTLY ONE WEEK.
WELL, ACTUALLY, IT'S "NEWSPAPER..." JUST THE LAGOON TRIBUNE.
CAROL, CAN YOU SCHEDULE ME A MEETING **DURING** THIS MEETING?
ON IT, SIR.

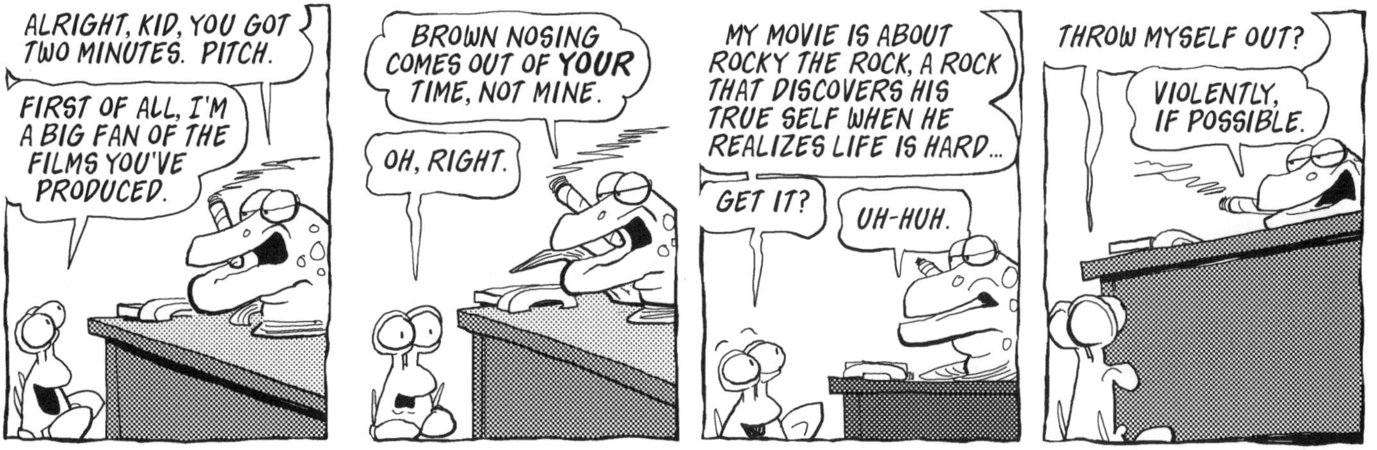
ALRIGHT, KID, YOU GOT TWO MINUTES. PITCH.
FIRST OF ALL, I'M A BIG FAN OF THE FILMS YOU'VE PRODUCED.
BROWN NOSING COMES OUT OF **YOUR** TIME, NOT MINE.
OH, RIGHT.
MY MOVIE IS ABOUT ROCKY THE ROCK, A ROCK THAT DISCOVERS HIS TRUE SELF WHEN HE REALIZES LIFE IS HARD...
GET IT?
UH-HUH.
THROW MYSELF OUT?
VIOLENTLY, IF POSSIBLE.

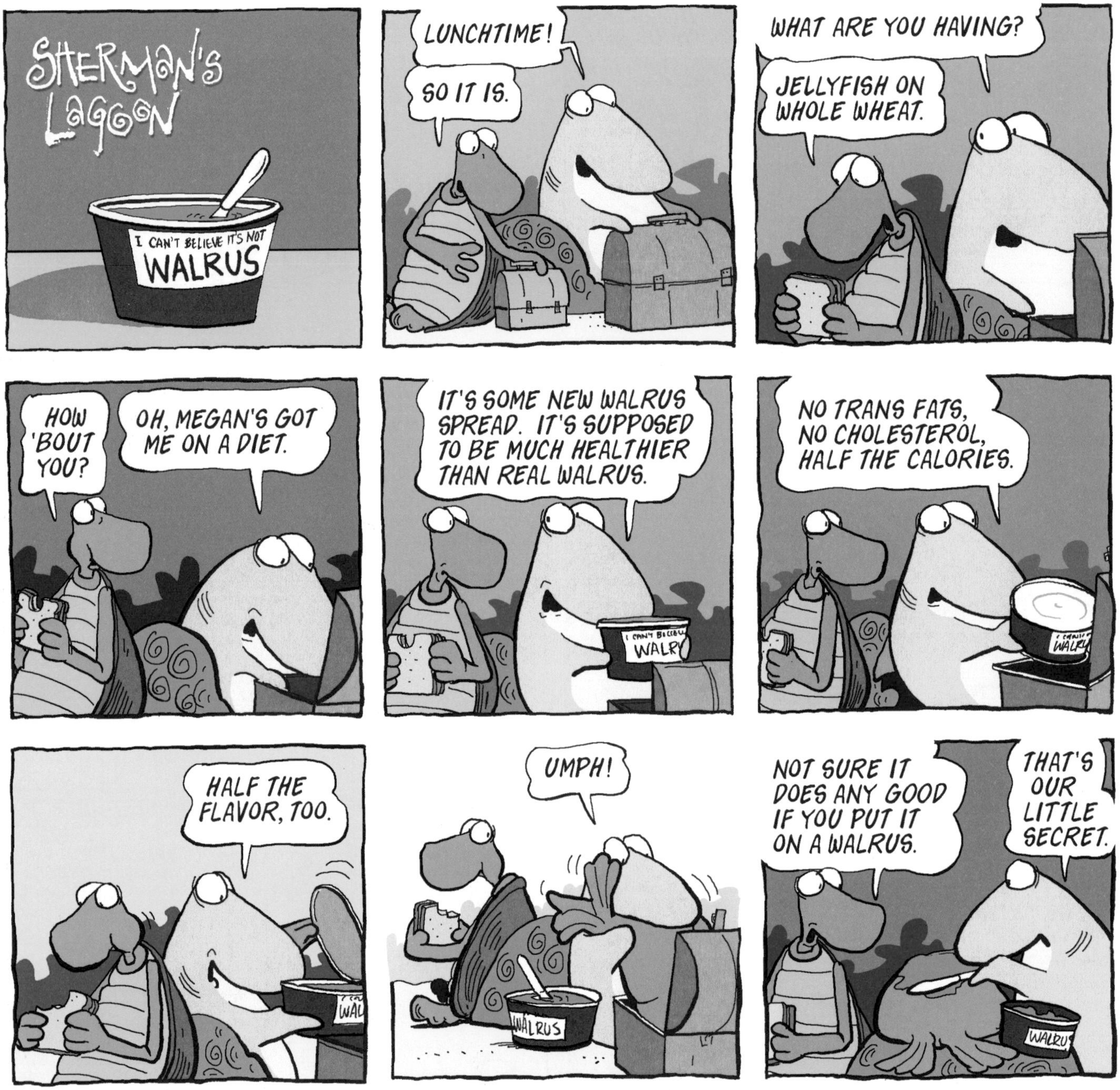
SHERMAN'S LAGOON
I CAN'T BELIEVE IT'S NOT WALRUS
LUNCHTIME!
SO IT IS.
WHAT ARE YOU HAVING?
JELLYFISH ON WHOLE WHEAT.
HOW 'BOUT YOU?
OH, MEGAN'S GOT ME ON A DIET.
IT'S SOME NEW WALRUS SPREAD. IT'S SUPPOSED TO BE MUCH HEALTHIER THAN REAL WALRUS.
NO TRANS FATS, NO CHOLESTEROL, HALF THE CALORIES.
HALF THE FLAVOR, TOO.
UMPH!
WALRUS
NOT SURE IT DOES ANY GOOD IF YOU PUT IT ON A WALRUS.
THAT'S OUR LITTLE SECRET.

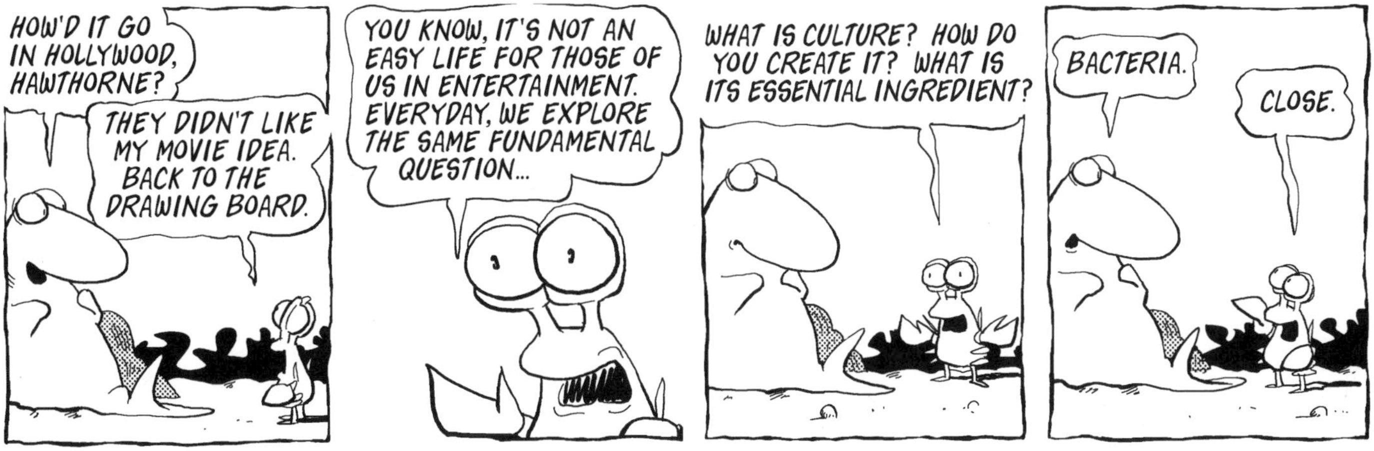
HOW'D IT GO IN HOLLYWOOD, HAWTHORNE?
THEY DIDN'T LIKE MY MOVIE IDEA. BACK TO THE DRAWING BOARD.
YOU KNOW, IT'S NOT AN EASY LIFE FOR THOSE OF US IN ENTERTAINMENT. EVERYDAY, WE EXPLORE THE SAME FUNDAMENTAL QUESTION...
WHAT IS CULTURE? HOW DO YOU CREATE IT? WHAT IS ITS ESSENTIAL INGREDIENT?
BACTERIA.
CLOSE.

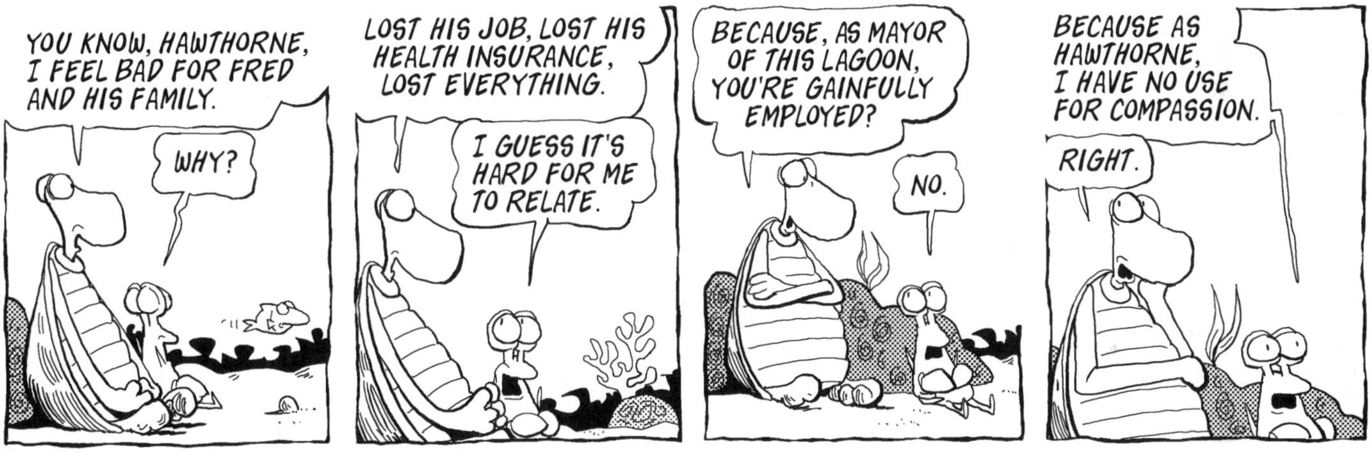
YOU KNOW, HAWTHORNE, I FEEL BAD FOR FRED AND HIS FAMILY.
WHY?
LOST HIS JOB, LOST HIS HEALTH INSURANCE, LOST EVERYTHING.
I GUESS IT'S HARD FOR ME TO RELATE.
BECAUSE, AS MAYOR OF THIS LAGOON, YOU'RE GAINFULLY EMPLOYED?
NO.
BECAUSE AS HAWTHORNE, I HAVE NO USE FOR COMPASSION.
RIGHT.

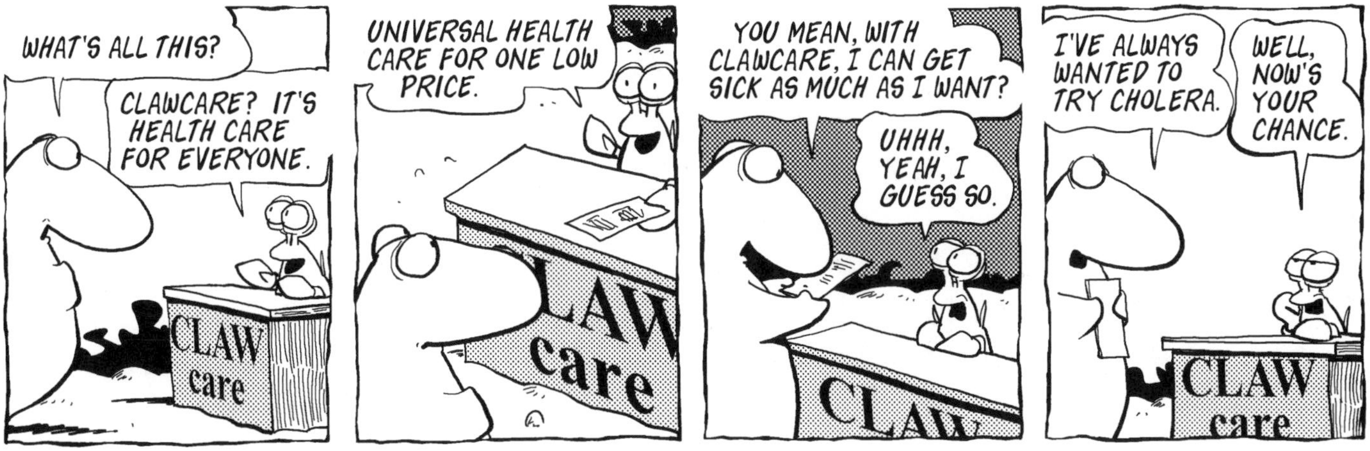
WHAT'S ALL THIS?
CLAWCARE? IT'S HEALTH CARE FOR EVERYONE.
CLAW care
UNIVERSAL HEALTH CARE FOR ONE LOW PRICE.
YOU MEAN, WITH CLAWCARE, I CAN GET SICK AS MUCH AS I WANT?
UHHH, YEAH, I GUESS SO.
I'VE ALWAYS WANTED TO TRY CHOLERA.
WELL, NOW'S YOUR CHANCE.
CLAW care

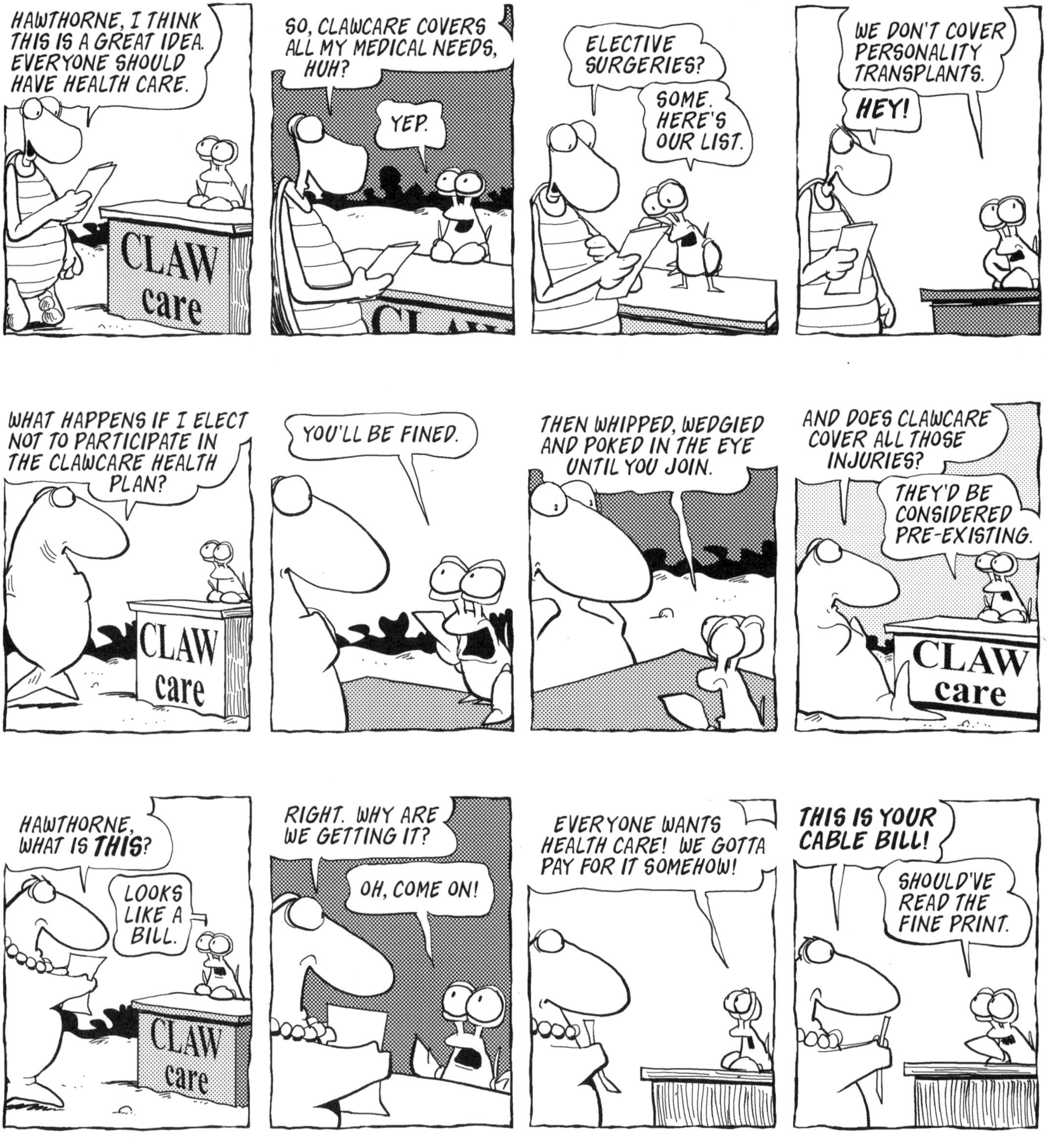
HAWTHORNE, I THINK THIS IS A GREAT IDEA. EVERYONE SHOULD HAVE HEALTH CARE.
CLAW care
SO, CLAWCARE COVERS ALL MY MEDICAL NEEDS, HUH?
YEP.
ELECTIVE SURGERIES?
SOME. HERE'S OUR LIST.
WE DON'T COVER PERSONALITY TRANSPLANTS.
HEY!
WHAT HAPPENS IF I ELECT NOT TO PARTICIPATE IN THE CLAWCARE HEALTH PLAN?
CLAW care
YOU'LL BE FINED.
THEN WHIPPED, WEDGIED AND POKED IN THE EYE UNTIL YOU JOIN.
AND DOES CLAWCARE COVER ALL THOSE INJURIES?
THEY'D BE CONSIDERED PRE-EXISTING.
CLAW care
HAWTHORNE, WHAT IS THIS?
LOOKS LIKE A BILL.
CLAW care
RIGHT. WHY ARE WE GETTING IT?
OH, COME ON!
EVERYONE WANTS HEALTH CARE! WE GOTTA PAY FOR IT SOMEHOW!
THIS IS YOUR CABLE BILL!
SHOULD'VE READ THE FINE PRINT.

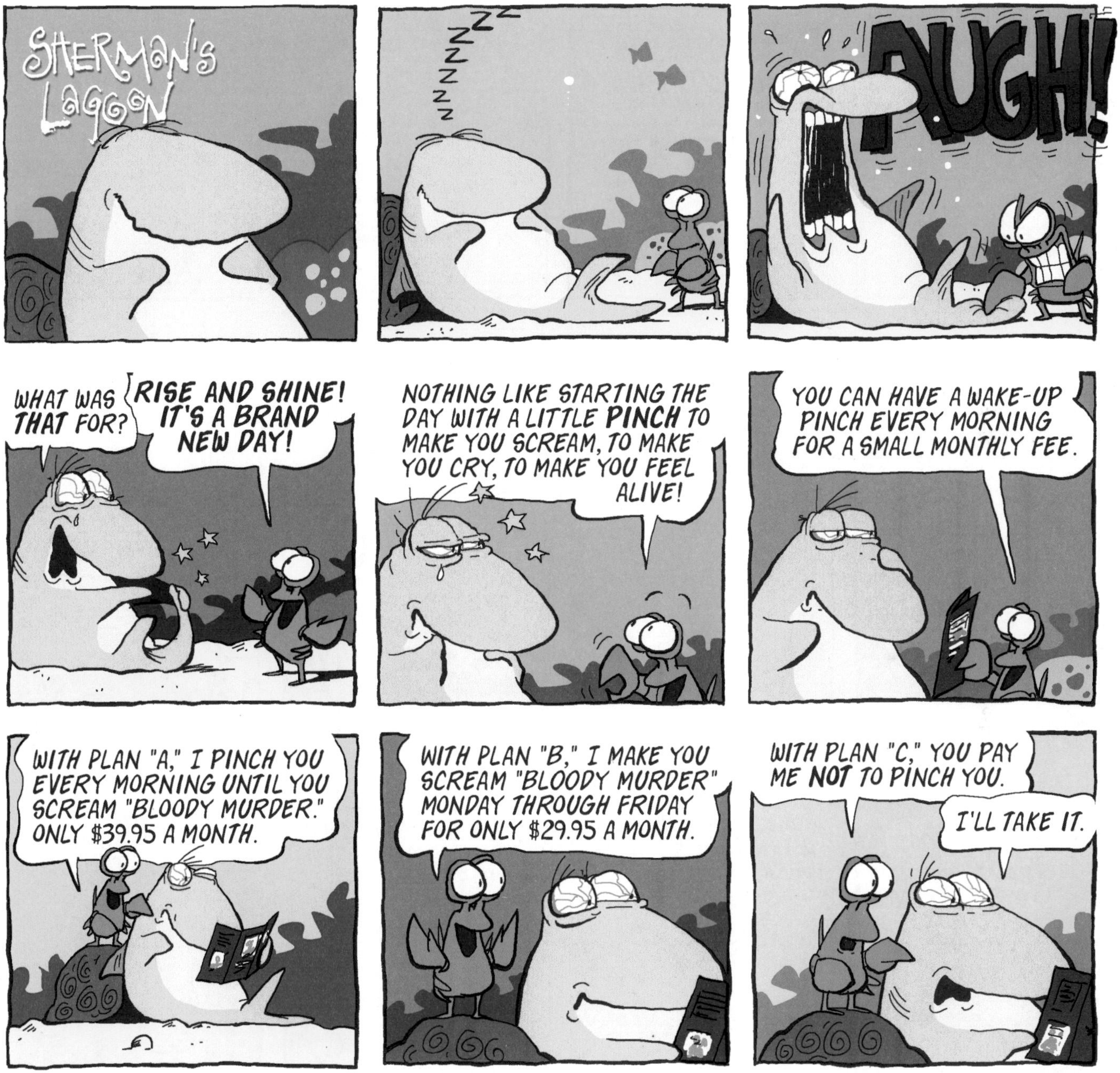
SHERMAN'S LAGOON
ZZZZZZZ
AUGH!
WHAT WAS THAT FOR?
RISE AND SHINE! IT'S A BRAND NEW DAY!
NOTHING LIKE STARTING THE DAY WITH A LITTLE PINCH TO MAKE YOU SCREAM, TO MAKE YOU CRY, TO MAKE YOU FEEL ALIVE!
YOU CAN HAVE A WAKE-UP PINCH EVERY MORNING FOR A SMALL MONTHLY FEE.
WITH PLAN "A," I PINCH YOU EVERY MORNING UNTIL YOU SCREAM "BLOODY MURDER." ONLY $39.95 A MONTH.
WITH PLAN "B," I MAKE YOU SCREAM "BLOODY MURDER" MONDAY THROUGH FRIDAY FOR ONLY $29.95 A MONTH.
WITH PLAN "C," YOU PAY ME NOT TO PINCH YOU.
I'LL TAKE IT.

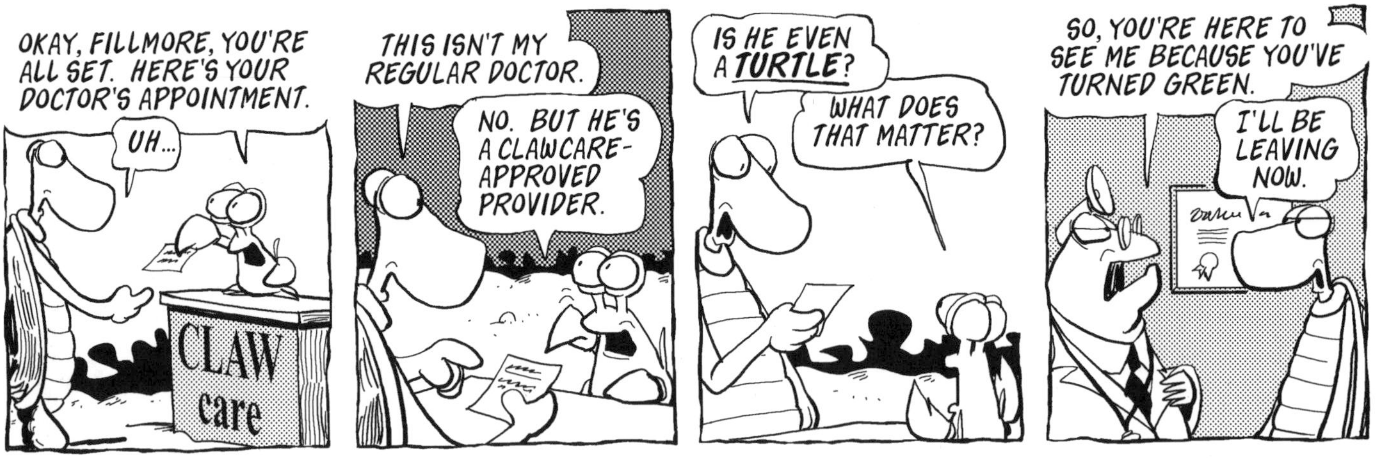
OKAY, FILLMORE, YOU'RE ALL SET. HERE'S YOUR DOCTOR'S APPOINTMENT.
UH...
CLAW care
THIS ISN'T MY REGULAR DOCTOR.
NO. BUT HE'S A CLAWCARE-APPROVED PROVIDER.
IS HE EVEN A TURTLE?
WHAT DOES THAT MATTER?
SO, YOU'RE HERE TO SEE ME BECAUSE YOU'VE TURNED GREEN.
I'LL BE LEAVING NOW.

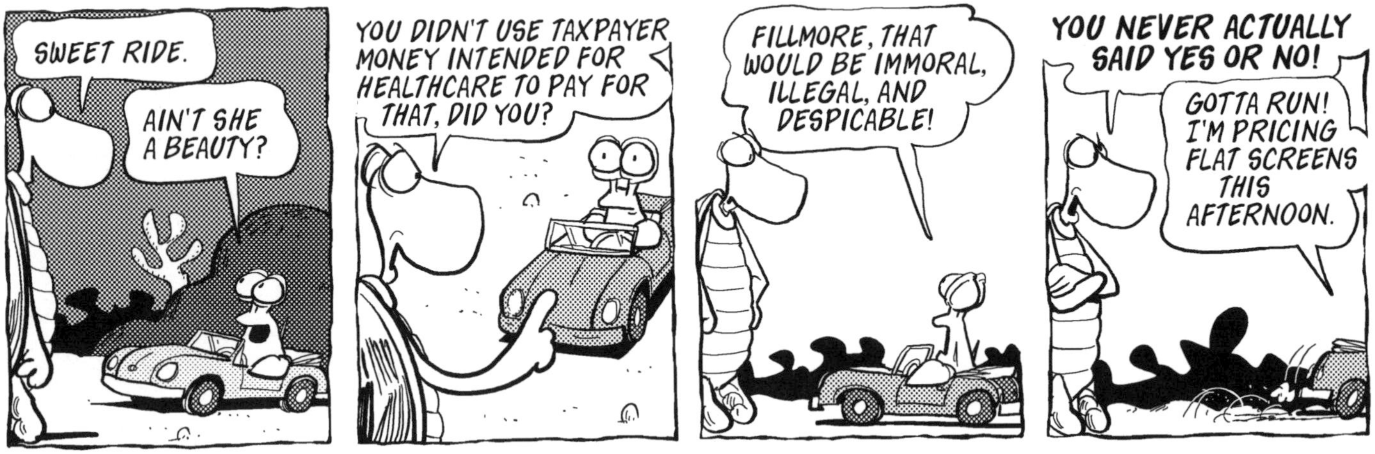
SWEET RIDE.
AIN'T SHE A BEAUTY?
YOU DIDN'T USE TAXPAYER MONEY INTENDED FOR HEALTHCARE TO PAY FOR THAT, DID YOU?
FILLMORE, THAT WOULD BE IMMORAL, ILLEGAL, AND DESPICABLE!
YOU NEVER ACTUALLY SAID YES OR NO!
GOTTA RUN! I'M PRICING FLAT SCREENS THIS AFTERNOON.

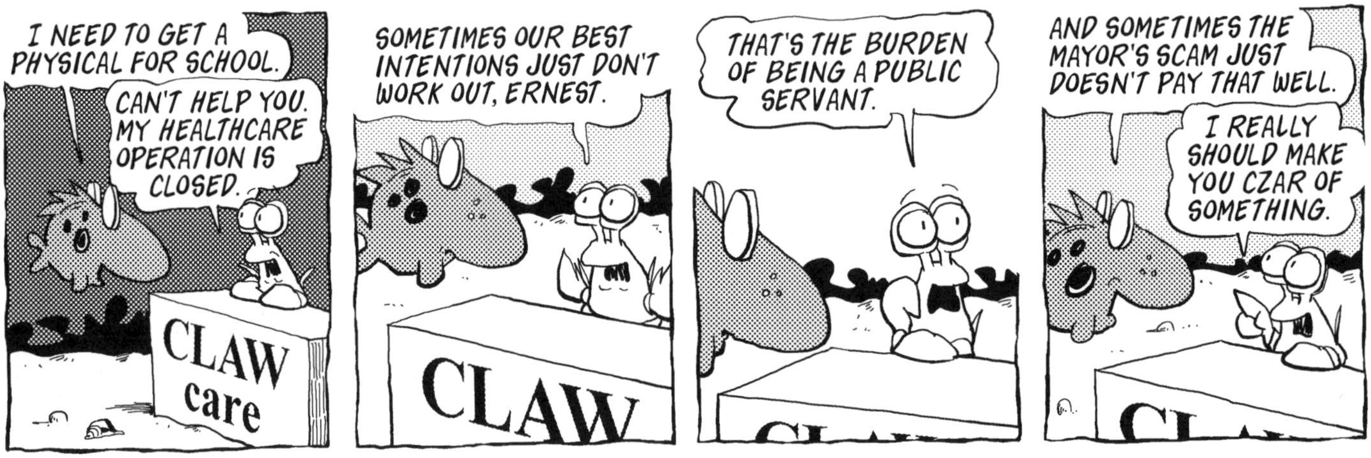
I NEED TO GET A PHYSICAL FOR SCHOOL.
CAN'T HELP YOU. MY HEALTHCARE OPERATION IS CLOSED.
CLAW care
SOMETIMES OUR BEST INTENTIONS JUST DON'T WORK OUT, ERNEST.
CLAW
THAT'S THE BURDEN OF BEING A PUBLIC SERVANT.
AND SOMETIMES THE MAYOR'S SCAM JUST DOESN'T PAY THAT WELL.
I REALLY SHOULD MAKE YOU CZAR OF SOMETHING.

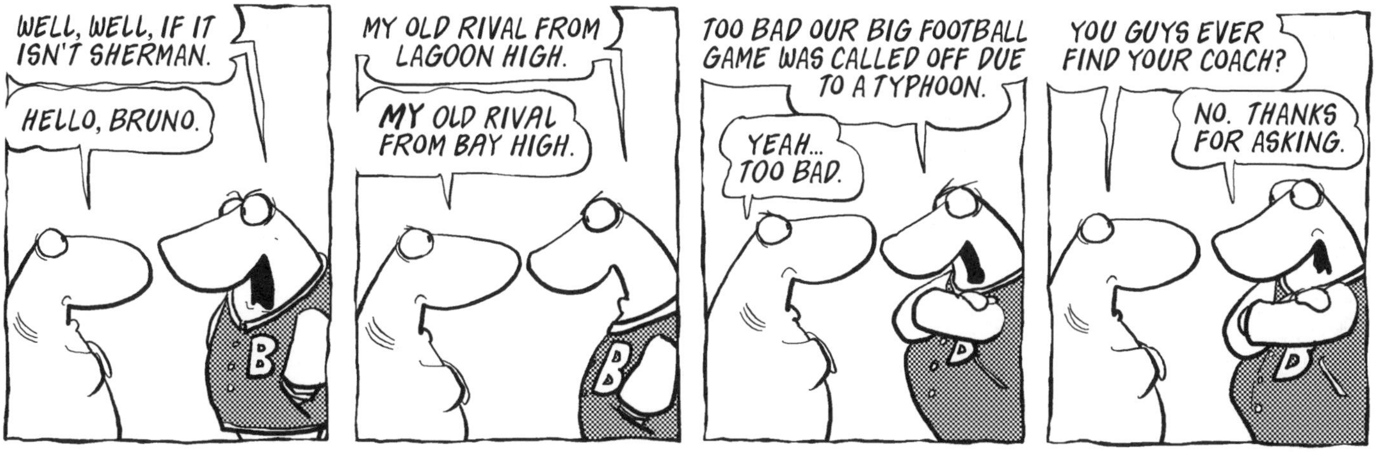
WELL, WELL, IF IT ISN'T SHERMAN.
HELLO, BRUNO.
MY OLD RIVAL FROM LAGOON HIGH.
MY OLD RIVAL FROM BAY HIGH.
TOO BAD OUR BIG FOOTBALL GAME WAS CALLED OFF DUE TO A TYPHOON.
YEAH... TOO BAD.
YOU GUYS EVER FIND YOUR COACH?
NO. THANKS FOR ASKING.

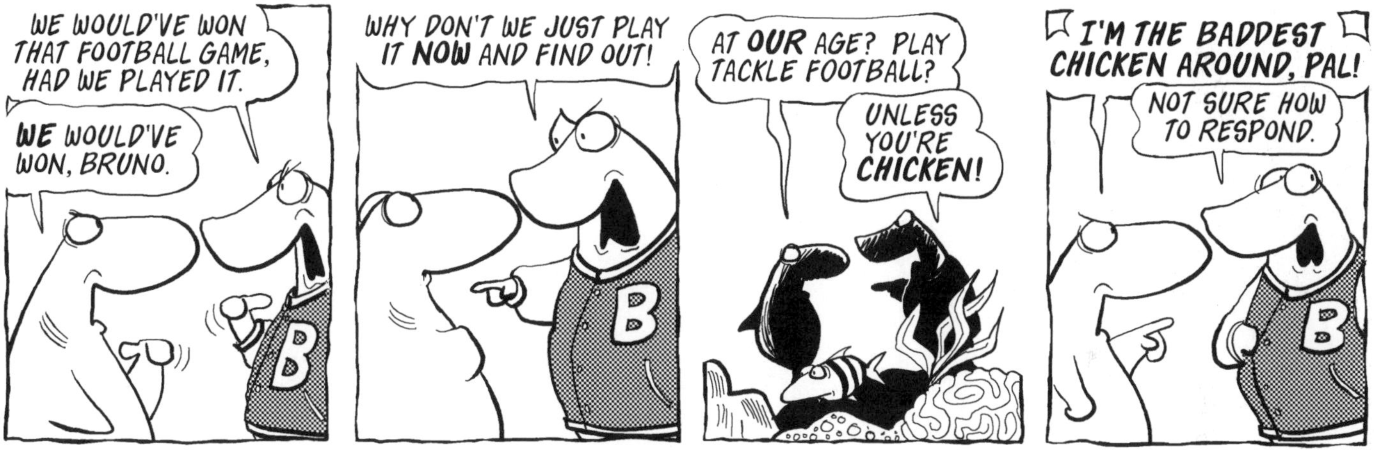
WE WOULD'VE WON THAT FOOTBALL GAME, HAD WE PLAYED IT.
WE WOULD'VE WON, BRUNO.
WHY DON'T WE JUST PLAY IT **NOW** AND FIND OUT!
AT **OUR** AGE? PLAY TACKLE FOOTBALL?
UNLESS YOU'RE **CHICKEN!**
I'M THE BADDEST CHICKEN AROUND, PAL!
NOT SURE HOW TO RESPOND.

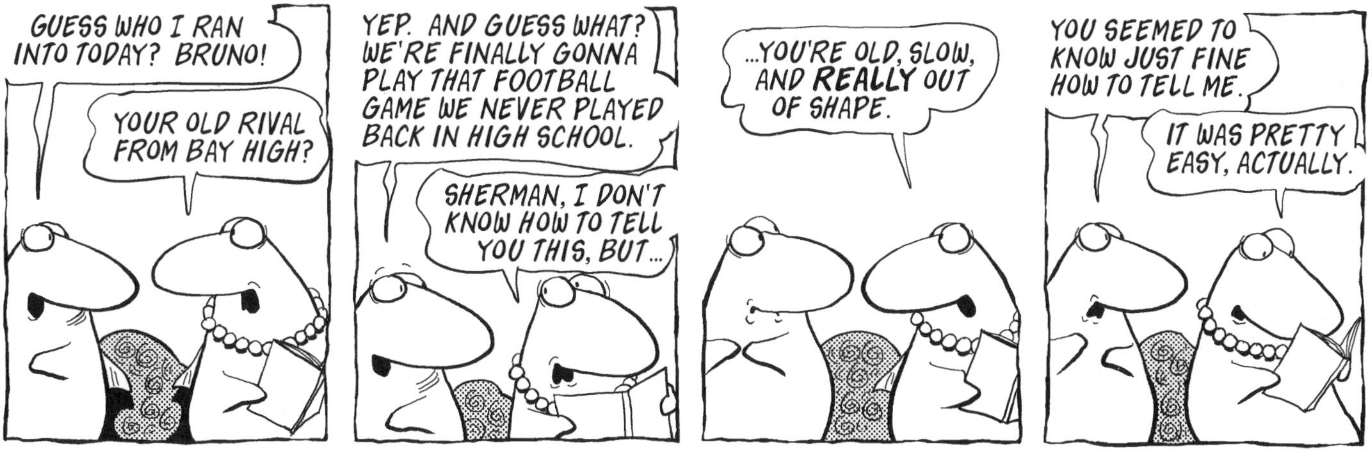
GUESS WHO I RAN INTO TODAY? BRUNO!
YOUR OLD RIVAL FROM BAY HIGH?
YEP. AND GUESS WHAT? WE'RE FINALLY GONNA PLAY THAT FOOTBALL GAME WE NEVER PLAYED BACK IN HIGH SCHOOL.
SHERMAN, I DON'T KNOW HOW TO TELL YOU THIS, BUT...
...YOU'RE OLD, SLOW, AND **REALLY** OUT OF SHAPE.
YOU SEEMED TO KNOW JUST FINE HOW TO TELL ME.
IT WAS PRETTY EASY, ACTUALLY.

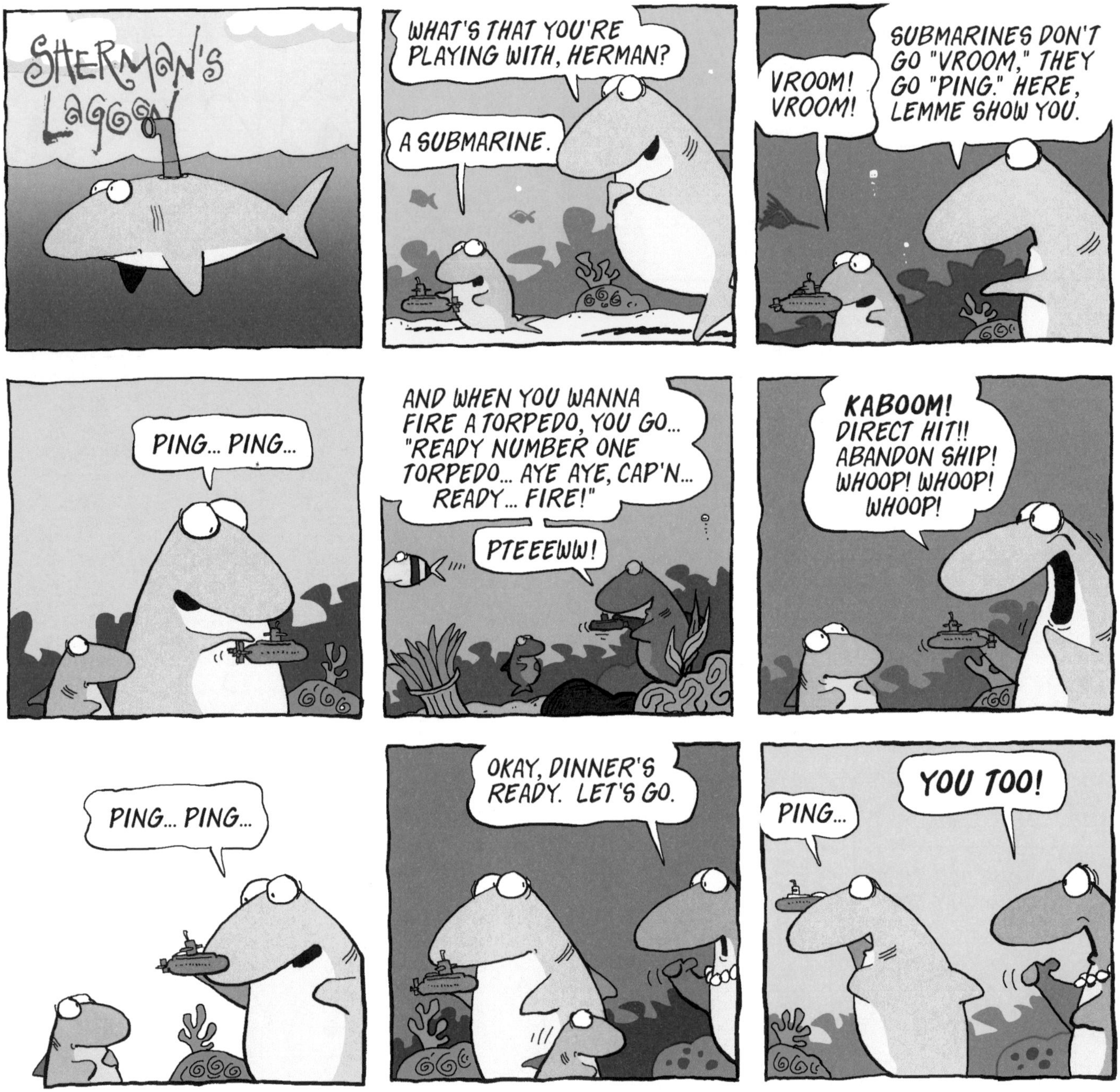
SHERMAN'S LAGOON
WHAT'S THAT YOU'RE PLAYING WITH, HERMAN?
A SUBMARINE.
VROOM! VROOM!
SUBMARINES DON'T GO "VROOM," THEY GO "PING." HERE, LEMME SHOW YOU.
PING... PING...
AND WHEN YOU WANNA FIRE A TORPEDO, YOU GO... "READY NUMBER ONE TORPEDO... AYE AYE, CAP'N... READY... FIRE!"
PTEEEWW!
KABOOM! DIRECT HIT!! ABANDON SHIP! WHOOP! WHOOP! WHOOP!
PING... PING...
OKAY, DINNER'S READY. LET'S GO.
PING...
YOU TOO!

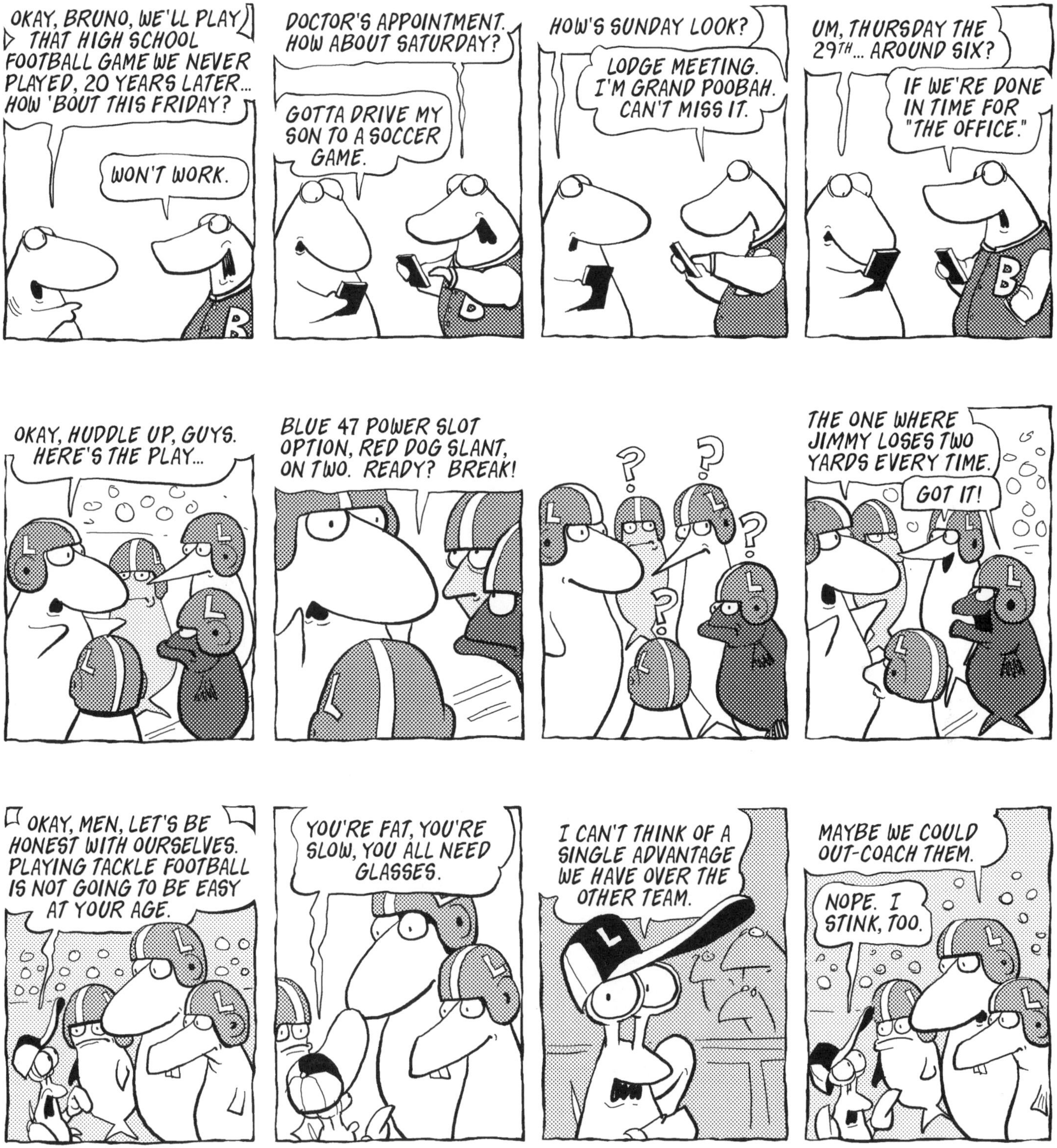
OKAY, BRUNO, WE'LL PLAY THAT HIGH SCHOOL FOOTBALL GAME WE NEVER PLAYED, 20 YEARS LATER... HOW 'BOUT THIS FRIDAY?
WON'T WORK.
DOCTOR'S APPOINTMENT. HOW ABOUT SATURDAY?
GOTTA DRIVE MY SON TO A SOCCER GAME.
HOW'S SUNDAY LOOK?
LODGE MEETING. I'M GRAND POOBAH. CAN'T MISS IT.
UM, THURSDAY THE 29TH... AROUND SIX?
IF WE'RE DONE IN TIME FOR "THE OFFICE."
OKAY, HUDDLE UP, GUYS. HERE'S THE PLAY...
BLUE 47 POWER SLOT OPTION, RED DOG SLANT, ON TWO. READY? BREAK!
?
?
?
?
THE ONE WHERE JIMMY LOSES TWO YARDS EVERY TIME.
GOT IT!
OKAY, MEN, LET'S BE HONEST WITH OURSELVES. PLAYING TACKLE FOOTBALL IS NOT GOING TO BE EASY AT YOUR AGE.
YOU'RE FAT, YOU'RE SLOW, YOU ALL NEED GLASSES.
I CAN'T THINK OF A SINGLE ADVANTAGE WE HAVE OVER THE OTHER TEAM.
MAYBE WE COULD OUT-COACH THEM.
NOPE. I STINK, TOO.

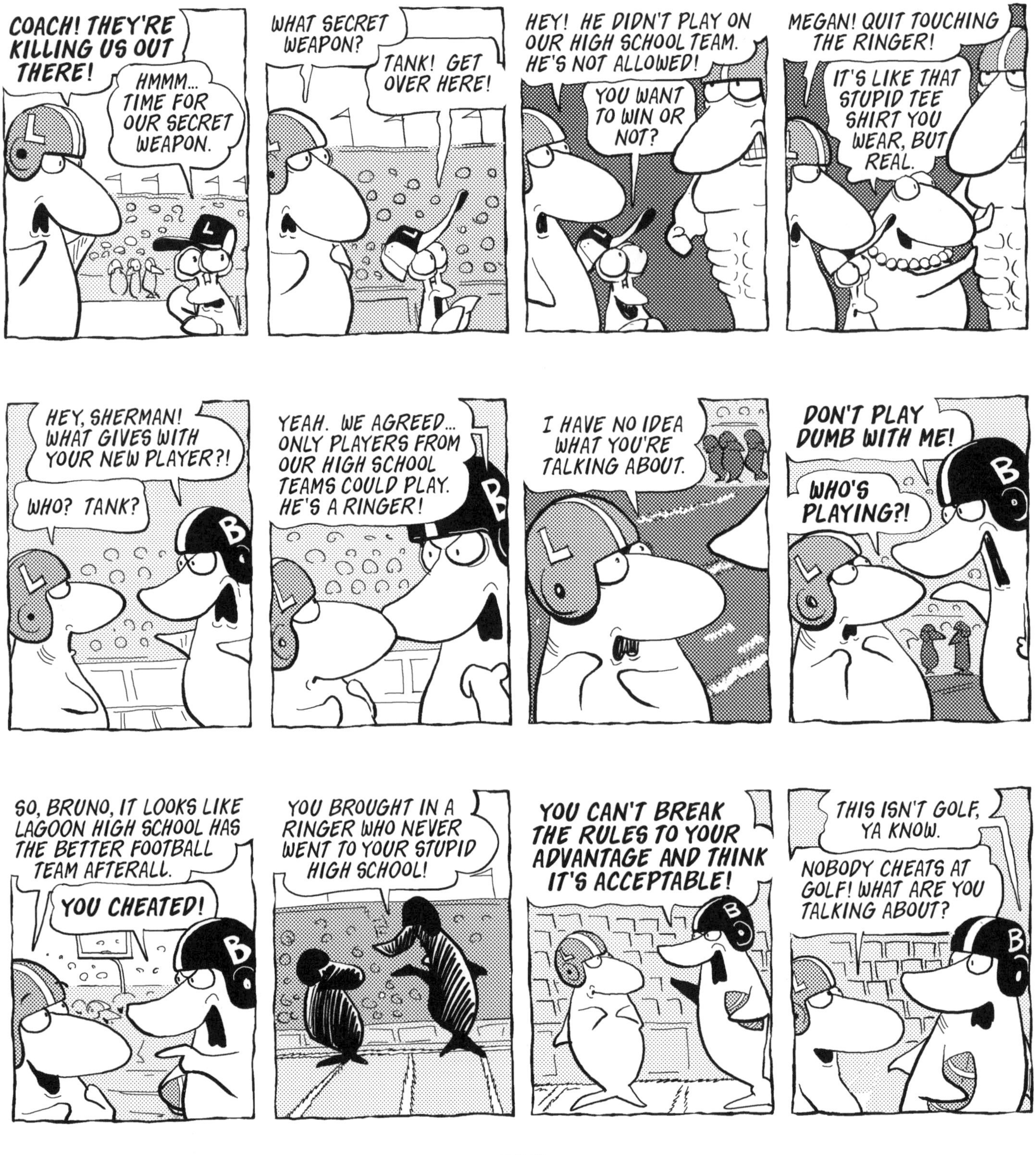
COACH! THEY'RE KILLING US OUT THERE!
HMMM... TIME FOR OUR SECRET WEAPON.
WHAT SECRET WEAPON?
TANK! GET OVER HERE!
HEY! HE DIDN'T PLAY ON OUR HIGH SCHOOL TEAM. HE'S NOT ALLOWED!
YOU WANT TO WIN OR NOT?
MEGAN! QUIT TOUCHING THE RINGER!
IT'S LIKE THAT STUPID TEE SHIRT YOU WEAR, BUT REAL.
HEY, SHERMAN! WHAT GIVES WITH YOUR NEW PLAYER?!
WHO? TANK?
YEAH. WE AGREED... ONLY PLAYERS FROM OUR HIGH SCHOOL TEAMS COULD PLAY. HE'S A RINGER!
I HAVE NO IDEA WHAT YOU'RE TALKING ABOUT.
DON'T PLAY DUMB WITH ME!
WHO'S PLAYING?!
SO, BRUNO, IT LOOKS LIKE LAGOON HIGH SCHOOL HAS THE BETTER FOOTBALL TEAM AFTERALL.
YOU CHEATED!
YOU BROUGHT IN A RINGER WHO NEVER WENT TO YOUR STUPID HIGH SCHOOL!
YOU CAN'T BREAK THE RULES TO YOUR ADVANTAGE AND THINK IT'S ACCEPTABLE!
THIS ISN'T GOLF, YA KNOW.
NOBODY CHEATS AT GOLF! WHAT ARE YOU TALKING ABOUT?

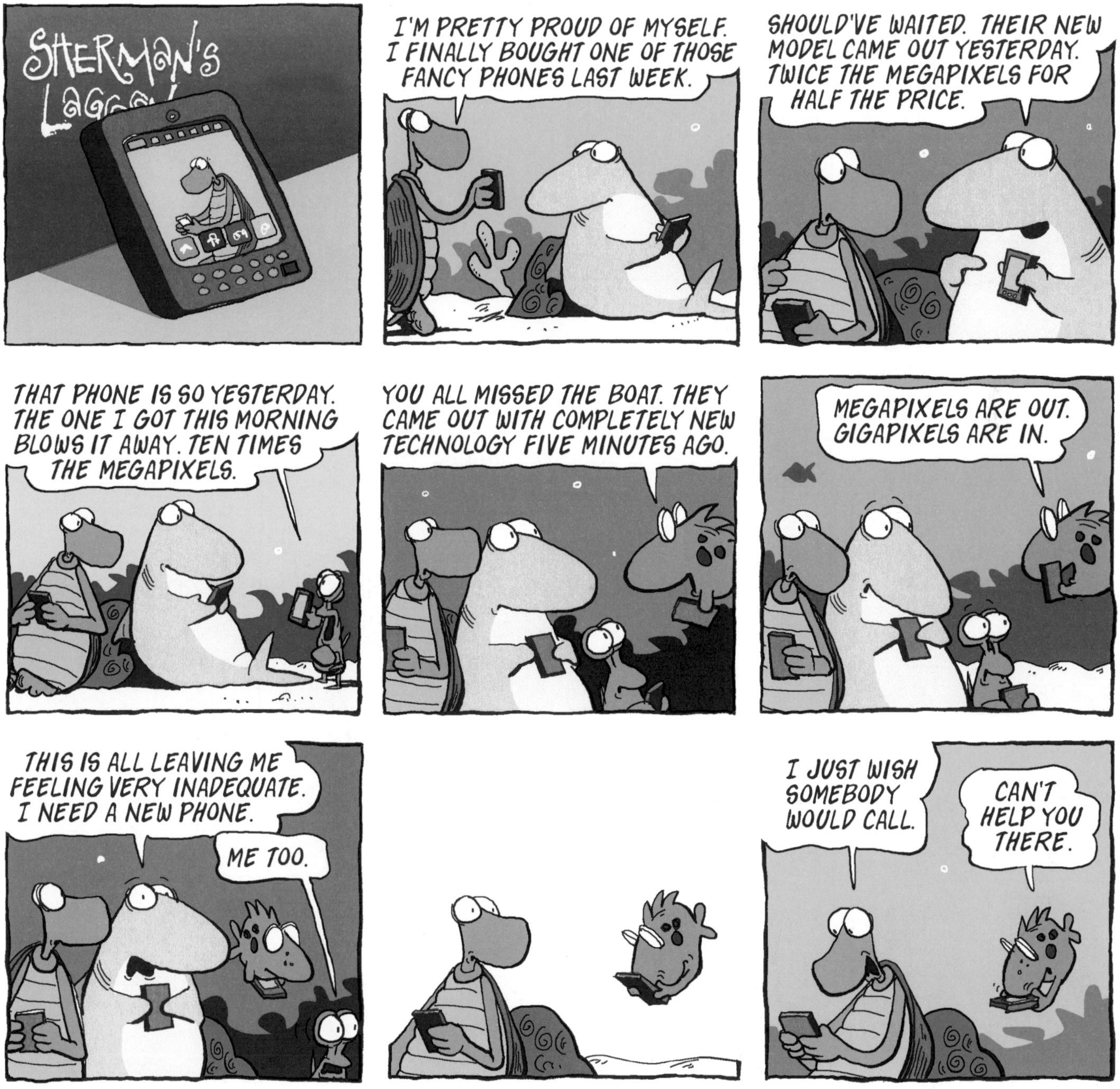
SHERMAN'S LAGOON
I'M PRETTY PROUD OF MYSELF. I FINALLY BOUGHT ONE OF THOSE FANCY PHONES LAST WEEK.
SHOULD'VE WAITED. THEIR NEW MODEL CAME OUT YESTERDAY. TWICE THE MEGAPIXELS FOR HALF THE PRICE.
THAT PHONE IS SO YESTERDAY. THE ONE I GOT THIS MORNING BLOWS IT AWAY. TEN TIMES THE MEGAPIXELS.
YOU ALL MISSED THE BOAT. THEY CAME OUT WITH COMPLETELY NEW TECHNOLOGY FIVE MINUTES AGO.
MEGAPIXELS ARE OUT. GIGAPIXELS ARE IN.
THIS IS ALL LEAVING ME FEELING VERY INADEQUATE. I NEED A NEW PHONE.
ME TOO.
I JUST WISH SOMEBODY WOULD CALL.
CAN'T HELP YOU THERE.

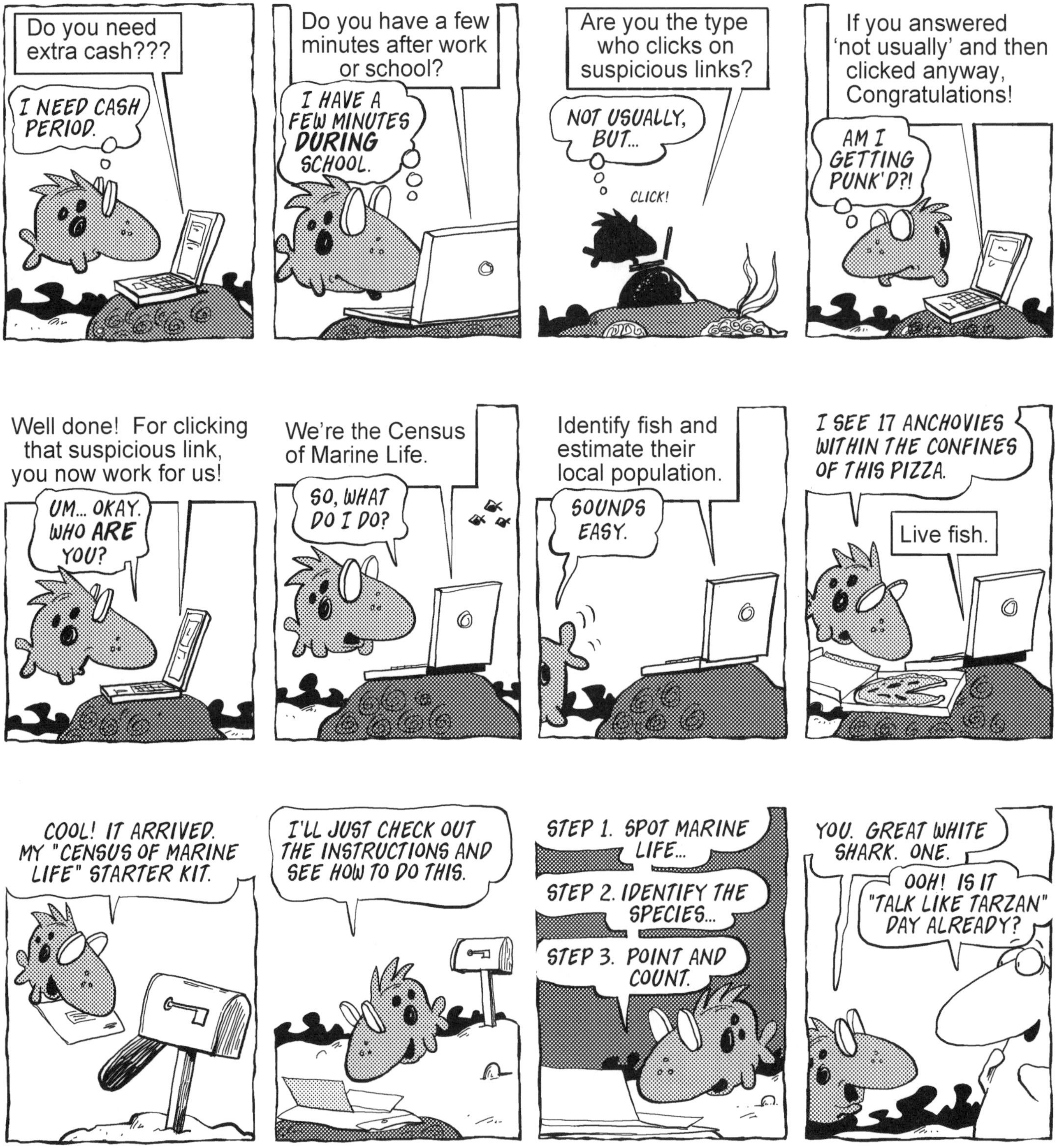
Do you need extra cash???
I NEED CASH PERIOD.
Do you have a few minutes after work or school?
I HAVE A FEW MINUTES DURING SCHOOL.
Are you the type who clicks on suspicious links?
NOT USUALLY, BUT...
CLICK!
If you answered 'not usually' and then clicked anyway, Congratulations!
AM I GETTING PUNK'D?!
Well done! For clicking that suspicious link, you now work for us!
UM... OKAY. WHO ARE YOU?
We're the Census of Marine Life.
SO, WHAT DO I DO?
Identify fish and estimate their local population.
SOUNDS EASY.
I SEE 17 ANCHOVIES WITHIN THE CONFINES OF THIS PIZZA.
Live fish.
COOL! IT ARRIVED. MY "CENSUS OF MARINE LIFE" STARTER KIT.
I'LL JUST CHECK OUT THE INSTRUCTIONS AND SEE HOW TO DO THIS.
STEP 1. SPOT MARINE LIFE...
STEP 2. IDENTIFY THE SPECIES...
STEP 3. POINT AND COUNT.
YOU. GREAT WHITE SHARK. ONE.
OOH! IS IT "TALK LIKE TARZAN" DAY ALREADY?

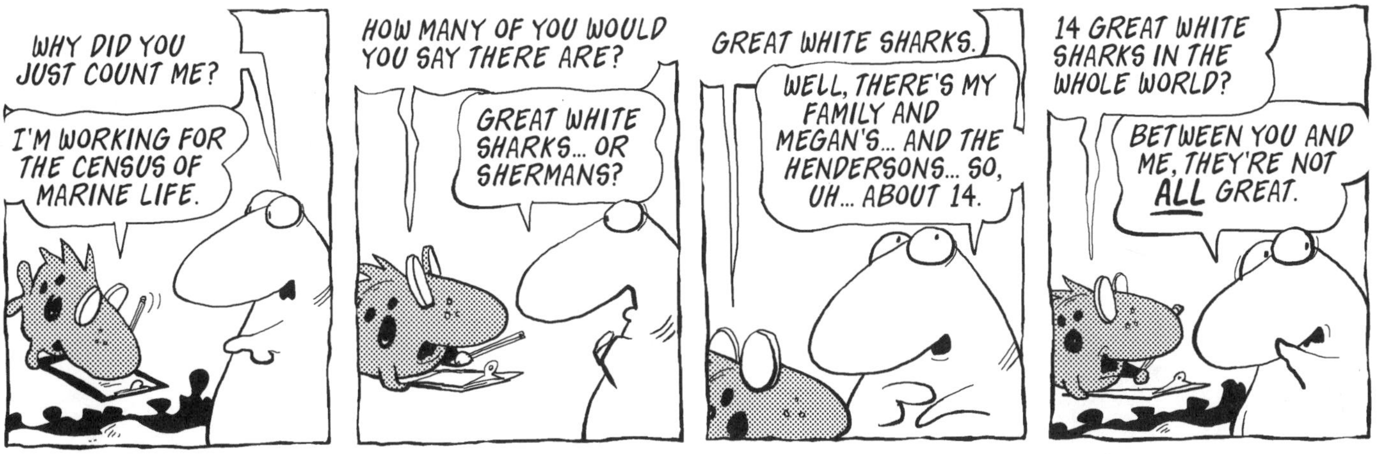
WHY DID YOU JUST COUNT ME?
I'M WORKING FOR THE CENSUS OF MARINE LIFE.
HOW MANY OF YOU WOULD YOU SAY THERE ARE?
GREAT WHITE SHARKS... OR SHERMANS?
GREAT WHITE SHARKS.
WELL, THERE'S MY FAMILY AND MEGAN'S... AND THE HENDERSONS... SO, UH... ABOUT 14.
14 GREAT WHITE SHARKS IN THE WHOLE WORLD?
BETWEEN YOU AND ME, THEY'RE NOT ALL GREAT.

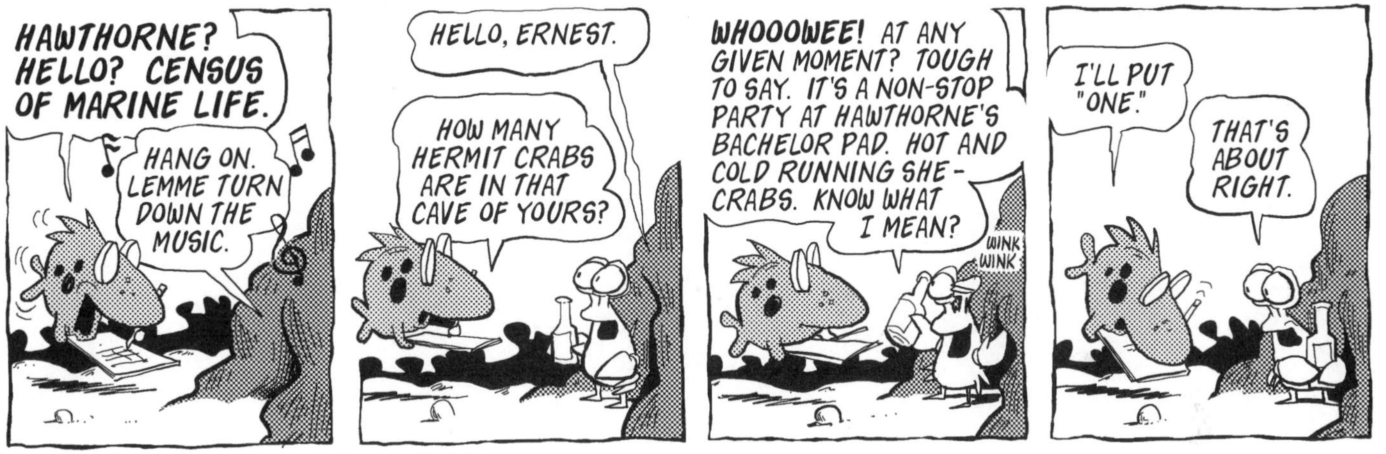
HAWTHORNE? HELLO? CENSUS OF MARINE LIFE.
HANG ON. LEMME TURN DOWN THE MUSIC.
HELLO, ERNEST.
HOW MANY HERMIT CRABS ARE IN THAT CAVE OF YOURS?
WHOOOWEE! AT ANY GIVEN MOMENT? TOUGH TO SAY. IT'S A NON-STOP PARTY AT HAWTHORNE'S BACHELOR PAD. HOT AND COLD RUNNING SHE-CRABS. KNOW WHAT I MEAN?
WINK WINK
I'LL PUT "ONE."
THAT'S ABOUT RIGHT.

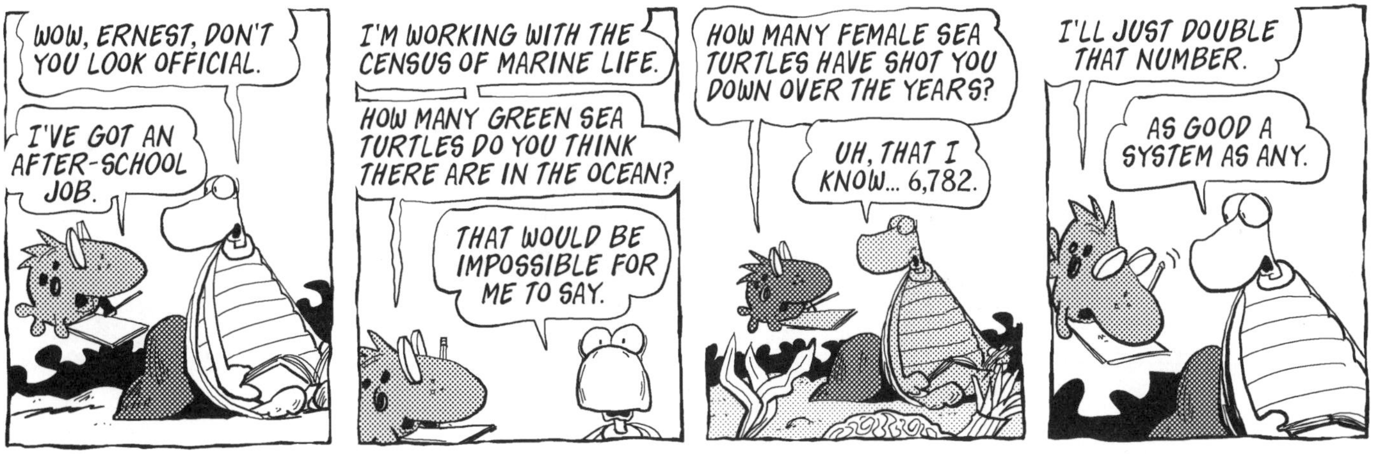
WOW, ERNEST, DON'T YOU LOOK OFFICIAL.
I'VE GOT AN AFTER-SCHOOL JOB.
I'M WORKING WITH THE CENSUS OF MARINE LIFE.
HOW MANY GREEN SEA TURTLES DO YOU THINK THERE ARE IN THE OCEAN?
THAT WOULD BE IMPOSSIBLE FOR ME TO SAY.
HOW MANY FEMALE SEA TURTLES HAVE SHOT YOU DOWN OVER THE YEARS?
UH, THAT I KNOW... 6,782.
I'LL JUST DOUBLE THAT NUMBER.
AS GOOD A SYSTEM AS ANY.

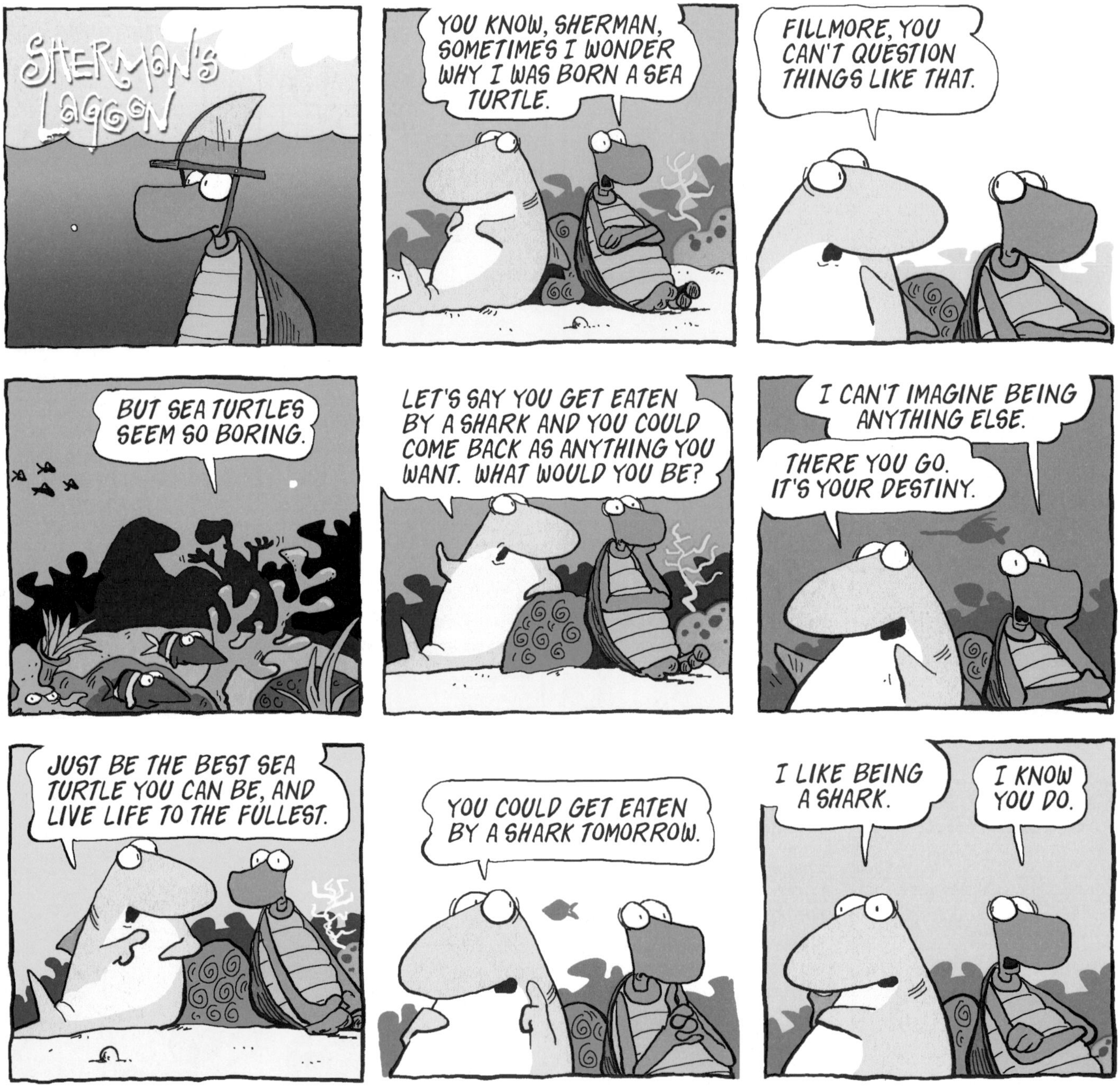
Sherman's Lagoon
YOU KNOW, SHERMAN, SOMETIMES I WONDER WHY I WAS BORN A SEA TURTLE.
FILLMORE, YOU CAN'T QUESTION THINGS LIKE THAT.
BUT SEA TURTLES SEEM SO BORING.
LET'S SAY YOU GET EATEN BY A SHARK AND YOU COULD COME BACK AS ANYTHING YOU WANT. WHAT WOULD YOU BE?
I CAN'T IMAGINE BEING ANYTHING ELSE.
THERE YOU GO. IT'S YOUR DESTINY.
JUST BE THE BEST SEA TURTLE YOU CAN BE, AND LIVE LIFE TO THE FULLEST.
YOU COULD GET EATEN BY A SHARK TOMORROW.
I LIKE BEING A SHARK.
I KNOW YOU DO.

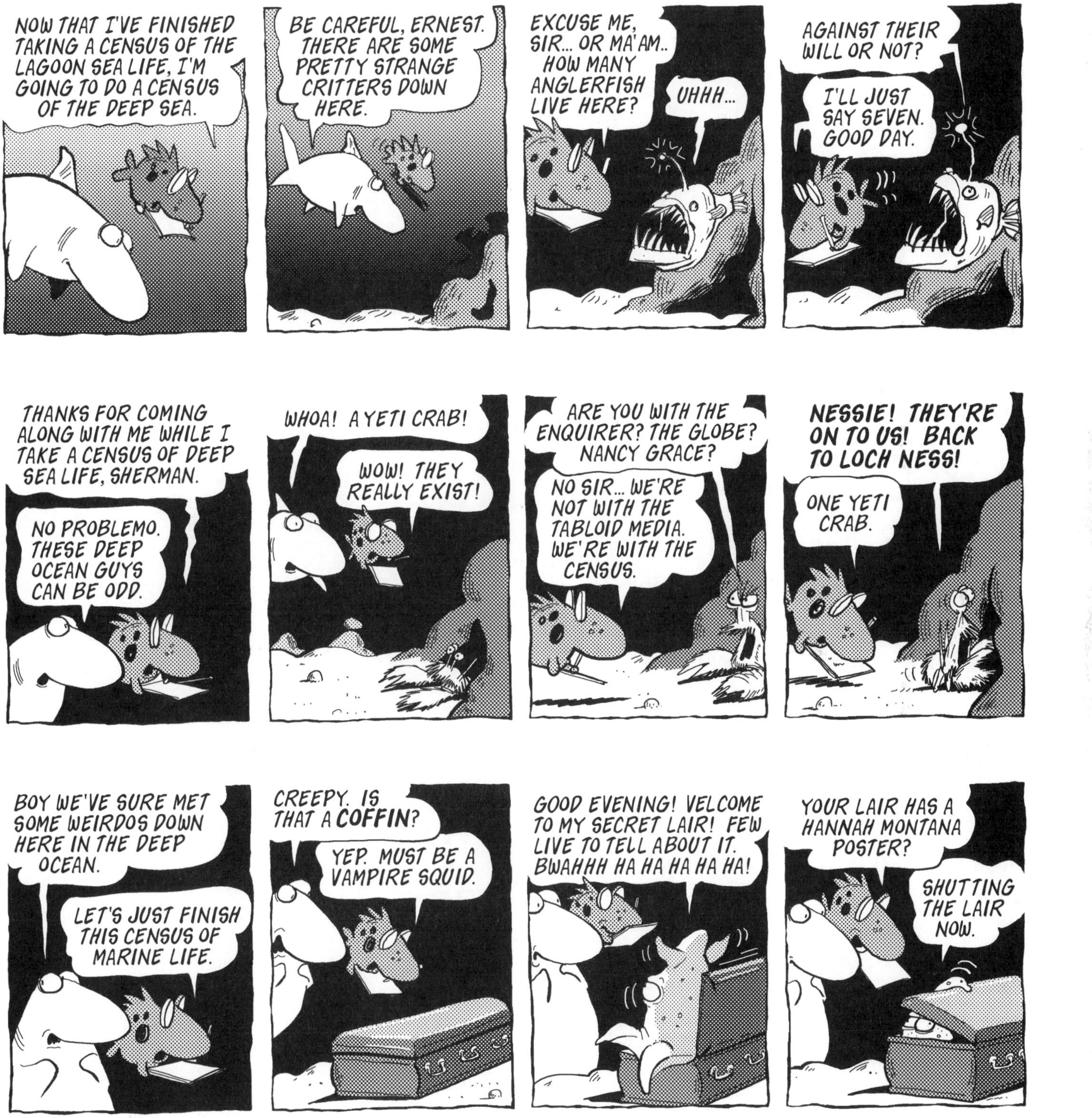
NOW THAT I'VE FINISHED TAKING A CENSUS OF THE LAGOON SEA LIFE, I'M GOING TO DO A CENSUS OF THE DEEP SEA.
BE CAREFUL, ERNEST. THERE ARE SOME PRETTY STRANGE CRITTERS DOWN HERE.
EXCUSE ME, SIR... OR MA'AM.. HOW MANY ANGLERFISH LIVE HERE?
UHHH...
AGAINST THEIR WILL OR NOT?
I'LL JUST SAY SEVEN. GOOD DAY.
THANKS FOR COMING ALONG WITH ME WHILE I TAKE A CENSUS OF DEEP SEA LIFE, SHERMAN.
NO PROBLEMO. THESE DEEP OCEAN GUYS CAN BE ODD.
WHOA! A YETI CRAB!
WOW! THEY REALLY EXIST!
ARE YOU WITH THE ENQUIRER? THE GLOBE? NANCY GRACE?
NO SIR... WE'RE NOT WITH THE TABLOID MEDIA. WE'RE WITH THE CENSUS.
NESSIE! THEY'RE ON TO US! BACK TO LOCH NESS!
ONE YETI CRAB.
BOY WE'VE SURE MET SOME WEIRDOS DOWN HERE IN THE DEEP OCEAN.
LET'S JUST FINISH THIS CENSUS OF MARINE LIFE.
CREEPY. IS THAT A COFFIN?
YEP. MUST BE A VAMPIRE SQUID.
GOOD EVENING! VELCOME TO MY SECRET LAIR! FEW LIVE TO TELL ABOUT IT. BWAHHH HA HA HA HA HA!
YOUR LAIR HAS A HANNAH MONTANA POSTER?
SHUTTING THE LAIR NOW.

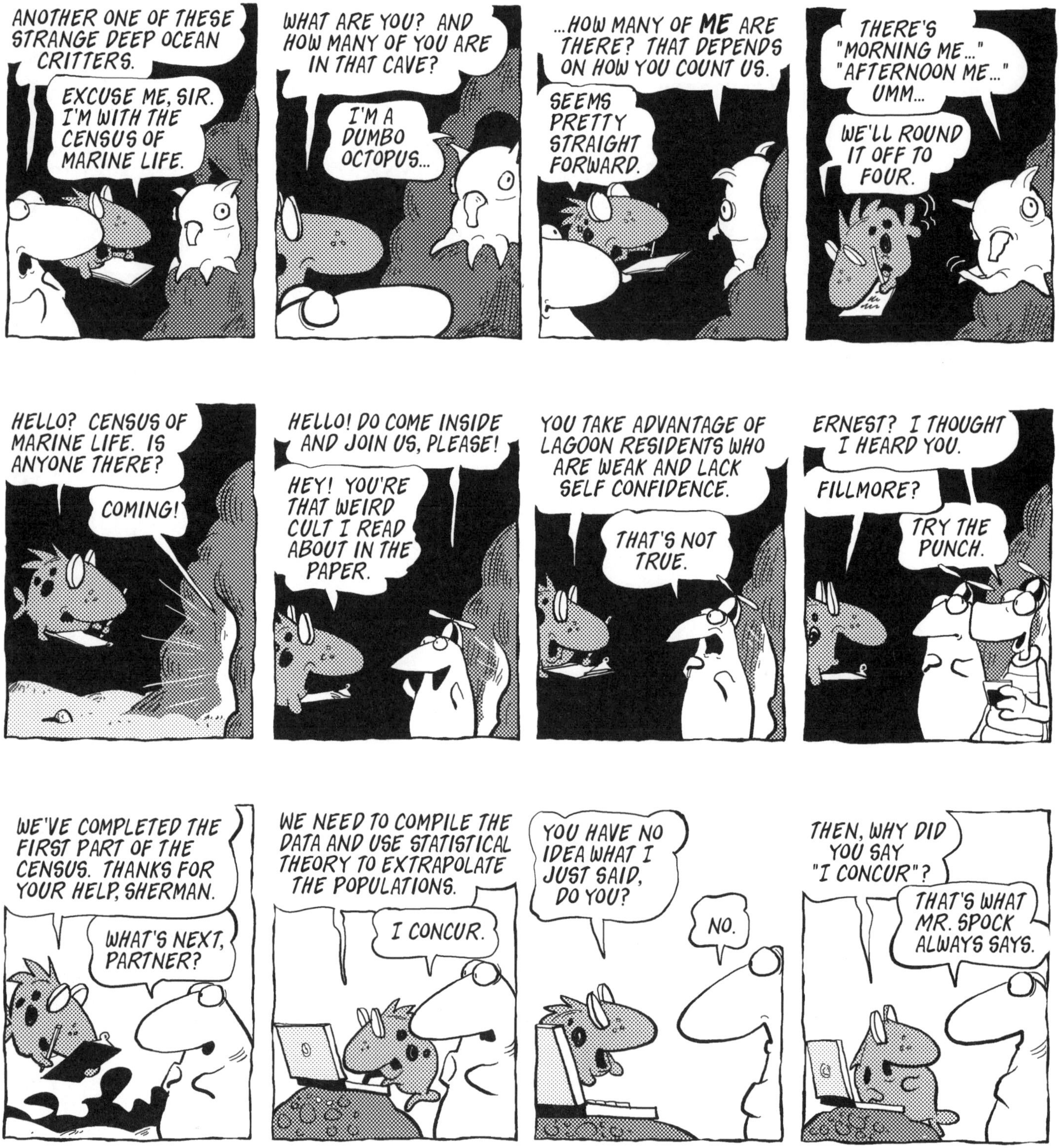
ANOTHER ONE OF THESE STRANGE DEEP OCEAN CRITTERS.
EXCUSE ME, SIR. I'M WITH THE CENSUS OF MARINE LIFE.
WHAT ARE YOU? AND HOW MANY OF YOU ARE IN THAT CAVE?
I'M A DUMBO OCTOPUS...
...HOW MANY OF **ME** ARE THERE? THAT DEPENDS ON HOW YOU COUNT US.
SEEMS PRETTY STRAIGHT FORWARD.
THERE'S "MORNING ME..." "AFTERNOON ME..." UMM...
WE'LL ROUND IT OFF TO FOUR.
HELLO? CENSUS OF MARINE LIFE. IS ANYONE THERE?
COMING!
HELLO! DO COME INSIDE AND JOIN US, PLEASE!
HEY! YOU'RE THAT WEIRD CULT I READ ABOUT IN THE PAPER.
YOU TAKE ADVANTAGE OF LAGOON RESIDENTS WHO ARE WEAK AND LACK SELF CONFIDENCE.
THAT'S NOT TRUE.
ERNEST? I THOUGHT I HEARD YOU.
FILLMORE?
TRY THE PUNCH.
WE'VE COMPLETED THE FIRST PART OF THE CENSUS. THANKS FOR YOUR HELP, SHERMAN.
WHAT'S NEXT, PARTNER?
WE NEED TO COMPILE THE DATA AND USE STATISTICAL THEORY TO EXTRAPOLATE THE POPULATIONS.
I CONCUR.
YOU HAVE NO IDEA WHAT I JUST SAID, DO YOU?
NO.
THEN, WHY DID YOU SAY "I CONCUR"?
THAT'S WHAT MR. SPOCK ALWAYS SAYS.

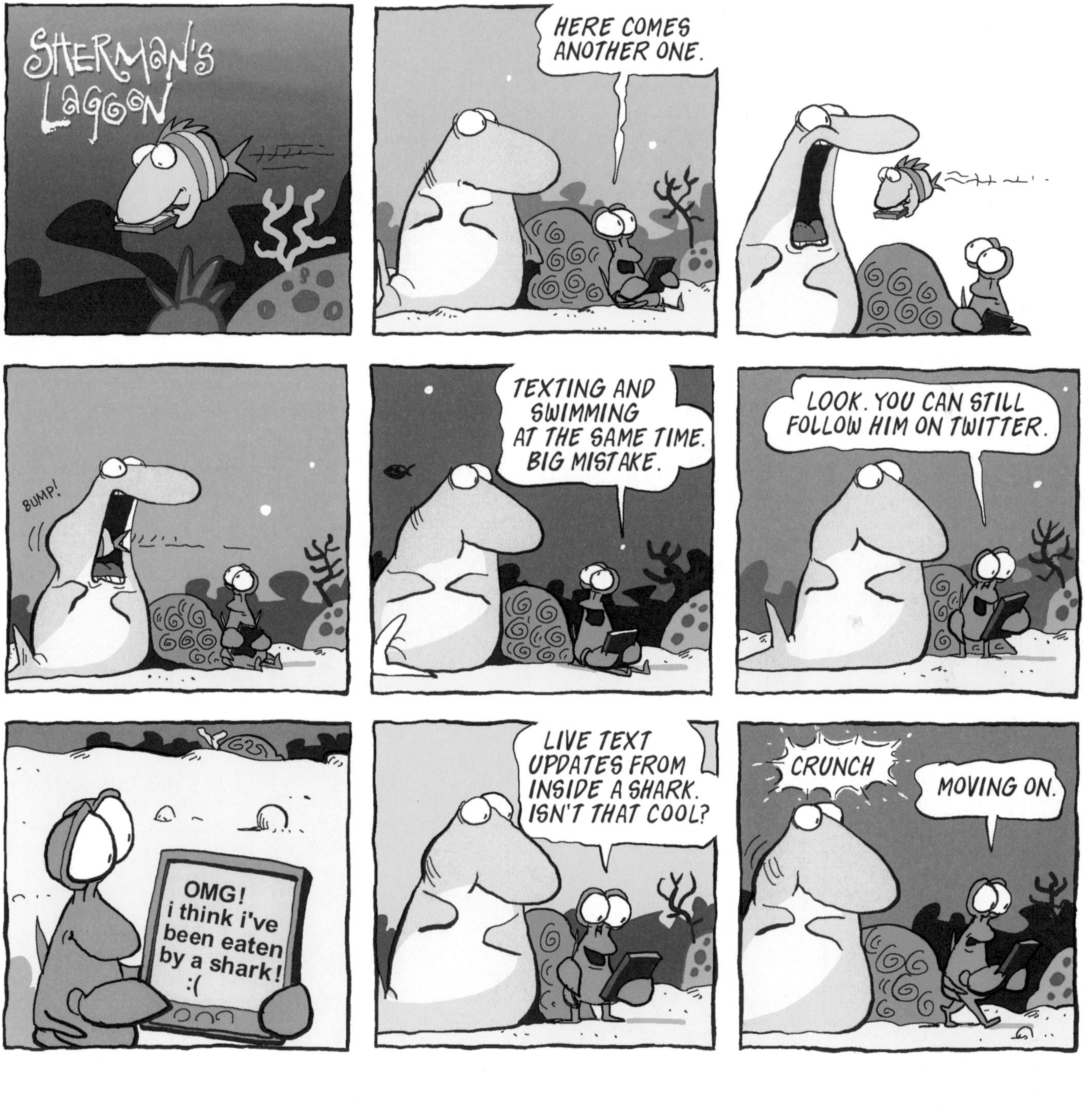
SHERMAN'S LAGOON
HERE COMES ANOTHER ONE.
BUMP!
TEXTING AND SWIMMING AT THE SAME TIME. BIG MISTAKE.
LOOK. YOU CAN STILL FOLLOW HIM ON TWITTER.
OMG! i think i've been eaten by a shark! :(
LIVE TEXT UPDATES FROM INSIDE A SHARK. ISN'T THAT COOL?
CRUNCH
MOVING ON.

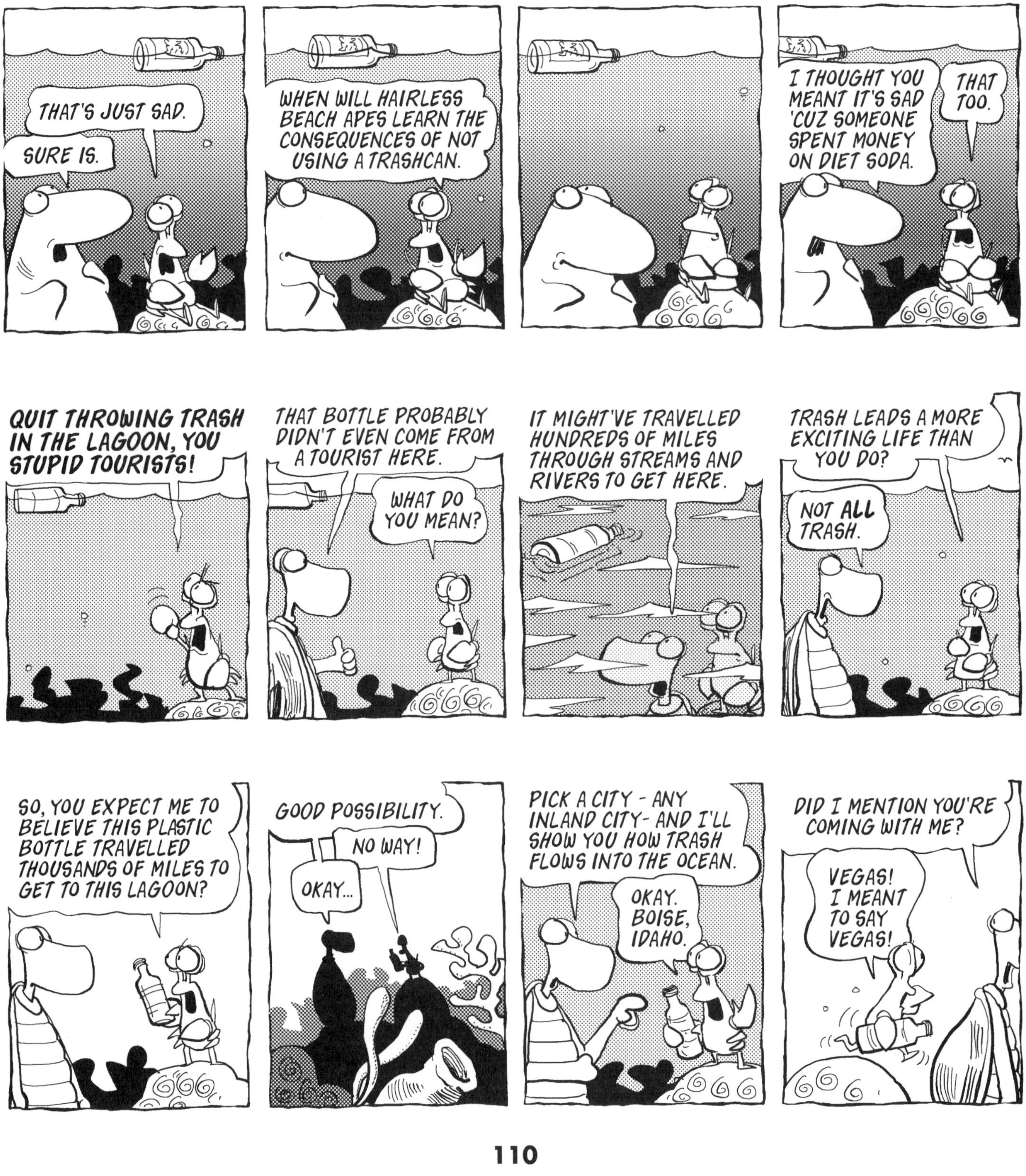
THAT'S JUST SAD.
SURE IS.
WHEN WILL HAIRLESS BEACH APES LEARN THE CONSEQUENCES OF NOT USING A TRASHCAN.
I THOUGHT YOU MEANT IT'S SAD 'CUZ SOMEONE SPENT MONEY ON DIET SODA.
THAT TOO.
QUIT THROWING TRASH IN THE LAGOON, YOU STUPID TOURISTS!
THAT BOTTLE PROBABLY DIDN'T EVEN COME FROM A TOURIST HERE.
WHAT DO YOU MEAN?
IT MIGHT'VE TRAVELLED HUNDREDS OF MILES THROUGH STREAMS AND RIVERS TO GET HERE.
TRASH LEADS A MORE EXCITING LIFE THAN YOU DO?
NOT ALL TRASH.
SO, YOU EXPECT ME TO BELIEVE THIS PLASTIC BOTTLE TRAVELLED THOUSANDS OF MILES TO GET TO THIS LAGOON?
GOOD POSSIBILITY.
NO WAY!
OKAY...
PICK A CITY - ANY INLAND CITY- AND I'LL SHOW YOU HOW TRASH FLOWS INTO THE OCEAN.
OKAY. BOISE, IDAHO.
DID I MENTION YOU'RE COMING WITH ME?
VEGAS! I MEANT TO SAY VEGAS!

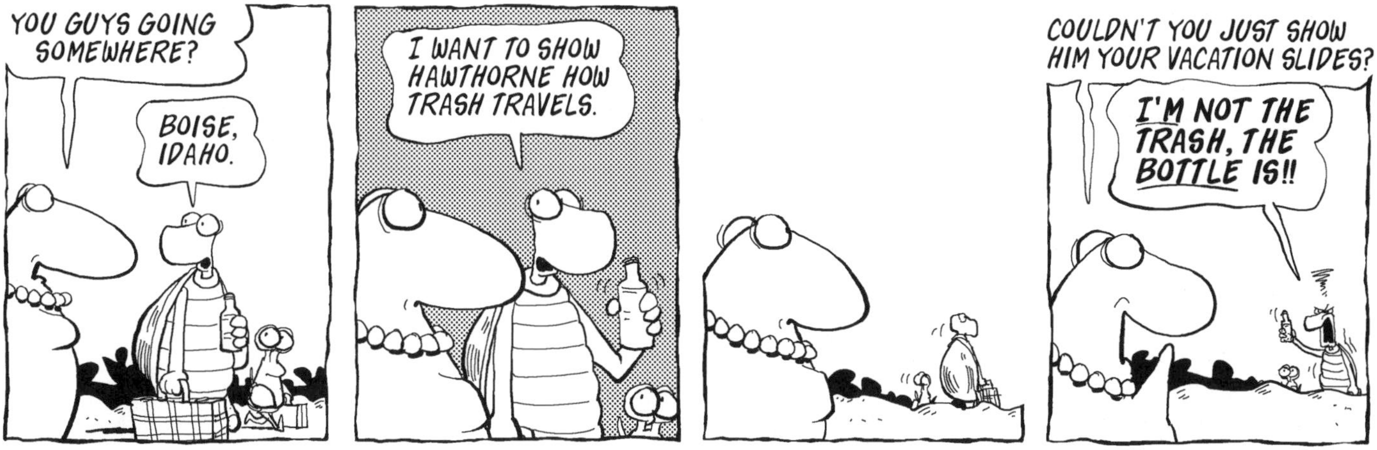
YOU GUYS GOING SOMEWHERE?
BOISE, IDAHO.
I WANT TO SHOW HAWTHORNE HOW TRASH TRAVELS.
COULDN'T YOU JUST SHOW HIM YOUR VACATION SLIDES?
I'M NOT THE TRASH, THE BOTTLE IS!!

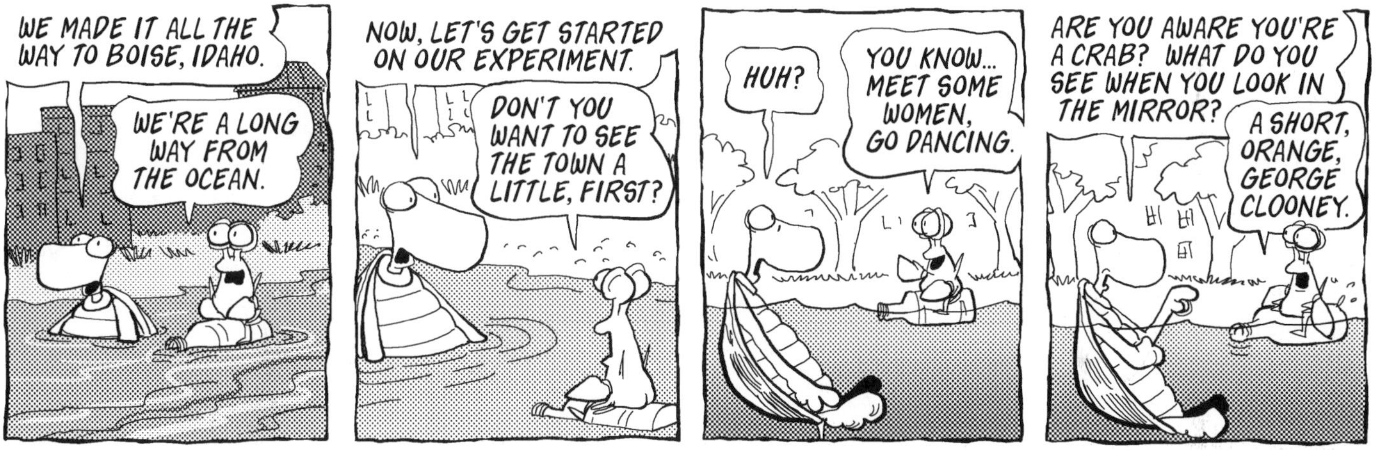
WE MADE IT ALL THE WAY TO BOISE, IDAHO.
WE'RE A LONG WAY FROM THE OCEAN.
NOW, LET'S GET STARTED ON OUR EXPERIMENT.
DON'T YOU WANT TO SEE THE TOWN A LITTLE, FIRST?
HUH?
YOU KNOW... MEET SOME WOMEN, GO DANCING.
ARE YOU AWARE YOU'RE A CRAB? WHAT DO YOU SEE WHEN YOU LOOK IN THE MIRROR?
A SHORT, ORANGE, GEORGE CLOONEY.

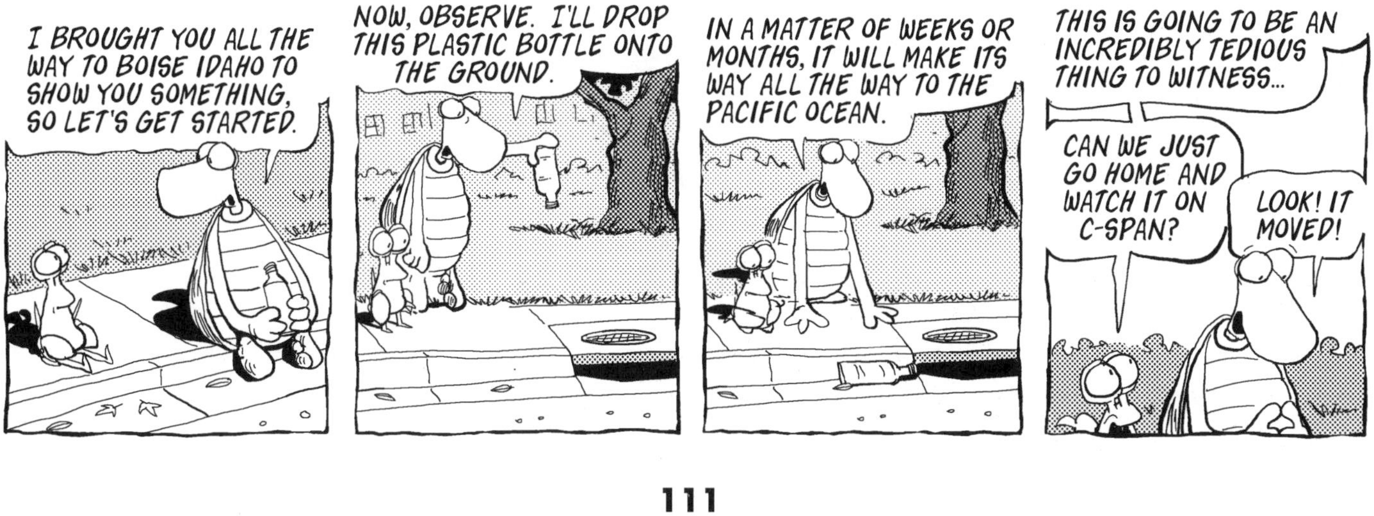
I BROUGHT YOU ALL THE WAY TO BOISE IDAHO TO SHOW YOU SOMETHING, SO LET'S GET STARTED.
NOW, OBSERVE. I'LL DROP THIS PLASTIC BOTTLE ONTO THE GROUND.
IN A MATTER OF WEEKS OR MONTHS, IT WILL MAKE ITS WAY ALL THE WAY TO THE PACIFIC OCEAN.
THIS IS GOING TO BE AN INCREDIBLY TEDIOUS THING TO WITNESS...
CAN WE JUST GO HOME AND WATCH IT ON C-SPAN?
LOOK! IT MOVED!

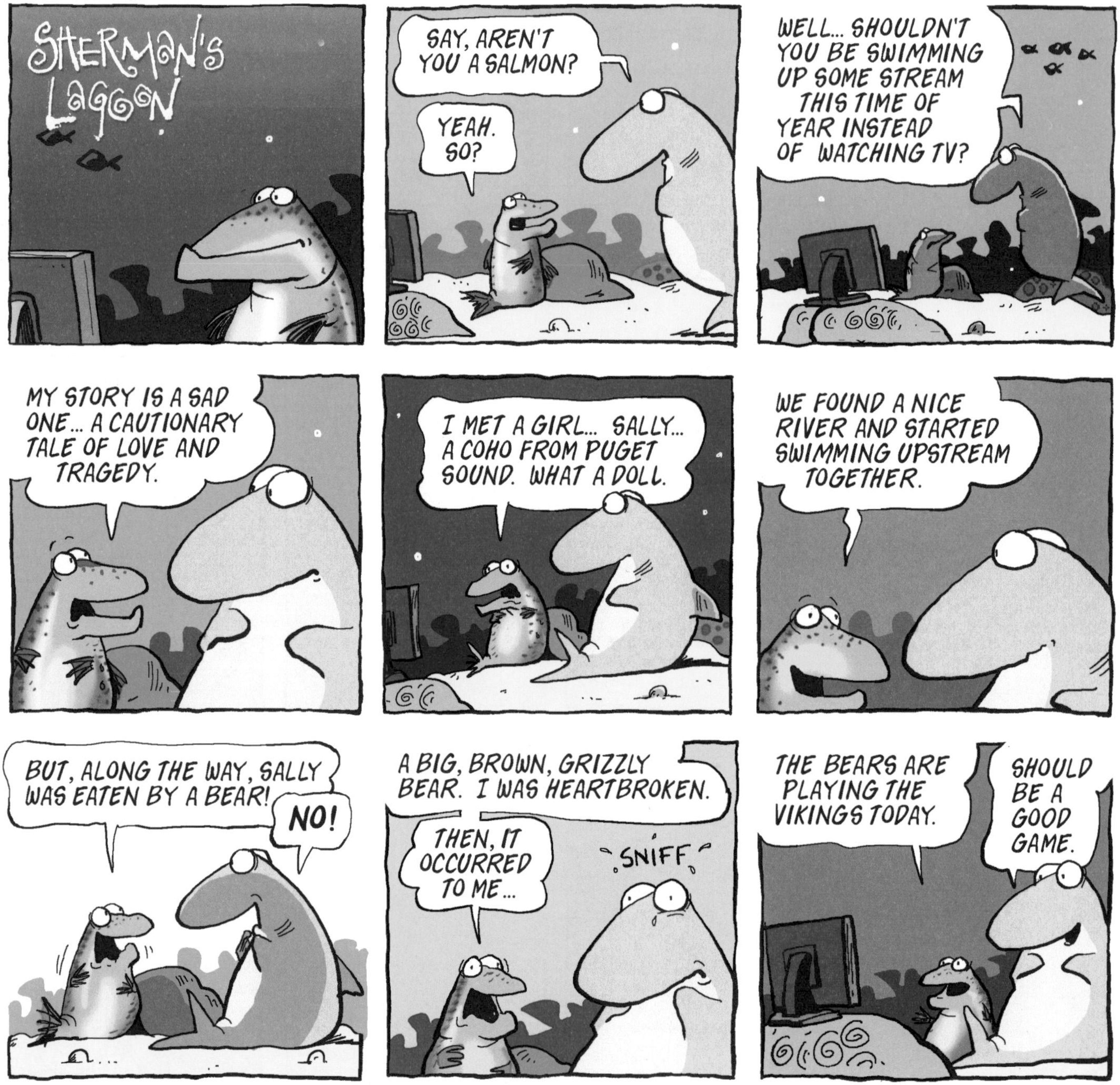
SHERMAN'S LAGOON
SAY, AREN'T YOU A SALMON?
YEAH. SO?
WELL... SHOULDN'T YOU BE SWIMMING UP SOME STREAM THIS TIME OF YEAR INSTEAD OF WATCHING TV?
MY STORY IS A SAD ONE... A CAUTIONARY TALE OF LOVE AND TRAGEDY.
I MET A GIRL... SALLY... A COHO FROM PUGET SOUND. WHAT A DOLL.
WE FOUND A NICE RIVER AND STARTED SWIMMING UPSTREAM TOGETHER.
BUT, ALONG THE WAY, SALLY WAS EATEN BY A BEAR!
NO!
A BIG, BROWN, GRIZZLY BEAR. I WAS HEARTBROKEN.
THEN, IT OCCURRED TO ME...
SNIFF
THE BEARS ARE PLAYING THE VIKINGS TODAY.
SHOULD BE A GOOD GAME.

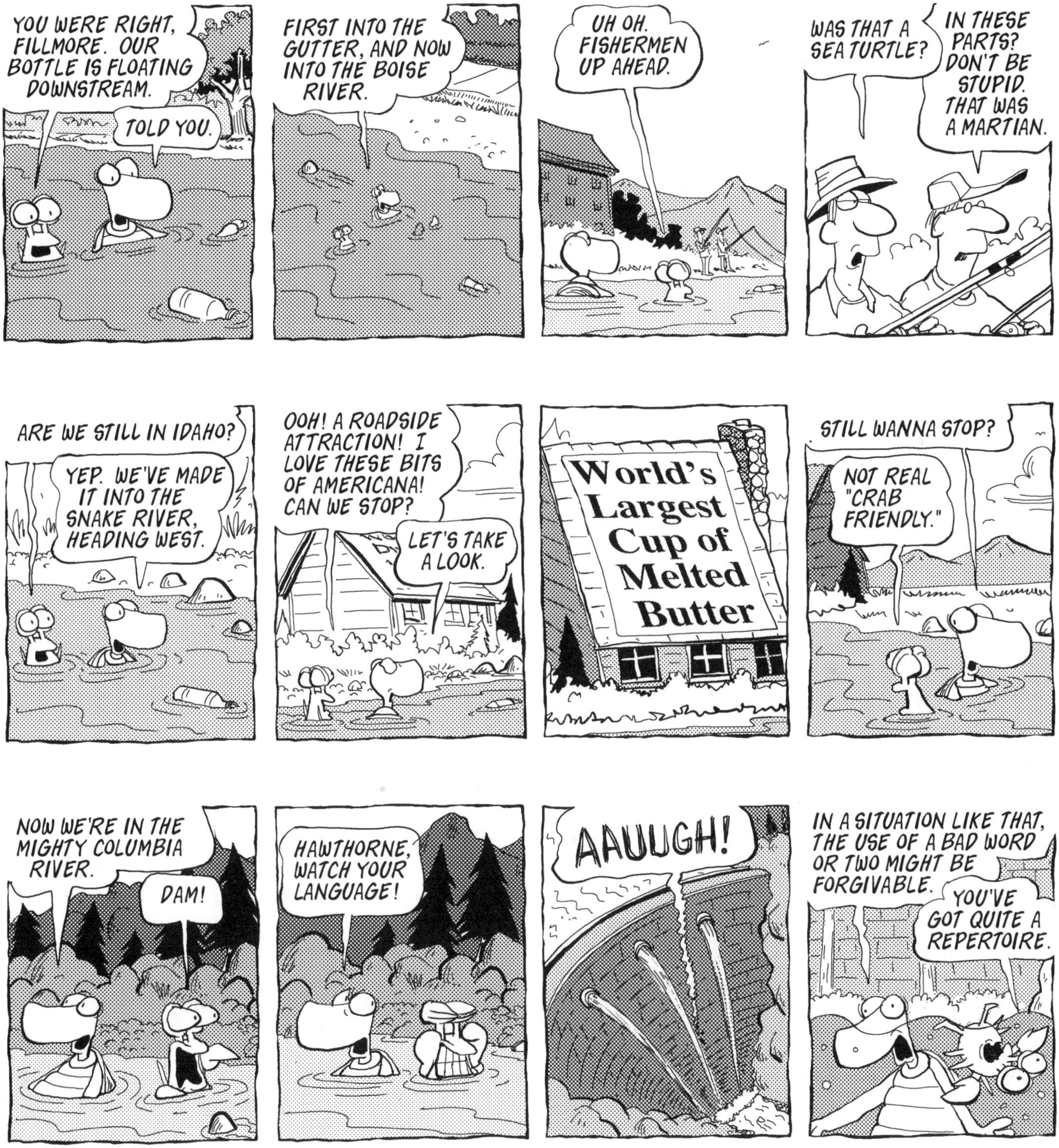
YOU WERE RIGHT, FILLMORE. OUR BOTTLE IS FLOATING DOWNSTREAM.
TOLD YOU.
FIRST INTO THE GUTTER, AND NOW INTO THE BOISE RIVER.
UH OH. FISHERMEN UP AHEAD.
WAS THAT A SEA TURTLE?
IN THESE PARTS? DON'T BE STUPID. THAT WAS A MARTIAN.
ARE WE STILL IN IDAHO?
YEP. WE'VE MADE IT INTO THE SNAKE RIVER, HEADING WEST.
OOH! A ROADSIDE ATTRACTION! I LOVE THESE BITS OF AMERICANA! CAN WE STOP?
LET'S TAKE A LOOK.
World's Largest Cup of Melted Butter
STILL WANNA STOP?
NOT REAL "CRAB FRIENDLY."
NOW WE'RE IN THE MIGHTY COLUMBIA RIVER.
DAM!
HAWTHORNE, WATCH YOUR LANGUAGE!
AAUUGH!
IN A SITUATION LIKE THAT, THE USE OF A BAD WORD OR TWO MIGHT BE FORGIVABLE.
YOU'VE GOT QUITE A REPERTOIRE.

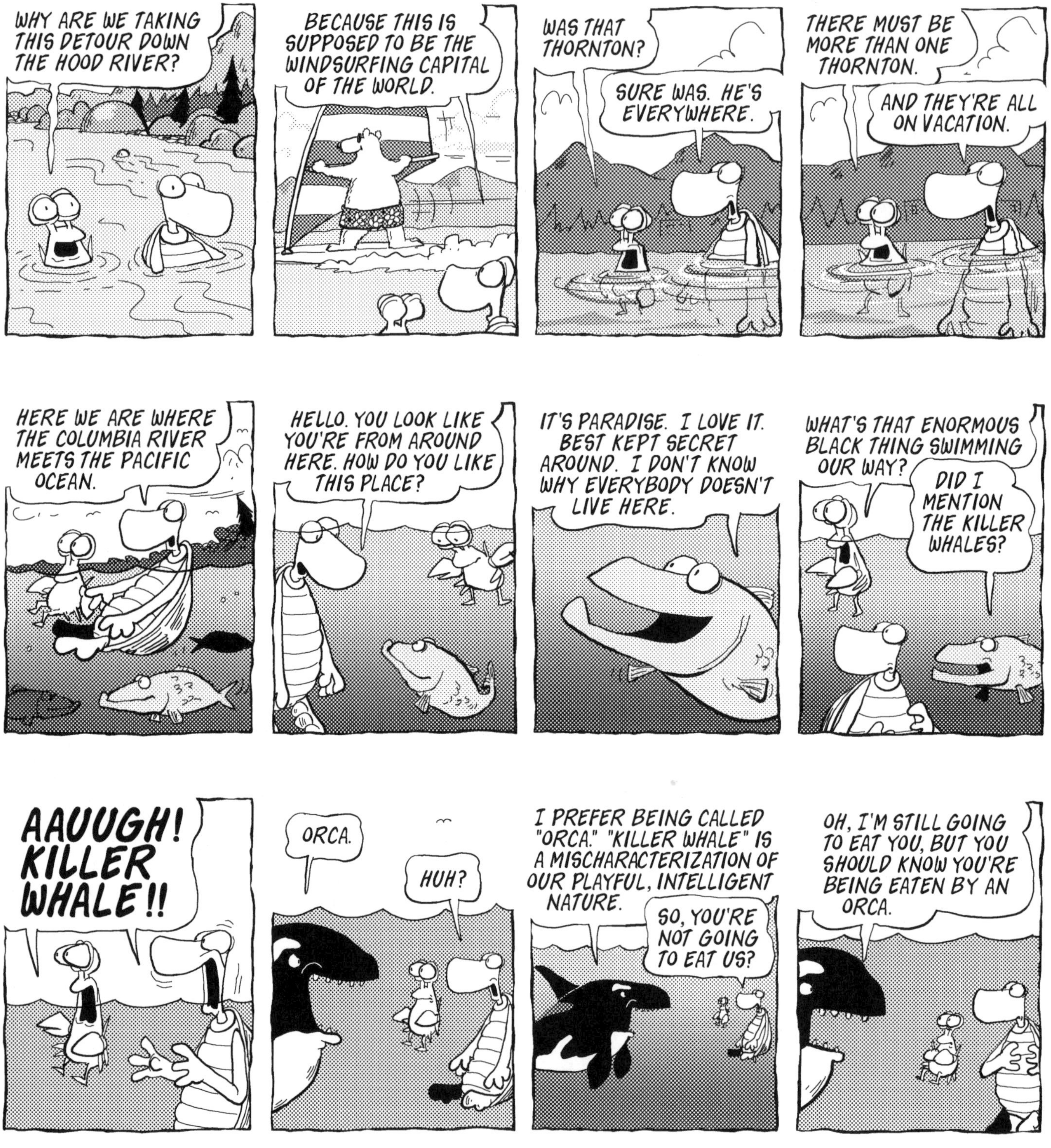
WHY ARE WE TAKING THIS DETOUR DOWN THE HOOD RIVER?
BECAUSE THIS IS SUPPOSED TO BE THE WINDSURFING CAPITAL OF THE WORLD.
WAS THAT THORNTON?
SURE WAS. HE'S EVERYWHERE.
THERE MUST BE MORE THAN ONE THORNTON.
AND THEY'RE ALL ON VACATION.
HERE WE ARE WHERE THE COLUMBIA RIVER MEETS THE PACIFIC OCEAN.
HELLO. YOU LOOK LIKE YOU'RE FROM AROUND HERE. HOW DO YOU LIKE THIS PLACE?
IT'S PARADISE. I LOVE IT. BEST KEPT SECRET AROUND. I DON'T KNOW WHY EVERYBODY DOESN'T LIVE HERE.
WHAT'S THAT ENORMOUS BLACK THING SWIMMING OUR WAY?
DID I MENTION THE KILLER WHALES?
AAUUGH! KILLER WHALE!!
ORCA.
HUH?
I PREFER BEING CALLED "ORCA." "KILLER WHALE" IS A MISCHARACTERIZATION OF OUR PLAYFUL, INTELLIGENT NATURE.
SO, YOU'RE NOT GOING TO EAT US?
OH, I'M STILL GOING TO EAT YOU, BUT YOU SHOULD KNOW YOU'RE BEING EATEN BY AN ORCA.

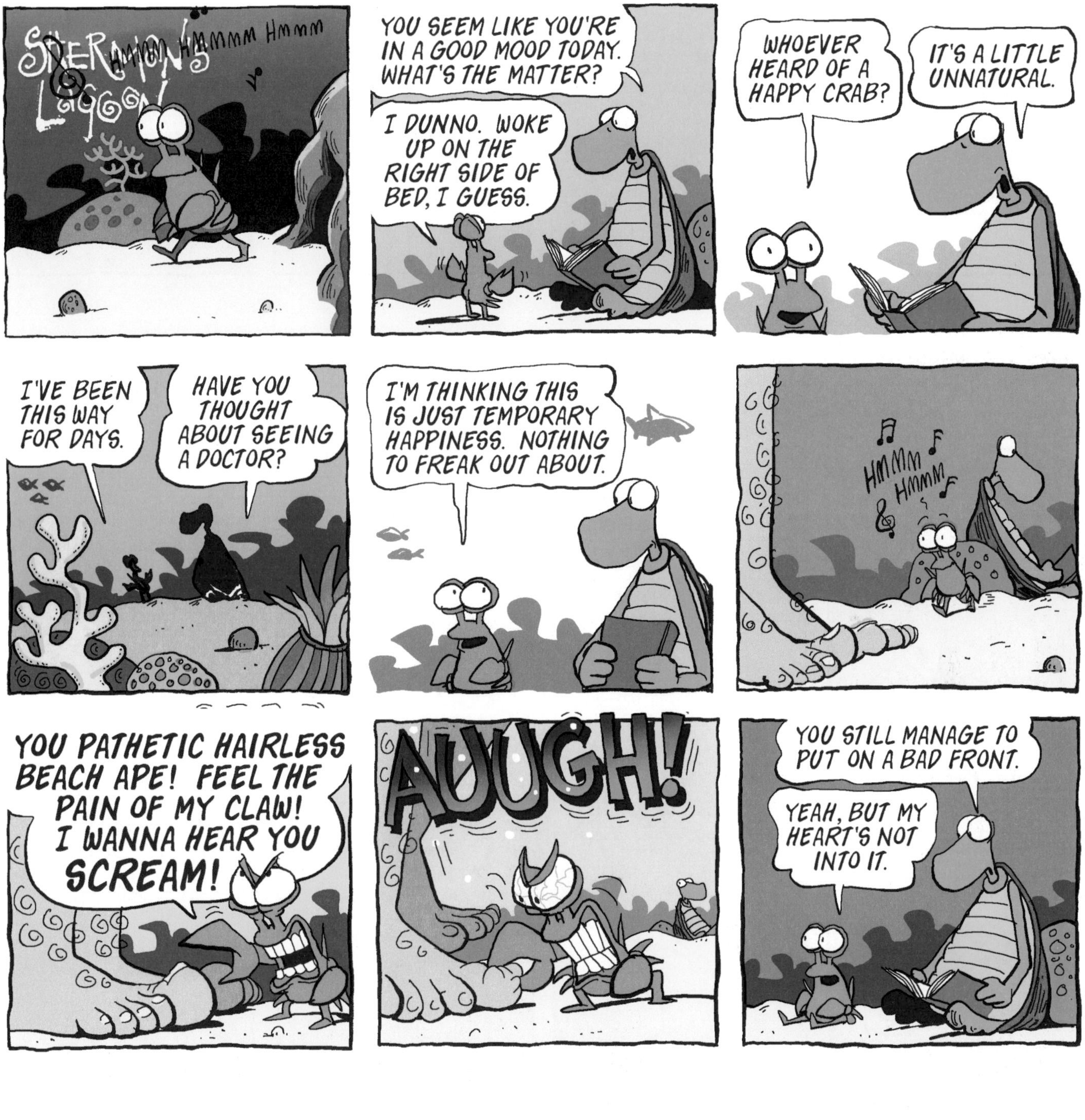

SHERMAN'S LAGOON
HMMM HMMMM HMMMM HMMM
YOU SEEM LIKE YOU'RE IN A GOOD MOOD TODAY. WHAT'S THE MATTER?
I DUNNO. WOKE UP ON THE RIGHT SIDE OF BED, I GUESS.
WHOEVER HEARD OF A HAPPY CRAB?
IT'S A LITTLE UNNATURAL.
I'VE BEEN THIS WAY FOR DAYS.
HAVE YOU THOUGHT ABOUT SEEING A DOCTOR?
I'M THINKING THIS IS JUST TEMPORARY HAPPINESS. NOTHING TO FREAK OUT ABOUT.
HMMM HMMM
YOU PATHETIC HAIRLESS BEACH APE! FEEL THE PAIN OF MY CLAW! I WANNA HEAR YOU SCREAM!
AUUGH!
YOU STILL MANAGE TO PUT ON A BAD FRONT.
YEAH, BUT MY HEART'S NOT INTO IT.

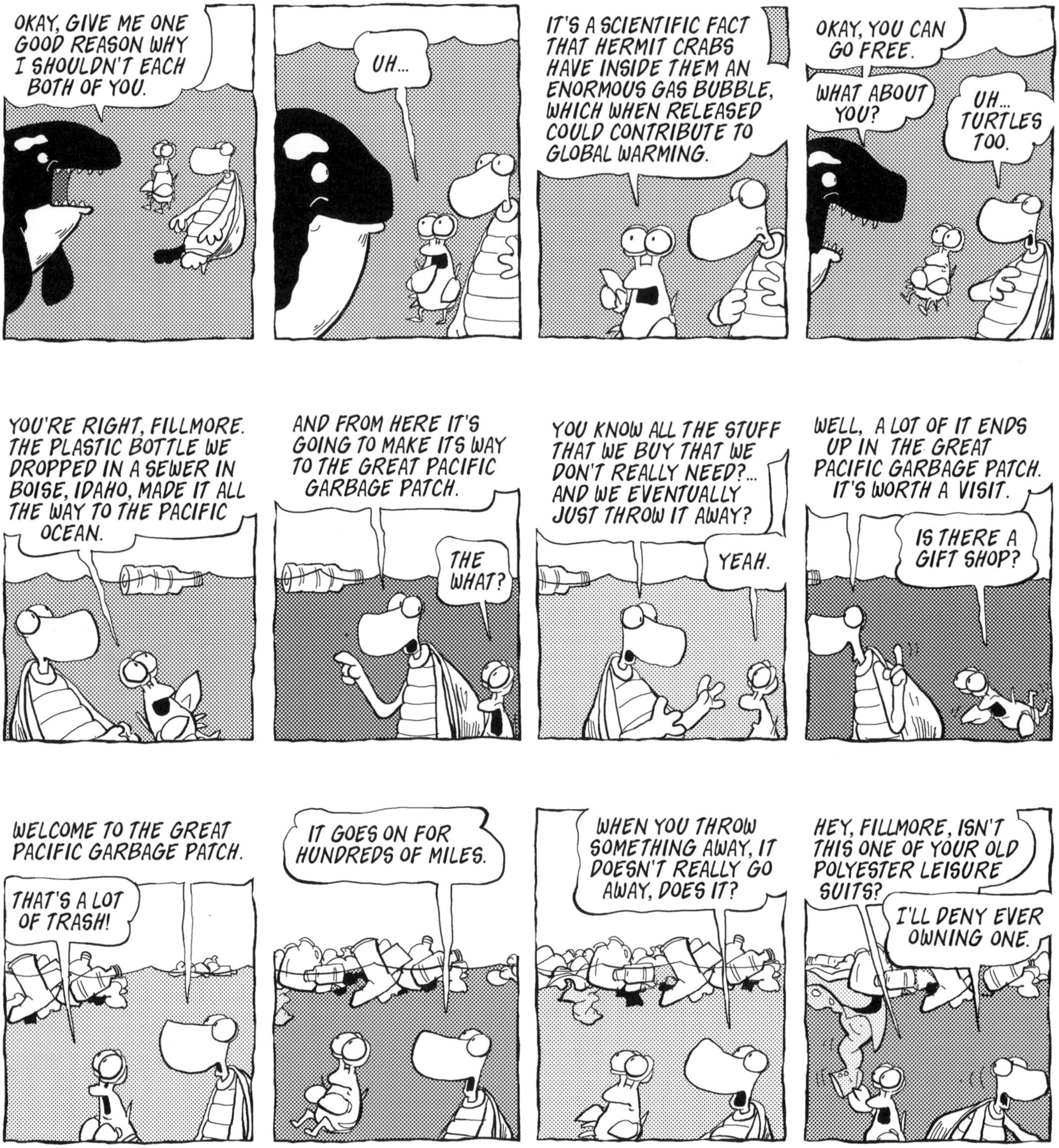
OKAY, GIVE ME ONE GOOD REASON WHY I SHOULDN'T EACH BOTH OF YOU.
UH...
IT'S A SCIENTIFIC FACT THAT HERMIT CRABS HAVE INSIDE THEM AN ENORMOUS GAS BUBBLE, WHICH WHEN RELEASED COULD CONTRIBUTE TO GLOBAL WARMING.
OKAY, YOU CAN GO FREE.
WHAT ABOUT YOU?
UH... TURTLES TOO.
YOU'RE RIGHT, FILLMORE. THE PLASTIC BOTTLE WE DROPPED IN A SEWER IN BOISE, IDAHO, MADE IT ALL THE WAY TO THE PACIFIC OCEAN.
AND FROM HERE IT'S GOING TO MAKE ITS WAY TO THE GREAT PACIFIC GARBAGE PATCH.
THE WHAT?
YOU KNOW ALL THE STUFF THAT WE BUY THAT WE DON'T REALLY NEED?... AND WE EVENTUALLY JUST THROW IT AWAY?
YEAH.
WELL, A LOT OF IT ENDS UP IN THE GREAT PACIFIC GARBAGE PATCH. IT'S WORTH A VISIT.
IS THERE A GIFT SHOP?
WELCOME TO THE GREAT PACIFIC GARBAGE PATCH.
THAT'S A LOT OF TRASH!
IT GOES ON FOR HUNDREDS OF MILES.
WHEN YOU THROW SOMETHING AWAY, IT DOESN'T REALLY GO AWAY, DOES IT?
HEY, FILLMORE, ISN'T THIS ONE OF YOUR OLD POLYESTER LEISURE SUITS?
I'LL DENY EVER OWNING ONE.

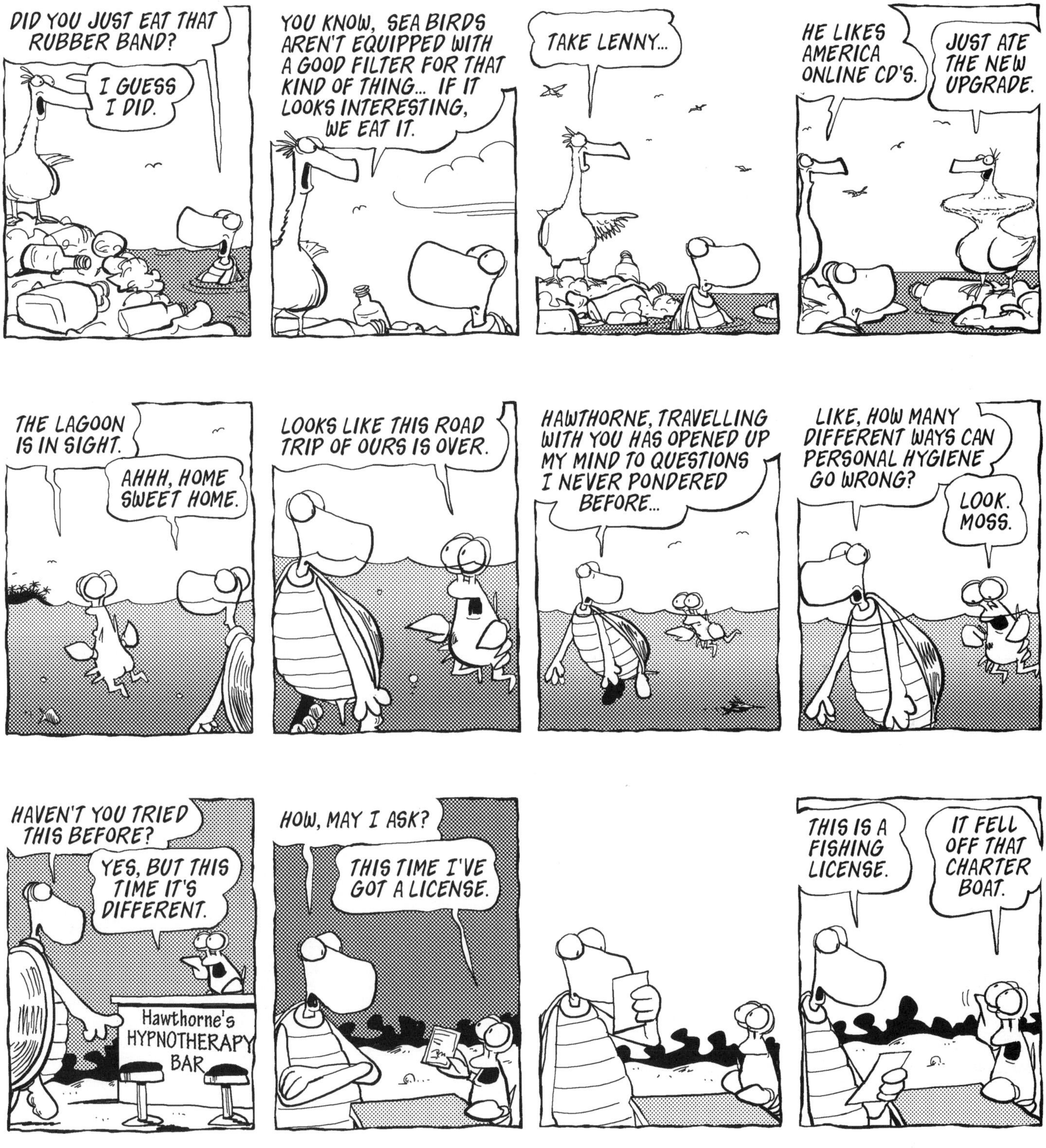
DID YOU JUST EAT THAT RUBBER BAND?
I GUESS I DID.
YOU KNOW, SEA BIRDS AREN'T EQUIPPED WITH A GOOD FILTER FOR THAT KIND OF THING... IF IT LOOKS INTERESTING, WE EAT IT.
TAKE LENNY...
HE LIKES AMERICA ONLINE CD'S.
JUST ATE THE NEW UPGRADE.
THE LAGOON IS IN SIGHT.
AHHH, HOME SWEET HOME.
LOOKS LIKE THIS ROAD TRIP OF OURS IS OVER.
HAWTHORNE, TRAVELLING WITH YOU HAS OPENED UP MY MIND TO QUESTIONS I NEVER PONDERED BEFORE...
LIKE, HOW MANY DIFFERENT WAYS CAN PERSONAL HYGIENE GO WRONG?
LOOK. MOSS.
HAVEN'T YOU TRIED THIS BEFORE?
YES, BUT THIS TIME IT'S DIFFERENT.
Hawthorne's HYPNOTHERAPY BAR
HOW, MAY I ASK?
THIS TIME I'VE GOT A LICENSE.
THIS IS A FISHING LICENSE.
IT FELL OFF THAT CHARTER BOAT.

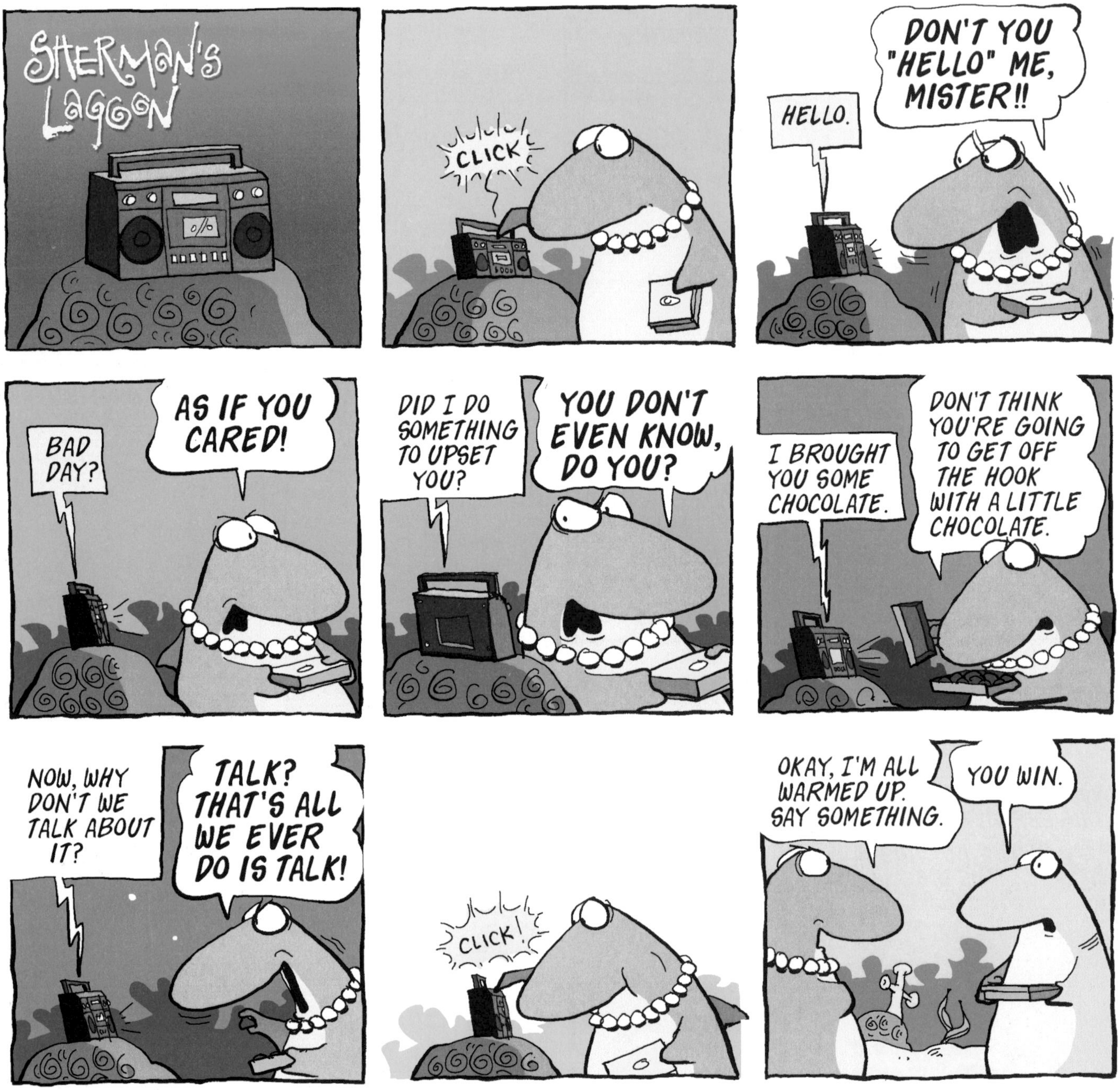
SHERMAN'S LAGOON
CLICK
HELLO.
DON'T YOU "HELLO" ME, MISTER!!
BAD DAY?
AS IF YOU CARED!
DID I DO SOMETHING TO UPSET YOU?
YOU DON'T EVEN KNOW, DO YOU?
I BROUGHT YOU SOME CHOCOLATE.
DON'T THINK YOU'RE GOING TO GET OFF THE HOOK WITH A LITTLE CHOCOLATE.
NOW, WHY DON'T WE TALK ABOUT IT?
TALK? THAT'S ALL WE EVER DO IS TALK!
CLICK!
OKAY, I'M ALL WARMED UP. SAY SOMETHING.
YOU WIN.

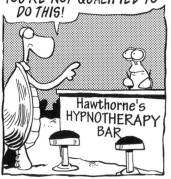

HAWTHORNE, YOU SHOULD BE ASHAMED OF YOURSELF! YOU'RE NOT QUALIFIED TO DO THIS!

Hawthorne's HYPNOTHERAPY BAR

I WANT TO HELP MY FELLOW LAGOONIES WITH THEIR HANG-UPS AND CHARACTER FLAWS. WHAT'S THE MATTER WITH THAT?

FOR INSTANCE, I COULD HELP YOU WITH YOUR SELF-ESTEEM ISSUES.

I DON'T HAVE "SELF-ESTEEM ISSUES."

REALLY? I DON'T SEE WHY YOU WOULDN'T.

HEY!

SO, WHAT HAPPENS HERE?

WELL, UNDER HYPNOSIS, I HELP YOU OVERCOME YOUR PROBLEMS.

Hawthorne's HYPNOTHERAPY BAR

LIKE, FOR INSTANCE, I COULD HELP YOU QUIT SMOKING.

BUT I DON'T SMOKE.

WELL, FIRST I COULD GET YOU TO SMOKE, AND THEN HELP YOU TO QUIT.

YOU'D DO ALL THAT FOR ME?

AT FAIRLY REASONABLE RATES.

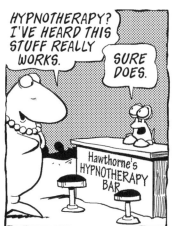

HYPNOTHERAPY? I'VE HEARD THIS STUFF REALLY WORKS.

SURE DOES.

Hawthorne's HYPNOTHERAPY BAR

I COULD DEFINITELY HELP YOU WITH YOUR WEIGHT ISSUES, MEGAN.

NOTE TO SELF: NEVER ASSUME WHAT A CLIENT NEEDS.

HEY, I KNOW THAT VOICE.

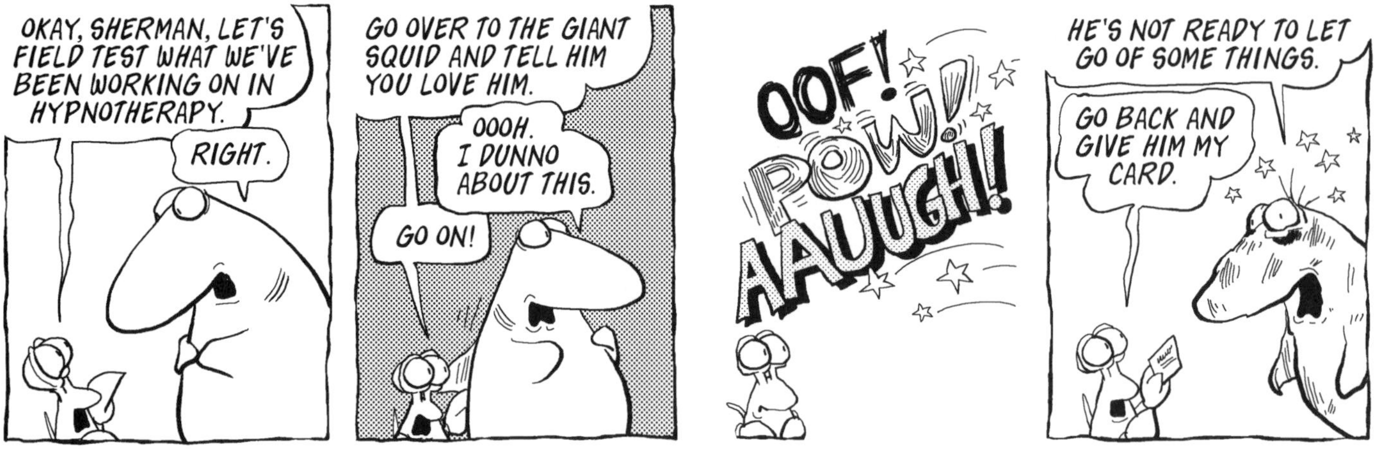
OKAY, SHERMAN, LET'S FIELD TEST WHAT WE'VE BEEN WORKING ON IN HYPNOTHERAPY.
RIGHT.
GO OVER TO THE GIANT SQUID AND TELL HIM YOU LOVE HIM.
OOOH. I DUNNO ABOUT THIS.
GO ON!
OOF! POW! AAUUGH!
HE'S NOT READY TO LET GO OF SOME THINGS.
GO BACK AND GIVE HIM MY CARD.

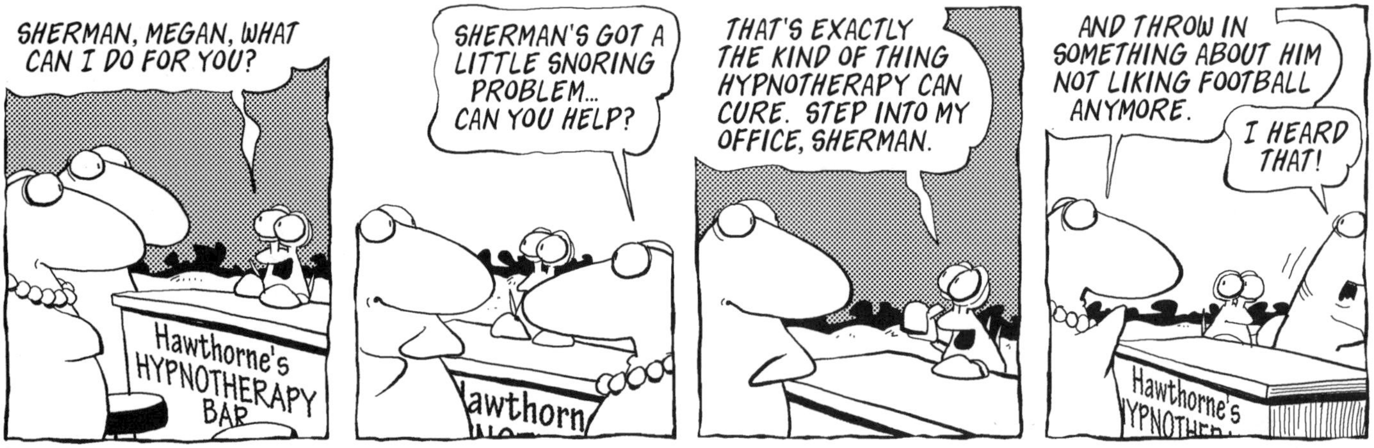
SHERMAN, MEGAN, WHAT CAN I DO FOR YOU?
Hawthorne's HYPNOTHERAPY BAR
SHERMAN'S GOT A LITTLE SNORING PROBLEM... CAN YOU HELP?
THAT'S EXACTLY THE KIND OF THING HYPNOTHERAPY CAN CURE. STEP INTO MY OFFICE, SHERMAN.
AND THROW IN SOMETHING ABOUT HIM NOT LIKING FOOTBALL ANYMORE.
I HEARD THAT!

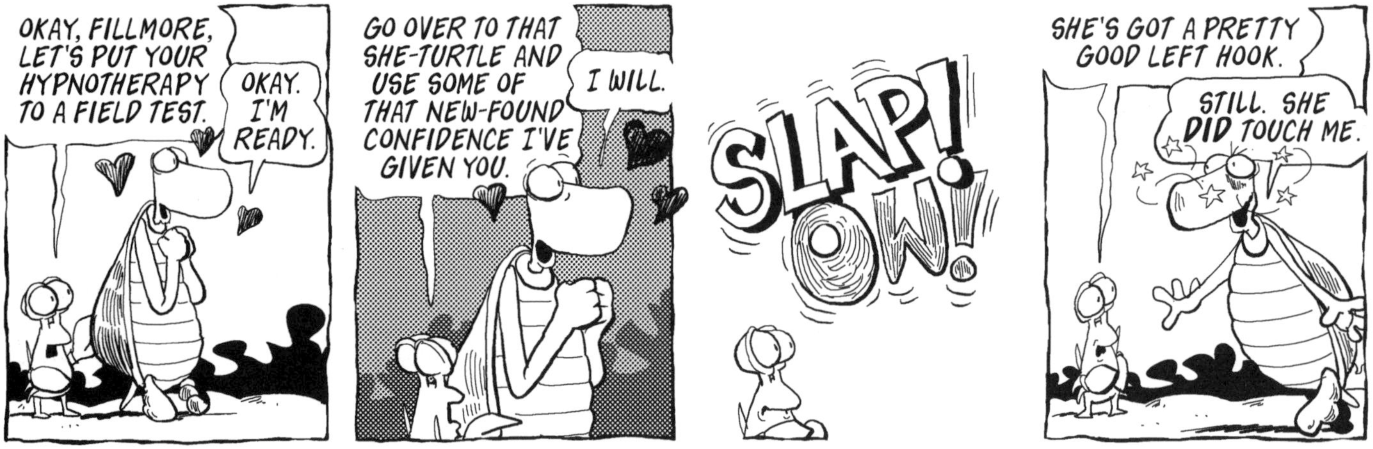
OKAY, FILLMORE, LET'S PUT YOUR HYPNOTHERAPY TO A FIELD TEST.
OKAY. I'M READY.
GO OVER TO THAT SHE-TURTLE AND USE SOME OF THAT NEW-FOUND CONFIDENCE I'VE GIVEN YOU.
I WILL.
SLAP! OW!
SHE'S GOT A PRETTY GOOD LEFT HOOK.
STILL. SHE **DID** TOUCH ME.

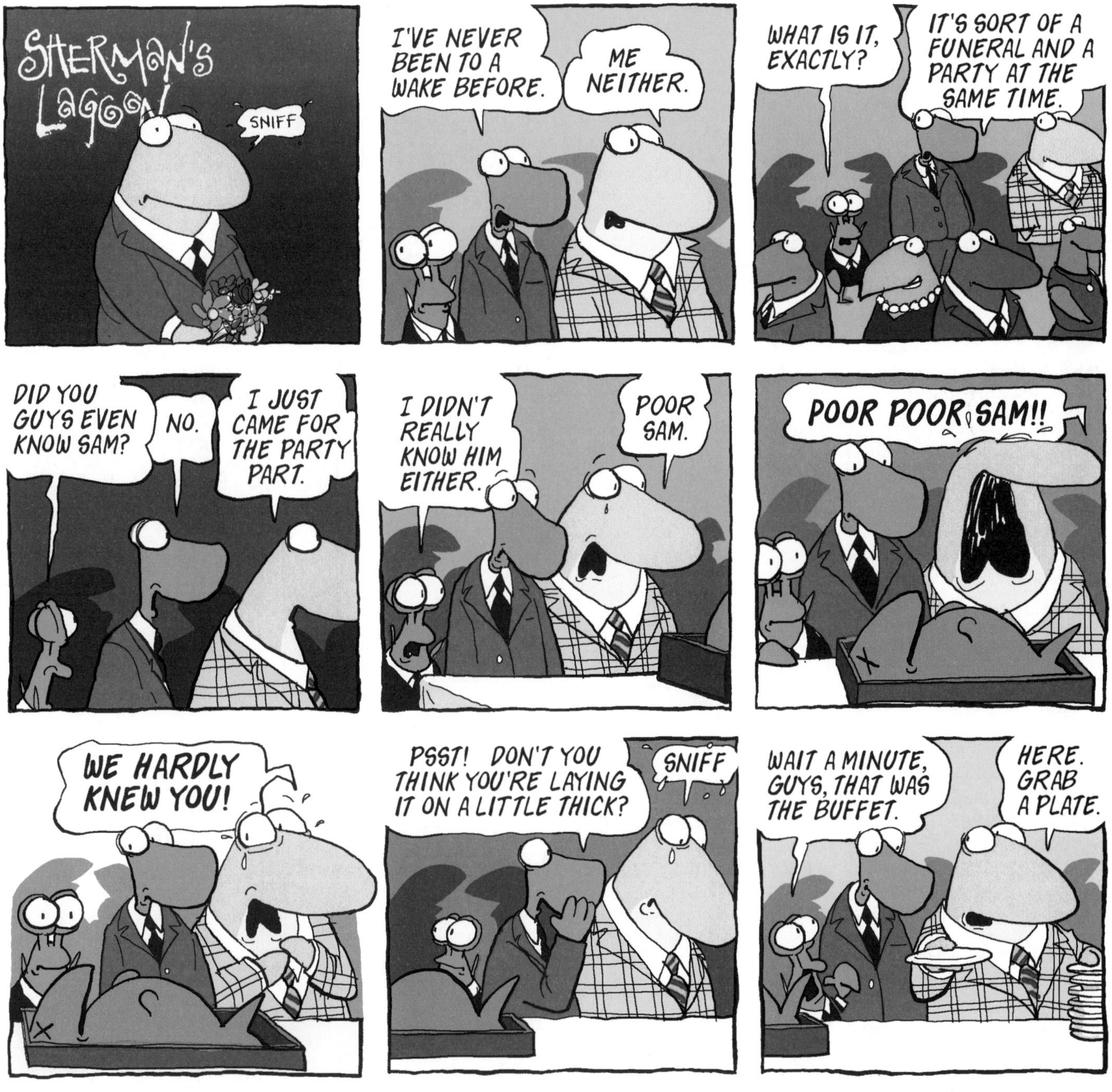
SHERMAN'S LAGOON
SNIFF
I'VE NEVER BEEN TO A WAKE BEFORE.
ME NEITHER.
WHAT IS IT, EXACTLY?
IT'S SORT OF A FUNERAL AND A PARTY AT THE SAME TIME.
DID YOU GUYS EVEN KNOW SAM?
NO.
I JUST CAME FOR THE PARTY PART.
I DIDN'T REALLY KNOW HIM EITHER.
POOR SAM.
POOR POOR SAM!!
WE HARDLY KNEW YOU!
PSST! DON'T YOU THINK YOU'RE LAYING IT ON A LITTLE THICK?
SNIFF
WAIT A MINUTE, GUYS, THAT WAS THE BUFFET.
HERE. GRAB A PLATE.

Panel 1: HEY THORNTON, CAN I INTEREST YOU IN A LITTLE HYPNOTHERAPY?
GO AWAY.

Panel 2: C'MON. WOULDN'T YOU LIKE A LITTLE MORE DRIVE? A LITTLE MORE MOTIVATION?
NO. BUG OFF.

Panel 3: BOING! BOING!

Panel 4: A LITTLE **LESS** THORNTON WOULDN'T HURT EITHER.
LAUNCHING IN 5... 4... 3...

Panel 5: OKAY, MEGAN, I'M GLAD YOU CAME TO HYPNOTHERAPY.
WELL, IT WAS SHERMAN'S IDEA.

Panel 6: HE THINKS I'M A CONTROL FREAK.
I SEE.

Panel 7: LIKE I CAN'T LET ANYONE DO ANYTHING WITHOUT FEELING THE NEED TO TELL THEM HOW TO DO IT.

Panel 8: I WANT YOU TO FOCUS ON THIS OBJECT.
NOT UNTIL YOU SIT UP STRAIGHT AND HOLD IT CORRECTLY.

Panel 9: I GAVE UP THE HYPNOTHERAPY PRACTICE.

Panel 10: ANOTHER ONE OF YOUR CAREERS COMES TO AN ABRUPT END... PITY... WHAT'S NEXT?

Panel 11: I WANT TO MAKE MONEY THE OLD FASHIONED WAY...

Panel 12: WITH A PRINTING PRESS.
I HEAR THAT'S ILLEGAL.

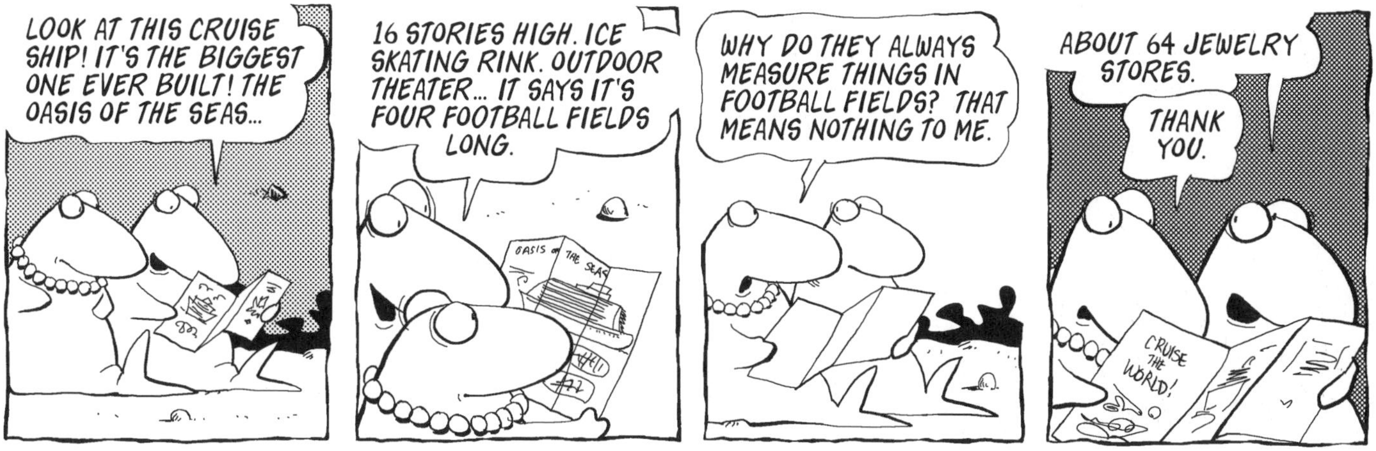
LOOK AT THIS CRUISE SHIP! IT'S THE BIGGEST ONE EVER BUILT! THE OASIS OF THE SEAS...
16 STORIES HIGH. ICE SKATING RINK. OUTDOOR THEATER... IT SAYS IT'S FOUR FOOTBALL FIELDS LONG.
WHY DO THEY ALWAYS MEASURE THINGS IN FOOTBALL FIELDS? THAT MEANS NOTHING TO ME.
ABOUT 64 JEWELRY STORES.
THANK YOU.
CRUISE THE WORLD!

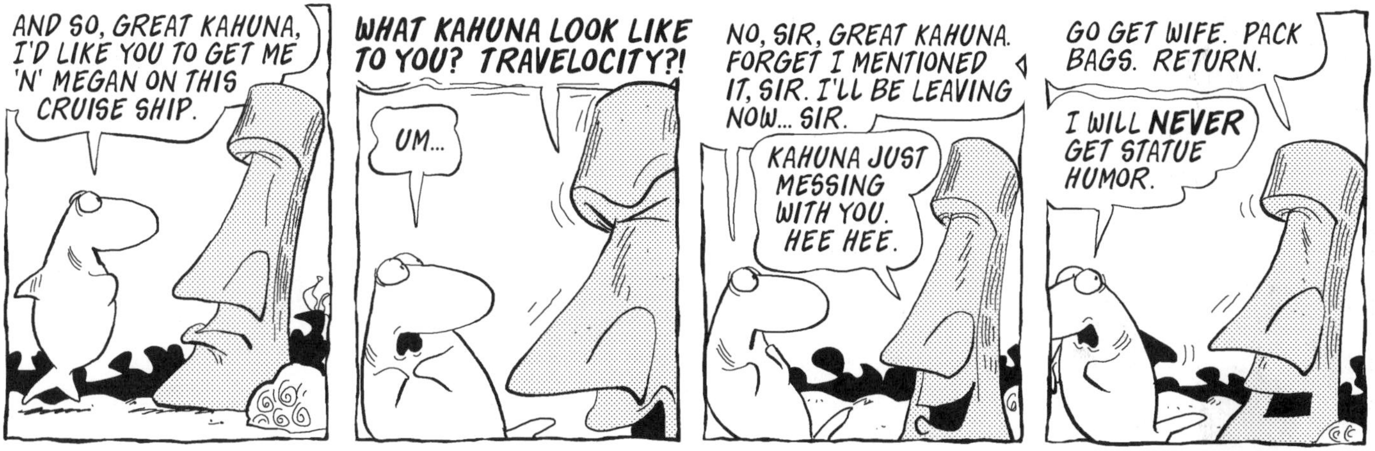
AND SO, GREAT KAHUNA, I'D LIKE YOU TO GET ME 'N' MEGAN ON THIS CRUISE SHIP.
WHAT KAHUNA LOOK LIKE TO YOU? TRAVELOCITY?!
UM...
NO, SIR, GREAT KAHUNA. FORGET I MENTIONED IT, SIR. I'LL BE LEAVING NOW... SIR.
KAHUNA JUST MESSING WITH YOU. HEE HEE.
GO GET WIFE. PACK BAGS. RETURN.
I WILL **NEVER** GET STATUE HUMOR.

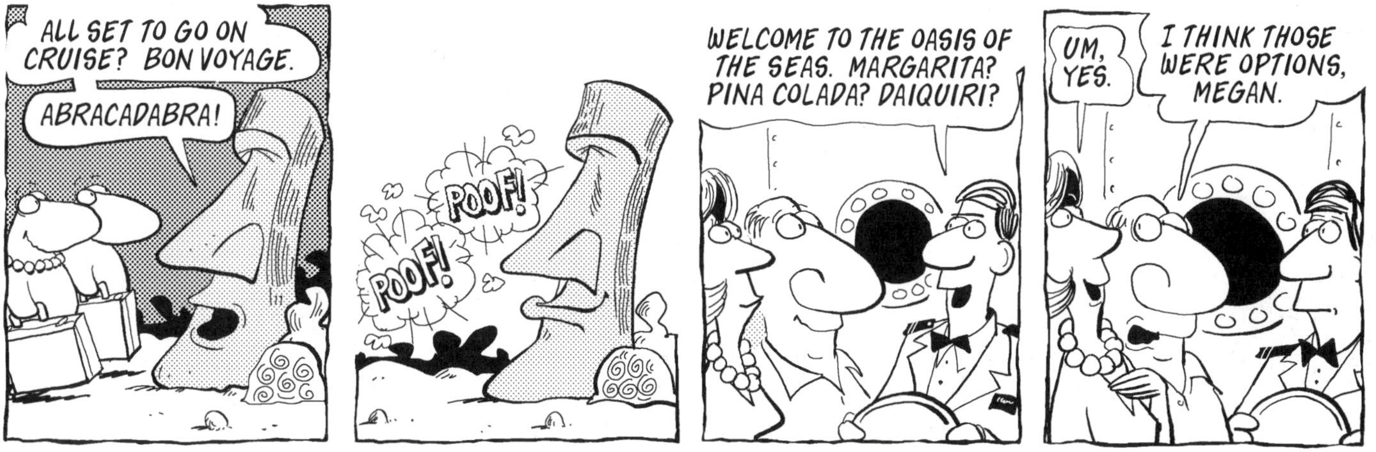
ALL SET TO GO ON CRUISE? BON VOYAGE.
ABRACADABRA!
POOF!
POOF!
WELCOME TO THE OASIS OF THE SEAS. MARGARITA? PINA COLADA? DAIQUIRI?
UM, YES.
I THINK THOSE WERE OPTIONS, MEGAN.

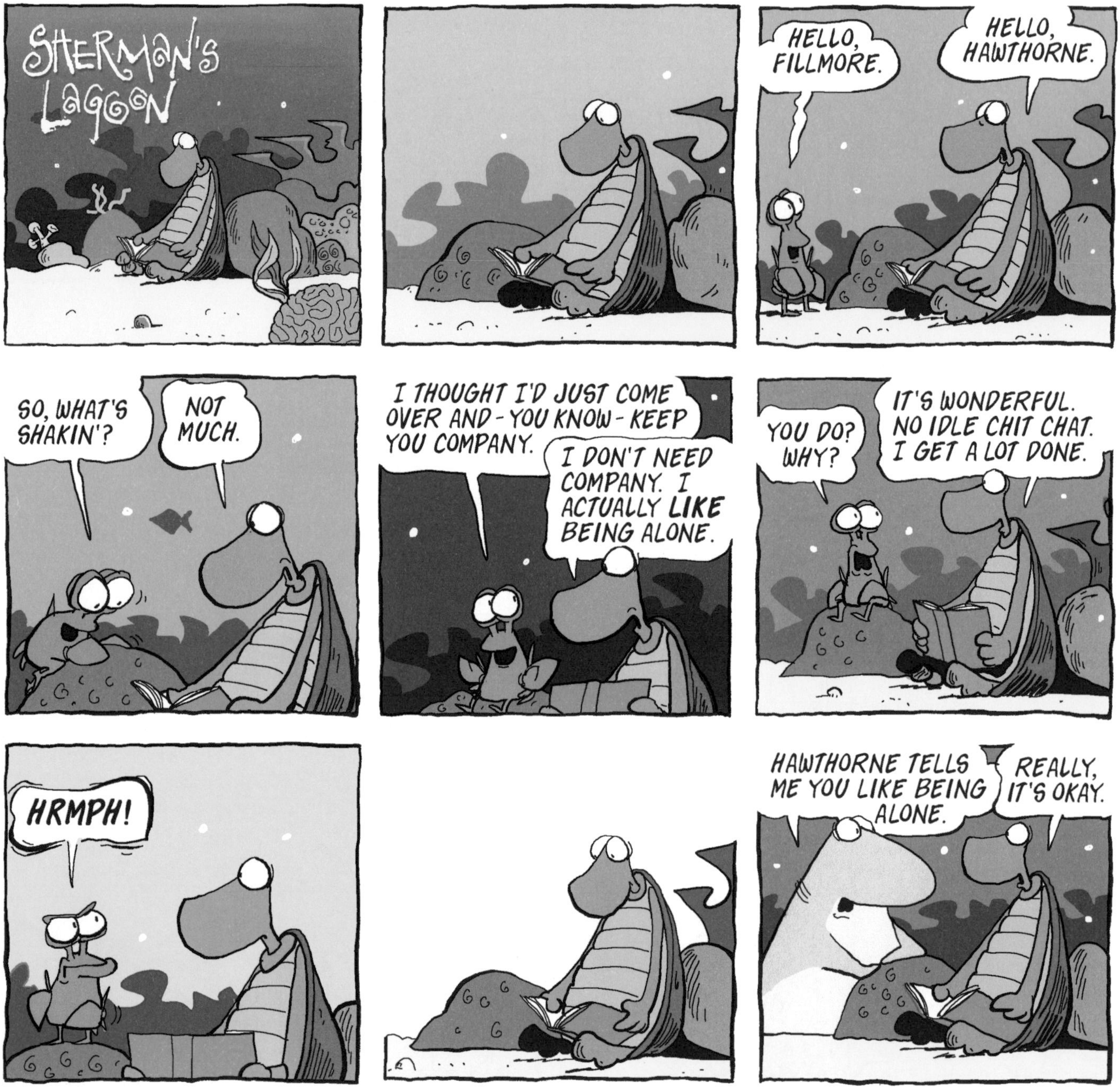
SHERMAN'S LAGOON
HELLO, FILLMORE.
HELLO, HAWTHORNE.
SO, WHAT'S SHAKIN'?
NOT MUCH.
I THOUGHT I'D JUST COME OVER AND - YOU KNOW - KEEP YOU COMPANY.
I DON'T NEED COMPANY. I ACTUALLY LIKE BEING ALONE.
YOU DO? WHY?
IT'S WONDERFUL. NO IDLE CHIT CHAT. I GET A LOT DONE.
HRMPH!
HAWTHORNE TELLS ME YOU LIKE BEING ALONE.
REALLY, IT'S OKAY.

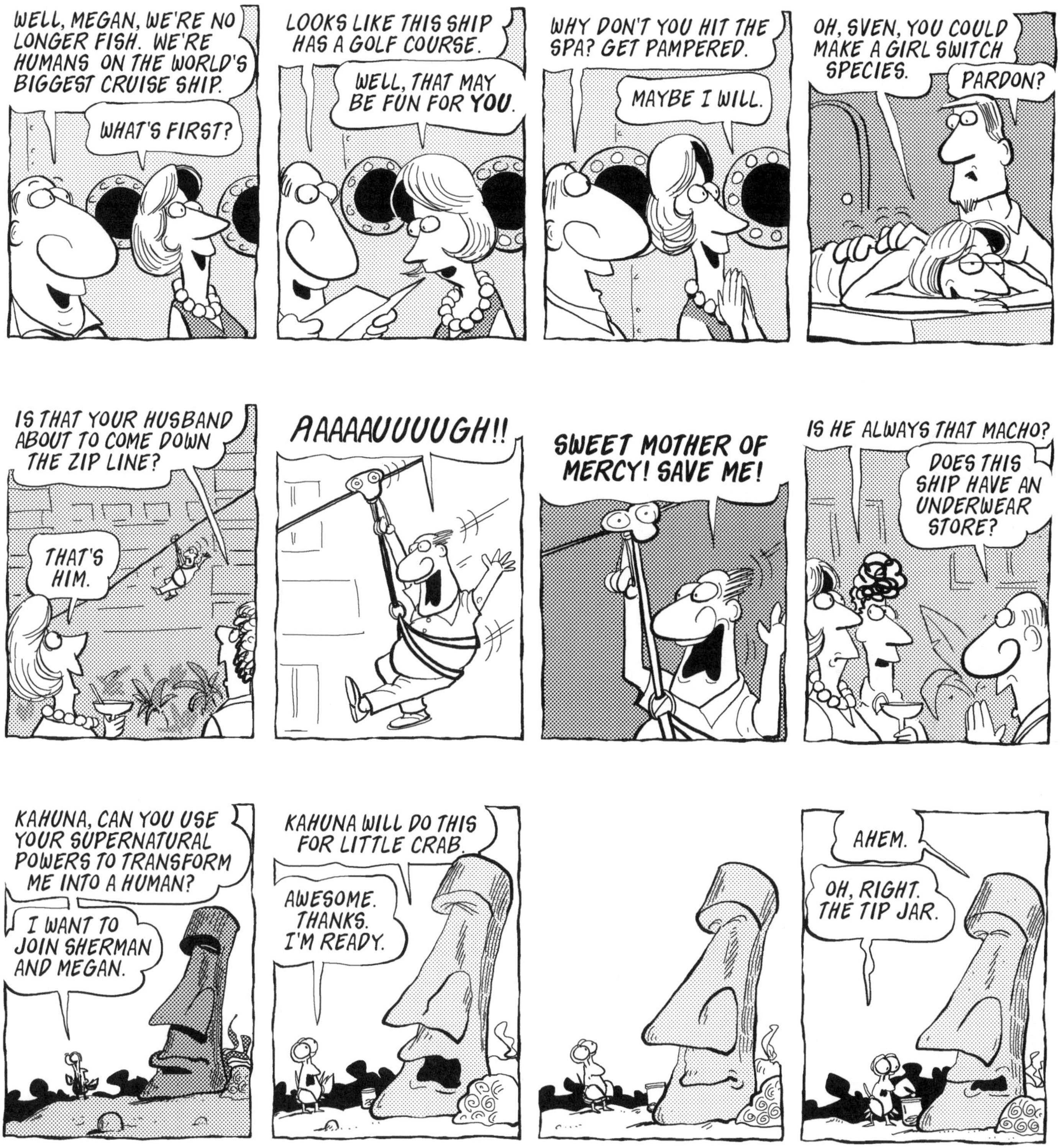
WELL, MEGAN, WE'RE NO LONGER FISH. WE'RE HUMANS ON THE WORLD'S BIGGEST CRUISE SHIP.
WHAT'S FIRST?
LOOKS LIKE THIS SHIP HAS A GOLF COURSE.
WELL, THAT MAY BE FUN FOR YOU.
WHY DON'T YOU HIT THE SPA? GET PAMPERED.
MAYBE I WILL.
OH, SVEN, YOU COULD MAKE A GIRL SWITCH SPECIES.
PARDON?
IS THAT YOUR HUSBAND ABOUT TO COME DOWN THE ZIP LINE?
THAT'S HIM.
AAAAAUUUUGH!!
SWEET MOTHER OF MERCY! SAVE ME!
IS HE ALWAYS THAT MACHO?
DOES THIS SHIP HAVE AN UNDERWEAR STORE?
KAHUNA, CAN YOU USE YOUR SUPERNATURAL POWERS TO TRANSFORM ME INTO A HUMAN?
I WANT TO JOIN SHERMAN AND MEGAN.
KAHUNA WILL DO THIS FOR LITTLE CRAB.
AWESOME. THANKS. I'M READY.
AHEM.
OH, RIGHT. THE TIP JAR.

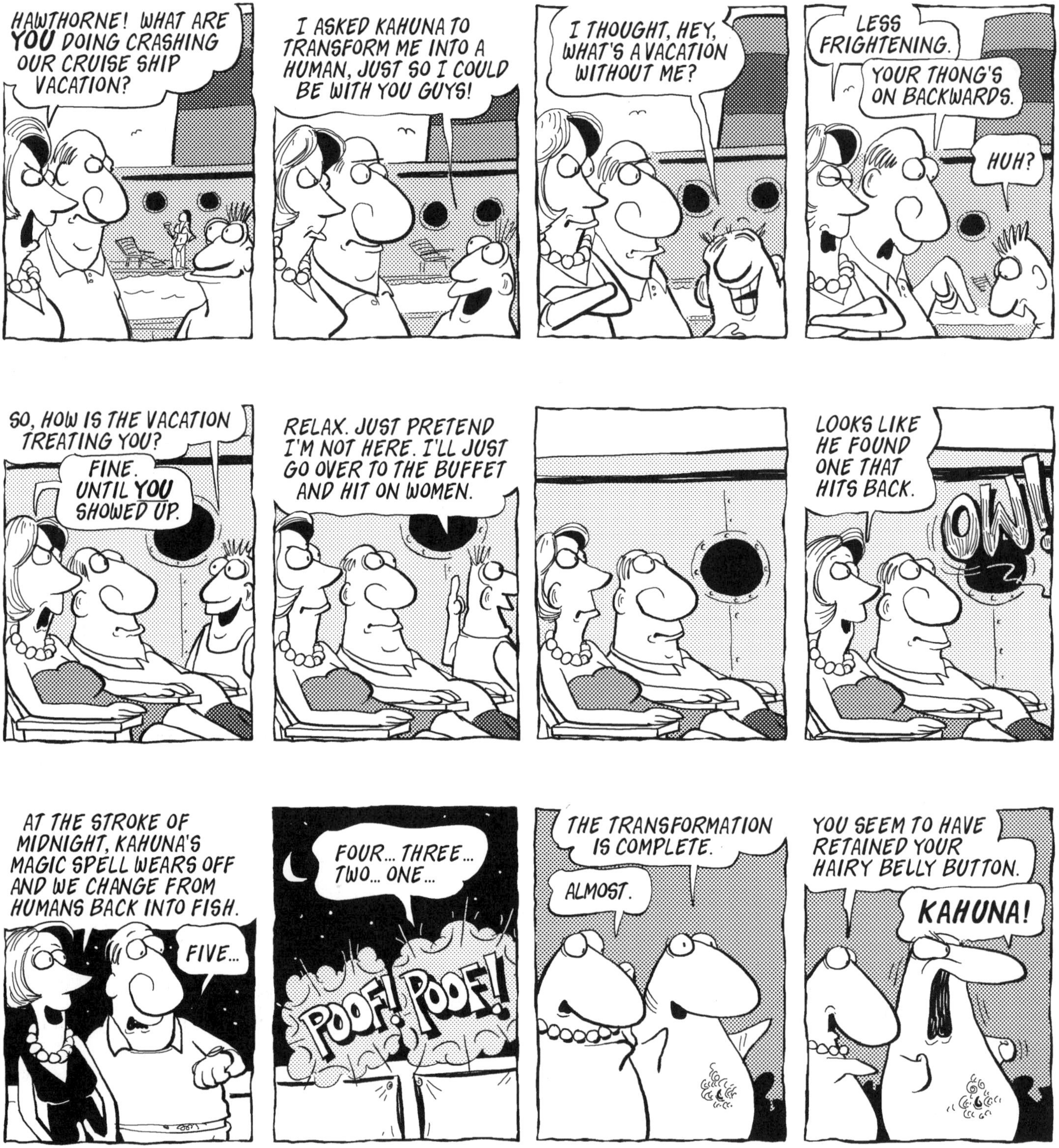
HAWTHORNE! WHAT ARE YOU DOING CRASHING OUR CRUISE SHIP VACATION?
I ASKED KAHUNA TO TRANSFORM ME INTO A HUMAN, JUST SO I COULD BE WITH YOU GUYS!
I THOUGHT, HEY, WHAT'S A VACATION WITHOUT ME?
LESS FRIGHTENING.
YOUR THONG'S ON BACKWARDS.
HUH?
SO, HOW IS THE VACATION TREATING YOU?
FINE. UNTIL YOU SHOWED UP.
RELAX. JUST PRETEND I'M NOT HERE. I'LL JUST GO OVER TO THE BUFFET AND HIT ON WOMEN.
LOOKS LIKE HE FOUND ONE THAT HITS BACK.
OW!
AT THE STROKE OF MIDNIGHT, KAHUNA'S MAGIC SPELL WEARS OFF AND WE CHANGE FROM HUMANS BACK INTO FISH.
FIVE...
FOUR... THREE... TWO... ONE...
POOF! POOF!
THE TRANSFORMATION IS COMPLETE.
ALMOST.
YOU SEEM TO HAVE RETAINED YOUR HAIRY BELLY BUTTON.
KAHUNA!

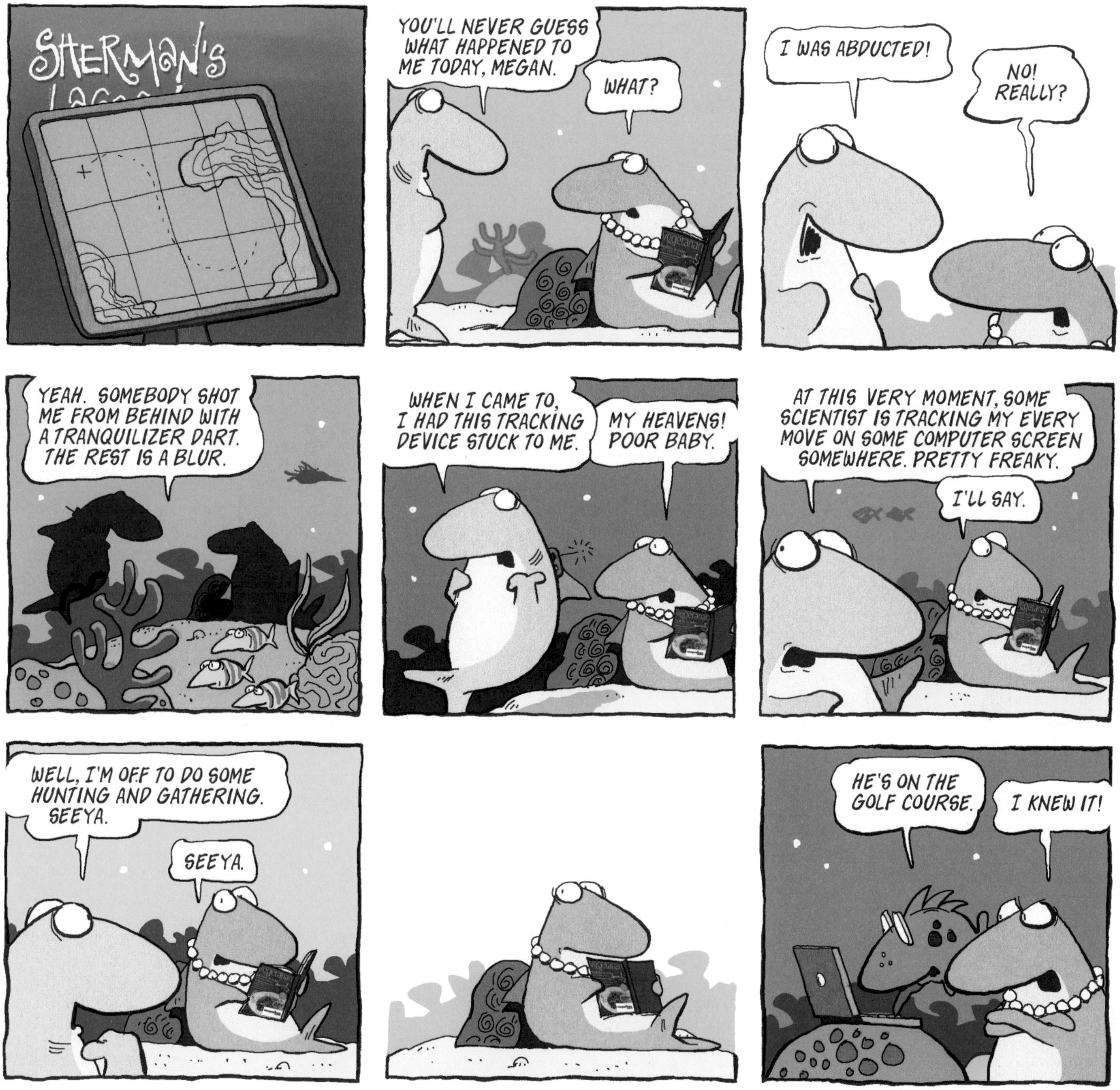
SHERMAN'S LAGOON
YOU'LL NEVER GUESS WHAT HAPPENED TO ME TODAY, MEGAN.
WHAT?
I WAS ABDUCTED!
NO! REALLY?
YEAH. SOMEBODY SHOT ME FROM BEHIND WITH A TRANQUILIZER DART. THE REST IS A BLUR.
WHEN I CAME TO, I HAD THIS TRACKING DEVICE STUCK TO ME.
MY HEAVENS! POOR BABY.
AT THIS VERY MOMENT, SOME SCIENTIST IS TRACKING MY EVERY MOVE ON SOME COMPUTER SCREEN SOMEWHERE. PRETTY FREAKY.
I'LL SAY.
WELL, I'M OFF TO DO SOME HUNTING AND GATHERING. SEEYA.
SEEYA.
HE'S ON THE GOLF COURSE.
I KNEW IT!